Yale Publications in Religion, 10

David Horne, editor

Published under the direction of the Divinity School

THE COMPOSITION AND ORDER

OF THE FOURTH GOSPEL

BULTMANN'S LITERARY THEORY

BY DWIGHT MOODY SMITH, JR.

NEW HAVEN AND LONDON, YALE UNIVESRITY PRESS, 1965

To Jane

Preface

The substance of this book was presented in slightly different form to the Graduate School of Yale University as a doctoral dissertation. As is doubtless the case with many dissertations, it grew out of a long-standing interest in the subject but developed in a way quite different from the author's original anticipations and intentions. In the beginning I had not even planned to concentrate upon Bultmann's work on the Fourth Gospel. But Professor Paul Schubert, whose counsel and instruction were invaluable at every stage of my graduate study, especially during the writing of the dissertation, convinced me that the projects which I had in mind would end in futility unless or until I dealt with Bultmann's treatment of the literary problems.

As the reader will notice, no attempt is made to set forth or defend a single thesis. The endeavor to show that Bultmann's literary and source criticism is simply a means of rationalizing and supporting his own theological views was abandoned at an early stage as both tendentious and unprofitable. His work is much more—and less—than that. Instead, I have striven to unfold in a systematic way Bultmann's many-faceted theses regarding the composition and order of John in order to make clear the issues raised and to draw some conclusions which I hope will be helpful for further research.

When I began work on this study in 1959, I expected Bultmann's commentary on the Johannine epistles and an English translation of the commentary on the gospel to appear before my study was completed, and I hoped to be able to take them into account. Since both seem to have been delayed, I have decided to go ahead with the publication of my study in the hopeful expectation that what value it has will not be too much diminished by their appearance.

I am particularly grateful to Professor Paul Meyer, who guided me in the actual writing of the dissertation, and less directly but nonetheless genuinely to my other teachers at Yale, Professors Paul S. Minear and Erwin R. Goodenough. It is naturally impossible for me to acknowledge all of my debts to my mentors in a preface. I am nevertheless unwilling to forgo the opportunity to mention Professor W. D. Davies, now of Union Theological Seminary, whose dedication to the tasks of New Testament scholarship played a large role in crystallizing my own aspirations when I was his student at Duke Divinity School. Lest it be suspected that my expressions of gratitude are merely covert attempts to implicate well-established scholars in my own errors, let me hasten to absolve those mentioned above of responsibility for any inaccuracies or misjudgments in this book.

Vandenhoeck and Ruprecht of Tübingen kindly gave me permission to quote from Prof. Bultmann's commentary on the Fourth Gospel, and *New Testament Studies* allowed me to use in Chapter 2 material which I had published previously in that journal. I naturally wish to thank both.

I should like also to thank the Samuel S. Fels Fund, whose generous assistance relieved me of financial worry during the writing of the dissertation on which this study is based. The generosity of the Methodist Theological School in Ohio and the Lilly Foundation in enabling me to have a leave of absence from my teaching responsibilities has made it possible for me to make some revisions in the manuscript and otherwise prepare it for publication; I am, of course, grateful to them as well. And last, but not least, thanks to my wife, whose support, consolation, tolerance, and endurance are gratefully recognized in the dedication of this book. She likewise is to be absolved from all responsibility for its contents, inasmuch as she has wisely and consistently devoted her attention to husband and family and not to this manuscript.

D. M. S., Jr.

November 1963

Contents

Introduction

By any reasonable assessment, Bultmann's commentary on the Fourth Gospel [1] is a monumental contribution to the study of that book. A notable example of the rigorous and consistent application of historical, literary, and philological criticism to an ancient document in order to achieve a genuine understanding, it displays both Bultmann's ability as a technical scholar and his acumen as a theological exegete whose interpretation arises from an analysis of an ancient text and an understanding of the milieu from which it stems and to which it belongs. This combination of technical thoroughness and theological perception is indeed impressive.[2]

1. *Das Evangelium des Johannes* (Göttingen, 1957). The *Ergänzungsheft* was revised for the 1957 edition.

2. Note K. Grobel's enthusiastic evaluation of the commentary in his review, *JBL*, 59 (1940), 434 f.: "Most commentaries on John may be classified as either philological prolegomena to true comment or as super-homilies upon the gospel. The one rarely crosses the threshold to actual elucidation of the author's thought; the other leaps across that threshold with high disdain of the critical steps by which, and by which alone, such a work should be circumspectly approached. Both are irresponsible—the one theologically, the other scientifically. Professor Bultmann's work . . . happily reconciles the mutual enmity between the two sorts of commentary by combining them—with the result that each acts as an antidote to the faults of the other." Cf. also Menoud, *L'Évangile de Jean d'après les recherches récentes*, p. 21; Haenchen, "Aus der Literatur zum Johannesevangelium 1929-56," *TR*, new ser. 23 (1955), 335; Jeremias, "Johanneische Literarkritik," *TB*, 20 (1941), 39; Käsemann, "Rudolf Bultmann, Das Evangelium des Johnnes," *VF*, *Theologischer Jahresbericht*, 3 (1942–46), 182 (published in 1947); and

The commentary is also a landmark in the study of the place and relations of the Gospel of John in the history of religions, inasmuch as it is a masterful assessment of the past half-century's achievements in this field as they bear upon the related problems of the background and interpretation of the Fourth Gospel. Bultmann stands in a succession of German historians of religion, including such notable scholars as Richard Reitzenstein and Wilhelm Bousset. Drawing upon their work and that of more recent scholars (especially his own students Günther Bornkamm, Heinrich Schlier, Hans Jonas, and Ernst Käsemann), he provides a comprehensive picture of the largely Gnostic religious and cultural milieu of the gospel. One may perhaps quarrel with this picture by taking issue with Bultmann at specific points or by questioning some of the assumptions, conclusions, or methods of the history of religion school. Nevertheless, the commentary itself stands as a model for any New Testament exegete who wishes to discharge his responsibility of producing a historically veracious interpretation of an ancient document. He must, like Bultmann, first of all attempt to understand the total context in which it emerged as well as the specific situation which called it forth.

It would be misleading to indicate Bultmann's relation and debt to other scholars without mentioning his own earlier work on the Fourth Gospel, which forms the background of, and in large measure lays the groundwork for, the commentary. The book is the fruition of years of intensive study of the gospel and its background, as is obvious both from Bultmann's bibliography and from the character and quality of the work itself.[3] This alone is enough to give the commentary a special significance.

Perhaps the single most distinctive feature of the commentary is Bultmann's handling of the much-discussed literary problem.[4] For years it has

---

Dibelius, "Ein neuer Kommentar zum Johannes-Evangelium," *TL*, 67 (1942), 257. All agree on the importance of Bultmann's commentary, and Haenchen assigns it a place alongside Barth's *Römerbrief*.

3. Bultmann's interest in the Fourth Gospel goes back at least as far as the early 1920s. See the bibliography for a list of his major works dealing with the gospel or its background.

4. For the history of the scholarly treatment of the literary problems of the Fourth Gospel see W. Bousset, "Ist das vierte Evangelium eine literarische Einheit?", *TR*, 12 (1909), 1 f., 39 ff.; W. F. Howard, *The Fourth Gospel in Recent Criticism and Interpretation*, pp. 19–175 passim, 276–303; Menoud, *L'Évangile de Jean*, pp. 8–29; Haenchen, *TR*, new ser. 23 (1955), 302–13; Menoud, "Les Études johanniques de Bultmann à Barrett," pp. 14–24; S. Schulz, *Untersuchungen zur Menschensohn-Christologie im Johannesevangelium*, pp. 41–81; and O. Merlier, *Le quatrième Évangile, la question johannique*, Connaissance de la Grèce XI, Études Néo-Testamentaires 2 (Paris, Presses Universitaires de France, 1961), 37–114. There is also most recently the excellent survey by W. G. Kümmel in his completely reworked edition of the Feine-Behm *Einleitung in das Neue Testament* (Heidelberg, Quelle & Meyer, 1963), pp. 135–49.

been widely recognized that interpretation of parts of the Fourth Gospel is difficult because the train of thought or sequence of narrative is either broken or obscure. Scholars before Bultmann have attempted to resolve such difficulties by theories of sources, redaction, or displacement. Bultmann's complete analysis involves his own variations of all three theories.

Assessing the evidence of confusion in the present text of the gospel, Bultmann concludes that the original order was disturbed at a very early date and the present one established by a redactor who found the text in fearful disarray. Bultmann proposes to rearrange, and thus restore, the text.[5] The fact that an allegedly superior textual order can be produced by rearrangement is taken to support the displacement theory. Bultmann apparently does not feel compelled to give a detailed account of whatever process resulted in the original displacement of much of the text. However such dislocations may have come about, he believes that their existence may be demonstrated exegetically.

Certain other difficulties in the gospel are resolved by the proposal that the evangelist wove together earlier written sources without being able to remove the traces of them completely. This source theory is the key to understanding both the composition of the gospel and the provenance of many of its ideas and ways of thought. Bultmann discerns five principal literary strata.

(1) He discovers in the prologue a *Vorlage* which the evangelist is said to have drawn from a written discourse source employed at many other points in the gospel.[6] Bultmann calls this source the *Offenbarungsreden* (revelation discourses). He identifies it primarily by its peculiar poetic structure, the Semitic quality of its language, and its Gnostic mythological motifs.

(2) Most of the narratives of chapters 1–12, especially the miracle stories, are said to have been taken by the evangelist from a second written source, called by Bultmann the *semeia*-source (sign source).[7]

(3) Another written source is said to lie at the base of the Johannine passion narrative (18:1–19:41).[8] Elements of resurrection tradition now found in chapter 20 had already been incorporated into that source before it came into the hand of the evangelist.[9]

(4) Another important element of the extant text of the Fourth Gospel, although not a source proper, is the material introduced into it by the same ecclesiastical redactor who is responsible for the present order of the gospel. Bultmann regards chapter 21 as an appendix and assigns it to this re-

---

5. Bultmann, *Johannes*, pp. 162 f.; p. 164 n. 2; p. 269 n. 1.   6. Ibid., 4 n. 5
7. Ibid., p. 78.   8. Ibid., pp. 489 ff.   9. Ibid., pp. 528 ff.

dactor.[10] The redactor is also held responsible for the interpolation of such passages as 6:51b–58; 5:28ff.; 12:48; and 19:34b, 35, which Bultmann believes espouse eschatological and sacramental doctrines foreign to the evangelist's thought. Bultmann's identification of the interpolations of the ecclesiastical redactor rests primarily and avowedly on theological considerations. In Bultmann's view, the redactor put the fragmented gospel into order as best he could and edited, annotated, and published it, adding chapter 21 as an attestation of its apostolic authenticity.

(5) Last but not least among the constituents of the Fourth Gospel is the work of the evangelist himself, whose literary skill and theological insight are manifest not only in the sections of the gospel which he freely composed but also in the way he wove the three principal written sources and other traditional materials into a harmonious whole, making them a vehicle for his own theological exposition. Bultmann identifies the work of the evangelist by contextual, stylistic, and theological criteria. Although the gospel shows traces of Semitic influence, even in those parts which Bultmann assigns to the evangelist, he regards it as certain that the author wrote in Greek rather than some Semitic tongue.

Thus, by a theory involving written sources, textual displacement, and redaction, Bultmann resolves the literary and related problems of the Fourth Gospel. Reactions to this particular aspect of his work—as well as to his commentary as a whole—have been mixed. Scholars have recognized that his proposals regarding the origin, order, editing, and publication of the gospel are as debatable as they are brilliant. It is therefore all the more remarkable that many subsequent studies of the Fourth Gospel, while paying proper tribute to Bultmann's scholarly accomplishment, have virtually bypassed many of the positions he sets forth and defends without seriously debating the questions and issues involved. For example, E. C. Colwell and E. L. Titus simply dismiss Bultmann's source and redaction theory with a conceivably valid but unelaborated objection:

> We reject Bultmann's elaborate identification of a Gnostic Sayings-Source and a Miracle-Source; as we do his suggestion that an editor is responsible for many of the agreements with the Synoptics. The possibility that an evangelist may not have achieved complete consistency is made probable by what we find to be true in Paul's thinking, and even in the work of the hypothetical editors.[11]

10. Ibid., pp. 543 ff.

11. *The Gospel of the Spirit, A Study in the Fourth Gospel* (New York, Harper, 1953), p. 31 n. 13.

In his revision of W. F. Howard's book, C. K. Barrett, who has proper respect for Bultmann's scholarship, nevertheless deals with his theory of displacement and redaction in summary fashion. He indicates a possible criticism of the displacement theory but draws a conclusion which he does not substantiate:

> It is doubtful whether any displacement or redaction theory has been worked out so completely and consistently as Dr. Bultmann's, and it is its very completeness which makes it impossible for a brief summary to do justice to it. It is however hardly unfair to say that the author never succeeds in giving a completely satisfying account of *how* the disruption took place, and, though his work is a monument of learning and acuteness, perhaps the most enduring lesson to be learnt from it is that such modest theories as those of Mr. Hoare and many of his predecessors are ultimately unsatisfying: we must either rearrange (with Dr. Bultmann) a good deal more—or else a good deal less.[12]

Now, as far as I know, Bultmann nowhere even attempts to give an account of *how* the disruption of the text took place. Therefore Barrett's statement is somewhat misleading, since it seems to imply that he has tried and failed. Moreover, it is not necessarily true that the lesson which we learn from Bultmann is that we must, following him, rearrange a good deal more than many of his predecessors or a good deal less. Barrett is quite correct about the consistency and completeness of Bultmann's displacement and redaction theories. It does not follow from this, however, that we must now either make many more or fewer rearrangements than Bultmann's more modest predecessors, but only that we must strive for equal consistency and completeness. In his commentary [13] Barrett seems to have rejected as unproved all the proposed rearrangements of the text of the gospel. Unfortunately, he does not argue the case against displacements with the same consistency and cogency with which Bultmann argued for them,[14] but such a comparable argumentation is precisely what is demanded. While Barrett's work has its own merits, it can scarcely be said to undertake a satisfactory examination of the problems of literary and historical criticism raised by Bultmann. Several other recent books in English take as little or less notice

12. Howard, *The Fourth Gospel*, p. 167.

13. *The Gospel According to St. John, An Introduction with Commentary and Notes on the Greek Text.*

14. Barrett presents some general arguments against the most common proposals for rearrangement (ibid., pp. 18 ff.) and at specific points indicates his rejection of Bultmann's proposals.

xvi
 INTRODUCTION

of Bultmann's work. Neither C. H. Dodd's magnum opus [15] nor R. H. Lightfoot's posthumously published commentary [16] takes it into account at all. While Titus refers to it in his recent commentary,[17] he gives neither the source theory nor the displacement theory very serious attention.

Recently there have been some serious and significant efforts on the part of several continental scholars to come to grips with the literary and related problems of the Fourth Gospel which have been either raised or brought into clearer focus by Bultmann's commentary. These have taken the form of either forthright debate with Bultmann or the presentation of new theories which complement or compete with his.[18] Such noteworthy studies, however, do not necessarily make superfluous another discussion of the same problems and, in particular, Bultmann's handling of them. But it is necessary at this point to indicate briefly the nature, purpose, and scope of this study.

It is a relatively modest undertaking. I shall first attempt to give a full and systematic presentation of Bultmann's literary-historical theory of the origins and earliest development of the Fourth Gospel in order to make clear his methods and their application. In doing this I do not presume to be presenting information which was hitherto unknown, but neither am I summarizing something with which everyone was already familiar. In examining this work carefully and without deliberate prejudgment, I hope to make some contribution to knowledge. In the course of the exposition of Bultmann's criteria and methods I shall reconstruct the hypothetical sources as they lay before the evangelist and the hypothetical original order of the gospel. This should serve as a basis for my own criticisms and tentative proposals and as a modest contribution to the advancement of the study of the origins and textual order of the Fourth Gospel.

The exposition of Bultmann's treatment of the problem of sources (Chapter 1) will be followed by a sketch of the scholarly discussion of Bultmann's work and some conclusions as to the present state of the problem (Chapter 2). The treatment of Bultmann's rearrangements (Chapter 3), which, surprisingly enough, do not seem to have been the subject of extensive and thorough discussion, will be accompanied by a series of critical exegetical observations dealing with his handling of the text and the problems that it raises and solves. After setting forth Bultmann's redaction theory (Chapter 4), I

15. *The Interpretation of the Fourth Gospel*, p. 121 n. 2.
16. *St. John's Gospel*, ed. C. F. Evans (Oxford, Clarendon Press, 1956).
17. *The Message of the Fourth Gospel, A New Commentary on the Gospel of John* (New York, Abingdon Press, 1957), p. 71 n. 3.
18. Below, Ch. 2.

shall examine it and the questions and issues it presents for the criticism and interpretation of the gospel as a whole.

One cannot undertake a study of Bultmann's work on John unaware of the author's pivotal importance in contemporary theological discussion. This study is in no way a direct contribution to that discussion, but any analysis and criticism of Bultmann's exegetical method are likely to have theological ramifications. This is especially true in the case of the *Johannesevangelium*, since it is not only Bultmann's most important exegetical work but deals with the New Testament book which Bultmann finds to be in closest agreement with his own theological position.[19] Indeed, the Gospel of John is thought to afford significant justification and encouragement for the task of demythologization. I shall not be so ambitious, however, as to attempt in this work to spell out in detail any implications of my investigation for Bultmann's demythologizing program, his understanding of the hermeneutical problem, or his theological position in general. Whether or not my study sheds any light on these problems, they will remain crucial for any reader of the Gospel of John or of the New Testament who is interested in understanding what the ancient writers themselves wished to say.

19. This is clear from the place enjoyed by Johannine theology in Bultmann's *Theology of the New Testament*. H. Ott, *Geschichte und Heilsgeschichte in der Theologie Rudolf Bultmanns*, Beiträge zur historischen Theologie, 19, ed. G. Ebeling, (Tübingen, J. C. B. Mohr, 1955) has called for a further investigation of the relation of the witness of John to the theology of Bultmann with the particular purpose of discovering how far the Johannine witness can be adequately comprehended by Bultmann's systematic presuppositions (p. 142; also p. 120 n. 1). Cf. also H. Diem, *Dogmatics*, trans. H. Knight (Edinburgh and London, Oliver and Boyd, 1959), pp. 244–52, where Bultmann's work on John is cited as a typical example of his exegetical method.

Abbreviations

Bibl	*Biblica*
BZ	*Biblische Zeitschrift*
CW	*Die Christliche Welt*
ET	*Evangelische Theologie*
GELNT	W. Bauer, *A Greek-English Lexicon of the New Testament*, trans. and ed. W. F. Arndt and F. W. Gringrich, Chicago, University of Chicago Press, 1937
GGA	*Göttingische Gelehrte Anzeigen*
Gn	*Gnomon*
JBL	*Journal of Biblical Literature*
JTS	*Journal of Theological Studies*
NEB	*The New English Bible, New Testament*, Oxford University Press, Cambridge University Press, 1961
NT	*Novum Testamentum*
NTA	*New Testament Abstracts*
NTS	*New Testament Studies*
OL	*Orientalische Literaturzeitung*
RGG	*Die Religion in Geschichte und Gegenwart, Handwörterbuch für Theologie und Religionswissenschaft*, Vol. 3, ed. K. Galling, Tübingen, J. C. B. Mohr, 1959
RSV	*The Holy Bible, Revised Standard Version*, New York, Thomas Nelson and Sons, 1952
TB	*Theologische Blätter*
TL	*Theologische Literaturzeitung*

TR   *Theologische Rundschau*
TS   *Theological Studies*
TTZ   *Trierer Theologische Zeitschrift*
TWNT   *Theologisches Wörterbuch zum Neuen Testament*, ed. G. Kittel and
            G. Friedrich, Stuttgart, W. Kohlhammer, from 1933
TZ   *Theologische Zeitschrift*
VF   *Verkündigung und Forschung*
ZNW   *Zeitschrift für die Neutestamentliche Wissenschaft*
ZTK   *Zeitschrift für Theologie und Kirche*

I

The Composition of the Gospel by the Evangelist

The Evangelist

Before turning to the evangelist's method and the criteria by which his hand is identified,[1] it is necessary to examine Bultmann's conception of the evangelist himself. The evangelist, the Christian circle from which he emerged, and the gospel he produced have their immediate background in the John the Baptist sect of Palestine and Syria. That such a Baptist sect continued to exist after the death of John the Baptist and that it was for a time a rival of the Christian sect (also a baptizing sect) is, according to Bultmann, clearly indicated by such passages as John 1:6–8, 1:15, 1:19–51, and 3:22–30 and Acts 18:25 and 19:1–7. Indeed, if any historical fact is represented in the Johannine account of John the Baptist, it is that the earliest disciples of Jesus had previously been disciples of the Baptist, or at least that a part of the Baptist sect had gone over to the early Christian congregation. The evangelist himself was probably a convert from this group.[2] Moreover, the tradition that Jesus

---

1. It will not be necessary to lay out the portions of the gospel assigned by Bultmann to the evangelist since they do not, like the semeia-source, the passion narrative, and the Offenbarungs-reden, constitute an independent, self-sufficient document when drawn together.

2. *Johannes*, p. 76. The less certainly 1:35–37 refers to a historical event in the life of Jesus, says Bultmann, the more certainly does it indicate the passing over of a group from the Baptist sect to the early Christian congregation.

was baptized by John may be taken as an indication that Jesus himself was for some time a disciple of the Baptist.[3] That Jesus actually baptized along-side of John as his rival, as is stated in 3:22, is probably a device of the evangelist to portray the rivalry of the two baptizing sects. Nevertheless, the possibility cannot be excluded that there is some traditional basis for the assertion of 3:22.[4] The original written source of the prologue, assigned by Bultmann to the Offenbarungsreden, is said to have been a cultic hymn of the Baptist congregation celebrating the pre-existent logos incarnate in John, who held a place of veneration in his sect somewhat analogous to that of Jesus in the early Christian community.[5] Verses 6–8 and 15 of chapter 1 are then naturally regarded as the evangelist's additions to this hymn. He applied the hymn to Jesus and made of John the witness to the incarnate logos rather than the incarnate logos himself. Thus, in making the transition from the Baptist sect to the Christian congregation, the evangelist and other former disciples of the Baptist did not abandon all their religious traditions and documents but adapted them for Christian use.[6]

Because of the manner in which the evangelist deals with the tradition, it is prima facie impossible that he could have been an eyewitness. Bultmann dismisses as superfluous the evidence brought forth to demonstrate that he was.[7] The suggestion, derived from the gospel itself, that the Beloved Disciple was an eyewitness and the author of the gospel (19:35; 21:24) is the work of the ecclesiastical redactor.[8] There is a sense in which the author did identify himself with the Beloved Disciple but without claiming to be an eyewitness or a member of the circle of the Twelve. The Beloved Disciple is not an historical figure at all, but an ideal figure. From the cross, Jesus assigns his mother to his care (19:26). Here the mother is Jewish Christianity and the disciple is pagan Christianity, as in 13:21–30 and 20:2–10 Peter is the symbol of Jewish Christianity and the Beloved Disciple is again the symbol of pagan Christian-

3. Ibid., p. 76 n. 4: "Die in ihrer Geschichtlichkeit nicht zu bestreitende Tatsache, dass sich Jesus von Johannes hat taufen lassen, beweist, dass Jesus eine Zeit lang zu den Täuferjüngern gehört hat."

4. Ibid., p. 122.

5. Ibid., p. 4 f.: "Das zu der Einfügung von. V. 6–8. 15 führende Motiv wird aus der polemischen Haltung der Verse deutlich; denn ihr Zweck ist nicht nur der positive, den Täufer als Zeugen für Jesus aufzubieten, sondern zugleich der polemische; die Autorität des Täufers als des Offenbarers zu bestreiten. Diese Autorität muss also von der Täufersekte ihrem Meister zugeschrieben worden sein; diese hat in Johannes das φῶς and damit dann doch wohl auch den fleischgewordenen präexistenten Logos gesehen" (cf. p. 29). Bultmann first expressed this view in his article "Der religionsgeschichtliche Hintergrund des Prologs des Johannes-Evangeliums," *Eucharisterion*, 2, 24.

6. *Johannes*, p. 5.

7. Ibid., p. 369 n. 5.

8. Ibid., p. 369.

ity.[9] How, then, does the evangelist identify himself with this Beloved Disciple? He does so only to the extent that he identifies himself with heathen Christianity and not in any personal historical sense.[10] Thus Bultmann disposes of the question of the apostolic authorship of the gospel. Of the theology, historical milieu, and literary method of the evangelist, Bultmann purports to know a great deal, but he does not answer and does not assign great importance to the usual questions of introduction which engrossed and vexed the Johannine scholarship of a previous generation. At least in this respect his viewpoint is similar to that of Dodd,[11] who likewise bypasses such conventional critical questions. According to Bultmann, nothing certain can be said about the author, the time of composition, or the place of composition of the gospel.[12]

We have already noted Bultmann's belief that the evangelist drew upon sources, weaving them into his composition and annotating them in order to express his own theological perspective and fulfill his purposes. It will now be necessary to see more precisely how the evangelist went about this task and how Bultmann attempts to identify exactly his compositions and annotations.

The Evangelist's Method and Bultmann's Criteria for Identifying His Work

The analysis of Bultmann's source criticism ought to begin where he begins or, at least, with one of his fundamental assumptions or principles. It is characteristic of Bultmann's commentary that his method is everywhere implicit and seldom if ever made explicit, but this deficiency is in some measure remedied by a recent encyclopedia article. According to his statement in this article, the separation of the work of the evangelist from the hypothetical sources is the initial step in his source-critical procedure. Bultmann writes:

> The question about the sources [of John] is . . . so difficult to answer because the speech of John seems to be so unified as to give no occasion for partitioning. The unity of speech, however, could have resulted from

9. Ibid., pp. 369 f.

10. "Will sich der Evglist selbst in dieser Gestalt [that of the Beloved Disciple] darstellen? In gewisser Weise wohl, sofern er eben in sich das Selbstbewusstsein und Überlegenheitsgefühl des freien Heidenchristentums trägt. Aber nicht seine Person, sondern seine Sache wird durch den Lieblingsjünger repräsentiert" (ibid., p. 370).

11. *Interpretation*, vii.

12. *RGG*, 3 (1959), 848 f. Here Bultmann nicely summarizes his position with respect to the authorship of John.

the evangelist's thorough editing. Close observation also shows considerable differences of speech in different sections, above all between the narrative reports and the speeches and discussions. Furthermore, certain expressions and passages may be recognized which are obviously to be traced back to the evangelist—transitions and explanations which stand out more or less clearly from the sources used. This is, for example, fully clear in the Passion Narrative, where traditional material has been reworked. But it is already clear from an analysis of the prologue, which is obviously based on a hymn upon which the evangelist has commented, so to speak, by means of interpolated notations. Further, the individual traits of the evangelist are recognizable in the distinct manner in which he constructs discussions between Jesus and the other persons, for example, the technique of misunderstanding. If in this fashion one has attained a picture of the individual style of the evangelist, he can with proper circumspection undertake a source analysis.[13]

In attempting to isolate and systematize various aspects of Bultmann's treatment of the problem of sources, we see the virture of his own procedure, which is to deal with all aspects of the source question as they arise in the course of actual exegesis. For while the identification of the style and method of the evangelist may, as Bultmann implies, be fundamental to the delineation of sources, it is not a task which can be carried out prior to or independently of source identification. We make a distinction here only for clarity in exposition. The attempt to identify the work of the evangelist tentatively assumes the evangelist's use of sources and the possibility of discerning a basic difference between such sources and editorial additions and transitions.[14] Like any good working hypothesis, this assumption is not arrived at arbitrarily but is based upon a preliminary examination of the evidence. Using this hypothesis in his analysis of the text, Bultmann separates the editorial work of the evangelist from his written sources. He obviously believes that the de-

13. Ibid., 842. While it is possible and profitable to approach Bultmann's work historically to see how his own previous research has shaped his commentary, my purpose is not to write the history of the development of this research. A glance at the bibliography will give some indication of it. Of crucial significance for Bultmann's source analysis of the gospel was his earlier analysis (1927) of the First Epistle, in which he began developing his method and criteria ("Analyse des ersten Johannesbriefes," *Jülicher Festgabe*, pp. 138–58). In fact, he undertook the study in preparation for the source criticism of the gospel (ibid., p. 138). In another article published about the same time, "Das Johannesevangelium in der neuesten Forschung," *CW*, 41 (1927), 502 f., Bultmann gives us an invaluable glimpse of his view of Johannine scholarship at that time. The article shows how the main lines of his approach to the gospel were already laid down ten years before the first fascicle of the commentary was published.

14. The possibility of the similar distinction between tradition and redaction has, of course, been of basic importance for Synoptic *Formgeschichte*.

tailed results of the analysis confirm the hypothesis and that he is able to carry through the separations with a high degree of accuracy. The importance of the distinction between editorial and traditional or source materials, which has been put to such far-reaching use in the investigation of the Pentateuch and the synoptic gospels, cannot be overemphasized. Together with the detection of patent difficulties in the text, it constitutes the starting point for Bultmann's comprehension and solution of the literary problems of the Fourth Gospel.

Bultmann at once distinguishes the hand of the evangelist in the prologue (1:1–18), where he discerns annotations (he uses the terms *Anmerkungen* and *Erläuterungen*) to a written source. His analysis of the prologue is typical and fundamental. It allows him to open up the whole question of the evangelist's use of sources and his method of annotating them and indicates the manner in which the source criticism of the gospel is to be carried out. Bultmann believes that certain difficulties of interpretation in the prologue are best resolved if 1:6–8, 15 are understood as additions by a later hand to a source document. If these verses are removed the difficulties disappear.[15] "These additions are not to be put aside as interpolations," says Bultmann, "rather they are the evangelist's explanations . . . as is confirmed by his way of working in the entire gospel." [16] The polemical nature of these verses is thoroughly consonant with the proposal that they have been added by the evangelist to a source. Not only is the theme of the witness of John the Baptist developed, but those who worship the Baptist as the incarnate logos are confuted.[17]

Another major criterion for the separation of source and evangelist in the prologue is the distinction between rhythmic and prosaic style. The style

15. *Johannes*, p. 3: "In die Aufgabe einer kritischen Analyse führt auch das Problem der sachlichen Gliederung. Wird v. 14 die Fleischwerdung des Logos berichtet, so muss vorher vom präexistenten Logos die Rede sein. Aber kann von diesen gesagt werden εἰς τὰ ἴδια ἦλθεν (V. 11)? So besteht der alte Streit der Exegeten, bis wie weit vom präexistenten Logos die Rede ist, von welchem Verse ab von seinem Auftreten im Fleisch. Die Frage findet leicht ihre Antwort, wenn man sieht, dass dem Prolog eine Quellenschrift zugrunde liegt, die der Evangelist mit seinen Anmerkungen versehen hat. Zu diesen gehören zunächst die vom Täufer handelnden Verse 6–8.15. Nach der vorliegenden Textfolge spricht der V. 15 redende Täufer auch die Worte von V. 16, die er doch von rechtswegen nicht sprechen kann; denn die ἡμεῖς von V. 16 müssen die von V. 14 sein. V. 15 sprengt den Zusammenhang und trennt die verbindenden Wörter πλήρης und ἐκ τοῦ πληρώματος; er ist eingefügt. Das Gleiche gilt dann auch für V. 6–8. V. 9 muss sich an V. 5 anschliessen. Wäre V. 6–8 ursprünglich im Text, so müsste V. 9–13 darauf in der Weise Bezug nehmen, dass gesagt würde: trotz dieses Zeugnisses fand der Logos keinen Glauben. Es heisst aber: obgleich die Welt durch den Logos geschaffen und sein Eigentum war . . . ; d.h. es wird auf V. 3 f. Bezug genommen."
16. Ibid., p. 4.
17. Ibid., p. 29. See also pp. 4 f.

of verses 6–8 is found to be wholly prosaic, in sharp contrast to the rhythmic, poetic quality of the neighboring verses, 1–5 and 9–12. This discovery supports the contention that 1:6–8 is an addition by the evangelist.[18] Failure to fit into the dominant poetic rhythm also calls attention to verse 12c, τοῖς πιστεύουσιν εἰς τὸ ὄνομα αὐτοῦ, and an examination of the context shows it to be impossible in the source in advance of verse 14.[19] Similarly, verse 13 is said to disrupt the rhythm of the neighboring verses and is ascribed to the evangelist.[20] The prosaic style of verse 18, with which verse 17 belongs, marks it as an interpolation of the evangelist.[21] Thus, it is established from the very beginning that the annotations of the evangelist are in prose, in contrast with at least one of his sources. It also begins to be clear how the evangelist edits and interpolates his sources. These are important insights. Henceforth, prose elements in the midst of a poetic text will immediately be suspected of being from the evangelist's hand. Interruptions in the progression of thought or narrative which occasion some difficulty of understanding or interpretation will also raise the possibility of interpolation by the evangelist in a source. While Bultmann is formulating criteria for distinguishing the work of the evangelist, he also begins to derive the characteristics of the poetic discourse behind the prologue, which he identifies as a portion of the Offenbarungsreden. As he discovers the characteristics of this source (and of the semeia-source and traditional passion narrative), they become negative criteria for the evangelist's work.

In analyzing the prologue,[22] Bultmann gathers other criteria. He discerns in the annotations of the prologue these recurring stylistic characteristics of the evangelist: (1) Old Testament or Hebraic modes of expression (1:6), (2) Rabbinic modes of expression (1:7), (3) the epexegetical ἵνα-clause (1:7), (4) antithetical constructions with successive clauses expressing the same idea first negatively and then positively (1:8), (5) the elliptical ἀλλ' ἵνα (1:8), (6) the stylized statement of identification (1:15), (7) λέγειν with the accusative meaning to say something about someone (1:15), (8) the demonstrative pronoun taking up the previously mentioned subject (1:18) or object.[23]

18. Ibid., p. 29 n. 1.
19. Ibid., p. 37 n. 4.
20. Ibid., p. 37 n. 5.
21. Ibid., p. 53 n. 5.
22. On the analysis of the prologue see Bultmann's earlier work in *Eucharisterion*. For an extensive discussion and criticism of Bultmann's analysis in the commentary, see Ruckstuhl, *Die literarische Einheit des Johannesevangeliums*, pp. 63–97. Cf. also R. Schnackenburg, "Logos-Hymnus und johanneischer Prolog," *BZ, 1* (1957), 69–109, whose position gives some support to Bultmann.
23. Bultmann, *Johannes:* (1) p. 29 n. 1. (2) p. 29 n. 1; p. 50 nn. 2, 6, 7; p. 53 n. 3. (3) p. 29 n. 1. (4) p. 29 n. 1; p. 53 n. 5. (5) p. 29 n. 1. (6) p. 50 n. 2. (7) p. 50 n. 2. (8) p. 53 n. 5.

Having already gathered this much evidence in the development of criteria for the identification of the evangelist, Bultmann is now prepared to identify the hand of the evangelist in the rest of the gospel and, in the course of doing so, to expand his set of criteria. We do not, of course, imagine that Bultmann analyzed the prologue without considerable prior knowledge of the theological and stylistic content of the rest of the gospel, for his identification of the stylistic characteristics of the evangelist in the prologue is based upon extensive familiarity with the style of the gospel as a whole. We have dealt with Bultmann's analysis of the prologue in some detail because it is the first instance of source criticism which the reader of the commentary encounters and because it affords an excellent example of his critical methodology at work. Bultmann's analysis of the prologue is not unprecedented and has been more widely accepted, in principle if not in detail, than many other aspects of his source criticism. It thus affords a good starting point for gaining insight into the way Bultmann develops his source-critical criteria. Historically, his separation of literary strata in the prologue [24] preceded both his analysis of the First Epistle [25] and his work on the rest of the gospel in preparation for his commentary.

Contextual Evidence for the Work of the Evangelist

As we examine Bultmann's analysis of the text,[26] his method of distinguishing the work of the evangelist from his sources becomes increasingly clear. With an uncanny sensitivity, he puts his finger on passages which on contextual grounds seem to be interpolations. Important clues for identifying such interpolations are: any difficulties or incongruities in a narrative or discourse, a passage's peculiar relation to its context, or the occurrence of an idea or motive known to be distinctive of the evangelist.

The contextual evidence cited by Bultmann as criteria for separating and identifying the work of the evangelist may be classified in several general categories. (1) Of particular importance, as we have noted, is the fact that the evangelist writes in prose.[27] Although this is properly a stylistic feature, it ought also to be included here, since, as in the case of 1:6–8, 15, it is often in contrast with the poetic or rhythmic style of the Offenbarungsreden source

---

24. *Eucharisterion* (1923), pp. 3–26.

25. *Jülicher Festgabe* (1927), pp. 138–58.

26. Cf. *Johannes*, p. 3, p. 68, p. 125 n. 4, p. 126 n. 2, p. 143 n. 1, p. 156 n. 5, p. 157 n. 8, pp. 160 f., p. 189 n. 2, p. 218 n. 9, pp. 241 f., p. 282 n. 3, p. 284 n. 3, p. 301 n. 4, p. 303 n. 6, p. 305 n. 4, p. 309 n. 2, p. 319, p. 361 n. 6, pp. 366 f., p. 394 n. 8, p. 459 n. 2, p. 474, p. 497, pp. 502 f., p. 505, pp. 515 ff., p. 520, p. 526, pp. 528 f., p. 534; also pp. 127 f., p. 128 n. 1, pp. 151 ff., pp. 208 f., p. 287.

27. Above, pp. 5 f.

in the same context that the individual editorial additions of the evangelist may be identified.[28] (2) It is also by the examination of the total context that the evangelist's method of making annotations (6:6) and explanations (10:13) and his penchant for broadening his sources by the addition of his own compositions is discovered. An understanding of the evangelist's method, which is theoretically one of the results of source criticism, actually helps in the task of source criticism itself. From a careful analysis of one part of the gospel, one learns what to expect from the evangelist and is able to recognize his redactional work elsewhere.[29] (3) Related to these annotations and compositions but distinguishable from them are the connective, transitional, introductory, or concluding passages such as 19:25–27, whose context and content help identify them as the evangelist's, and certain words, phrases, or statements (e.g., 11:4) which prepare for the introduction of a new motif or source material.[30] (4) Also to be attributed to the evangelist is most of the dialogue between Jesus and his questioners and opponents, which is characterized by the recurring motif of misunderstanding on the part of Jesus' interlocutors.[31] Such dialogue is not always the free composition of the evangelist but is often constructed by him out of segments from the Offenbarungsreden put into the mouth of Jesus, and thus historicized.[32] (5) The dates and place names (e.g., 6:4) that appear out of place or unnecessary in the context of traditional source materials are often recognizably the evangelist's additions, particularly when they betray his peculiar interests.[33] (6) Finally, in at least two instances (6:22–26 and 8:44), Bultmann is able to separate the work of the evangelist from an underlying source by his discovery, through a close examination of the total context, that the evangelist has actually misunderstood his source.[34]

Those passages which on contextual grounds appear to stem from the evangelist serve as the basis for the establishment of a set of stylistic criteria by which Bultmann is able not only to confirm but also to define more exactly the evangelist's use of written sources. On the one hand, since these

28. Cf. *Johannes*, p. 37 nn. 4, 5; p. 117 n. 1, p. 207 n. 1, p. 385 n. 5, p. 394 n. 8, p. 413 n. 1, p. 414 n. 1, p. 424 n. 1; also p. 29 n. 1, p. 53 n. 5, p. 110 n. 3, p. 170 n. 2, p. 199 n. 7, p. 262 n. 7, p. 198 n. 8, p. 200 n. 5, where Bultmann notes the prosaic style of the evangelist.

29. On the redactional work of the evangelist, ibid., p. 3, p. 86, p. 93, p. 141 n. 1, p. 157 n. 1, pp. 177 ff., p. 178, p. 201, pp. 208 f., p. 218 n. 6, p. 262 n. 7, p. 273, p. 276 n. 5, p. 282 n. 3, p. 284 n. 3, p. 321, p. 323, p. 340 n. 1, p. 343, p. 364, p. 366, p. 374, p. 459 n. 2, p. 474, p. 502, p. 503.

30. Ibid., p. 127, p. 346, p. 401 n. 5, p. 520; also p. 85 n. 5, p. 86, p. 137, p. 142, p. 264, p. 302 n. 7, p. 323, p. 343, p. 401 n. 5, p. 503.

31. See below, p. 11.

32. Ibid., p. 93.

33. Ibid., p. 68; p. 156; p. 503; p. 515.

34. Ibid., pp. 160 f.; pp. 241 f.

passages taken as a whole show similar stylistic characteristics, the contextual evidence is confirmed. On the other, the stylistic features attain an independent status and are then used to make further and more precise identifications of the redactional work of the evangelist. While Bultmann's insight into the separation of sources from the work of the evangelist on the basis of the study of the relation of elements in the same context to one another is logically prior to his gathering of stylistic characteristics, the latter, when assembled, confirm the initial findings and in turn become independent criteria. With the development of stylistic criteria for the evangelist, portions of the gospel which are not original with him become more easily discernible. The distinct characteristics of the evangelist's hand become negative criteria for the identification of the sources.

Stylistic Characteristics of the Evangelist's Work

Some of the criteria of style and speech said to be characteristic of the evangelist appear to be much more important than others, and Bultmann does not always permit one to be sure whether or not he himself has decided that a trait characteristic of the evangelist is clearly enough defined to be used in identifying passages as stemming from him. As a general rule, those characteristics to which Bultmann refers most frequently are the ones that are decisive for establishing the style of the evangelist and are therefore the most useful criteria for separating his own work from his sources.[35]

The specific and general stylistic characteristics of the evangelist most frequently cited by Bultmann include the following (only one example of each given in parentheses): (1) prosaic style (1:6–8), (2) Old Testament and Rabbinic modes of expression and Semitisms in general, (3) the frequent use of the epexegetical ἵνα-clause explicating a demonstrative (1:7), (4) the epexegetical ἵνα-clause itself (4:34), (5) stylized statements of definition (6:50) and identification (1:15), (6) the antithetical construction with a positive statement preceded by its negative counterpart (1:8) and (7) frequently employing the οὐ (κ) . . . ἀλλά construction, (8) the emphatic ἐκεῖνος (1:8), (9) the elliptical ἀλλ' ἵνα (1:8), (10) λέγειν with the accusative meaning to say something about someone (1:15), (11) the pronoun taking up the preceding subject or object in the same sentence (1:18), (12) οὐ(κ) . . .

---

35. These characteristics may be classified further as lexical, stylistic, and syntactical. Bultmann, however, does not attempt to classify the characteristics of the evangelist in this way, but uses the terms *sprachlich* and *stilistisch* to cover a multitude of phenomena. Consequently, I have adopted no system of classification. The order in which the characteristics are presented is approximately the order of their importance. I have attempted to group related characteristics together.

ἀλλά ... and similar constructions with a negative and ἀλλά (1:31), (13) the explanatory διὰ τοῦτο or, when the reason given follows rather than precedes, διὰ τοῦτο ... ὅτι ... (1:31), (14) the explanatory (and causal) ὅτι-clause (3:18), (15) ἐν (ἐκ or διὰ) τούτῳ (9:30), (16) a pair of verbs introduced by καί meaning "and so" and bound together by καί meaning "and" (1:34), (17) (the twofold ἀμὴν ἀμήν introducing the words of Jesus (1:51), (18) μετὰ τοῦτο (μετὰ ταῦτα) as a transitional formula (2:12), (19) stylized formulas used in introducing scripture quotations (2:17), (20) transitional ὡς δέ and ὡς οὖν (2:23), (21) αὐτὸς δέ and αὐτὸς γάρ (2:24), (22) οὐ(δὲ) γάρ (3:17), (23) οὖν connective (3:25), (24) ὡς οὖν (4:40), (25) ὅτι οὖν (6:24), (26) questions (of Jesus) introduced by οὐ(κ) (4:35), (27) separation of the nominative from the modifying genitive by the finite verb (4:39), (28) ταῦτα εἶπεν, τοῦτο δὲ ἔλεγεν, etc. (in different tenses and number), sometimes with ὅτι or ἵνα following (6:6), (29) ταῦτα εἰπών as a transitional formula (13:21), (30) neutral πᾶν (6:37), (31) οἶδα ὅτι (4:42), (32) causal καθώς (10:15).[36] As a rule Bultmann does not identify a passage as the evangelist's on the basis of a single stylistic feature. In assigning a passage (e.g., 1:6–8) to the evangelist he is

36. All page references are to *Johannes* unless otherwise stated. (1) p. 29 n. 1, p. 53 n. 5, p. 110 n. 3, p. 170 n. 2, p. 199 n. 7, p. 198 n. 8, p. 200 n. 5. Bultmann also comments upon the evangelist's simplicity of style (p. 122 n. 1). (2) p. 29 n. 1. See also index, p. 560. (3) p. 29 n. 1, p. 170 nn. 2, 3 (6:50). See (5) below. (4) p. 29 n. 1, p. 302 n. 7, p. 362 n. 6, p. 378 n. 8. See (5) below. (5) Typical of the evangelist's style is what Bultmann calls the *Definitionsatz*. It takes a variety of syntactical forms but is usually marked by the demonstrative, which lifts out something previously mentioned in order that it may be explained more fully. The epexegetical ἵνα-clause explicating a demonstrative usually serves the purpose of definition (p. 174 nn. 1, 3, p. 378 n. 1, p. 389 n. 4, p. 417 n. 1). Other constructions used for the same purpose include: οὕτως ... ὥστε ..., αὕτη ... ὅτι ..., and in the case of something hypothetical, ἐν τούτῳ ... (ἐάν ...) (p. 110 n. 3, p. 403 n. 2). Of a similar genre is the *Identificationsatz* (p. 50 n. 2), in which a person, e.g. Jesus in 1:15, is emphatically singled out by the use of the demonstrative and identified. (6) p. 29 n. 1, p. 53 n. 5, p. 60 n. 3, p. 110 n. 3, p. 173 nn. 1, 7; p. 292 n. 1, p. 452 n. 1. (7) See (12) below. (8) p. 29 n. 1, p. 53 n. 5, p. 64 n. 1, p. 89 n. 1, p. 126 n. 6, p. 181 n. 7, p. 221 n. 8, p. 239 n. 4, p. 257 n. 6, p. 262 n. 7, p. 366. (9) p. 29 n. 1, p. 63 n. 6, p. 251 n. 4, p. 313 n. 2, p. 311 n. 6, p. 318 n. 5, p. 389 n. 1, p. 424 n. 9. (10) p. 50 n. 2. (11) p. 53 n. 5, p. 117 n. 1, p. 125 n. 4, p. 173 n. 1, p. 199 n. 7, p. 200 n. 5, p. 207 n. 1, p. 263 n. 4, p. 275 n. 8, p. 377 n. 5, p. 397 n. 6. (12) p. 29 n. 1, p. 63 n. 6, p. 177 n. 5, p. 292 n. 1, p. 302 n. 7, p. 313 n. 2, p. 318 nn. 1, 5; p. 389 n. 1, p. 392 n. 4. (13) p. 63 n. 6, p. 177 n. 5, p. 254 n. 10, p. 292 n. 1, p. 319 n. 3, p. 340 n. 1, p. 346 n. 4, p. 361 n. 1, p. 422 n. 3. (14) p. 110 n. 3, p. 478 n. 7. (15) p. 255 n. 5, p. 403 n. 2, p. 414 n. 7. (16) p. 64 n. 1, p. 257 n. 6. (17) p. 74 n. 3. (18) p. 85 n. 6, p. 122 n. 1. (19) γεγραμμένον ἐστίν: p. 87 n. 4; ἵνα πληρωθῇ: p. 346 n. 4, p. 385 n. 5, p. 424 n. 9. (20) p. 91 n. 3. (21) p. 91 n. 3, p. 157 n. 1. (22) p. 110 n. 3, p. 111 n. 1, p. 119 n. 1, p. 239 n. 4, p. 262 n. 7. (23) p. 122 n. 1. (24) p. 148 n. 3. (25) p. 160 n. 7, p. 361 n. 6. (26) p. 143 n. 1. (27) p. 148 n. 3. (28) p. 157 n. 1, p. 164 n. 1, p. 174 n. 5, p. 198 n. 8, p. 254 n. 10, p. 313 n. 2, p. 386 n. 3, p. 416 n. 9, p. 428 n. 1, p. 452 n. 1. (29) p. 367 n. 1. (30) p. 173 n. 6, p. 377 n. 5. (31) p. 148 n. 3, p. 198 nn. 1, 6; p. 422 n. 2. (32) p. 291 n. 3, p. 362 n. 6, p. 376 n. 1, p. 377 n. 5, p. 389 n. 4, p. 403 n. 2.

often able to cite several stylistic characteristics as well as contextual or other evidence.[37]

In addition to the stylistic criteria noted,[38] there are a number of characteristic literary techniques or expressions which help identify the evangelist's work. Especially important is the frequent motif of misunderstanding found in discussions involving Jesus and his interlocutors. After a statement of Jesus, the interlocutor asks a question that reflects a serious misunderstanding (e.g., 3:4), usually based upon his failure to grasp the Johannine dualism.[39] Jesus corrects the interlocutor and uses the question as the springboard for the continuing discussion or discourse. Sometimes Jesus is made to ask questions designed to provide occasions for him to reproach his interlocutors rather than to evoke a genuine answer (3:10).[40] Occasionally the evangelist has Jesus cite something he himself has said earlier in the gospel (8:24).[41] The recurring summary assertion that many believed in Jesus is also characteristic of the evangelist (2:23).[42]

The Evidence of Theological Motifs and Terminology

Bultmann believes that theological considerations confirm his identification of the work of the evangelist. He identifies common theological terms or

37. *Johannes*, p. 29 n. 1, p. 110 nn. 3, 5.

38. The above list by no means exhausts Bultmann's collection of the characteristics which mark the style of the evangelist. I have included those which seem to me to be the most important. Bultmann also cites the following other characteristics: μέντοι after negation (p. 221 n. 8); ἤδη-clause (p. 254 n. 10); ἵνα ἐάν (p. 254 n. 10; p. 316 n. 2); ταύτην τὴν ἐντολήν (p. 292 n. 1); πρὸς θάνατον, ὑπὲρ τῆς δόξης, ὑπὲρ τοῦ ὀνόματος, δι᾽ αὐτῆς (p. 302 n. 7); ὧν (p. 313 n. 2; ἦν δὲ ἐγγύς with following Jewish festival (p. 316 n. 2); statements of date after καί (p. 316 n. 2); ἐζήτουν οὖν καὶ ἔλεγον (p. 316 n. 2); ἦν δὲ καί (p. 122 n. 1); οὐ χρείαν ἔχειν ἵνα (p. 91 n. 3, p. 92 n. 5, p. 357 n. 4); causal ὅτι-clause at the conclusion of a statement (p. 318 n. 5); τούτου with τοῦ κόσμου (p. 330 n. 1); ἤδει γάρ (p. 361 n. 1); χαρὰ πεπληρωμένη (p. 386 n. 3); θέλω ἵνα (p. 397 n. 6); a clause taking up some word or element from the latter half of the immediately preceding clause (p. 506 n. 2); εἰδώς (p. 522 n. 1); a verb immediately following the ἀλλά in an adversative clause (p. 160 n. 6); ἔλεγεν δέ (p. 340 n. 1); τινὲς γὰρ ἐδόκουν (p. 366 n. 4); τότε (p. 366 n. 5).

The characteristics I have classified under style already include some items which might better be called "speech" or "vocabulary." There are other words or expressions which Bultmann regards as characteristic of the evangelist: μονογενὴς υἱός (p. 110 n. 3); σωτὴρ τοῦ κόσμου and ἵνα σώσω τὸν κόσμον (p. 148 n. 3); ἀπὸ του οὐρανοῦ or ἐκ τοῦ οὐρανοῦ (p. 173 n. 7); διάβολος instead of σατανᾶς (p. 366); τεκνία—found frequently in the epistles but only at 13:33 in the gospel—(p. 402 n. 5); the simple Ἰουδαῖοι of Jesus' opponents (p. 59, p. 174, p. 502 n. 4, p. 503 n. 2, p. 516 n. 5); ἐν τῷ νόμῳ αὐτῶν (p. 59 n. 2, p. 424 n. 9). See also Ruckstuhl, *Einheit*, pp. 26 f.

39. Johannes, p. 175 n. 5.

40. Ibid., p. 143 n. 1.

41. Ibid., p. 265 n. 2, p. 340 n. 1.

42. Ibid., p. 91 n. 3.

motifs in passages which may be ascribed to the evangelist on other grounds. These in turn become additional criteria for source criticism. Theological considerations thus support the contextual and stylistic evidence and make possible or more certain further identification of the work of the evangelist. There is a certain amount of circularity involved here, but it is not as if Bultmann were identifying passages as the evangelist's because of their theological content while using these same passages to determine the theology of the evangelist. The latter is determined by the perspective and thrust of the gospel as a whole as well as by the purpose and interests of the material assigned specifically to him.

Bultmann finds the following theological ideas and terminology significant for source criticism: (1) the precise use of "Son of Man" as a title for Jesus in his capacity as "the One sent by God walking upon earth" (1:51), (2) the positive use of Old Testament quotations and motifs (3:14), particularly in contrast with the Offenbarungsreden, (3) a sophisticated conception of the σημεῖα of Jesus fundamentally different from the naive view of signs found in the semeia-source, (4) the theme of μαρτυρία, especially the μαρτυρία of the Baptist and the Father to Jesus (5:33–35), (5) μένειν ἐν used of the abiding of the word in the hearer (5:38), (6) Jesus' διδαχή (7:16), (7) the problem of those who hear the gospel at second hand (4:39–42), (8) the obedience of Jesus to the Father (12:49 f.), (9) Jesus as ὁ προφήτης (1:21, 6:14), (10) the question of the origin of Jesus (2:9), (11) the redeemer's sending of the elect into the world to witness (17:18), (12) the ἀγάπη motif (13:34), and (13) an overall subtlety and theological sophistication displayed in the use of sources.[43]

The Method of the Evangelist

Supported by this ever-broadening base of evidence, Bultmann is able to comment extensively on the methods which the evangelist uses to exploit his sources to the best effect. The evangelist interprets them, annotates them, expands them, and supplements them in order to put them at the service of his own viewpoint. He actually demythologizes the semeia-source and, especially, the Offenbarungsreden so as to make them vehicles of his own theology. He rejects and transforms the primitive miracle faith of the semeia-

___

43. All page references are to *Johannes*. (1) p. 74 n. 4, p. 76, p. 107 n. 4, p. 110 n. 5, p. 257. "Son of Man" also appears in the discourse source but not in the same sense. The redactor also uses the title (6:27, 51–58), but his use of it to refer to the exalted Lord gives him away. The term is not used by the evangelist of any pre-existent logos or Urmensch. (2) p. 109 n. 1, p. 172, p. 205 n. 2. (3) pp. 149 f., p. 152 f., pp. 157 ff., p. 346. (4) p. 198 n. 8, p. 275 n. 8. (5) p. 200 n. 5, p. 414 n. 1. (6) p. 206 n. 4. (7) p. 148. (8) p. 263. (9) p. 58. The evangelist also coordinates the title ὁ χριστός with ὁ προφήτης (1:21, 7:40 f.). (10) p. 82 n. 9, p. 255 n. 5. (11) p. 390 n. 4. (12) p. 403 n. 2, p. 415 nn. 1, 3. (13) pp. 75 f., p. 138, pp. 157 ff., p. 148.

source, understanding the miracles as signs which do not in and of themselves evoke faith—and are not conditioned by faith, as in the synoptics—but which place the one who confronts them in the position of deciding whether Jesus is the revelation of God. He rejects and transforms the Gnostic mythology of the Offenbarungsreden, historicizing the discourses by placing them in the mouth of Jesus, where they do not purport to tell of the nature of a divine being, his descent to earth, and ascent to the Father but rather indicate the significance of Jesus as the revealer and place man in the crisis of decision, in which he must decide whether he believes that the man Jesus is the revelation of God.[44] In the finished gospel, the signs and discourses have the same purpose and effect, different as they are in origin and substance. They do not afford external legitimation of the revelation of God in Jesus. Rather, they are used by the evangelist to express a purified idea of revelation, and, in the preaching of the Fourth Gospel, they become the vehicle of the event in which revelation occurs again and again. In function they are fundamentally and essentially the same, for neither has any meaning for the evangelist except as it speaks to man's actual (existential) situation and places him in the moment of decision.

Bultmann indicates a number of techniques and peculiarities characteristic of the evangelist's handling of his sources:[45] (1) the use of annotations and transitions; (2) the abridgment, transposition, and excision of sources; (3) the taking up, in advance, of a theme or motif which is to be brought in later by the use of source material; (4) the imitation of the style of the source (particularly the Offenbarungsreden); and (5) the symbolic understanding and interpretation of the events or sayings found in the source.[46] He also notes that the evangelist knew and used traditional materials other than those contained in the discourse, sign, and passion sources.[47]

44. It is nevertheless true that the theological perspective of the evangelist has strong affinities with that of the Offenbarungsreden. In Bultmann's view their religious and cultural milieus are similar: *Johannes*, p. 354 n. 3, p. 39 n. 5, p. 119 n. 1, p. 220 nn. 1, 5; p. 239 n. 4, p. 263 n. 4, p. 264 n. 5, p. 271 n. 2, p. 287, p. 395 n. 2.

45. Bultmann repeatedly refers to and describes the evangelist's method of employing his sources: ibid., p. 103, p. 128, p. 136 n. 5, p. 173, p. 178, p. 217 n. 2, p. 220 n. 5, p. 224 n. 1, p. 262 n. 6, p. 264 n. 2, p. 303 n. 6, p. 304 n. 1, p. 321, p. 323, p. 337, p. 354 n. 3, p. 374, pp. 421 ff., p. 478 n. 7, pp. 500 f., pp. 502 f., p. 503, p. 526, pp. 528 f., p. 534, p. 536, pp. 537 f., p. 541. On the evangelist's use of the semeia-source see e.g. pp. 78 f.; on his use of the Offenbarungsreden source see p. 93, p. 95 n. 5.

46. (1) see p. 8. (2) *Johannes*, p. 142, p. 161, p. 170 n. 1, p. 177, p. 478 n. 3, p. 502, p. 536. (3) see above, p. 8. (4) *Johannes*, p. 220 nn. 1, 5; p. 264 n. 5, p. 409 n. 2. (5) *Johannes*, p. 86 n. 2, p. 89, p. 161, p. 253 n. 3, p. 351, pp. 365 ff.

47. For example, the evangelist is said to use what appear to be traditional words of the Lord that we know in somewhat different form from the synoptic tradition: p. 88 n. 7, p. 95 n. 5, p. 352. He also reflects some knowledge of the synoptic tradition itself: p. 325 n. 5, p. 326 n. 3, p. 340 n. 1, p. 343 n. 6. Below pp. 51–3.

A Preliminary Question about Bultmann's Method

Against Bultmann's source analysis, it may be argued that his method is circular and therefore invalid. He has only the somewhat ambiguous internal evidence of the document itself and no external evidence upon which to base his arguments. On the other hand, it must be conceded that in principle his procedure is no more circular than, for example, the source criticism of the Pentateuch (the results of which are much less secure, however, than they were thought to be several decades ago). In each case, the source critic is forced to proceed without external evidence, i.e. other ancient documents which give an indication of having been incorporated in the document upon which he is working. (Contrast the situation of synoptic source criticism.) In each case, contextual, stylistic, and theological (or other *sachlich*) considerations, used in conjunction with one another, lead to the separation of sources. The significant difference is that in the case of the Pentateuch one is presumably dealing with a document which grew by accretion, the various contributors having no foreknowledge of what the actual end product would be and caring little for stylistic homogeneity, while in the case of the Gospel of John one is dealing with something much more in the nature of a literary product, to which an author gave very careful attention in order to give the impression of unity.[48] Therefore the task of documentary criticism would be much more difficult in the latter case, even if the correctness of Bultmann's general hypothesis of written sources were granted. But that hypothesis itself is much harder to establish convincingly because of the very nature of the gospel.

Against the charge of circularity Bultmann would doubtless maintain that all historical reason is strongly circular,[49] and this certainly cannot be unconditionally denied. Indeed, all scientific reason involves the gathering of data around a hypothesis or the formulation of a hypothesis on the basis of data. In the testing of the hypothesis against this evidence the hypothesis proves itself valid or invalid. There is a sense in which this moving from evidence to hypothesis or hypothesis to evidence may be termed a circular process. But in the case of the physical sciences the results can be tested by continuing experience and experiment, whereas in the case of historical research the only test of a hypothesis is its capacity for explaining all the evidence which gave rise to the hypothesis in the first place. This, however, does not necessarily

48. Cf. Howard, *The Fourth Gospel*, p. 101; also the perceptive remarks of B. H. Streeter, *The Four Gospels: A Study of Origins* (4th rev. impression, London, Macmillan, 1930), p. 378.

49. Cf. his *Die Geschichte der synoptischen Tradition* (4th ed. Göttingen, Vandenhoeck und Ruprecht, 1958), p. 5.

constitute indubitable proof that the hypothesis, that is, the historical theory, corresponds to the reality of the past. More than one hypothesis may explain all the evidence equally well in the opinion of different scholars, or none may. Nor does historical research offer the kind of opportunity for correction and modification that is possible in the experimental sciences. Therefore, even if we should find it necessary to say that Bultmann's hypothesis about the origin of the Fourth Gospel explains the available evidence most comprehensively and coherently, this would not necessarily permanently validate it. It would, however, give it the authority of the most probable historical explanation. This would be nothing to take lightly, since historical science can only, with respect to matters of historical fact, deal in degrees of probability—granted that a high degree of probability may be imperceptibly close to certainty.

But the door must always remain open for another hypothesis which would explain the evidence equally well or better, perhaps taking into account factors that had been previously overlooked or given an improper evaluation. To be more specific, even if Bultmann's hypothesis explained with greatest consistency the evidence as he gathers and evaluates it, there remains always the possibility of introducing further evidence or, from a different perspective, evaluating the available evidence differently. For example, one might concede that Bultmann has made as thorough an investigation of the literary character of the Fourth Gospel as anyone could demand and, at the same time, ask whether he has not allowed his literary analysis to dictate an understanding of the historical process through which the gospel emerged in its present form without making sufficient allowance for other factors which deserve consideration. It is conceivable that Bultmann has adopted a perspective which predisposes him to think in terms of literary analysis and literary sources as the key to the solution of Johannine problems. Whether, or to what extent, this is the case will be an important question for the subsequent chapters of this study.

The Sources Used by the Evangelist

The Offenbarungsreden

I have indicated that the identification or separation of sources is the obverse of the identification of the work of the evangelist, the criteria for the delineation of the one becoming negative criteria for the other. I have dealt first with the evangelist for reasons already cited and because in this case Bultmann establishes the most elaborate set of criteria—particularly stylistic characteristics—by which he proposes to separate the various literary strata.

The Offenbarungsreden compose what is in many respects the evangelist's most important source. We have already indicated that this source first appears in the prologue. It distinguishes itself on stylistic and contextual grounds from the evangelist's work and at the same time has the closest relation to his own *Denkweise* and theology.[50] This is not surprising, since both the evangelist and his source spring from a common cultural and religious milieu, although the evangelist is, of course, Christian while the source is not.[51] The evangelist writes in a partially Semitizing Greek, while the source was originally composed in Aramaic.[52] Whether that document was translated by the evangelist himself or came into his hands already translated is a question which, according to Bultmann, cannot be decided.[53] The proximate origin of the Johannine Offenbarungsreden is the same circle of Baptist adherents from which the evangelist himself was converted (the prologue, which is regarded as the hymn-like introduction to the collected discourses, is explicitly said to stem from the Baptist sect [54]), but the ultimate origin of these discourses is to be located in a peculiar type of Oriental Gnosticism that supposedly manifested itself in such groups as the Baptist sect.[55]

50. Above, p. 13 n. 44.

51. On the common cultural and religious milieu see *Johannes*, pp. 4 f. The non-Christian origin of the Offenbarungsreden does not in principle exclude the possibility that this material was used in the Christian cultus before being incorporated in the Gospel of John. Bultmann nevertheless makes the evangelist himself responsible for the Christianizing of the discourses. The revealer who is spoken of and speaks in the source is only identified with Jesus by the evangelist.

52. *Johannes*, p. 5.

53. *RGG*, 3 (1959), 844.

54. *Johannes*, p. 5. On the integral relation of the source of the prologue to the subsequent Offenbarungsreden see p. 4 n. 5, p. 93. On the relation of the revelation discourses as a whole to the Baptist circle see p. 125 n. 7.

55. In defining and categorizing this Gnosis, Bultmann cites the work of his student, H. Jonas, *Gnosis und spätantiker Geist* (Göttingen, Vandenhoeck und Ruprecht, 1934).

Bultmann's identification of the Gnostic background of the Fourth Gospel has a long history. In 1923 he published the article, "Der religionsgeschichtliche Hintergrund des Prologs zum Johannesevangelium," in which he found a Vorlage in the prologue and tried to ascertain its place in the history of religions. At that time he related it closely to Hellenistic-Jewish wisdom speculation influenced by Oriental mythology. Two years later there appeared an extensive and important article, "Die Bedeutung der neuerschlossen en mandäischen und mani-chäischen Quellen für das Verständnis des Johannes-Evangeliums" [*ZNW*, 24 (1925), 100–46], in which Bultmann compared passages in the Gospel of John with Mandaean, Manichaean, and other Gnostic sources. He found twenty-eight central motifs in the gospel which could be closely paralleled from these sources, and he concluded that the Gnostic redeemer myth to which they attest is the key to the understanding of the Fourth Gospel. The redeemer myth is held to be earlier than the Fourth Gospel even though most of the literary evidence for it is demonstrably later. Bultmann would establish this conclusion by showing that assertions of John may be explained on the basis of this myth, while the converse is not true.

Bultmann attempts to define precisely the Gnosticism of this source. Since the Offenbarungsreden represent Oriental Gnosis (Jonas' category), there is nothing in them about the role of the sphere hostile to God in the self-unfolding process of the Godhead. There is, of course, a dualism, but, as in most of the Mandaean documents, there is no speculation about the origin of the sphere of darkness in a primeval fall. Although, in keeping with the character of Oriental Gnosis, darkness appears as an active power opposed to God, its role is reduced to a minor one, since this Gnosis, like that of the Odes of Solomon, is subject to the restraining influences of Old Testament faith. Moreover, only the logos, and no elaborate system of emanations, stands between God and the world. This fact reflects in part the relation of the Offenbarungsreden to an earlier form of Gnosis in which such speculations had not developed (e.g. the Mandaean literature) and in part its relation to a later form in which, under the influence of the Old Testament, they had been reduced (e.g. the Odes of Solomon). Within the gospel itself, only the references to the angels (1:51) and to the many μοναί in the Father's house (14:2) betray the fact that in the Gnostic thought-world of the Offenbarungsreden heaven has more inhabitants than the prologue of the gospel implies, i.e. God and the logos.

In the prologue there is no attempt to describe or conceptualize in any way the procession of the logos from the Father. Neither the creation of the world nor that of man is described as a tragedy. At this point, according to Bultmann, the distance from most forms of Gnosis is greatest. Creation is attributed to the Godhead, as in Iranian Gnosis generally, where it is a battle against darkness. Here, however, the role of darkness has been sharply reduced, again under the influence of the Old Testament, and the battle motif has disappeared. As in the Odes of Solomon the dualism here defines only the soteriology, not the cosmology; the world is created by God or his word.

In his article, "Analyse des ersten Johannesbriefes," he discovered a Vorlage in the First Epistle that presumably stems from the same milieu as the speeches of John. Interestingly enough, while the source of the First Epistle bears many similarities to the Offenbarungsreden of the Fourth Gospel, there is at least one striking difference. Apart from 2:23; 5:10, 12 (II John 9), where Father and Son are mentioned, there is little suggestion of a revealer or redeemer myth in the source of I John. Bultmann himself does not say more than that the sources of the two documents are related in form and content (RGG, 3, 1959, 837). Like its counterpart, the source of I John is originally non-Christian. While his commentary was appearing, Bultmann published the review article "Johanneische Schriften und Gnosis," in which he vigorously defended his view of the Gnostic background of the Fourth Gospel against the attack of E. Percy in Untersuchungen über den Ursprung der johanneischen Theologie, zugleich ein Beitrag zur Frage nach der Entstehung des Gnostizismus (Lund, Gleerupska, 1939). For Bultmann's own views on Gnosis see also his Gnosis and his Primitive Christianity in Its Contemporary Setting, pp. 162–71.

The distinction of the demiurge from the logos (found in Mandaean texts) is absent from the prologue along with any theory of the origin of souls in an *Urmensch*. In general, the mythological aspect of this Gnosis is quite restrained, and interest in the relation of man to the revelation of God, i.e. the soteriological interest, is predominant.[56]

This Gnostic Denkweise of the Offenbarungsreden is defined by Bultmann on the basis of a comparison of the prologue and other Johannine speeches with other Gnostic documents, particularly the Odes of Solomon and the Mandaean literature. He has also investigated a variety of Gnostic or quasi-Gnostic materials including the Naasene hymn, the Ignatian corpus, and certain early Christian writings from the so-called apocryphal New Testament. In the first place, these documents are supposed to demonstrate the existence of a thought world which could, and did, produce religious texts not unlike the hypothetical Offenbarungsreden. Furthermore, they manifest a form and a poetic structure that show a certain kinship with the style of the speeches of the Gospel of John. Thus, both the substantial and formal characteristics of parallel documents are taken to support the contention that a text such as the Johannine Offenbarungsreden existed independently before the composition of the Fourth Gospel. So Bultmann is able to make the claim that the identification of the Offenbarungsreden is not solely dependent on the internal evidence of the gospel but draws support also from the existence of a religious Denkweise and of documents which can be traced to a time nearly contemporary with the Fourth Gospel.[57]

Bultmann is able to distinguish between the theology of the Offenbarungsreden and that of the evangelist despite their similarities or agreements on many points. He observes such divergences as the following: the difference in the use of the title Son of Man, which for the evangelist is Jesus as the revealer in his mission on earth, but for the source is the Urmensch in whom the revealer and believers find their true origin and unity; the difference in the use of the Old Testament, which the source, in contrast with the evangelist, never refers to in a favorable light; their different application of the concept μένειν ἐν, used in the source in the strongly mystical sense of the abiding of God in the believer but by the evangelist in the sense of the abiding of the word in the hearer.[58] Furthermore, in the evangelist's thought there is only

---

56. For this and the preceding assertions about the Gnosis of the Offenbarungsreden see Bultmann, *Johannes*, pp. 13 ff.

57. In separating the Offenbarungsreden from the remainder of the gospel, Bultmann frequently cites as supporting evidence passages from one or more of these supposedly related Gnostic documents. See ibid., pp. 2 f., pp. 4 f., pp. 13 f., p. 11 n. 3, p. 112 n. 1, p. 113 n. 1, p. 119 n. 3, p. 332 n. 4, p. 338 n. 6, pp. 277 ff., p. 322, p. 329 n. 4, p. 395 n. 2, p. 462 n. 1.

58. Above, p. 12 and n. 43.

one sent from God, namely Jesus, while in the source the revealer speaks in the first person plural including with himself others also sent by God.[59] Most important is the distinction between the mythological character of the language in the source and the evangelist's more sophisticated use of this language as he, so to speak, demythologizes the source and historicizes it by putting it into the mouth of Jesus.[60] For source-critical purposes, however, the primary distinctions between the evangelist and the source are not substantial and theological but formal and stylistic.

The difference between the discourse and the narrative portions of the Fourth Gospel has previously been recognized and even attributed to different strata or sources, but Bultmann has broken new ground in his distinction between a speech source and the annotations of the evangelist interwoven with it. He gave the first indication of his speech source theory in a 1923 article on the prologue, in which he separated a Vorlage from the work of the evangelist and noted the recurrence throughout the gospel of motifs akin to those of this source.[61] Then in 1927 he attempted to establish such a distinction between source and author-annotator in his analysis of the First Epistle. In this article he made clear the importance of this document for the source analysis of the Fourth Gospel, which he had already undertaken.[62] Bultmann identifies in the epistle most of the main characteristics of speech and style which enable him to separate source from evangelist in the gospel. In the analysis of the epistle as in the commentary on the gospel Bultmann establishes on formal or contextual grounds that a certain section belongs to the source or to the evangelist and proceeds on the basis of this section to begin formulating a set of stylistic characteristics to serve as criteria for further source separations.[63] He first discovers grounds for believing that 1:5b–10 is from a Vorlage and 2:1, 2 from the author of the finished document and then

59. *Johannes*, p. 104.

60. On the evangelist's important differences from pagan Gnostic mythological thinking see pp. 38 f., pp. 41 f., p. 104, pp. 188 f., p. 191 n. 5. On his historicization of the Offenbarungsreden see p. 93.

61. *Eucharisterion*, especially pp. 23–26.

62. *Jülicher Festgabe*, p. 138: "Meine Vermutung, dass der Johannesevangelist ausser anderer Tradition eine Quelle verarbeitet hat, die Offenbarungsreden enthielt, suchte ich durch stilkritische Untersuchungen zu stützen. Diese dehnte ich auf die Johannesbriefe aus und fand bald zum eigenen Erstaunen, dass auch der Verfasser des ersten Briefes jene Redensammlung benutzt hat."

63. Ibid., p. 138. "Hat man Grund, zunächst an einer bestimmten Stelle eine Quelle zu vermuten (für mich war es 1, 5–2, 2), so wird man die hier zu erhebenden stilkritischen Beobachtungen für die weitere Analyse fruchtbar machen. Man wird zumal die hier gefundenen Wendungen der redaktionellen Technik des Verfassers in Zusammenhang mit seiner Schreibweise bringen, die aus den zweifellos von ihm stammenden Teilen des 'Briefes' erkenntlich ist."

begins to formulate stylistic criteria and to make other such source-critical distinctions on the basis of them.[64]

In the separation of sources in the gospel Bultmann brings together a rather considerable collection of formal and stylistic criteria for the Offenbarungs-reden. Of greatest importance is the rhythmic, poetic style of the discourses, which, when grasped, makes them appear to stand out from the context in which they are set and which contrasts strikingly with the prose style of the evangelist. (The verses of the Offenbarungsreden are printed as poetry throughout the commentary.) When Bultmann first encounters material from the Offenbarungsreden in the prologue he recognizes it to be cultic-liturgical poetry. As in the Odes of Solomon, two short clauses are linked together in a double verse which gives expression to one thought. Sometimes the second member of the double verse leads the thought further (verses 1, 4, 14a, 16). Sometimes the members stand in parallelism (verse 3) or in antithesis (verses 5, 10, 11). This form of versification is common in Semitic poetry. In the prologue, however, it is executed in a particularly strict and artful way. In each member of a double verse there are two words of emphasis. The second word in the first member usually becomes the first in the second member, the second in that member becomes the first in the first member of the next verse, and so on in chainlike succession (ἐν ἀρχῇ ἦν ὁ λόγος / καὶ ὁ λόγος ἦν πρὸς τὸν θεόν. / καὶ θεὸς ἦν ὁ λόγος.).[65] Bultmann believes that the same gen-

---

64. Interestingly enough, one of Bultmann's prime criteria for the separation of the Offen-barungsreden source in the epistle is his conjecture—substantiated to his satisfaction through close examination of the text—that in 2:1, 2 there is a significant misunderstanding of 1:5b–10. He construes this misunderstanding as follows: the passage 1:5b–10 simply states in apodictic and unconditional fashion the difference between two forms of human existence, the Christian and the non-Christian. The verses of 2:1, 2 (along with 1:7b and 9b, which interrupt the rhythm and must be bracketed as interpolations) show no real understanding of this distinc-tion, but, in concern over the operation of continuing forgiveness through Christ in the church, make out of the source's apodictic assertions, which do not describe possibilities but simply state facts, conditions under which forgiveness may or may not be obtained. This sort of misunderstanding of the Offenbarungsreden is apparently not attributed to the evangelist, yet the stylistic characteristics of the author of I John are substantially the same as those ascribed to the evangelist in the commentary. The kind of ecclesiastical orthodox interest which Bultmann there attributes to the redactor of the gospel is here assigned to the author of the epistle! After the publication of his commentary on the gospel, Bultmann found it necessary to review his earlier work on the epistle. On second look he discovered there, also, the work of the same ecclesiastical redactor who edited the gospel. He thus clears up the potential difficulty by assigning to this redactor the more blatant assertions about the forgive-ness of sin (distinctions between "sins unto death" and "sins not unto death" and references to the cleansing power of Christ's blood) and futuristic apocalyptic eschatology. The redactor's work includes 1:7b; 2:2 and 5:14–21. His hand is also detected in 2:28; 3:2; 4:10 and 4:17. For Bultmann's theory of the redaction of the First Epistle, see "Die kirchliche Redaktion des ersten Johannesbriefes."

65. *Johannes*, pp. 2 f. See 1:1 and 4 f. Käsemann notices that this chainlike succession does

eral poetic structure found in the prologue can be seen in the rest of the gospel, where it indicates the evangelist's continued use of the same source. The doublets are frequently antithetical.[66] Sometimes the second line of a doublet stands in antithesis to the first (3:6); sometimes an entire doublet is the antithesis of the one preceding it (4:13 f.). The separate verses or clause of the doublets are generally apodictic, without condition or subordination (3:6).[67] Consequently, clauses are frequently merely bound together by καί (1:5).[68] Other characteristics also identify a passage as stemming from the Offenbarungsreden or confirm such an identification: (1) Semitisms (3:27), (2) the ἐγώ εἰμι sayings of Jesus (chapter 10), (3) a superfluous third line after a double verse marking the end of a discourse (1:14e), (4) πᾶς (ν) with the participle as the subject of a clause (8:34) or (5) sometimes replaced by a relative clause or an ἐάν-clause as in 4:14.[69]

The evangelist almost always puts the Offenbarungsreden into the mouth of Jesus, except in the prologue. He comments upon the words of the Offenbarungsreden in such fashion that they really become texts for his preaching.[70] He artfully employs the source to express his own ideas.[71] When necessary he alters its sequence, breaking up continuous speeches and rearranging single sentences.[72] He also imitates the style of the source so that it is not always possible to distinguish between the two.[73] At some points Bultmann's separation of the Offenbarungsreden is conveniently supported by his rearrangement of the order of the text (e.g., 8:12, 12:44-50). So while the source

---

not recur in the discourses elsewhere in the gospel and maintains that Bultmann does not succeed in answering the inevitable question of why it does not: *VF, 3* (1942–46), 187.

66. *Johannes*, p. 100 n. 2, p. 136 n. 5, p. 111 n. 3, p. 113 n. 7, p. 117 n. 1, p. 264 n. 5. *Jülicher Festgabe*, p. 141.

67. *Johannes*, p. 100 n. 2, p. 224 n. 1. *Jülicher Festgabe*, p. 141. Bultmann refuses to apply this criterion with pedantic consistency, however (ibid., p. 152).

68. *Johannes*, p. 28, p. 51 n. 4.

69. All page references are to *Johannes*. (1) p. 5, p. 125 n. 7, p. 207 n. 1, p. 224 n. 1. (2) p. 168 n. 1, p. 170 n. 1, p. 260 n. 3, p. 262 n. 1, p. 276, n. 5, p. 412 n. 7, p. 413 n. 1. The self-predication is usually followed by a promise to the believer. When the promise precedes, Bultmann proposes that the evangelist has reversed the order of the verses (ibid., p. 170 n. 1 [6:47 f.], p. 228 n. 7, p. 262 n. 1). An ἐγώ εἰμι saying may stand as a single line at the beginning of a discourse in contrast to the double verses of the rest of the discourse (ibid., p. 260 n. 3 [8:12]). (3) p. 51 n. 5, p. 203 n. 5, p. 271 n. 2. (4) p. 241 n. 6, p. 335 n. 3, p. 409 n. 2, p. 413 n. 1. (5) p. 413 n. 1.

70. Ibid., p. 93.

71. Ibid., p. 103.

72. Ibid., p. 170 n. 1 (6:47, 48), p. 202 n. 4, p. 210 n. 3, p. 245 n. 4, p. 264 n. 5, p. 274, p. 304 n. 1, p. 307 n. 1, p. 323.

73. Ibid., p. 220 nn. 1, 5 (7:6 f.), p. 264 n. 5. For this and other reasons Bultmann voices some hesitancy and uncertainty in his source criticism (p. 220 n. 1, p. 382 n. 6, p. 443 n. 6), but he nevertheless believes that it must be attempted and can be carried through: ibid., passim; *RGG, 3* (1959), 842; *Jülicher Festgabe*, p. 139.

theory and the redaction theory have to do with two clearly distinct stages in the *Entstehungsgeschichte* of the gospel, the evidence for them is not entirely independent.[74]

In summary it cannot be overemphasized that in the case of the Offenbarungsreden, as in the case of the evangelist, Bultmann identifies literary strata so that his criteria for identifying one become negative criteria for the other. The occurrence of a number of the stylistic characteristics of the evangelist in a passage indicates that the passage in question does not stem from any of the sources, unless characteristics of the source also appear. In such cases it usually becomes necessary to make separations within the passage, since the evangelist has evidently reworked, expanded, or annotated his source, imparting to it traces of his own style. In 11:9 f., for example, we have a doublet of verses in antithetical parallelism preceded by a line which does not fall into the rhythm. Each line of the doublet is followed by a ὅτι-clause, which fits into the rhythm fairly well, but the ὅτι-clause itself is characteristic of the evangelist. Bultmann holds the doublet in parallelism to be "without doubt" from the Offenbarungsreden, while the ὅτι-clauses, one of which contains the characteristic τοῦ κόσμου τούτου, are assigned to the evangelist. The initial clause of verse 9, actually a question, is said to be a composition of the evangelist also.[75] So Bultmann proceeds throughout the gospel.

The source criticism of John is then primarily a matter of the separation of the annotations and compositions of the evangelist from the written sources which he employed. There is no problem of separating source from source as, for example, in the Pentateuch. The very nature of the major sources determines in advance where one will usually find them and makes it unlikely that they will be often found together.[76] The Offenbarungsreden forms the basis of the discourses, the semeia-source the basis of most of the miracle stories, and the passion source the basis of the crucifixion and resurrection narratives. Because the identification of sources consists almost exclusively in the separation of sources from the work of the evangelist, it becomes clear why the establishment of criteria for the identification of the evangelist's hand is so important. Bultmann can be relatively sure that he can identify his sources and accurately define their limits only if he can be confident of his identification of the evangelist's work. He therefore develops a long list of

---

74. *Johannes*, p. 262 n. 1, p. 271 n. 2, p. 274, p. 294 n. 1.

75. Ibid., p. 304 n. 1.

76. There are exceptions, of course. For example, in 11:9 f. and 24 f. we have excerpts from the Offenbarungsreden in the midst of a story taken from the semeia-source. But even here they are embedded in compositions of the evangelist, which in turn are set in the semeia-source.

characteristics of speech and style which are typical of the evangelist. The characteristics of the sources are not elaborated to the same degree—possibly they could not be.[77] One suspects that Bultmann relies to some extent on the absence of those characteristics which are typical of the evangelist for the identification of the sources. However, he never relies on such negative stylistic criteria alone. He can always introduce contextual and theological criteria to buttress his separation of sources at points where positive stylistic criteria are wanting.

The Offenbarungsreden[1]   1–57

1:

1 Εν αρχη ην ο λογος,   5

    και ο λογος ην προς τον θεον,

  και θεος ην ο λογος.

2   [ουτος ην εν αρχη προς τον θεον.]

3 παντα δι αυτου εγενετο,   19

    και χωρις αυτου εγενετο ουδε εν

4 ο γεγονεν, εν αυτω ζωη ην,

    και η ζωη ην το φως των ανθρωπων·

5 και το φως εν τη σκοτια φαινει,   26

    και η σκοτια αυτο ου κατελαβεν.

9 ην το φως το αληθινον,

    ο φωτιζει παντα [ανθρωπον], ερχομενον εις τον κοσμον.   31

10 [εν τω κοσμω ην, και] ο κοσμος δι αυτου εγενετο,   33

    και ο κοσμος αυτον ουκ εγνω.

11 εις τα ιδια ηλθεν,   34

    και οι ιδιοι αυτον ου παρελαβον.

12 οσοι δε ελαβον αυτον,   35

    εδωκεν αυτοις [εχουσιαν] τεκνα θεου γενεσθαι,

[1] Numbers along the righthand margin refer to the pages of Bultmann's *Das Evangelium des Johannes* that deal with the lines to which the numbers are keyed. They are intended as a guide and are not necessarily complete. Underlined numbers refer to the pages in Bultmann in which he deals with the entire section of text that follows, up to the next underlined numbers.

In the text, source material about which there is considerable undertainty is in square brackets. Points at which the evangelist has omitted part of the source are indicated by three ellipsis dots. Bultmann's conjectured reconstructions of such portions of the source are enclosed in pointed brackets (< >). Chapter and verse numbers are in the lefthand margin. In general, the style of the Nestle text has been followed in matters of spelling, capitalization, and punctuation, except where Bultmann alters it.

77. Cf. Ruckstuhl, pp. 104 f.

14 Και ο λογος σαρξ εγενετο   38
    και εσκηνωσεν εν ημιν,
  και εθεασαμεθα την δοξαν αυτου,
    δοξαν ως μονογενους παρα πατρος.
  <ην> πληρης χαριτος και αληθειας.
16   <και> εκ του πληρωματος αυτου ημεις παντες ελαβομεν,   51
    και χαριν αντι χαριτος·

3:

                                           92–121

6 το γεγεννημενον εκ της σαρκος σαρξ εστιν,   100
    και το γεγεννημενον εκ του πνευματος πνευμα εστιν.
8 το πνευμα οπου θελει πνει,   101
    και την φωνην αυτου ακουεις,
αλλ ουκ οιδας ποθεν ερχεται
    και που υπαγει·
11 ο οιδαμεν λαλουμεν και ο εωρακαμεν μαρτυρουμεν.   103
12 ει τα επιγεια ειπον υμιν και ου πιστευετε,   105
    πως εαν ειπω υμιν τα επουρανια πιστευσετε;
13 και ουδεις αναβεβηκεν εις τον ουρανον,   107
    ει μη ο εκ του ουρανου καταβας,
    [ο υιος του ανθρωπου].
18 [ο πιστευων εις αυτον ου κρινεται·   111
    ο μη πιστευων ηδη κεκριται.
20 πας γαρ ο φαυλα πρασσων μισει το φως   113
    και ουκ ερχεται προς το φως,
21 ο δε ποιων την αληθειαν ερχεται προς το φως.]
31 ο ων εκ της γης εκ της γης εστιν   116
    ο εκ του ουρανου ερχομενος επανω παντων εστιν.
32 ο εωρακεν και ηκουσεν, [τουτο] μαρτυρει,   117
    και την μαρτυριαν αυτου ουδεις λαμβανει.
33 ο λαβων αυτου την μαρτυριαν   118
    εσφραγισεν οτι ο θεος αληθης εστιν.
  ον γαρ απεστειλεν ο θεος
34   τα ρηματα του θεου λαλει·
35 ο πατηρ αγαπα τον υιον,   119
    και παντα δεδωκεν εν τη χειρι αυτου.
36 ο πιστευων εις τον υιον εχει ζωην αιωνιον·   121
    ο δε απειθων τω υιω ουκ οψεται ζωην,
      αλλ η οργη του θεου μενει επ αυτον.[1]

---

[1] Bultmann, *Johannes*, pp. 121 ff., believes 3:22–30 is based on old baptist traditional material. Although v. 27 looks like *Offenbarungsreden* material, and Bultmann sets it forth in strophic form (p. 125), he apparently does not designate it as such.

7: 37–38 εαν τις διψα, ερχεσθω [προς με],   136 n. 5; 228 n. 7
και πινετω ο πιστευων εις εμε.

4: 13 πας ο πινων εκ του υδατος τουτου   136 n. 5
διψησει παλιν·
14 ος δ αν πιη εκ του υδατος ου εγω δωσω αυτω,
ου μη διψησει εις τον αιωνα.
αλλα το υδωρ ο δωσω αυτω
γενησεται εν αυτω πηγη υδατος αλλομενου εις ζωην αιωνιον
23 [αλλα ερχεται ωρα και νυν εστιν,   114 n. 1
οτε οι αληθινοι προσκυνηται προσκυνησουσιν τω πατρι εν
πνευματι και αληθεια·
24 πνευμα ο θεος,
και τους προσκυνουντας εν πνευματι και αληθεια δει προσκυνειν]

6: 27 εργαζεσθε μη την βρωσιν την απολλυμενην,   161–74
αλλα την βρωσιν την μενουσαν εις ζωην αιωνιον,   164
35 εγω ειμι ο αρτος της ζωης·   168
ερχομενος προς εμε ου μη πειναση,
και ο πιστευων εις εμε ου μη διψησει πωποτε.
33   [ο γαρ αρτος του   168 n. 1
θεου εστιν ο καταβαινων εκ του ουρανου και ζωην διδους τω κοσμω.]
48 Εγω ειμι ο αρτος της ζωης.   170
47   ο πιστευων εχει <εις εμε> ζωην αιωνιον.
44 Ουδεις δυναται ελθειν προς με   171
εαν μη [ο πατηρ ο πεμψας] με ελκυση αυτον.
45 πας ο ακουσας παρα του πατρος και μαθων   172
ερχεται προς εμε.
37 και τον ερχομενον προς με
ου μη εκβαλω εξω.

5: 17 [ο πατηρ μου [εως αρτι] εργαζεται, καγω εργαζομαι·]   183 n. 6
                                                                 185–209
19 ου δυναται ο υιος ποιειν αφ εαυτου ουδεν,   186
αν μη τι βλεπη τον πατερα ποιουντα·
α γαρ αν εκεινος ποιη,
ταυτα και ο υιος ομοιως ποιει.
20 ο γαρ πατηρ φιλει τον υιον   189
και παντα δεικνυσιν αυτω α αυτος ποιει,
[και μειζονα τουτων δειξει αυτω εργα. ινα υμεις θαυμαζητε]
21 ωσπερ γαρ ο πατηρ εγειρει τους νεκρους και ζωοποιει,   192
ουτως και ο υιος ους θελει ζωοποιει.

24 ο τον λογον μου ακουων   193
    και πιστευων τω πεμψαντι με
εχει ζωην αιωνιον,
    και εις κρισιν ουκ ερχεται,
αλλα μεταβεβηκεν
    εκ του θανατου εις την ζωην.

25 ερχεται ωρα και νυν εστιν   194
οτε οι νεκροι ακουσουσιν της φωνης του υιου του θεου
    και οι ακουσαντες ζησουσιν.

26 ωσπερ γαρ ο πατηρ εχει ζωην εν εαυτω   195
    ουτως και τω υιω εδωκεν ζωην εχειν εν εαυτω.

11: 25 εγω ειμι η αναστασις και η ζωη.   307
    ο πιστευων εις εμε καν αποθανη ζησεται,

5: 26 και πας ο ζων [και πιστευων εις εμε] ου μη αποθανη εις τον αιωνα.

30 Ου δυναμαι εγω ποιειν.   197
    απ εμαυτου ουδεν·
καθως ακουω κρινω,
    και η κρισις η εμη δικαια εστιν,
οτι ου ζητω το θελημα το εμον,
    αλλα το θελημα του πεμψαντος με.

31 Εαν εγω μαρτυρω περι εμαυτου,   198
    η μαρτυρια μου ουκ εστιν αληθης·

32 αλλος εστιν ο μαρτυρων περι εμου.
    και [οιδα οτι] αληθης εστιν η μαρτυρια,
    ην μαρτυρει περι εμου.

37 ουτε φωνην αυτου πωποτε ακηκοατε   200 n. 5
    ουτε ειδος αυτου εωρακατε,

39 ερευνατε τας γραφας,   201
    οτι υμεις δοκειτε εν αυταις ζωην αιωνιον εχειν·

40 και ου θελετε ελθειν προς με
7:   ινα ζωην εχητε.

16 η εμη [διδαχη][1] ουκ εστιν εμη   205
    αλλα του πεμψαντος με·

17 εαν τις θελη το θελημα αυτου ποιειν,   206
    γνωσεται περι της [διδαχης]
ποτερον εκ του θεου εστιν,
    η εγω απ εμαυτου λαλω.

18 ο αφ εαυτου λαλων   206 f.
    την δοξαν την ιδιαν ζητει·
ο δε ζητων την δοξαν του πεμψαντος αυτον,
    ουτος αληθης εστιν.

5: 41 Δοξαν παρα ανθρωπων ου λαμβανω.   202 f.

[1] Bultmann, *Johannes*, p. 206 n. 5, believes that λογος stood originally in the source.

42 αλλα εγνωκα υμας,   202 n. 4
     οτι την αγαπην του θεου ουκ εχετε εν εαυτοις.
43 εγω εληλυθα εν τω ονοματι του πατρος μου,
     και ου λαμβανετε με·
     εαν αλλος ελθη εν τω ονοματι τω ιδιω,
     εκεινον λημψεσθε.
44 πως δυνασθε υμεις πιστευσαι,
     δοξαν παρα αλληλων λαμβανοντες,
     και την δοξαν την παρα του μονου θεου ου ζητειτε;

8: 14 καν εγω μαρτυρω περι εμαυτου,   209–46
     αληθης εστιν η μαρτυρια μου,   210
   οτι οιδα ποθεν ηλθον και που υπαγω·
     υμεις δε ουκ οιδατε ποθεν ερχομαι η που υπαγω.
 16 και εαν κρινω δε εγω,   211
     η κρισις η εμη αληθινη εστιν,
   οτι μονος ουκ ειμι,
     αλλ εγω και ο πεμψας με.
 19 ουτε εμε οιδατε ουτε τον πατερα μου·   213
     ει εμε ηδειτε, και τον πατερα μου αν ηδειτε.

7: 6 [ο καιρος ο εμος ουπω παρεστιν,   220 n. 1
     ο δε καιρος ο υμετερος παντοτε εστιν ετοιμος.
 7 ου δυναται ο κοσμος μισειν υμας,   220 n. 5
     εμε δε μισει,
   οτι εγω μαρτυρω περι αυτου
     οτι τα εργα αυτου πονηρα εστιν.]
 28 και απ εμαυτου ουκ εληλυθα,   224, esp. n. 1
     αλλ εστιν αληθινος ο πεμψας με,
     [ον υμεις ουκ οιδατε·]
 29   εγω οιδα αυτον,
   [οτι παρ αυτου ειμι]
     κακεινος με απεστειλεν.

7: 33 ετι χρονον μικρον μεθ υμων ειμι
     και υπαγω προς τον πεμψαντα με.
 34 ζητησετε με και ουχ ευρησετε
     και οπου ειμι εγω υμεις ου δυνασθε ελθειν.

8: 50 εγω δε ου ζητω την δοξαν μου·   226
     εστιν ο ζητων και κρινων.
 54 εαν εγω δοξασω εμαυτον,
     η δοξα μου ουδεν εστιν·
   εστιν ο πατηρ μου ο δοξαζων με,
     ον υμεις λεγετε οτι θεος ημων εστιν.

55 και ουκ εγνωκατε αυτον,
     εγω δε οιδα αυτον.
    [καν ειπω οτι ουκ οιδα αυτον,
     εσομαι ομοιος υμιν ψευστης·]
   αλλα οιδα αυτον
     και τον λογον αυτου τηρω.   232

43 δια τι την λαλιαν την εμην ου γινωσκετε;   245 n. 4
    οτι ου δυνασθε ακουειν τον λογον τον εμον.

42 εγω γαρ εκ του θεου εξηλθον και ηκω,

44   υμεις εκ του πατρος <υμων> του διαβολου εστε.
    εκεινος ανθρωποκτονος ην απ αρχης
    και εν τη αληθεια ουκ εστηκεν.
    <ο λαλων> το ψευδος εκ των ιδιων λαλει,
    [οτι ψευστης εστιν και ο πατηρ αυτου.][1]

47 ο ων εκ του θεου τα ρηματα του θεου ακουει·

45   εγω δε οτι την αληθειαν λεγω, ου πιστευετε μοι.
   τις εξ υμων ελεγχει με περι αμαρτιας;

46   ει αληθειαν λεγω, δια τι υμεις ου πιστευετε μοι;

51 εαν τις τον εμον λογον τηρηση,
    θανατον ου μη θεωρηση εις τον αιωνα.

8: 12 [παλιν ουν αυτοις ελαλησεν ο Ιησους λεγων.]   260–72
    εγω ειμι το φως του κοσμου·   260
     ο ακολουθων μου ου μη περιπατηση εν τη σκοτια,
     αλλ εξει το φως της ζωης.

12: 44 ο πιστευων εις εμε   262
    [ου] πιστευει εις [εμε αλλα εις] τον πεμψαντα με,
   45 και ο θεωρων εμε
    θεωρει τον πεμψαντα με.

9: 39 <εγω ειμι το φως του κοσμου>   258; 262
    εις κριμα εγω εις τον κοσμον τουτον ηλθον,   n. 6
   ινα οι μη βλεποντες βλεπωσιν
    και οι βλεποντες τυφλοι γενωνται.

12: 47 και εαν τις μου ακουση των ρηματων και μη φυλαξη,   262
    εγω ου κρινω αυτον·

48 ο αθετων εμε και μη λαμβανων τα ρηματα μου
    εχει τον κρινοντα αυτον·

49 οτι εγω εξ εμαυτου ουκ ελαλησα.

[1] Bultmann, *Johannes*, p. 245 n. 4, thinks that this clause may be from the evangelist and that the source originally read: εγω δε τα ρηματα του θεου λαλω.

8: 50   αλλα καθως ειρηκεν μοι ο πατηρ, ουτως λαλω.

23 [υμεις εκ των κατω εστε,   264

      εγω εκ των ανω ειμι,

υμεις εκ τουτου του κοσμου εστε,

      εγω ουκ ειμι εκ του κοσμου τουτου.]

28 και απ εμαυτου ποιω ουδεν,   269

29   αλλα ο πεμψας με μετ εμου εστιν.

     ουκ αφηκεν με μονον.

       οτι εγω τα αρεστα αυτω ποιω παντοτε.

9: 5 οταν εν τω κοσμω ω,   251 f.; 304 n. 1

        φως ειμι του κοσμου.

4 δει εργαζεσθαι εως ημερα εστιν·

       ερχεται νυξ οτε ουδεις δυναται εργαζεσθαι.

11: 9 εαν τις περιπατη εν τη ημερα, ου προσκοπτει,   304

12: 10   εαν δε τις περιπατη εν τη νυκτι, προσκοπτει.

35 [ετι μικρον χρονον το φως εν υμιν εστιν.]   271

   περιπατειτε ως το φως εχετε,

      ινα μη σκοτια υμας καταλαβη·

   και ο περιπατων εν τη σκοτια

      ουκ οιδεν που υπαγει.

36 ως το φως εχετε,

     πιστευετε εις το φως,

       ινα υιοι φωτος γενησθε.

                                                             272—95, esp. 274

10: 11   Εγω ειμι ο ποιμην ο καλος. ο ποιμην ο καλος την ψυχην αυτου

12 τιθησιν υπερ των προβατων· ο μισθωτος και ουκ ων ποιμην, ου

ουκ εστιν τα προβατα ιδια, θεωρει τον λυκον ερχομενον και

αφιησιν τα προβατα και φευγει, — και ο λυκος αρπαζει αυτα

1 και σκορπιζει· ὁ μη εισερχομενος δια της θυρας εις την αυλην   283 n. 3

των προβατων αλλα αναβαινων αλλαχοθεν, εκεινος κλεπτης

2 εστιν και ληστης· ο δε εισερχομενος δια της θυρας ποιμην εστιν

3 των προβατων. τουτω ο θυρωρος ανοιγει, και τα προβατα της φω-

νης αυτου ακουει, και τα ιδια προβατα φωνει κατ ονομα και εξαγει

4 αυτα. οταν τα ιδια παντα εκβαλη, εμπροσθεν αυτων πορευεται,

και τα προβατα αυτω ακολουθει, οτι οιδασιν την φωνην αυτου·

8 παντες οσοι ηλθον προ εμου κλεπται εισιν και λησται· αλλ ουκ   284 n. 3

10 ηκουσαν αυτων τα προβατα. ο κλεπτης ουκ ερχεται ει μη ινα

κλεψη και θυση και απολεση· εγω ηλθον ινα ζωην εχωσιν και

14 περισσον εχωσιν. εγω ειμι ο ποιμην ο καλος, και γινωσκω τα

15 εμα και γινωσκουσι με τα εμα, καθως γινωσκει με ο πατηρ καγω

27 γινωσκω τον πατερα. τα προβατα τα εμα της φωνης μου ακου-   294 n. 1

28 ουσιν, καγω γινωσκω αυτα, και ακολουθουσιν μοι, καγω διδωμι
   αυτοις ζωην αιωνιον, και ου μη απολωνται εις τον αιωνα, και
29 ουχ αρπασει τις αυτα εκ της χειρος μου. ο πατηρ μου ο δεδωκεν
30 μοι παντων μειζον εστιν. και ουδεις δυναται αρπαζειν εκ της
 9 χειρος του πατρος. εγω και ο πατηρ εν εσμεν. [εγω ειμι η θυρα·   287 n. 7
   δι εμου εαν τις εισελθη, σωθησεται.]¹

12: 27   321–31
   νυν η ψυχη μου τεταρακται, και τι ειπω; πατερ, σωσον με εκ
   της ωρας ταυτης. [αλλα δια τουτο ηλθον εις την ωραν ταυτην.] 323; 327 n. 3
28 πατερ, δοξασον σου το ονομα. ηλθεν ουν φωνη εκ του ουρανου·
29 και εδοξασα και παλιν δοξασω. [ο ουν οχλος ο εστως και ακουσας   329
   ελεγεν βροντην γεγονεναι· αλλοι ελεγον· αγγελος αυτω λελα-
23, 31 ληκεν.] εληλυθεν η ωρα ινα δοξασθη ο υιος του ανθρωπου. νυν 323, 330 n. 1
   κρισις εστιν του κοσμου²· νυν ο αρχων του κοσμου εκβληθησεται
32 εξω· καγω εαν υψωθω εκ της γης, παντας ελκυσω προς εμαυτον.

8: 31   332–39
   εαν υμεις μεινητε εν τω λογω τω εμω,   332 n. 4
      αληθως μαθηται μου εστε,
32 και γνωσεσθε την αληθειαν,
      και η αληθεια ελευθερωσει υμας.
34 πας ο ποιων την αμαρτιαν δουλος   335 n. 3
      <. . . ?>
35 ο [δε] δουλος [ου?] μενει εν τη οικια εις τον αιωνα,   337 n. 3
      ο <δε> υιος <ου?> μενει εις τον αιωνα.
38 α εγω εωρακα παρα τω πατρι λαλω·   338
      και υμεις [ουν] α ηκουσατε παρα του πατρος ποιειτε.

17: 1   374–97
   πατερ, εληλυθεν η ωρα·   374
      δοξασον σου τον υιον,
         ινα ο υιος δοξαση σε.
 4 εγω σε εδοξασα επι της γης,   378
      το εργον τελειωσας ο δεδωκας μοι
 5 και νυν δοξασον με συ, πατερ, παρα σεαυτω
      τη δοξη η ειχον παρα σοι.
 6 Εφανερωσα σου το ονομα τοις ανθρωποις,   380
      ους εδωκας μοι εκ του κοσμου.
   σοι ησαν καμοι αυτους εδωκας,
      και τον λογον σου τετηρηκαν,

¹ The position of this verse in the source is apparently undetermined.
² Here, as elsewhere, Bultmann attributes the τουτου to the evangelist.

9   εγω περι αυτων ερωτω, οτι σοι εισιν,   382

10   [και τα εμα παντα σα εστιν και τα σα εμα.]
        και δεδοξασμαι εν αυτοις.   383

11   και ουκετι ειμι εν τω κοσμω,
        και αυτοι εν τω κοσμω εισιν,
        καγω προς σε ερχομαι.
        πατερ αγιε, τηρησον αυτους   285 n. 2
            εν τω ονοματι σου ω δεδωκας μοι,

12 οτε ημην μετ αυτων   385
        εγω ετηρουν αυτους και εφυλαξα,
        και ουδεις εξ αυτων απωλετο
            ει μη ο υιος της απωλειας,

13 νυν δε προς σε ερχομαι,   386 n. 3
        <και αυτοι εν τω κοσμω εισιν>

14 εγω δεδωκα αυτοις τον λογον σου,   338
        και ο κοσμος εμισησεν αυτους.

16 εκ του κοσμου ουκ εισιν.   389
        καθως εγω ουκ ειμι εκ του κοσμου.

17 αγιασον αυτους εν τη αληθεια·
        ο λογος ο σος αληθεια εστιν.

20   [Ου περι τουτων δε ερωτω μονον, αλλα και περι των πιστευοντων   392 n. 6
21 δια του λογου αυτων εις εμε, ινα παντες εν ωσιν, καθως συ, πατηρ,
        εν εμοι καγω εν σοι, ινα και αυτοι εν ημιν ωσιν, ινα ο κοσμος
22 πιστευη οτι συ με απεστειλας.   καγω την δοξαν ην δεδωκας μοι
23 δεδωκα αυτοις, ινα ωσιν εν καθως ημεις εν· εγω εν αυτοις και συ
        εν εμοι, ινα ωσιν τετελειωμενοι εις εν, ινα γινωσκη ο κοσμος οτι
        συ με απεστειλας και ηγαπησας αυτους καθως εμε ηγαπησας.]¹

13:
                                                                 401–59
31 νυν εδοξασθη ο υιος [του ανθρωπου,]   401
        και ο θεος εδοξασθη εν αυτω·

32 ει ο θεος εδοξασθη εν αυτω,
        και ο θεος δοξασει αυτον εν αυτω,

15:
1   Εγω ειμι η αμπελος η αληθινη,   406
        και ο πατηρ μου ο γεωργος εστιν,

2   παν κλημα εν εμοι μη φερον καρπον,   409
        αιρει αυτο,
    και παν το καρπον φερον,
        καθαιρει αυτο ινα καρπον πλειονα φερη.

---

¹ It is not clear whether vv. 20–23 or only vv. 21–23 are based on the source. Bultmann indicates the former (*Johannes*, p. 392 n. 6), but also says that v. 20 is clearly a *Bildung* of the evangelist (p. 392 n. 4; cf. p. 394 n. 8).

4 μεινατε εν εμοι,   411
   καγω εν υμιν.

5 εγω ειμι η αμπελος.   412
   υμεις τα κληματα.
ο μενων εν εμοι καγω εν αυτω
   ουτος φερει καρπον πολυν,

6 εαν μη τις μενη εν εμοι,   413
   εβληθη εξω ως το κλημα [και εξηρανθη.]

9 καθως ηγαπησεν με ο πατηρ,   415
   καγω υμας ηγαπησα
μεινατε εν τη αγαπη τη εμη.

10   καθως εγω μενω αυτου εν τη αγαπη.

14 υμεις φιλοι μου εστε   415 n. 1;
   εαν ποιητε ο εγω εντελλομαι υμιν   418 n. 1
ουχ υμεις με εξελεξασθε,
   αλλ εγω εξελεξαμην υμας,

16 και εθηκα υμας ινα υμεις υπαγητε
   και καρπον φερητε
      και ο καρπος υμων μενη,

18 Ει ο κοσμος υμας μισει,   422
   [γινωσκετε οτι] εμε πρωτον υμων μεμισηκεν.

19 ει εκ του κοσμου ητε,
   ο κοσμος αν το ιδιον εφιλει·

20 ει εμε εδιωξαν,
   και υμας διωξουσιν·
ει τον λογον μου ετηρησαν,
   και τον υμετερον τηρησουσιν.

22 ει μη ηλθον και ελαλησα αυτοις,   424
   αμαρτιαν ουκ ειχοσαν·
νυν δε προφασιν ουκ εχουσιν
   περι της αμαρτιας αυτων.[1]

24 ει τα εργα μη εποιησα εν αυτοις
   αμαρτιαν ουκ ειχοσαν·
νυν δε και εωρακασιν και μεμισηκασιν
   και εμε και τον πατερα μου.

26 Οταν ελθη ο παρακλητος   425 n. 4
   ο <s> παρα του πατρος εκπορευεται,

16:

μαρτυρησει περι εμου
8   <και> ελεγξει τον κοσμον περι αμαρτιας

---

[1] Bultmann, *Johannes*, p. 424 n. 1, thinks that v. 23 may have been inserted from another point in the source; but it could also be a composition of the evangelist.

12 [Ετι πολλα εχω υμιν λεγειν,   441
       αλλ ου δυνασθε βασταζειν αρτι·]

13 οταν δε ελθη <ο παρακλητας>,   442
       οδηγησει υμας εις την αληθειαν πασαν·
   ου γαρ λαλησει αφ εαυτου,   443
       αλλ οσα ακουει λαλησει,

14 εκ του εμου λημψεται
       και αναγγελει υμιν.

16 Μικρον και ουκετι θεωρειτε με,   444
       και παλιν μικρον και οψεσθε με.

20 κλαυσετε και θρηνησετε υμεις,   445
       ο δε κοσμος χαρησεται·
   υμεις λυπηθησεσθε,
       αλλ η λυπη υμων εις χαραν γενησεται.

21 [η γυνη οταν τικτη λυπην εχει, οτι ηλθεν η ωρα αυτης· οταν δε   446 n. 5
   γεννηση το παιδιον, ουκετι μνημονευει της θλιψεως δια την χαραν
   οτι εγεννηθη ανθρωπος εις τον κοσμον.]

22 και υμεις ουν νυν μεν λυπην εχετε·   447
       παλιν δε οψομαι υμας,
   και χαρησεται υμων η καρδια,
       και την χαραν υμων ουδεις αιρει αφ υμων.

23 και [εν εκεινη τη ημερα] εμε ουκ ερωτησετε ουδεν.   449 n. 3
24   ινα η χαρα υμων η πεπληρωμενη.

28 εξηλθον εκ του πατρος και εληλυθα εις τον κοσμον·   454
       παλιν αψιημι τον κοσμον και πορευομαι προς τον πατερα.

14:   459-89
                                                                    462
  1 Μη ταρασσεσθω υμων η καρδια·
       πιστευετε εις τον θεον, και εις εμε πιστευετε.

  2 εν τη οικια του πατρος μου μοναι πολλαι εισιν,
       <και> πορευομαι ετοιμασαι τοπον υμιν

  3 και εαν πορευθω και ετοιμασω τοπον υμιν,
       παλιν ερχομαι και παραλημψομαι υμας προς εμαυτον,

  4 ινα οπου ειμι εγω και υμεις ητε.
       Και οπου εγω υπαγω οιδατε την οδον.

  6 εγω ειμι η οδος και η αληθεια και η ζωη·   467
       ουδεις ερχεται προς τον πατερα ει μη δι εμου.

  7 <γινωσκων> με, και τον πατερα μου αν <γινωσκει>   469 n. 3

  9   <και> ο εωρακως εμε εωρακεν τον πατερα·

 10 εγω εν τω πατρι και ο πατηρ εν εμοι εστιν;   470 n. 7
       [τα ρηματα α εγω λεγω υμιν απ εμαυτου ου λαλω· ο δε πατηρ

 12 εν εμοι μενων ποιει τα εργα αυτου. ο πιστευων εις εμε τα εργα α 471 n. 4
   εγω ποιω κακεινος ποιησει, και μειζονα τουτων ποιησει, οτι εγω

14 προς τον πατερα πορευομαι· εαν τι αιτησητε με εν τω ονοματι   473 n. 1
   μου, εγω ποιησω.]

16 καγω ερωτησω τον πατερα,   475
   και αλλον παρακλητον δωσει υμιν,[1]

17 ο<ν> ο κοσμος ου δυναται λαβειν,   476
   υμεις <δε> γινωσκετε αυτο<ν>.

18 Ουκ αφησω υμας ορφανους,   477
   ερχομαι προς υμας.

19 ετι μικρον και ο κοσμος με ουκετι θεωρει,   478
   υμεις δε θεωρειτε με.

26 [ο δε παρακλητος] υμας διδαξει παντα   484 n. 7
   και υπομνησει υμας παντα α ειπον υμιν εγω.

27 Ειρηνην αφιημι υμιν,   485
   ειρηνην την εμην διδωμι υμιν·
   ου καθως ο κοσμος διδωσιν
   εγω διδωμι υμιν.
   μη ταρασσεσθω υμων η καρδια
   μηδε δειλιατω.

18: 37 [εγω εις τουτο γεγεννημαι και εις τουτο εληλυθα   506 n. 8
   εις τον κοσμον, ινα μαρτυρησω τη αληθεια·]

[1] According to Bultmann, *Johannes*, p. 475 n. 7 (cf. p. 350 n. 3, p. 475 n. 4), 14:16 actually was the first reference to the παρακλητος in the source. Thus at this point the source is apparently not in its original order. Becker's reconstruction of the source, however, places 15:26 before 14:16 (*Reden*, 135 f.).

The Semeia-Source

The evangelist draws his miracle stories from a semeia-source which Bultmann attempts to distinguish from both the work of the evangelist and from other narrative tradition. The suggestion that a source containing miracle stories lies behind the Fourth Gospel is not original with Bultmann. He himself cites the earlier work of A. Faure.[78] It remains, however, for Bultmann to redefine the exact limits of this document and interpret it in the context of the gospel. He assigns to the semeia-source the tradition behind the following narrative and other materials: the calling of the disciples, 1:35–51 (probable); the miracle at Cana, 2:1–12; the story of the Samaritan woman, 4:1–42 (probable); the healing of the ruler's son, 4:43–54 (cf. Matt. 8:5–13, Luke 7:1–10); the feeding of the multitude, 6:1–14 (cf. Matt. 14:13–21, 15:32–39; Mark 6:32–44, 8:1–10; Luke 9:10–17); Jesus' walking on the water, 6:16–26 (cf. Matt. 14:22–32, Mark 6:45–52); Jesus' conversation with

78. *Johannes*, p. 78 n. 4 (*ZNW*, 21, 1922, 107–12).

his brothers, 7:1–13; [79] the healing of the impotent man, 5:1–16; the healing of the man blind from birth, 9:1–39; the transition in 10:40–42 (probable); the raising of Lazarus, 11:1–44; the conclusion of the first half of the gospel, 12:37–38; and the conclusion of the whole gospel, 20:30–31.[80] It goes without saying that the evangelist has made a number of annotations and expansions in the semeia-source.

As in the case of the work of the evangelist and the Offenbarungsreden, Bultmann first identifies the semeia-source with the help of general contextual evidence.[81] Using this as a guide, he is then able to find, in the source, characteristic traits of speech and style which confirm the identification already tentatively made and which permit further source separations. An important clue appears in 2:11, where the changing of water into wine is called $\dot{\eta}$ $\dot{\alpha}\rho\chi\dot{\eta}$ $\tau\hat{\omega}\nu$ $\sigma\eta\mu\epsilon\dot{\iota}\omega\nu$ (the first of the signs) suggesting that this is the beginning of a sign source.[82] Bultmann then notices that after 2:11 the healing of the ruler's son in chapter 4 is called the second sign (4:54) in clear contradiction to 2:23 and 4:45, which speak in general terms of intervening signs.[83] The qualification "when he had come from Judea into Galilee" is put aside as a gloss of the evangelist. It is therefore probable that 2:11 and 4:54 are from a common source in which the signs were enumerated. Bultmann also points out that 20:30 f., which refers to the "many other signs which Jesus did," is in all probability the conclusion of this semeia-source, and he conjectures that, since 2:1–12 shows a kinship in style to 1:35–51, the latter may well have been the introduction. This conjecture is supported by the appropriateness of verse 50 ($\mu\epsilon\dot{\iota}\zeta\omega$ $\tau\sigma\dot{\upsilon}\tau\omega\nu$ $\ddot{o}\psi\eta$) as the climax of such an introduction.[84] Moreover, it is not unlikely that a source lies at the base of 4:1–42, where, as in 1:35–52, Jesus reveals himself to men as $\theta\epsilon\hat{\iota}\sigma\varsigma$ $\ddot{\alpha}\nu\theta\rho\omega\pi\sigma\varsigma$ by means of his supernatural knowledge. If the source of 1:35–52 is the semeia-source, then it could be supposed that the material underlying 4:1–42 is from the same place. If the latter is from the semeia-source, this would explain the present

---

79. In the semeia-source this pericope is probably the introduction to 5:1–16 (*Johannes*, p. 217 n. 1).

80. Note that some of the pericopes of the semeia-source have almost exact parallels in the synoptics, e.g. the feeding of the multitude, while others are vaguely reminiscent, e.g. the healing of the impotent man and the man born blind. Still others stand in the place of synoptic accounts of the same event, e.g. the calling of the disciples, while others are completely without precedent in the synoptics, e.g. the wine miracle at Cana.

81. Cf. Ruckstuhl, p. 98.

82. For this and the following assertions, see *Johannes*, pp. 78 f. and the appropriate places in the commentary.

83. The references to other signs occur in summary sections, which Bultmann assigns to the evangelist.

84. Ibid., p. 78.

position of 4:43–54, which, according to Bultmann, cannot otherwise be understood.[85] The pericope was simply left by the evangelist where he found it in the semeia-source directly after the story of the Samaritan woman.[86] Although Bultmann obviously believes it is most probable that the tradition behind 1:35–52 and 4:1–42 stems from the semeia-source, he never commits himself unequivocally to this judgment.

The stylistic characteristics of the semeia-source are relatively few in comparison with those of the evangelist.[87] The source was written in a Semitizing Greek, and many of its stylistic characteristics are Semitisms.[88] (Bultmann is quite certain, however, that the present source was not translated directly out of a Semitic original.[89] For one thing, a Greek translator would have probably introduced connective particles, but in the semeia-source such particles are either lacking altogether or are used in a quite primitive fashion. [90]) The verb is often placed at the beginning of a clause, a typically Semitic construction (e.g., 1:37 f.).[91] The use of ποιεῖν reflects the Semitic causative construction (6:10),[92] and the repetition of the genitive of the personal pronoun with two or more nouns reflects the Semitic pronominal suffix (6:3 ff.).[93] The semeia-source contains other non-Greek and Semitic constructions and expressions: (1) ἦν δὲ σάββατον ἐν ἐκείνῃ τῇ ἡμέρᾳ (5:9); (2) ἐν τῇ ἀσθενείᾳ αὐτοῦ (5:5); (3) the superfluous ἡμεῖς (9:24); (4) the taking up of the object in advance by αὐτόν (9:13); (5) the use of ἴδε, ἔρχου καὶ ἴδε, the absolute ἀποστέλλειν, and φωνῇ μεγάλῃ (11:3 ff.); (6) the statement of time in 11:17.[94]

85. Ibid., p. 131.

86. Ibid., pp. 131, 149 f. That 4:43–54 is from the semeia-source is shown by the designation of the miracle as the "second sign" (v. 54). In the course of exegetical analysis Bultmann is led to make other observations about the structure of the semeia-source. He notes, for example, the relationship and similarities of the healing stories in chapters 5 and 9 (ibid., pp. 178, 250).

87. Although at one point Bultmann asserts that the style of the semeia-source stands out clearly from that of the evangelist, the Offenbarungsreden, and even the miracle stories of the synoptics (ibid., p. 78), he nevertheless grants that the *sprachlich* criteria for the semeia-source are not able to stand alone (but only serve as a confirmation) and that the styles of the evangelist and of the semeia-source are not in every case easily differentiated (p. 301 n. 4).

88. The evangelist, as well as some of the minor sources which I have not yet dealt with, shows a significant number of Semitisms, including some which Bultmann specifies as distinctive of the semeia-source. See the severe criticism of Ruckstuhl on this point, pp. 98–111.

89. *Johannes,* p. 68 n. 7, p. 131 n. 5, et passim.

90. Ibid., p. 68 n. 7, p. 131 n. 5, p. 155 n. 5, p. 177 n. 4, p. 250 n. 1, p. 301 n. 2. An absence of translation errors is also noted.

91. Ibid., p. 68 n. 7, p. 131 n. 5, p. 155 n. 5, p. 177 n. 4, p. 301 n. 2.

92. Ibid., p. 155 n. 5, p. 301 n. 2.

93. Ibid., p. 155 n. 5, p. 250 n. 1.

94. Ibid.: (1) p. 177 n. 4. (2) p. 177 n. 4. (3) p. 250 n. 1. (4) p. 253 n. 8. (5) p. 301 n. 2. (6) p. 301 n. 2 (cf. p. 180 n. 6).

Aside from these stylistic features, Bultmann also takes note of distinctive motifs or details of the narrative in the semeia-source which cannot be attributed to the evangelist because they do not embody any of his interests and yet are different from the synoptics. For example, in 6:1–26 the following items are noted: [95] Jesus' seizing the initiative and his complete control of the situation, the contrasting embarrassment of the disciples, the designation by name of the disciples participating in the event described, the statement that 200 denarii of bread would not be sufficient for the crowd (whereas in Mark 6:37 that is the amount specified as needed), and the more extensive use of direct speech than in Mark. Therefore, despite the similarity of this and other miracle stories of John to the synoptics, Bultmann is quite certain that they are not derived from the synoptic gospels but from the special semeia-source. The basic contention is that the many various divergences from the synoptics cannot be accounted for by the evangelist's own interests and are explicable only on the assumption that the evangelist used not the synoptics but another written source of tradition.[96] But some of the material given us by the synoptic gospels is also found, perhaps in somewhat different form, in the semeia-source,[97] and the motifs and interests of the individual narratives and formulations within the narratives (e.g. the techniques of healing) are sometimes similar to those in the synoptics.[98] Thus, Bultmann can classify narratives from the semeia-source according to his form-critical categories (5:1 ff.).[99] Yet the narratives of the semeia-source not only show variations from the comparable synoptic accounts but sometimes manifest a later stage in the development of the tradition (9:1–7).[100]

In the exact delineation of the semeia-source the criteria that enable Bultmann to identify the evangelist's additions and notations play a significant role, as in the case of the separation of the Offenbarungsreden. They serve as a confirmation and a check on the identification of the source through internal criteria. Here as elsewhere Bultmann does not first identify the hand of the evangelist and then the source but rather identifies one in contrast with the other in the same context.[101]

The origins of the semeia-source are apparently obscure. It represents a tradition which was transmitted independently of the synoptics, developing in a similar way but with marked dissimilarities. Perhaps it was originally a

95. Ibid., p. 155.

96. Ibid., p. 78.

97. Ibid., pp. 151, 155.

98. Ibid., p. 177 n. 3, p. 181 n. 2, p. 253.

99. Ibid., p. 178 n. 4, p. 180 n. 7.

100. Ibid., p. 250, p. 302 nn. 1, 3.

101. Ibid., p. 131, pp. 149 f., p. 155, p. 221 n. 8, p. 299 n. 2, p. 301 n. 4, p. 310 n. 3 for examples of Bultmann's identification of the source over against the work of the evangelist.

propaganda document of the circle of former Baptist disciples by whom the evangelist, himself a onetime member of the Baptist sect, was converted.[102] It is not to be highly valued as a record of the deeds of the historical Jesus, since on the whole it represents a stage in the development of the tradition later than the synoptic narrative material.[103]

The evangelist's use of the semeia-source is somewhat analogous to his use of the Offenbarungsreden. He does not take it at its face value. In the case of the Offenbarungsreden he altered the significance of the mythological language; here he does away with primitive and naive *Wunderglaube* which sees Jesus as a divine or supernatural man ($\theta\epsilon\hat{\iota}os$ $\check{a}\nu\theta\rho\omega\pi os$) and understands the signs of Jesus as the symbolic representations of him as the revealer.[104] Like the words of Jesus, they do not compel faith in the supernatural or other-worldly but demand existential decision about himself. Jesus' signs and words are fundamentally the same, so the evangelist can close his gospel with a passage drawn from the semeia-source (20:30 f.) that refers to the work of Jesus as the "signs which he did" and, with this, indicate, in his own frame of reference, the words of Jesus as well.[105]

The Semeia-Source [1]

1:
35 ... Ειστηκει ο Ιωαννης και εκ των μαθητων αυτου δυο, και   68–76

36 εμβλεψας τω Ιησου περιπατουντι λεγει· ιδε ο αμνος του θεου.

37 και ηκουσαν οι δυο μαθηται αυτου λαλουντος και ηκολουθησαν

38 τω Ιησου. στραφεις δε ο Ιησους και θεασαμενος αυτους ακο-
    λουθουντας λεγει αυτοις· τι ζητειτε; οι δε ειπαν αυτω· ρ α β ι

39 ... που μενεις; λεγει αυτοις· ερχεσθε και οψεσθε. ηλθαν ουν και   68 n. 6
    ειδαν που μενει, και παρ αυτω εμειναν την ημεραν εκεινην· [ωρα ην   68 n. 5

40 ως δεκατη.] Ην Ανδρεας ο αδελφος Σιμωνος Πετρου εις εκ των
    δυο των ακουσαντων παρα Ιωαννου και ακολουθησαντων αυτω·

41 ευρισκει ουτος πρωτον τον αδελφον τον ιδιον Σιμωνα και λεγει

[1] See p. 23 n. 1. As previously noted, the assignment of 1:35–52 and 4:1–42 to the source remains uncertain.

102. Ibid., p. 76 n. 6. This would certainly make the Baptist sect the most important, if not the only, element of the gospel's immediate milieu. (Above, pp. 1 f.).

103. Cf. *RGG*, *3* (1959), 842.

104. *Johannes*, pp. 78 f.: "... dieser Begriff [$\sigma\eta\mu\epsilon\hat{\iota}o\nu$] nicht der eindeutige der naiven Wundererzählung ist. Vielmehr ist deutlich—und wird durch die Exegese vollends deutlich werden—, dass sich die Begriffe $\sigma\eta\mu\epsilon\hat{\iota}a$ und $\dot{\rho}\dot{\eta}\mu\alpha\tau\alpha$ ($\lambda\dot{o}\gamma o\iota$) gegenseitig bestimmen; das $\sigma\eta\mu\epsilon\hat{\iota}o\nu$ ist keine blosse Demonstration, sondern redender Hinweis, Symbol, und das $\dot{\rho}\hat{\eta}\mu\alpha$ ist nicht Lehre als Mitteilung eines Gedankengehalts, sondern geschehendes Wort, Ereignis der Anrede." Furthermore, Bultmann does not believe that one can in every case assume that the evangelist regarded his narrative as the account of an actual historical event (*Johannes*, p. 83 n. 4).

105. Ibid., pp. 78 f., 540 f. On the place of the miracles in the theology of the evangelist see pp. 78 f., 152 f., 161, 173, 346.

42 αυτω· ευρηκαμεν τον Μ ε σ σ ι α ν . . . . ηγαγεν αυτον προς   68 n. 6
   τον Ιησουν. εμβλεψας αυτω ο Ιησους ειπεν· συ ει Σιμων ο υιος

43 Ιωαννου, συ κληθηση Κ η φ α s . . . . [ηθελησεν εξελθειν εις   68 n. 6
   την Γαλιλαιαν·] και[1] ευρισκει Φιλιππον. και λεγει αυτω ο   68 n. 5

44 Ιησους· ακολουθει μοι. ην δε ο Φιλιππος απο Βηθσαιδα, εκ της

45 πολεως Ανδρεου και Πετρου. ευρισκει Φιλιππος τον Ναθαναηλ και
   λεγει αυτω· ον εγραψεν Μωυσης εν τω νομω και οι προφηται

46 ευρηκαμεν, Ιησουν υιον του Ιωσηφ τον απο Ναζαρεθ. και ειπεν
   αυτω Ναθαναηλ· εκ Ναζαρεθ δυναται τι αγαθον ειναι; λεγει

47 αυτω ο Φιλιππος· ερχου και ιδε. ειδεν Ιησους τον Ναθαναηλ
   ερχομενον προς αυτον και λεγει περι αυτου· ιδε αληθως Ισραη-

48 λιτης, εν ω δολος ουκ εστιν. λεγει αυτω Ναθαναηλ· ποθεν με
   γινωσκεις; απεκριθη Ιησους και ειπεν αυτω· προ του σε Φιλιππον

49 φωνησαι οντα υπο την συκην ειδον σε. απεκριθη αυτω Ναθαναηλ·   74 n. 1
   ρ α β β ι, [συ ει ο υιος του θεου·] συ βασιλευς ει του Ισραηλ.   68 (Ergän-
                                                                        zungsheft)

2:

                                                                        78–85
1 Και [τη ημερα τη τριτη] γαμος εγενετο εν Κανα της Γαλιλαιας,   79
2 και ην η μητηρ του Ιησου εκει· εκληθη δε και ο Ιησους και [οι   79
3 μαθηται αυτου] εις τον γαμον. και υστερησαντος οινου λεγει η
4 μητηρ του Ιησου προς αυτον· οινον ουκ εχουσιν. και λεγει αυτη
5 ο Ιησους· τι εμοι και σοι. γυναι ουπω ηκει η ωρα μου. λεγει η
6 μητηρ αυτου τοις διακονοις· ο τι αν λεγη υμιν ποιησατε. ησαν
   δε εκει λιθιναι υδριαι εξ κατα τον καθαρισμον των Ιουδαιων
7 κειμεναι, χωρουσαι ανα μετρητας δυο η τρεις. λεγει αυτοις ο
   Ιησους· γεμισατε τας υδριας υδατος. και εγεμισαν αυτας εως ανω.
8 και λεγει αυτοις· αντλησατε νυν και φερετε τω αρχιτρικλινω.
9 οι δε ηνεγκαν. ως δε εγευσατο ο αρχιτρικλινος το υδωρ οινον   79
10 γεγενημενον, . . . φωνει τον νυμφιον ο αρχιτρικλινος και λεγει
   αυτω· πας ανθρωπος πρωτον τον καλον οινον τιθησιν, και οταν
   μεθυσθωσιν τον ελασσω· συ τετηρηκας τον καλον οινον εως αρτι.
11 Ταυτην εποιησεν αρχην των σημειων ο Ιησους εν Κανα της Γαλιλαιας [και εφανερωσεν την δοξαν αυτου, και επιστευσαν εις αυτον   79
   <οι μαθηται αυτου>].[2]
12 [Μετα τουτο] κατεβη εις Καφαρναουμ αυτος και η μητηρ   85 n. 6
   αυτου και οι αδελφοι και εκει εμειναν [ου πολλας ημερας.]   85 n. 5

4:

                                                                        127–49
4 [Εδει δε αυτον διερχεσθαι δια της Σαμαρειας.] ερχεται ουν   128 n. 4
5 εις πολιν της Σαμαρειας λεγομενην Συχαρ, πλησιον του χωριου

[1] Bultmann, *Johannes*, p. 68, believes the subject of the verb ευρισκει
was originally one of the previously called disciples.

[2] Bultmann, *Johannes*, p. 79 (*Ergänzungsheft*), thinks perhaps only the
phrase "his disciples" in v. 11 is a later addition to the story.

6 ὁ εδωκεν Ιακωβ [τω] Ιωσηφ τω υιω αυτου· ην δε εκει πηγη του
　　Ιακωβ. ο ουν Ιησους κεκοπιακως εκ της οδοιπορίας εκαθεζετο ουτως
7 επι τη πηγη· ωρα ην ως εκτη. ερχεται γυνη εκ της Σαμαρειας
9 αντλησαι υδωρ. λεγει αυτη ο Ιησους· δος μοι πειν. . . . λεγει　　　128, 130
　　ουν αυτω η γυνη η Σαμαριτις· πως συ Ιουδαιος ων παρ εμου πειν
16 αιτεις γυναικος Σαμαριτιδος ουσης; . . . λεγει αυτη· υπαγε φωνη-　　128
17 σον τον ανδρα σου και ελθε ενθαδε. απεκριθη η γυνη και ειπεν·
　　ουκ εχω ανδρα. λεγει αυτη ο Ιησους· καλως ειπες οτι ανδρα ουκ
18 εχω· πεντε γαρ ανδρας εσχες, και νυν ον εχεις ουκ εστιν σου ανηρ·
19 τουτο αληθες ειρηκας. λεγει αυτω η γυνη· κυριε, θεωρω οτι
25 προφητης ει συ. . . . [λεγει αυτω η γυνη· οιδα οτι Μ ε σ σ ι α ς　　128
　　ερχεται, ο λεγομενος χριστος· οταν ελθη εκεινος, αναγγελει ημιν　　131; 139
　　　　　　　　　　　　　　　　　　　　　　　　　　　　　　　　　　n. 1
26 απαντα. λεγει αυτη ο Ιησους· εγω ειμι, ο λαλων σοι.] . . .　　128
28 Αφηκεν ουν την υδριαν αυτης η γυνη και απηλθεν εις την πολιν,
29 και λεγει τοις ανθρωποις· δευτε ιδετε ανθρωπον ος ειπεν μοι
30 παντα α εποιησα· μητι ουτος εστιν ο χριστος; εξηλθον εκ της
40 πολεως και . . . ηρωτων αυτον μειναι παρ αυτοις· και εμεινεν εκει　　128 n. 1
　　δυο ημερας.

　　　　　　　　　　　　　　　　　　　　　　　　　　　　　　　　　151–54
　　　　　　　　　　　　　　　　　　　　　　　　　　　　　　　　　151; 152
46 Και ην τις βασιλικος ου ο υιος ησθενει εν Καφαρναουμ· ουτος　　　n. 2
47 ακουσας οτι Ιησους ηκει . . . απηλθεν προς αυτον και ηρωτα ινα　　151
50 . . . ιασηται αυτου τον υιον· ημελλεν γαρ αποθνησκειν. . . . λεγει　　151; 152
　　αυτω ο Ιησους· πορευου ο υιος σου ζη. επιστευσεν ο ανθρωπος τω
51 λογω ον ειπεν αυτω ο Ιησους, και επορευετο. ηδη δε αυτου κατα-
　　βαινοντος οι δουλοι υπηντησαν αυτω λεγοντες οτι ο παις αυτου ζη.
52 επυθετο ουν την ωραν παρ αυτων εν η κομψοτερον εσχεν· ειπαν ουν
53 αυτω οτι . . . ωραν εβδομην αφηκεν αυτον ο πυρετος. εγνω ουν　　152
　　ο πατηρ οτι εκεινη τη ωρα εν η ειπεν αυτω ο Ιησους· ο υιος σου ζη.
54 και επιστευσεν αυτος και η οικια αυτου ολη. Τουτο [δε] παλιν
　　δευτερον σημειον εποιησεν ο Ιησους ελθων εκ της Ιουδαιας εις την
　　Γαλιλαιαν.

　　　　　　　　　　　　　　　　　　　　　　　　　　　　　　　　　155–61
6:　　　　　　　　　　　　　　　　　　　　　　　　　　　　　　　156 n. 2
1 Μετα ταυτα απηλθεν ο Ιησους περαν της θαλασσης της
2 Γαλιλαιας. . . . ηκολουθει δε αυτω οχλος πολυς. . . . ανηλθεν　　156 n. 3
3 δε εις το ορος Ιησους, και εκει εκαθητο μετα των μαθητων
5 αυτου. . . . επαρας ουν τους οφθαλμους ο Ιησους και θεασαμενος　　155
　　οτι πολυς οχλος ερχεται προς αυτον, λεγει προς Φιλιππον· ποθεν
7 αγορασωμεν αρτους ινα φαγωσιν ουτοι; . . . απεκριθη αυτω ο　　155
　　Φιλιππος· διακοσιων δηναριων αρτοι ουκ αρκουσιν αυτοις, ινα
8 εκαστος βραχυ τι λαβη. λεγει αυτω εις εκ των μαθητων αυτου,
9 Ανδρεας ο αδελφος Σιμωνος Πετρου· εστιν παιδαριον ωδε ος εχει
　　πεντε αρτους κριθινους και δυο οψαρια· αλλα ταυτα τι εστιν εις

10 τοσουτους; ειπεν ο Ιησους· ποιησατε τους ανθρωπους αναπεσειν.
ην δε χορτος πολυς εν τω τοπω. ανεπεσαν ουν οι ανδρες τον
11 αριθμον ως πεντακισχιλιοι. ελαβεν ουν τους αρτους ο Ἰησους
και ευχαριστησας διεδωκεν τοις ανακειμενοις, ομοιως και εκ των
12 οψαριων οσον ηθελον. ως δε ενεπλησθησαν, λεγει τοις μαθηταις
αυτου· συναγαγετε τα περισσευσαντα κλασματα, ινα μη τι
13 αποληται. συνηγαγον ουν, και εγεμισαν δωδεκα κοφινους
κλασματων εκ των πεντε αρτων των κριθινων α επερισσευσαν
16 τοις βεβρωκοσιν. . . . Ὡς δε οψια εγενετο, κατεβησαν οι μαθηται   155, 157
17 αυτου επι την θαλασσαν, και εμβαντες εις πλοιον ηρχοντο περαν
της θαλασσης εις Καφαρναουμ. και σκοτια ηδη εγεγονει και ουπω
18 εληλυθει προς αυτους ο Ιησους, η τε θαλασσα ανεμου μεγαλου
19 πνεοντος διηγειρετο. εληλακοτες ουν ως σταδιους εικοσι πεντε η
τριακοντα θεωρουσιν τον Ιησουν περιπατουντα επι της θαλασσης
20 και εγγυς του πλοιου γινομενον, και εφοβηθησαν. ο δε λεγει
21 αυτοις· εγω ειμι· μη φοβεισθε. ηθελον ουν λαβειν αυτον εις το
πλοιον, και ευθεως εγενετο το πλοιον επι της γης εις ην υπηγον.
22 Τη επαυριον ο οχλος ο εστηκως περαν της θαλασσης ειδον οτι
πλοιαριον αλλο ουκ ην εκει ει μη εν, και οτι ου συνεισηλθεν τοις
μαθηταις αυτου ο Ιησους εις το πλοιον αλλα μονοι οι μαθηται   155; 160
25 αυτου απηλθον . . . και ευροντες αυτον περαν της θαλασσης   n. 5
ειπον αυτω· ρ α β β ι, ποτε ωδε γεγονας; . . .   161

7:   216–22
2 [Ην δε εγγυς η εορτη των Ιουδαιων η σκηνοπηγια.] ειπον   218 n. 5
3 ουν προς αυτον οι αδελφοι αυτου· μεταβηθι εντευθεν και υπαγε
εις την Ιουδαιαν, ινα και . . . θεωρησουσιν τα εργα σου α ποιεις·   218 n. 9
                                                            217 n. 2;
4 ουδεις γαρ τι εν κρυπτω ποιει και ζητει αυτος εν παρρησια ειναι.   218 n. 6
6, 8 λεγει ουν αυτοις ο Ιησους· . . . υμεις αναβητε εις την εορτην·   217 n. 2
9 εγω ουκ αναβαινω εις την εορτην ταυτην, . . . ταυτα δε ειπων   217 n. 2
10 αυτοις εμεινεν εν τη Γαλιλαια. Ὡς δε ανεβησαν οι αδελφοι αυτου
εις την εορτην, τοτε και αυτος ανεβη, . . .   217 and
                                                            n. 2; 221

5:   177–85
2 Εστιν δε εν τοις Ιεροσολυμοις επι τη προβατικη κολυμβηθρα,   179
3 η επιλεγομενη Εβραιστι Βηθζαθα, πεντε στοας εχουσα. εν
ταυταις κατεκειτο πληθος των ασθενουντων, τυφλων, χωλων,
[1]5 ξηρων. ην δε τις ανθρωπος εκει τριακοντα και οκτω ετη εχων εν
6 τη ασθενεια αυτου· τουτον ιδων ο Ιησους κατακειμενον, και γνους
οτι πολυν ηδη χρονον εχει, λεγει αυτω· θελεις υγιης γενεσθαι;
7 απεκριθη αυτω ο ασθενων· κυριε, ανθρωπον ουκ εχω, ινα οταν
ταραχθη το υδωρ βαλη με εις την κολυμβηθραν· εν ω δε ερχομαι

[1] V. 4 is almost certainly not a part of the original text and is omitted
by Nestle.

8 εγω, αλλος προ εμου καταβαινει. λεγει αυτω ο Ιησους· εγειρε

9 αρον τον κραβατον σου και περιπατει. και ευθεως εγενετο υγιης

    ο ανθρωπος, και ηρεν τον κραβατον αυτου και περιεπατει. Ην

10 δε σαββατον εν εκεινη τη ημερα. ελεγον ουν οι Ιουδαιοι τω

    τεθεραπευμενω· σαββατον εστιν, και ουκ εξεστιν σοι αραι τον

11 κραβατον. ος δε απεκριθη αυτοις· ο ποιησας με υγιη, . . .   181 n. 7

12 μοι ειπεν· αρον τον κραβατον σου και περιπατει. ηρωτησαν

    αυτον· τις εστιν ο ανθρωπος ο ειπων σοι· αρον και περιπατει;

13 ο δε ιαθεις ουκ ηδει τις εστιν· ο γαρ Ιησους εξενευσεν οχλου οντος

14 εν τω τοπω. μετα ταυτα ευρισκει αυτον ο Ιησους εν τω ιερω

    και ειπεν αυτω· ιδε υγιης γεγονας· μηκετι αμαρτανε, ινα μη χειρον

15 σοι τι γενηται. απηλθεν ο ανθρωπος και ειπεν τοις Ιουδαιοις οτι

[cf. 16, 18 Ιησους εστιν ο ποιησας αυτον υγιη. <και δια τουτο εζητουν οι

    Ιουδαιοι αποκτειναι τον Ιησουν οτι ταυτα εποιει εν σαββατω> . . .   177

7:

19 τι με ζητειτε αποκτειναι, . . . εν εργον εποιησα και παντες   <u>208 f.</u>

21 θαυμαζετε. δια τουτο Μωυσης δεδωκεν υμιν την περιτομην, . . .

22 και εν σαββατω περιτεμνετε ανθρωπον. ει περιτομην λαμβανει

23 [ο] ανθρωπος εν σαββατω ινα μη λυθη ο νομος Μωυσεως, εμοι

    χολατε οτι ολον ανθρωπον υγιη εποιησα εν σαββατω;

9:

                                                                    <u>249-57</u>

1, 2   Και παραγων ειδεν ανθρωπον τυφλον εκ γενετης. και

    ηρωτησαν αυτον οι μαθηται αυτου λεγοντες· ρ α β β ι, τις

3 ημαρτεν, ουτος η οι γονεις αυτου, ινα τυφλος γεννηθη; απεκριθη   250; 252

6 Ιησους· ουτε ουτος ημαρτεν ουτε οι γονεις αυτου, . . . ταυτα ειπων   n. 1

    επτυσεν χαμαι και εποιησεν πηλον εκ του πτυσματος, και επεθηκεν

7 αυτου τον πηλον επι τους οφθαλμους, και ειπεν αυτω· υπαγε νιψαι

    εις την κολυμβηθραν του Σιλωαμ. . . . απηλθεν ουν και ενιψατο,   253

8 και ηλθεν βλεπων. Οι ουν γειτονες και οι θεωρουντες αυτον το

    προτερον, οτι προσαιτης ην, ελεγον· ουχ ουτος εστιν ο καθημενος

9 και προσαιτων; αλλοι ελεγον οτι ουτος εστιν· αλλοι ελεγον·

    ουχι, αλλα ομοιος αυτω εστιν. εκεινος ελεγεν οτι εγω ειμι.

10 ελεγον ουν αυτω· πως [ουν] ηνεωχθησαν σου οι οφθαλμοι;

11 απεκριθη εκεινος· ο ανθρωπος ο λεγομενος Ιησους πηλον εποιησεν

    και επεχρισεν μου τους οφθαλμους και ειπεν μοι οτι υπαγε εις τον

12 Σιλωαμ και νιψαι· απελθων ουν και νιψαμενος ανεβλεψα. και

13 ειπαν αυτω· που εστιν εκεινος; λεγει· ουκ οιδα. Αγουσιν αυτον

14 προς τους Φαρισαιους, τον ποτε τυφλον. ην δε σαββατον εν η

    ημερα τον πηλον εποιησεν ο Ιησους και ανεωξεν αυτου τους

    οφθαλμους. παλιν ουν ηρωτων αυτον και οι Φαρισαιοι πως

    ανεβλεψεν. ο δε ειπεν αυτοις· πηλον επεθηκεν μου επι τους

16 οφθαλμους, και ενιψαμην, και βλεπω. ελεγον ουν εκ των Φαρι-   254 n. 1
   σαιων τινες· [ουκ εστιν ουτος παρα θεου ο ανθρωπος] οτι το

17 σαββατον ου τηρει. . . . λεγουσιν ουν τω τυφλω παλιν· τι συ   254 n. 4

18 λεγεις περι αυτου, οτι ηνεωξεν σου τους οφθαλμους; . . . <και>   254 n. 4
   ουκ επιστευσαν . . . περι αυτου οτι ην τυφλος και ανεβλεψεν,

19 εως οτου εφωνησαν τους γονεις αυτου του αναβλεψαντος και
   ηρωτησαν αυτους λεγοντες· ουτος εστιν ο υιος υμων, ον υμεις

20 λεγετε οτι τυφλος εγεννηθη; πως ουν βλεπει αρτι; απεκριθησαν
   ουν οι γονεις αυτου και ειπαν· οιδαμεν οτι ουτος εστιν ο υιος ημων

21 και οτι τυφλος εγεννηθη· πως δε νυν βλεπει ουκ οιδαμεν, η τις
   ηνοιξεν αυτου τους οφθαλμους ημεις ουκ οιδαμεν· αυτον ερωτησατε,

24 ηλικιαν εχει, αυτος περι εαυτου λαλησει. . . . Εφωνησαν ουν   250, 254
   τον ανθρωπον εκ δευτερου ος ην τυφλος, και ειπαν αυτω· δος
   δοξαν τω θεω· ημεις οιδαμεν οτι ουτος ο ανθρωπος αμαρτωλος

25 εστιν. απεκριθη ουν εκεινος· ει αμαρτωλος εστιν ουκ οιδα· εν

26 οιδα, οτι τυφλος ων αρτι βλεπω. ειπαν ουν αυτω· τι εποιησεν

27 σοι; πως ηνοιξεν σου τους οφθαλμους; απεκριθη αυτοις· ειπον
   υμιν ηδη και ουκ ηκουσατε· τι παλιν θελετε ακουειν; μη και υμεις

28 θελετε αυτου μαθηται γενεσθαι; και ελοιδορησαν αυτον και   250; 255
   ειπαν· συ μαθητης ει εκεινου, ημεις δε του Μωυσεως εσμεν   n. 5

34, 35 μαθηται· . . . και εξεβαλον αυτον εξω. [Ηκουσεν Ιησους οτι   256 n. 7
   εξεβαλον αυτον εξω, και ευρων αυτον ειπεν· συ πιστευεις εις τον

36 υιον του ανθρωπου; απεκριθη εκεινος και ειπεν· και τις εστιν,

37 κυριε, ινα πιστευσω εις αυτον; ειπεν αυτω ο Ιησους· και εωρακας

38 αυτον και ο λαλων μετα σου εκεινος εστιν. ο δε εφη· πιστευω,
   κυριε· και προσεκυνησεν αυτω.[1]]

10:

40 [Και απηλθεν παλιν περαν του Ιορδανου εις τον τοπον οπου   299 n. 2

41 ην Ιωαννης το πρωτον βαπτιζων, και εμενεν εκει. και πολλοι
   ηλθον προς αυτον και ελεγον οτι Ιωαννης μεν σημειον εποιησεν

42 ουδεν, παντα δε οσα ειπεν Ιωαννης περι τουτου αληθη ην. και
   πολλοι επιστευσαν εις αυτον εκει.]

11:

                                                                      300–13,
2 Ην δε τις ασθενων, Λαζαρος απο Βηθανιας, εκ της κωμης esp. 301 n. 4

3 Μαριας και Μαρθας της αδελφης αυτης. . . . απεστειλαν ουν   302 n. 1
   αι αδελφαι προς αυτον λεγουσαι· κυριε, ιδε ον φιλεις ασθενει. . . .   302 n. 7

5 ηγαπα δε ο Ιησους [την Μαρθαν και την αδελφην αυτης και] τον

6 Λαζαρον. ως ουν ηκουσεν οτι ασθενει, τοτε μεν εμεινεν εν ω ην

---

[1] Bultmann, *Johannes*, p. 256 n. 7, thinks it impossible to distinguish
sharply between source and evangelist in this section (the same is perhaps
true of vv. 31–34). He notes, ibid., p. 257 n. 6, that v. 37 reflects the
evangelist's style.

7, 11 τοπω δυο ημερας· επειτα . . . μετα τουτο λεγει αυτοις· Λαζαρος   303 n. 6
ο φιλος ημων κεκοιμηται· αλλα πορευομαι ινα εξυπνισω αυτον.
12 ειπαν ουν οι μαθηται αυτω· κυριε, ει κεκοιμηται, σωθησεται.
13 ειρηκει δε ο Ιησους περι του θανατου αυτου· εκεινοι δε εδοξαν
14 οτι περι της κοιμησεως του υπνου λεγει. τοτε ουν ειπεν αυτοις ο
15 Ιησους παρρησια· Λαζαρος απεθανεν, και χαιρω δι υμας, [ινα   305 n. 1
πιστευσητε,] οτι ουκ ημην εκει· αλλα αγωμεν προς αυτον. . . .   305 n. 4
17 Ελθων ουν ο Ιησους ευρεν αυτον τεσσαρας ηδη ημερας εχοντα
18 εν τω μνημειω. ην δε Βηθανια εγγυς των Ιεροσολυμων ως απο
19 σταδιων δεκαπεντε. πολλοι δε εκ των Ιουδαιων εληλυθεισαν
προς την Μαρθαν και Μαριαμ, ινα παραμυθησωνται αυτας περι
33 του αδελφου. . . . Ιησους ουν ως ειδεν αυτην κλαιουσαν και τους   305 n. 9;
συνελθοντας αυτη Ιουδαιους κλαιοντας, ενεβριμησατο τω πνευματι   311 n. 3
34 και εταραξεν εαυτον, και ειπεν· που τεθεικατε αυτον; λεγουσιν
38 αυτω· κυριε, ερχου και ιδε. . . . Ιησους ουν ερχεται εις το   310 n. 3
39 μνημειον· ην δε σπηλαιον, και λιθος επεκειτο επ αυτω. λεγει ο   311 n. 4
Ιησους· αρατε τον λιθον. λεγει αυτω η αδελφη του τετελευτη-
41 κοτος Μαρθα· κυριε, ηδη οζει· τεταρταιος γαρ εστιν. . . . ηραν   310 n. 3;
43 ουν τον λιθον. . . . . [και] φωνη μεγαλη εκραυγασεν· Λαζαρε,   311 n. 6
44 δευρο εξω. εξηλθεν ο τεθνηκως δεδεμενος τους ποδας και τας
χειρας κειριαις, και η οψις αυτου σουδαριω περιεδεδετο. λεγει
αυτοις ο [Ιησους]· λυσατε αυτον και αφετε αυτον υπαγειν.   311 n. 6

12:
                                                                    346, esp.
37 Τοσαυτα δε αυτου σημεια πεποιηκοτος εμπροσθεν αυτων ουκ   n. 4
38 επιστευον εις αυτον, ινα ο λογος Ησαιου του προφητου πληρωθη
ον ειπεν· κυριε, τις επιστευσεν τη ακοη ημων; και ο βραχιων
κυριου τινι απεκαλυφθη;

20:
                                                                    78, 541 n. 2
30 Πολλα μεν ουν και αλλα σημεια εποιησεν ο Ιησους ενωπιον
των μαθητων, α ουκ εστιν γεγραμμενα εν τω βιβλιω τουτω·
31 ταυτα δε γεγραπται ινα πιστευητε οτι Ιησους εστιν ο χριστος ο
υιος του θεου, [και ινα πιστευοντες ζωην εχητε εν τω ονοματι   541 f.
αυτου.]

The Passion Source

Although the evangelist follows the familiar tradition in the passion and Easter narratives, his source is not the synoptic gospels. That this source is nevertheless a written document is shown by the many details and statements which are of no use to the evangelist theologically and by the evangelist's

additions, which often stand out clearly from the source.[106] Bultmann concedes that the existence of a passion source can be only partially supported
by stylistic criteria, since the characteristics of the evangelist do not always
stand out pronouncedly from it.[107] Although there is no compelling proof that
the evangelist used a single, unified written source for the passion and Easter
stories, this is altogether probable, since the passion was the first part of the
history of Jesus to be brought together in a continuous and complete narrative.
Since a passion narrative would have scarcely circulated without an Easter
story, the latter, too, must have been a part of the single written source upon
which the evangelist worked.[108]

The style of the passion narrative is an easy Semitizing Greek. Bultmann
makes an extensive catalogue of the stylistic characteristics of the passion
narrative but, significantly, does not attempt to separate the characteristics
of the source from those of the evangelist.[109] As is obvious from his list, many
of the characteristics which appear in the source also turn up in the material
assigned to the evangelist. Therefore stylistic criteria cannot be decisive for
source criticism.

Aside from those passages, unparalleled in the synoptics and not attributable
to the evangelist, which suggest a written, non-synoptic source, Bultmann
finds contextual grounds to support and delineate such a source. His arguments center upon the incongruities or inconsistencies which he finds in the
text. Here, as in the case of other sources, he assumes that, when a writer
follows a written source and copies large portions of it, he is not able to
remove every trace of that source with complete success but leaves behind
telltale clues: fissures in the continuity of the narrative, unnecessary repeti-
tions, inconsistencies and non sequiturs of one sort or another.[110] Also, here
as elsewhere, Bultmann is aided in delimiting the source by his ability to

106. Ibid., p. 491: "Dass er einer schriftlichen Quelle folgt, ergibt sich 1. daraus, dass er
Stücke und Einzelangaben bringt, die er nicht im Sinne seiner Theologie auswertet, wie die
Verleugnung des Petrus, die Verlosung des Mantels Jesu, die Ortsangabe 19:13; 2. daraus, dass
sich seine Zusätze von einer zugrunde liegenden Vorlage manchmal deutlich abheben.—Deutlich
ist auch, dass seine Quelle nicht die Synoptiker sind, bsw. einer von ihnen."
For examples of Bultmann's perspicuity in discerning the difficulties in the narrative and
other clues (e.g. style and interests of the evangelist) which lead to the separation of the passion source, see ibid., pp. 492 f., pp. 496 f., pp. 502 f., p. 510 n. 7, p. 518 n. 1, pp. 519 ff., p. 529,
p. 532 nn. 1, 3, p. 535 nn. 1, 5.
107. Ibid., p. 491 n. 9; "Die Analyse kann nur z.T. durch sprachliche Kriterien gestützt
werden, da die stilistischen Eigenarten des Evangelisten in der Erzählung nicht ausgeprägt sind."
108. Ibid., p. 491.
109. Ibid., pp. 491 f.
110. Ibid., pp. 493, 497, 502 f., 515, 528, 534, 537.

recognize the evangelist's method of editing and annotating his sources. A good example of Bultmann's total procedure is to be found in his analysis of 19:16a–37:

> The evangelist follows his source farther; his additions stand out from it. The report of the source is similar to that of the synoptics, agreeing in many details, in others characteristically diverging. . . . First of all it appears that vv. 20–22 should stem from the evangelist, since the motif of vv. 12b, 15c occurs here. Also the beginning of v. 23 shows that vv. 20–22 are an interruption. The evangelist must recover the connection with v. 19 through the introduction of ὅτε ἐσταύρωσαν τὸν Ἰησοῦν [in v. 23].
>
> The source then runs from v. 23 to v. 25. Mk. 15:40 f. shows that the tradition early reported that women were witnesses of the crucifixion. It is probable that the evangelist has moved this notice [v. 25]—which in the source, as in Mark, would have stood at the conclusion—forward in order to gain a point of contact for vv. 26 f., which is his own composition. In this case the conclusion of v. 24 (οἱ μὲν οὖν στρατιῶται ταῦτα ἐποίησαν) is also his composition. In the source vv. 28–30 then followed [v. 24]. In v. 28 the λεγει . διψῶ stems from two motivations, the first (εἰδὼς . . . ὅτι ἤδη πάντα τετέλεσται) is from the evangelist, while the second (ἵνα τελειωθῇ ἡ γραφή) is provided by the source. But then the τετέλεσται of v. 30 will stem from the evangelist, who substituted it for a word of the source.
>
> The sections vv. 31–37 and 38–42 stand in a certain rivalry, since in vv. 31–37 the descent from the cross is accomplished through the Roman soldiers, while according to v. 38 Joseph of Arimathea takes Jesus down from the cross. But it is improbable that one of these sections has been introduced by the evangelist into his source; rather it is much more likely that they already lay before the evangelist in this combination. The specifically Johannine ideas are found neither in the one nor in the other section.[111]

Assuming quite rightly the continuity of any traditional passion narrative, Bultmann suspects from the beginning of his analysis of one section (18:28–19:16a) that the source has been used there simply because it has been discovered in the previous section (18:1–27).[112] Although contending that the source of the Johannine passion narrative was not one or more of the

---

111. Ibid., pp. 515 f. For an even more extensive example of Bultmann's method cf. his analysis of 20:1–18 (pp. 528 f.).

112. Ibid., pp. 502, 534.

synoptics, he uses instances of parallelism with the synoptic accounts to buttress his theory of an independent passion source.[113] The similarities to the synoptic tradition and the recognizably similar structure and sequence demonstrate the traditional nature of the Johannine passion account; the differences which cannot be attributed to the evangelist necessitate the hypothesis of a written source. Bultmann tends to assume that a recognizable parallel to the synoptic account stems from the source rather than the evangelist. Once this assumption is granted, it becomes a valuable means for recognizing and substantiating the existence of the source.

There is a variety of other subsidiary criteria for the identification of the source. In contrast with the evangelist, who usually refers simply to the Jews, the source makes distinctions among the Jews (19:6).[114] The legendary manner of reporting the appearance of the risen Jesus identifies 20:19 f. as a part of the source.[115] A *hapax legomenon* places one passage (18:38b, 39) under suspicion of being from the source.[116] The occurrence of strange theological terminology ($\dot{\alpha}\phi\iota\acute{\epsilon}\nu\alpha\iota$, $\kappa\rho\alpha\tau\epsilon\hat{\iota}\nu$) in 20:23, the demonstration of the resurrection by corporeal evidence (20:24–29), and the mention of the Twelve (20:19 f.), otherwise rare in John, also serve as supporting evidence for the identification of the source.[117]

While Bultmann is confident of the existence of the traditional written source, he is somewhat less certain of his ability to set its exact limits at every point.[118] Doubtless this is due in considerable measure to the lack of clearly defined differences between the style of the evangelist and the style of the source—a deficiency which Bultmann himself is willing to admit.[119]

The method of the evangelist in employing and annotating the source is already implied in what has been said here and in previous sections. Of special interest is Bultmann's proposal that the evangelist omits portions of his source and substitutes his own compositions. For example, Bultmann conjectures that the evangelist has broken away the conclusion of the traditional story of Mary at the tomb and has substituted the commission motif contained in 20:14–18.[120] The evangelist is also said to develop motifs of the source in line with his own interests. He takes the traditional idea that Jesus was accused as one who claimed to be a $\beta\alpha\sigma\iota\lambda\epsilon\acute{\upsilon}\varsigma$ and places it at the center of the

113. But not, of course, as direct evidence for it. Ibid., p. 502 n. 6, p. 515, p. 534, p. 537.
114. Ibid., p. 502 n. 6.
115. Ibid., p. 535.
116. Ibid., p. 503 n. 4.
117. Ibid., pp. 534 ff., 537.
118. Ibid., pp. 502; cf. 537.
119. Ibid., p. 491 n. 9; see above p. 45.
120. Ibid., p. 529.

passion narrative, where he develops it by means of the dialogue between Jesus and Pilate (18:28–19:22). In this manner he makes clear his own understanding of the paradoxical character of the kingly claims of Jesus.[121]

The Passion Source [1]

491 f.
492–96

18:

1 [Ταυτα ειπων Ιησους εξηλθεν συν τοις μαθηταις αυτου περαν του χειμαρρου του Κεδρων, οπου ην κηπος, εις ον εισηλθεν αυτος
2 και οι μαθηται αυτου. ηδει δε και Ιουδας ο παραδιδους αυτον τον τοπον, οτι πολλακις συνηχθη Ιησους εκει μετα των μαθητων
4 αυτου.] ... Ιησους ουν ... εξηλθεν και λεγει αυτοις· τινα   494 n. 10
5 ζητειτε; απεκριθησαν αυτω· Ιησουν τον Ναζωραιον. λεγει   495
αυτοις· εγω ειμι. ειστηκει δε και Ιουδας ο παραδιδους αυτον μετ
10 αυτων. ... Σιμων ουν Πετρος εχων μαχαιραν ειλκυσεν αυτην   495–501
και επαισεν τον του αρχιερεως δουλον και απεκοψεν αυτου το
11 ωταριον το δεξιον· ην δε ονομα τω δουλω Μαλχος. ειπεν ουν ο
Ιησους τω Πετρω· βαλε την μαχαιραν εις την θηκην· το ποτηριον
12 ο δεδωκεν μοι ο πατηρ, ου μη πιω αυτο; ουν οι υπηρεται των   496–501
Ιουδαιων συνελαβον τον Ιησουν και εδησαν αυτον, και ηγαγον
15 προς Ανναν. Ηκολουθει δε τω Ιησου Σιμων Πετρος και αλλος   499 n. 1
μαθητης. ο δε μαθητης εκεινος ην γνωστος τω αρχιερει, και
συνεισηλθεν τω Ιησου εις την αυλην του αρχιερεως, ο δε Πετρος
17 ειστηκει προς τη θυρα εξω. λεγει ουν τω Πετρω η παιδισκη η   449 n. 8
θυρωρος· μη και συ εκ των μαθητων ει του ανθρωπου τουτου;
18 λεγει εκεινος· ουκ ειμι. ειστηκεισαν δε οι δουλοι και οι υπηρεται
ανθρακιαν πεποιηκοτες, οτι ψυχος ην, και εθερμαινοντο· ην δε
19 και ο Πετρος μετ αυτων εστως και θερμαινομενος. Ο ουν αρχιερευς ηρωτησεν τον Ιησουν περι των μαθητων αυτου και περι της
20 διδαχης αυτου. απεκριθη αυτω Ιησους· εγω παντοτε εδιδαξα εν   500
συναγωγη και εν τω ιερω, οπου παντες οι Ιουδαιοι συνερχονται.
21 τι με ερωτας; ερωτησον τους ακηκοοτας τι ελαλησα αυτοις· ιδε
22 ουτοι οιδασιν α ειπον εγω. ταυτα δε αυτου ειποντος εις παρεστηκως των υπηρετων εδωκεν ραπισμα τω Ιησου ειπων· ουτως
23 αποκρινη, τω αρχιερει; απεκριθη αυτω Ιησους· ει κακως ελαλησα,
25 μαρτυρησον περι του κακου· ει δε καλως, τι με δερεις; ... Ην δε   501
Σιμων Πετρος εστως και θερμαινομενος. ειπον ουν αυτω· μη και
συ εκ των μαθητων αυτου ει; ηρνησατο εκεινος και ειπεν· ουκ
26 ειμι. λεγει εις εκ των δουλων του αρχιερεως, συγγενης ων ου
απεκοψεν Πετρος το ωτιον· ουκ εγω σε ειδον εν τω κηπω μετ
27 αυτου; παλιν ουν ηρνησατο Πετρος, και ευθεως αλεκτωρ εφωνησεν.

[1] See p. 23 n. 1.
121. Ibid., p. 503.

28, 29   Αγουσιν ουν τον Ιησουν εις το πραιτωριον· ην δε πρωι· και

19:   13   εξηλθεν ουν ο Πιλατος εξω προς αυτους· [και εκαθισεν επι βηματος
εις τοπον λεγομενον Λιθοστρωτον, Εβραιστι δε Γ α β β α θ α.]

29   και φησιν· τινα κατηγοριαν φερετε του ανθρωπου τουτου; . . .

15   . . . [αρον αρον, σταυρωσον αυτον.] . . . . . . [τον βασιλεα υμων

38, 39   σταυρωσω;] . . . εγω ουδεμιαν ευρισκω εν αυτω αιτιαν. εστιν
δε συνηθεια υμιν ινα ενα απολυσω υμιν εν τω πασχα· βουλεσθε

40   ουν απολυσω υμιν τον βασιλεα των Ιουδαιων; εκραυγασαν ουν
παλιν λεγοντες· μη τουτον, αλλα τον Βαραββαν. ην δε ο

6   Βαραββας ληστης. [οτε ουν ειδον αυτον οι αρχιερεις και οι

1   υπηρεται, εκραυγασαν λεγοντες· σταυρωσον σταυρωσον.] Τοτε

16   ουν ελαβεν ο Πιλατος τον Ιησουν και εμαστιγωσεν. . . . [τοτε

2   ουν] παρεδωκεν αυτον αυτοις ινα σταυρωθη. και οι στρατιωται
πλεξαντες στεφανον εξ ακανθων επεθηκαν αυτου τη κεφαλη, και

3   ιματιον πορφυρουν περιεβαλον αυτον, και ηρχοντο προς αυτον
και ελεγον· χαιρε ο βασιλευς των Ιουδαιων· και εδιδοσαν αυτω
ραπισματα.[1]

17   Παρελαβον ουν τον Ιησουν· και βασταζων εαυτω τον σταυρον
εξηλθεν εις τον λεγομενον κρανιου τοπον, ο λεγεται Εβραιστι

18   Γ ο λ γ ο θ α, οπου αυτον εσταυρωσαν, και μετ αυτου αλλους

19   δυο εντευθεν και εντευθεν, μεσον δε τον Ιησουν. εγραψεν δε και
τιτλον ο Πιλατος και εθηκεν επι του σταυρου· ην δε γεγραμμενον·
ΙΗΣΟΥΣ Ο ΝΑΖΩΡΑΙΟΣ Ο ΒΑΣΙΛΕΥΣ ΤΩΝ ΙΟΥΔΑΙΩΝ.

23   Οι ουν στρατιωται, ελαβον τα ιματια αυτου και εποιησαν τεσσερα
μερη, εκαστω στρατιωτη μερος, και τον χιτωνα. ην δε ο χιτων

24   αρραφος, εκ των ανωθεν υφαντος δι ολου. ειπαν ουν προς αλλη-
λους· μη σχισωμεν αυτον, αλλα λαχωμεν περι αυτου τινος εσται·
ινα η γραφη πληρωθη· διεμερισαντο τα ιματια μου εαυτοις και
επι τον ιματισμον μου εβαλον κληρον. Μετα τουτο ο Ιησους, ινα
τελειωθη η γραφη, λεγει· διψω. σκευος εκειτο οξους μεστον·
σπογγον ουν μεστον του οξους υσσωπω περιθεντες προσηνεγκαν

30   αυτου τω στοματι. οτε ουν ελαβεν το οξος [ο] Ιησους ειπεν· . . .

25   και κλινας την κεφαλην παρεδωκεν το πνευμα. ειστηκεισαν δε
παρα τω σταυρω του Ιησου [η μητηρ αυτου και] η αδελφη της
μητρος αυτου, Μαρια η του Κλωπα και Μαρια η Μαγδαληνη.]

31   Οι ουν Ιουδαιοι, επει παρασκευη ην, ινα μη μεινη επι του

---

[1] According to Bultmann, *Johannes*, p. 502, John 19:4–16a is a construction of the evangelist containing several source fragments which appeared
earlier (before 1–3) in the original account. Bultmann is necessarily
somewhat indefinite about the exact content of the source from 18:28
through 19:3. I have reconstructed it here as best I can.

σταυρου τα σωματα εν τω σαββατω, ην γαρ μεγαλη η ημερα
εκεινου του σαββατου, ηρωτησαν τον Πιλατον ινα κατεαγωσιν
32 αυτων τα σκελη και αρθωσιν. ηλθον ουν οι στρατιωται, και
του μεν πρωτου κατεαξαν τα σκελη και του αλλου του συσταυρω-
33 θεντος αυτω· επι δε τον Ιησουν ελθοντες, ως ειδον ηδη αυτον
34 τεθνηκοτα, ου κατεαξαν αυτου τα σκελη, αλλ εις των στρατιωτων
36 λογχη αυτου την πλευραν ενυξεν. εγενετο γαρ ταυτα ινα η γραφη   525 ff.
37 πληρωθη· οστουν ου συντριβησεται αυτου. και παλιν ετερα γραφη
38 λεγει· οψονται εις ον εξεκεντησαν. Μετα δε ταυτα ηρωτησεν
τον Πιλατον Ιωσηφ απο Αριμαθαιας, [ων μαθητης του Ιησου
κεκρυμμενος δε δια τον φοβον των Ιουδαιων] ινα αρη το σωμα του   527
39 Ιησου· και επετρεψεν ο Πιλατος. [ηλθεν]¹ ουν και [ηρεν]¹ το σωμα   527 n. 1
αυτου. [φερων] μιγμα σμυρνης και αλοης ως λιτρας εκατον.
40 ελαβον ουν το σωμα του Ιησου και εδησαν αυτο οθονιοις μετα
των αρωματων, καθως εθος εστιν τοις Ιουδαιοις ενταφιαζειν.
41 ην δε εν τω τοπω οπου εσταυρωθη κηπος, και εν τω κηπω μνη-
42 μειον καινον, εν ω ουδεπω ουδεις ην τεθειμενος· εκει ουν δια την
παρασκευην των Ιουδαιων, οτι εγγυς ην το μνημειον, εθηκαν τον
Ιησουν.

20:

528–34

1 Τη δε μια των σαββατων Μαρια η Μαγδαληνη ερχεται πρωι
σκοτιας ετι ουσης εις το μνημειον, και βλεπει τον λιθον ηρμενον εκ
6, 7 του μνημειου [και θεωρει τα οθονια κειμενα, και το σουδαριον, ο
ην επι της κεφαλης αυτου, ου μετα των οθονιων κειμενον αλλα
11 χωρις εντελυλιγμενον εις ενα τοπον.] Μαρια δε ειστηκει προς   530 f
τω μνημειω εξω κλαιουσα. ως ουν εκλαιεν, παρεκυψεν εις το
12 μνημειον, και θεωρει δυο αγγελους εν λευκοις καθεζομενους, ενα
προς τη κεφαλη και ενα προς τοις ποσιν, οπου εκειτο το σωμα
13 του Ιησου. και λεγουσιν αυτη εκεινοι· γυναι, τι κλαιεις: λεγει
αυτοις οτι ηραν τον κυριον μου, και ουκ οιδα που εθηκαν αυτον. . . .
19 [Ουσης ουν οψιας] τη μια σαββατων, και των θυρων κεκλεισμενων   534–40
οπου ησαν οι μαθηται δια τον φοβον των Ιουδαιων, ηλθεν ο Ιησους   535 n. 3
20 και εστη εις το μεσον, και λεγει αυτοις· ειρηνη υμιν. και τουτο
ειπων εδειξεν και τας χειρας και εχαρησαν ουν οι μαθηται ιδοντες   535 n. 8.
23 τον κυριον. αν τινων αφητε τας αμαρτιας, αφεωνται αυτοις·   536
αν τινων κρατητε, κεκρατηνται.

537–40

[24 Θωμας δε εις εκ των δωδεκα, ο λεγομενος Διδυμος, ουκ ην μετ
25 αυτων οτε ηλθεν Ιησους. ελεγον ουν αυτω οι αλλοι μαθηται·
εωρακαμεν τον κυριον. ο δε ειπεν αυτοις· εαν μη ιδω εν ταις χερσιν
αυτου τον τυπον των ηλων και βαλω τον δακτυλον μου εις τον

---

¹ Bultmann, *Johannes*, p. 527 n. 1, believes the plural, attested in the
case of ηλθον and ηραν by ℵ N pc it sa, is original in all three cases,
including the participle, which would then have read φεροντες.

26 τοπον των ηλων ου μη πιστευσω. Και μεθ ημερας οκτω παλιν
   ησαν εσω οι μαθηται αυτου, και Θωμας μετ αυτων. ερχεται ο
   Ιησους των θυρων κεκλεισμενων, και εστη εις το μεσον και ειπεν·
27 ειρηνη υμιν. ειτα λεγει τω Θωμα· φερε τον δακτυλον σου ωδε και
28 ιδε τας χειρας μου, [και μη γινου απιστος αλλα πιστος. απεκριθη
   Θωμας και ειπεν αυτω· ο κυριος μου και ο θεος μου.]

Other Sources and Traditions

Bultmann believes that at a number of places in the gospel the evangelist
used traditions or sources which cannot be ascribed to any of the three major
source documents.[122] Such scattered materials can best be dealt with by classi-
fying them according to their relation to the synoptic gospels. First, there
are extensive sections recognizably parallel to the synoptic accounts. These
include the sources or traditions used in 2:13–22 (the temple-cleansing
scene),[123] 12:1–11 (the anointing of Jesus at Bethany), [124] 12:12–19 (the entrance into Jerusalem),[125] and 13:21–30 (the prediction of the betrayal).[126]
In all four cases Bultmann decides against direct dependence upon the synoptic accounts, since in each case there are divergences from the synoptics which
cannot be satisfactorily accounted for by ascribing them to the evangelist.
Bultmann favors the hypothesis of written sources for 2:13–22, 12:1–11, and
12:12–19, especially for the first two passages. In the case of 13:21–30 he
is unable to decide between a written source and oral tradition, because he
cannot distinguish clearly between source and evangelist. The latter's stylistic characteristics are everywhere apparent.[127]

Bultmann calls attention to several other points in the gospel which reflect
the evangelist's knowledge and use of the synoptic tradition in some form.
In 12:24–26 the evangelist has introduced such traditional material, which
he has reworked and annotated.[128] Verses 25 f. are his reformulations of
traditional words of the Lord, known to us from the synoptics, while verse

---

122. For the purpose of this presentation I shall not consider 1:35–52 and 4:1–42, which
Bultmann believes are probably based on sections from the semeia-source, although he does not
claim certainty on this point. At least the stories show the same leitmotif (Jesus' supernatural
knowledge) and stylistic characteristics (ibid., p. 131 n. 5) and probably belong together
whether or not they are from the semeia-source. Their position, relation, and style are best
explained, in Bultmann's terms, by supposing that they are.

123. Ibid., pp. 85 f.

124. Ibid., pp. 315 f., p. 316 n. 8.

125. Ibid., pp. 315 f., p. 319. Possibly the accounts of the anointing and the entrance stem
from the same source (p. 319 n. 3) and stood there in this order, which is the reverse of the
synoptics'. For the evangelist, however, this order has a more profound significance (p. 316).

126. Ibid., pp. 366 f.

127. Ibid., p. 366.

128. Ibid., p. 321.

24 is a traditional image which was apparently widely used in primitive Christianity.[129] In 12:27 f. Bultmann notes no direct dependence upon the synoptics or even synoptic-like tradition but simply knowledge of, and allusion to, the synoptic traditions of the prayer in the garden of Gethsemane and the transfiguration scene.[130] Likewise, 1:33 presupposes knowledge of the synoptic tradition of the baptism of Jesus by John the Baptist.[131] Again in 6:60–71, which he removes from its present position to the end of the first half of the gospel, Bultmann does not see direct dependence upon the synoptics but believes the passage nevertheless indicates knowledge, common also to the synoptics, of the confession of Peter as a turning point in Jesus' ministry.[132]

The foot-washing scene in 13:1–20 is foreign to the synoptic tradition, and Bultmann believes that it is based on a traditional written source. The identification of this source begins with the recognition that there are two somewhat conflicting interpretations of the act of foot-washing in verses 7–11 and 12–20. In 13:7 Jesus tells Peter that he, Peter, will know what he has done to him μετὰ ταῦτα, which, according to Bultmann, means after the resurrection and cannot refer to the interpretation given a few verses further on (12–20). The brief account of the act itself (verses 4, 5) and this second interpretation (verses 12–20) are from the source, which is to be classified form-critically as a relatively late *Apopthegma*.[133] Stylistic evidence is adduced in support of this. The source is said to be written in a Semitizing Greek, which is apparently similar to that of the semeia-source.[134] Despite the fact that this story is without parallel in the synoptics, it contains several *logia* or allusions to *logia* which are found in Matthew and Luke.[135] Peter's pledge of allegiance to Jesus and Jesus' immediate prediction of his denial (13:36–38) mirror the account of these events which is given in the synop-

129. Ibid., p. 325 n. 1. It is, of course, an image of the resurrection.

130. Ibid., p. 327 n. 7. Bultmann explores the possible relation to Mark. John 12:28 could have Mark 9:2–8 in view, unless the transfiguration was known to the evangelist in its original form as a resurrection story. Also, the word of the Lord in John 12:25 f. could be a Johannine formulation of Mark 8:34 f., and John 12:27 may betray knowledge of Mark 14:36 as well as the Gethsemane tradition in general. The ἦλθεν ἡ ὥρα of John 12:23 recalls Mark 14:41 and could be another link between the two gospels. Bultmann does not close off any of these possibilities but does not embrace them either.

131. Ibid., p. 63 n. 8.

132. Ibid., p. 340. It should not be inferred that Bultmann believes that this knowledge is historically correct.

133. Ibid., pp. 351 f.

134. Ibid., p. 352 n. 3. The evangelist's Greek also shows Semitic coloring (including, for example, the placing of the verb first, which Bultmann has already identified as a stylistic characteristic of the semeia-source, ibid., p. 68 n. 7).

135. Ibid., p. 352.

tics.[136] John 16:32 is also clearly the Johannine counterpart of the report of Jesus' prediction of the scattering of the disciples which appears in Matthew and Mark but not in Luke.[137] In both cases the evangelist has recast the sayings in his own style.

In summary, it appears that, by Bultmann's own reckoning, the evangelist is acquainted with a rather broad range of the synoptic tradition. This is especially true when one takes into consideration the many affinities to synoptic tradition and the style of the synoptic pericopes in the semeia-source. While Bultmann can in most cases show that even when John uses the synoptic tradition he does not quote directly from any of the synoptics (or from any extant non-canonical gospel), he does not absolutely exclude the possibility that he knew of them. In fact, he seems expressly to leave open the possibility that he knew Mark.[138] But he certainly lays no stress on this possibility.

A couple of other conjectural source fragments not related to the synoptics must be mentioned. Finding real difficulties of interpretation in 3:22–30 (especially verse 25), Bultmann decides that there is a piece of Baptist tradition at the root of this passage. That the evangelist would have drawn on Baptist tradition is, on Bultmann's terms, most probable.[139] After a lengthy analysis setting forth the various possibilities, he concludes that a high degree of certainty cannot be attained and that, in any event, the exact determination of the possible source at this point is of little importance for the understanding of the passage in the sense of the evangelist.[140] There is also the possibility that 12:20–22 is a fragment of some source, since the request of the Greeks to see Jesus (verse 21) is never answered directly. Bultmann leaves the question open, however, granting that the request of the Greeks could have been the evangelist's own device for introducing what immediately follows, namely, the proclamation that the hour of the glorification of the Son of Man has arrived. (Jesus is made known to the Greeks only after his glorification, that is, his crucifixion and resurrection.) He interprets the section on the assumption that the evangelist deliberately placed 12:20–22 where it now stands, whatever its ultimate origin. Nevertheless, the lack of continuity between 12:20–22 and what follows raises the question of displacement, which cannot be easily put aside, since it is possible that a section has fallen out after verse 22.[141] I shall turn to this whole problem of displacement and redactional rearrangement in Chapter 3.

136. Ibid., p. 459 n. 2.
137. Ibid., p. 456 n. 6.
138. Ibid., p. 327 n. 7.
139. Ibid., pp. 5, 76.
140. Ibid., pp. 121–23. Although Bultmann refers to a traditional source for verse 25, he does not specify a written source.
141. Ibid., pp. 321 f.

Other Sources and Traditions [1]

Synoptic-like Tradition

85–91

2:

14 και ευρεν εν τω ιερω τους πωλουντας βοας και προβατα και
περιστερας και τους κερματιστας καθημενους, και ποιησας

15 φραγελλιον εκ σχοινιων παντας εξεβαλεν εκ του ιερου. και ειπεν·   86 n. 10

16 αρατε ταυτα εντευθεν, μη ποιειτε τον οικον του πατρος μου οικον

18 εμποριου. απεκριθησαν ουν οι Ιουδαιοι και ειπαν αυτω· τι σημειον   87

19 δεικνυεις ημιν, οτι ταυτα ποιεις; απεκριθη Ιησους και ειπεν αυτοις·
λυσατε τον ναον τουτον, και εν τρισιν ημεραις [εγερω] . . .
αυτον.

Baptist Tradition

123–27

3:

22 [Μετα ταυτα ηλθεν ο Ιησους και οι μαθηται αυτου εις την

23 Ιουδαιαν γην, και εκει διετριβεν μετ αυτων και εβαπτιζεν. ην
δε και Ιωαννης βαπτιζων εν Αινων εγγυς του Σαλιμ, οτι υδατα

25 πολλα ην εκει, και παρεγινοντο και εβαπτιζοντο·] Εγενετο ουν
ζητησις εκ των μαθητων Ιωαννου μετα Ιουδαιου περι καθαρισμου.

27 ου δυναται ανθρωπος λαμβανειν ουδεν εαν μη η δεδομενον αυτω

29 εκ του ουρανου. ο εχων την νυμφην νυμφιος εστιν· ο δε φιλος του
νυμφιου, ο εστηκως και ακουων αυτου, χαρα χαιρει δια την φωνην
του νυμφιου.

Synoptic-like Tradition

316–18

12:

1 Ο ουν Ιησους [προ εξ ημερων του πασχα] ηλθεν εις Βηθανιαν.   317 n. 10

2, 3 εποιησαν ουν αυτω δειπνον εκει, και η Μαρθα διηκονει. η ουν   316 n. 8
Μαριαμ λαβουσα λιτραν μυρου ναρδου πιστικης πολυτιμου   316 n. 8
ηλειψεν τους ποδας του Ιησου [και εξεμαξεν ταις θριξιν αυτης τους   317 n. 3

4 ποδας αυτου·] η δε οικια επληρωθη εκ της οσμης του μυρου. λεγει
δε Ιουδας ο Ισκαριωτης εις των μαθητων αυτου, ο μελλων αυτον

5 παραδιδοναι· δια τι τουτο το μυρον ουκ επραθη τριακοσιων

7 δηναριων και εδοθη πτωχοις; ειπεν ουν ο Ιησους· αφες αυτην, ινα   317 f.
εις την ημεραν του ενταφιασμου μου τηρηση αυτο·

Synoptic-like Tradition

319–21

12:

12 Τη επαυριον ο οχλος πολυς ο ελθων εις την εορτην, ακουσαντες

13 οτι ερχεται Ιησους εις Ιεροσολυμα, ελαβον τα βαια των φοινικων
και εξηλθον εις υπαντησιν αυτω, και εκραυγαζον·
ω σ α ν ν α,

[1] See p. 23 n. 1.

ευλογημενος ο ερχομενος εν ονοματι κυριου,
    και ο βασιλευς του Ισραηλ.

14 [ευρων δε ο Ιησους οναριον εκαθισεν επ αυτο, καθως εστιν
    γεγραμμενον·
15   μη φοβου, θυγατηρ Σιων·
    ιδου ο βασιλευς σου ερχεται,
    καθημενος επι πωλον ονου.]

Source Fragment?   321 f.

12:

20 [Ησαν δε Ελληνες τινες εκ των αναβαινοντων ινα προσκυνησωσιν
21 εν τη εορτη· ουτοι ουν προσηλθον Φιλιππω τω απο Βηθσαιδα της
    Γαλιλαιας, και ηρωτων αυτον λεγοντες· κυριε, θελομεν τον
22 Ιησουν ιδειν. ερχεται ο Φιλιππος και λεγει τω Ανδρεα· ερχεται
    Ανδρεας και Φιλιππος και λεγουσιν τω Ιησου.]

Synoptic-like Tradition   321, 324 ff.

12:

24 [[Αμην αμην λεγω υμιν, εαν μη ο κοκκος του σιτου πεσων εις
    την γην αποθανη, αυτος μονος μενει· εαν δε αποθανη, πολυν
25 καρπον φερει,][1] ο φιλων την ψυχην αυτου απολλυει αυτην, και ο
26 μισων την ψυχην αυτου. φυλαξει αυτην. εαν εμοι τις διακονη,
    εμοι ακολουθειτω,]

Traditional Segment   351–65

13:

4 Εγειρεται και τιθησιν τα ιματια, και λαβων λεντιον διεζωσεν
5 εαυτον· ειτα βαλλει υδωρ εις τον νιπτηρα, και ηρξατο νιπτειν
    τους ποδας των μαθητων και εκμασσειν τω λεντιω ω ην διεζω-
12 σμενος. <ειτα> ελαβεν τα ιματια αυτου και ανεπεσεν· παλιν   361 n. 6
13 ειπεν αυτοις· γινωσκετε τι πεποιηκα υμιν; υμεις φωνειτε με·   361 n. 7
14 ο διδασκαλος και ο κυριος, και καλως λεγετε· ειμι γαρ. ει ουν
    εγω ενιψα υμων τους ποδας ο κυριος και ο διδασκαλος, και υμεις
16 οφειλετε αλληλων νιπτειν τους ποδας· αμην αμην λεγω υμιν,   362 n. 6
    ουκ εστιν δουλος μειζων του κυριου αυτου, ουδε αποστολος μειζων   363 n. 6
17 του πεμψαντος αυτον. ει ταυτα οιδατε, μακαριοι εστε εαν ποιητε
20 αυτα. αμην αμην λεγω υμιν, ο λαμβανων αν τινα πεμψω εμε   364 n. 6
    λαμβανει, ο δε εμε λαμβανων λαμβανει τον πεμψαντα με.

Synoptic-like Source (oral?)   365–68,
                                                                  esp. 366 f.

13:

21, 22 Αμην αμην λεγω υμιν οτι εις εξ υμων παραδωσει με. εβλεπον

---

[1] 12:24 is a traditional *Bildwort* (Bultmann, *Johannes*, pp. 324 f.), not
a piece of synoptic tradition.

23 εις αλληλους οι μαθηται απορουμενοι περι τινος λεγει. ην
ανακειμενος εις εκ των μαθητων αυτου εν τω κολπω του Ιησου,
24 νευει ουν τουτω Σιμων Πετρος και λεγει αυτω· ειπε τις εστιν περι
25 ου λεγει. αναπεσων εκεινος [ουτως] επι το στηθος του Ιησου
26 λεγει αυτω· κυριε, τις εστιν; αποκρινεται ουν ο Ιησους· εκεινος
εστιν ω εγω βαψω το ψωμιον και δωσω αυτω. βαψας ουν [το]
27 ψωμιον λαμβανει και διδωσιν Ιουδα Σιμωνος Ισκαριωτου. και
30 μετα το ψωμιον εισηλθης εις . . . ο σατανας. λαβων ουν το
ψωμιον εξηλθεν ευθυς.

Evangelical Tradition

459 n. 2

13: 36 [Λεγει αυτω Σιμων Πετρος· κυριε, που υπαγεις; απεκριθη
Ιησους· οπου υπαγω ου δυνασαι μοι νυν ακολουθησαι, ακολουθησεις
37 δε υστερον. λεγει αυτω [ο] Πετρος· κυριε, δια τι ου δυναμαι σοι
38 ακολουθησαι αρτι; την ψυχην μου υπερ σου θησω. αποκρινεται
Ιησους· την ψυχην σου υπερ εμου θησεις; αμην αμην λεγω σοι,
ου μη αλεκτωρ φωνηση εως ου αρνηση με τρις.][1]

[1] Although based on tradition, this passage owes its present form to
the evangelist.

2

The Discussion of Bultmann's Theory of Sources

The Testing and Evaluation of Bultmann's Method of Identifying and Separating Sources

Before the final fascicles of the commentary had appeared, J. Jeremias was already calling attention to Bultmann's theories about the Fourth Gospel.[1] Pointing to Bultmann's identification of the Offenbarungsreden source and his far-reaching rearrangement of the text as the really new features of his work, Jeremias at the same time expressed his own doubts about both. In questioning the source theory, he resorted to considerations of style. Having chosen several Johannine stylistic characteristics from a list compiled by E. Schweizer,[2] he showed that they are not in any way limited by the literary strata delineated by Bultmann but seem to occur in random distribution in the Offenbarungsreden, the work of the evangelist, and elsewhere. This apparent deficiency in stylistic support for Bultmann's source theory led Jeremias to doubt the existence of the Offenbarungsreden source. He maintained that if the indecisive character of the stylistic evidence can only be explained by

1. "Johanneische Literarkritik," *TB*, 20 (1941), 33–46, especially 39–43. The commentary began to appear in 1937 and was completed in 1941.
2. *Ego Eimi*, pp. 82–112; see below pp. 66 ff.

the contention that the evangelist imitated his source, this confirms the elusive-
ness of the distinction between the evangelist and the Offenbarungsreden.
Granting that the evangelist may have used a source in his prologue, Jeremias
doubts that Bultmann has successfully demonstrated that this source continues
throughout the gospel. He also suggests that one could question Bultmann's
thesis that some of the Johannine speeches have their roots in a Gnostic milieu.[3]

Soon after the completion of the commentary, an important review by
Martin Dibelius appeared.[4] Like Jeremias, Dibelius pays tribute to Bultmann's
achievement as a landmark of scholarship. On the whole his judgments are
highly favorable, despite his doubts about the helpfulness of technical existentialist terminology in exegesis. He does, however, indicate his skepticism
of Bultmann's source theory.[5] While agreeing with Bultmann that there are
probably written sources behind the Fourth Gospel, Dibelius believes that
Bultmann tries for an unattainable precision in defining them. It is regrettable
that Dibelius did not see fit to enter into more extensive debate with Bultmann on these matters, but he had the whole commentary to review, and
this is only one important aspect of it.

It is not necessary to mention every review of Bultmann's commentary,
since most of them seem to express the same admiration and the same misgivings. We may, however, note the initial reaction in the United States. In
1940 K. Grobel reviewed as much of the commentary as had appeared up
to that time,[6] but, since he only intended to call attention to the scope and
significance of the work and to present its main features, he did not enter
into discussion with Bultmann on specific issues. Immediately after World
War II, B. S. Easton made a more extensive presentation of Bultmann's work
with special attention to the theory of the Offenbarungsreden source.[7] Easton
thought Bultmann's identification of this source was of great importance and

3. For Jeremias' specific criticisms of Bultmann's source theory, see *TB, 20* (1941), 40 f.
4. *TL, 67* (1942), 257–63.
5. With regard to the semeia-source Dibelius comments (ibid., col. 259): "Ich bin nicht
überzeugt, dass alle diese Erzählungen aus der gleichen Quelle stammen müssen. Die Ver-
wandtschaft des Stiles liesse sich aus dem Typus begreifen; auch glaube ich gar nicht, dass wir
den Wortlaut der Quelle immer so genau, Vers für Vers, herausarbeiten können, wie dies B.
annimmt." Dibelius is also skeptical of Bultmann's attempt to recover the Offenbarungsreden:
"das ist nicht immer überzeugend" (col. 260). The passion source is regarded as more probable,
however: "Weit sicherer als diese Hypothese der Offenbarungsreden scheint mir die Annahme,
dass der johanneischen Passion eine vorjohanneische Leidensgeschichte zugrunde liegt. Denn
hier bietet das wesentliche Argument die Beobachtung, dass die johanneische Leidensgeschichte
gewisse Elemente enthält, die vom Evangelisten gar nicht ausgewertet, sondern einfach weiter-
gegeben werden (Verleugnung, Verlosung des Mantels, Begräbnis)" (col. 260).
6. *JBL, 59* (1940), 434–36.
7. *JBL, 65* (1946), 73–81 and "Bultmann's RQ Source," ibid., 143–56.

published this document (in English translation) in the form in which Bultmann recovered it from the gospel. Although not engaging in extensive debate with Bultmann, he indicated some questions raised by the identification
of this hypothetical speech source and suggested that most of what Bultmann
assigned to this source might have been compiled by the evangelist himself,
perhaps using extracts of one or more Gnostic works.[8] This is an interesting
suggestion, but Easton did not develop it further.

Ph.-H. Menoud, in the second edition (1947) of his noteworthy volume
on Johannine scholarship,[9] also expresses doubts about the validity of Bultmann's attempt to distinguish sources behind the Fourth Gospel. Like
Jeremias, he grants that the author probably used a source in the prologue,
but doubts that it is part of a continuous Offenbarungsreden which can be
traced throughout the gospel. Like Jeremias, he brings the stylistic work of
Schweizer to bear on Bultmann's source analysis. While Jeremias tests the
sources of Bultmann against six of the characteristics set forth by Schweizer,
plus one he himself added, Menoud claims to have done the same with forty
Johannine characteristics. (Schweizer himself had only thirty-three.) He
gives the results of only seven.[10] His results are approximately the same as
those of Jeremias. The Johannine characteristics appear in all of Bultmann's
hypothetical sources. Menoud's conclusions are therefore negative as far as
they go, but he does not claim absolute finality for them.

At about the same time that the second edition of Menoud's study was
published, there appeared in Germany a brilliant and extensive review of
Bultmann's commentary by his pupil Ernst Käsemann.[11] Käsemann also takes
issue with Bultmann on the question of source criticism, expressing misgivings particularly about his attempt to identify an Offenbarungsreden source
running throughout the gospel. He raises the pertinent question of whether
the evidence of style and content adduced by Bultmann really indicates two
separate literary strata (source and evangelist) or merely the evangelist's use
of Gnostic modes of expression.[12] Käsemann's skepticism as to Bultmann's

8. Ibid., p. 156.
9. "Les Études johanniques," pp. 12–26. On the literary problem see pp. 12–26, on Bultmann
pp. 17–21.
10. Ibid., p. 19, 2. 2: ἐμός, (ἐ)άν (μή) τις, οὐ(κ) · · · οὐδείς, ἀφ᾽ ἑαυτοῦ, ὑπάγω, πιστεύειν εἰς
τινα, ἀπεκρίθη καί εἶπεν·
11. VF, 3 (1942–46), 182–201. The publication of the review was obviously delayed by the
war.
12. Ibid., p. 188: "Auffällige Differenzen stilistischer wie inhaltlicher Art sollen im Ev. damit
keineswegs geleugnet werden. Und die Beobachtungen des Kommentars dürften hier durchweg
zutreffen und uns den Blick für eins der vielen Rätsel des Ev. schärfen. Es fragt sich nur, ob
man diese Differenzen quellenmässig auflösen kann oder ob sie nicht einfach Index der Tatsache
sind, dass das 4. Ev. sich aufs stärkste an Stil und Vorstellungen gnostischer Offenbarungsreden

speech source apparently has not diminished but, if anything, grown stronger, as his more recent references to Bultmann's work on John show. He also continues to be very doubtful of Bultmann's whole conception of what the evangelist was trying to accomplish through his use of sources. For example, he believes that Bultmann assigns too much theological sophistication to the evangelist in supposing that, in order to present a purified conception of revelation, he intentionally demythologizes sources which in themselves are either miraculous or mythical in character.[13]

In an extended note in an article on the problem of Johannine authorship, Käsemann attempts to show that Bultmann's hypothesis of a pre-Christian Gnostic source for the First Epistle and gospel involves the allegedly incredible corollary that the theological idea *simul iustus simul peccator* originated in pagan Gnosis.[14] For, in Bultmann's analysis of I John 1:5–10, this basic theological thought is assigned to the non-Christian Gnostic source, which is the same or similar to the speech source of the gospel. Käsemann complains that such a theological position can scarcely be assigned to such a source. The Offenbarungsreden upon which the author comments in the gospel and epistle must already be a Christian Gnostic document, as the theological analysis of I John 1:5–10 shows. If this much is granted, there would be nothing to prevent one's supposing that the author composed it himself. Käsemann believes this to be most likely. He also proposes to remove the exegetical grounds for Bultmann's separation of source and homiletician in the First Epistle by showing that 2:1, 2 is not, as Bultmann has maintained, an editorial misinterpretation of the source of 1:5–10 but an "antithetical continuation of the thought of 1:8 f.," presumably from the same author. Neither in the First Epistle nor in the gospel do Bultmann's stylistic criteria necessitate or legitimate source criticism. They merely show that the author was capable of more than one form of expression. Furthermore, Käsemann finds it difficult to believe that a Christian evangelist, even one with decided Gnostic tendencies, would have used a pagan Gnostic source as the theological backbone of his gospel.[15]

---

anlehnt und gleichzeitig in seinem Kerygma vom Mythos dieser Offenbarungsreden abrückt. Ich kann die Frage hier nur offenlassen."

13. Ibid., pp. 198 ff. See also Käsemann's article "Neutestamentliche Fragen von Heute," *ZTK*, *54* (1957), 15 f.

14. "Ketzer und Zeuge," *ZTK*, *48* (1951), p. 306 n. 2.

15. *ZTK*, *54* (1957), 16: "Ich muss gestehen, dass ich mich nicht vom Vorliegen der behaupteten Offenbarungsquelle überzeugen kann und es nicht bloss anstössig, sondern auch unglaubwürdig finde, wenn faktisch aus dem Evangelisten auf weiteste Strecken der christliche Kommentator einer heidnischen Quelle gemacht wird."

In 1939 Schweizer suggested that the evangelist either reworked a Christian speech source,

Käsemann subsequently turned his attention to Bultmann's analysis and interpretation of the prologue, with which he disagrees on several important points. Like Bultmann, he thinks that the evangelist used an earlier hymn as the basis of the prologue.[16] Unlike Bultmann, he believes that this was not a pre-Christian Gnostic hymn but one already in Christian use before the evangelist adopted it. In some contrast to Bultmann, who identified the hymn in verses 1(2?)–5, 9–12, 14, and 16, Käsemann finds it only in 1(2?)–5 and 10–12.[17] Most important, verses 14–18 without exception are assigned to the evangelist. Repeating his doubts about the possibility of satisfactorily showing the connection between the source of the prologue and the hypothetical collection of Offenbarungsreden underlying the speeches throughout the gospel,[18] Käsemann points out that even in the prologue one cannot discern the same rhythmic structure in verses 14–18 which is present in the earlier portion. Moreover, there is in verse 14 a significant change from the third person to the confessional first person plural. In developing and applying the criterion of rhythm, Bultmann relies to a considerable extent upon the theory of the Aramaic origin of the prologue source, which at one or two crucial points gets him out of difficulty. But in Käsemann's judgment the theory that the source was originally in Aramaic is not sufficiently well established to play a fundamental role in the analysis of the prologue and to serve as the

---

closely akin to the Mandaean texts, or that he composed such a document himself (*Ego Eimi*, p. 108). Braun, while in large measure accepting Bultmann's source analysis of I John, maintains that the Vorlage is already Christian (*ZTK*, *48*, 1951, especially pp. 264–70). Nauck, in *Die Tradition und der Charakter des ersten Johannesbriefes*, argues that the author utilizes his own earlier strophic composition as the basis for his epistle. Although Nauck's analysis of the epistle is illuminating and his attempt to relate it to the Qumran Manual of Discipline is significant, the theory that the author made use of his own earlier material does not overcome the difficulties facing Bultmann's source theory, which Nauck rejects. Since Nauck must forego theological and stylistic criteria and rely mainly on structural evidence derived from the nature of the stophes, his results appear even more problematic than Bultmann's.

For the history of the criticism and interpretation of I John see Haenchen, "Neuere Literatur zu den Johannesbriefen." *TR*, new ser. *26* (1960), 1–43, 267–91. Haenchen is dubious of Bultmann's attempt to separate a written discourse source in I John (cf. pp. 19 f.). He also disagrees with Käsemann's understanding of the theology of I John and its place in the development of early Christian thought. With H. Conzelmann ("Was vom Anfang war," *Neutestamentliche Studien für Rudolf Bultmann*, ed. W. Eltester, Beihefte zur Zeitschrift für die Neutestamentliche Wissenschaft und die Kunde der älteren Kirche, *21*, Berlin, Alfred Töpelmann, 1954, 194–201), he sees the First Epistle as a Johannine pastoral letter. Haenchen considers it even more deeply imbued with early Catholicism than the Pauline pastorals (cf. pp. 30–40, especially pp. 38 ff.). Against Käsemann cf. also G. Bornkamm, πρεσβύτερος, *TWNT*, *6* (1959), especially 671 n. 121.

16. "Aufbau und Anliegen."

17. Ibid., pp. 85 ff.

18. Ibid., p. 78. Cf. *VF*, *3* (1942–46), 187 f.

basis for other hypotheses. The use of the Aramaic theory to establish the rhythm of the prologue is especially questionable.[19]

Käsemann believes that the evangelist, who introduced the Baptist interpolation of 1:6–8, already understood verse 5 as a reference to the incarnation. Thus in his view the statement that the word became flesh in verse 14 does not mark the great turning point of the prologue.

Most fundamental therefore is Käsemann's criticism of Bultmann's interpretation of 1:14, which Käsemann assigns to the evangelist.[20] Whereas Bultmann, along with many earlier exegetes and a long tradition of Christian theological interpretation, has seen the point of emphasis in the καὶ ὁ λόγος σὰρξ ἐγένετο, Käsemann proposes that this assertion is merely the necessary presupposition of the ἐθεασάμεθα τὴν δόξαν αὐτοῦ. Bultmann, taking his cue from the ὁ λόγος σὰρξ ἐγένετο, understands the Fourth Gospel as the gospel of the revelation of the Word in the man Jesus and renders a Kierkegaardian interpretation of the incarnation as the incognito of the revealer. From the perspective proposed by Käsemann, Bultmann has really obscured the leitmotif of the gospel, which is the glorious character of the incarnation as the presence and activity of God upon earth in the person of Jesus.[21] This view of the Christology of the gospel, which is really the obverse of Bultmann's, has some very important implica-

19. Käsemann points out that in two cases (ἄνθρωπον in vs. 9b and ἐξουσία in vs. 12b) Bultmann improves the rhythm by supposing that words which do not fit were added to the Aramaic Vorlage by the translator ("Aufbau und Anliegen," pp. 77 f.).

20. Ibid., p. 85. Although the idea of incarnation is admittedly not uniquely Christian, Käsemann believes that the *formulation* of the idea in verse 14 is: "Wenn Bultmann V. 14 für seine gnostische Täuferquelle reklamiert, so wird dieser damit nicht nur die Anschauung von der Präexistenz des Täufers, sondern auch die von der Inkarnation des Offenbarers zugeschrieben. Ist aber die vorchristliche Verwendung des Themas der Fleischwerdung in seiner johanneischen Formulierung und Intention wirklich glaubhaft? Das Motiv ist, wie W. Bauer eingehend dargetan hat als solches griechisch. Doch liegt der Ton der hellenistischen Epiphaniegeschichten nicht so sehr auf dem Moment der Inkarnation als auf dem der Verhüllung der sich herablassenden Gottheit. In reinem Judentum kann der erschienene Messias überhaupt nicht verkündigt werden, und für die Gnosis müssten Parallelen zur johanneischen Formulierung und Paradoxie doch wohl noch erst beigebracht werden. Wird man aus diesem Tatbestand nicht zu folgern haben, dass die Betonung der Inkarnation als das Medium der Offenbarung ein Charakteristikum des Christentums sei?"

21. Ibid., pp. 90–94. The word becoming flesh in the Fourth Gospel signifies for Bultmann the revealer's pure humanity: "Der Offenbarer ist nichts als ein Mensch" (Bultmann, *Johannes*, p. 40; cited by Käsemann, "Aufbau und Anliegen," p. 91). Against this interpretation Käsemann maintains (p. 94): "Fleisch ist für den Evangelisten hier nichts anderes als die Möglichkeit der Kommunikation des Logos als des Schöpfers und Offenbarers mit den Menschen. 14a ist eine Aufnahme von 10a und Übergang zum folgenden. Das Thema, das mit diesem Übergangssatz vorbereitet wird, steht in 14c: 'Wir sahen seine Herrlichkeit.' Dieses Thema ist zugleich das des gesamten Evangeliums, in welchem es durchweg und allein um die praesentia dei in Christus geht."

tions for source criticism. Bultmann's source analysis enables him to assign the cruder mythological and miraculous elements of the gospel to the speech and sign sources, which the evangelist is supposed to have used in a very artful way, employing their language, narrative, or imagery to express his own more sophisticated point of view. This disposition of the miraculous and mythical elements, which puts a certain distance between their original meaning and the use to which they are put in the gospel, is precisely what is demanded if Bultmann's interpretation is to stand.[22] But the effect of Käsemann's interpretation of the prologue, especially verse 14, is to remove the inner theological justification and motivation of the source theory. Given Käsemann's understanding of the evangelist's perspective, the source theory, which for Bultmann was a key to the proper understanding of the gospel, becomes superfluous. If the evangelist's thought follows the lines laid down by Käsemann, he could perfectly well have composed the speeches of Jesus in the gospel as the definitive expression of his Christology. It would not be necessary to suppose that he had adopted a document whose conceptualizations he took seriously but not literally. The proposal of a semeia-source is perhaps not quite so seriously affected by this sort of criticism; the evangelist could have employed such a document, understanding it historically as well as theologically. This is, in fact, what Käsemann himself proposes.[23]

22. Käsemann, ZTK, 54 (1957), 15 f.: "Bultmanns Deutung, mit der ich mich hier allein befasse, steht und fällt mit der Theorie, dass der Evangelist eine heidnische Quelle von Offenbarungsreden benutzt, überarbeitet und kommentiert habe und sich gleichzeitig einer Zeichenquelle bediene, um mit Wundern die Gabe und den Anspruch des Offenbarers zu illustrieren. Nur so kann Bultmann sowohl das unbestreitbar im Evangelium vorliegende mythologische Gut wie den krassen Mirakelglauben vom Evangelisten distanzieren. Nur so kann er daran festhalten, dass die Fleischwerdung des Wortes das Thema des Evangeliums sei, im Sinne Kierkegaards die Fleischwerdung das Inkognito des Offenbarers wahren und mit diesem Inkognito das Ärgernis der Welt erregen lassen." See also VF, 3 (1942–46), 198 ff.

23. It would be wrong to leave the impression that Käsemann has departed completely from his teacher in his understanding of the Fourth Gospel, even though he rejects major aspects of his literary theory and overall interpretation. His appreciation of Bultmann's accomplishment is apparent in his reviews of the works of other scholars. For Käsemann's review of Barrett's The Gospel According to St. John and of the latter's revision of Howard's The Fourth Gospel in Recent Criticism and Interpretation see GGA, 211 (1957–58), 145–60. For his review of Dodd's The Interpretation of the Fourth Gospel see Gn, 28 (1956), 321–26. Käsemann accepts in principle the necessity of making rearrangements in the order of the gospel (although he probably would not go so far as Bultmann), believes that one cannot dismiss the possibility of redactions, and thinks traditions lie behind the gospel.

Only after this book was in the press did I become aware of a very recent article by E. Haenchen which challenges the prologue analysis of both Käsemann and Bultmann ("Probleme des johanneischen Prologs," ZTK, 60, 1963, 305–34). Haenchen believes that the source or hymn on which the prologue is based was already Christian, and in this respect agrees with Käsemann. Yet he does not agree that a reference to the incarnation is to be seen as early as

A decade after the completion of Bultmann's commentary, E. Ruckstuhl, a Swiss Catholic, launched a full-scale attack on the source and redaction theory in the most comprehensive evaluation of Bultmann made up to that time. The title of Ruckstuhl's work, *Die literarische Einheit des vierten Evangeliums* (*The Literary Unity of the Fourth Gospel*), reveals the author's own position. It is both his strength and his weakness that he seems to approach Bultmann's work with the assumption, or at least the hypothesis, that the gospel is a literary unit. Perhaps for this reason Ruckstuhl leaves the not altogether felicitous impression that he has an equally strong case against Bultmann at every point. Nevertheless, it cannot be denied that at many points Ruckstuhl does present significant evidence against the source theory.

In beginning his own analysis, Ruckstuhl recalls that in 1927 Bultmann himself asserted that a set of suitable stylistic criteria was the prime requisite for the source criticism of the Fourth Gospel.[24] He concludes the examination of his work with the claim that Bultmann has not, in fact, been able to produce such a suitable set of criteria. Therefore his attempt to separate sources must be regarded as unsuccessful, and, in view of the collapse of this most carefully worked out source theory, one can only conclude that the Fourth Gospel is the original creation of a single author.[25] According to Ruckstuhl, stylistic criteria are brought forth in impressive array only in the case of the evangelist. The stylistic characteristics of the sources do not distinguish themselves sufficiently from those of the evangelist and are far fewer in number. This deficiency is not to be ascribed to Bultmann's negligence. He has investigated the material diligently but has made the error of ascribing passages with the

---

verse 5, but only in verse 14 (p. 322: "Es ist die Schwäche der auch von Käsemann übernommenen Interpretation von v. 5, dass sie die Menschwerdung des Logos wie etwas Selbstverständliches behandelt, statt als das Unerhörte, für das der Weisheitsmythos keine Parallele mehr bot."). The Baptist interpolation of 1:6–8, which has led some commentators to see the incarnation in verse 5, is not the work of the evangelist, but of a later redactor (along with verses 12–13, 15). When these passages are excised, the high point of the hymn and of the prologue is clearly the statement of the incarnation in verse 14. Only verse 18 is the interpolation of the evangelist.

If Haenchen's analysis of the prologue is accepted, this exegetical basis of Käsemann's grasp of Johannine theology is threatened. It is impossible to adjudicate the question here, but I should like to mention several aspects of Haenchen's theory which merit further critical examination: his argument that verses 6–8, 15 run counter to the evangelist's understanding of the Baptist and therefore cannot be ascribed to him; his explanations of why a redactor would have made such interpolations; his virtual exclusion of all stylistic and rhythmic considerations as criteria for the literary analysis. While, as Haenchen points out, some early Christian hymns do not display a definite strophic pattern, the fact that such a pattern does occur in the early verses of the prologue makes their later absence striking.

24. Ruckstuhl, p. 39. He refers to Bultmann's article in *CW, 41* (1927), 502–11.
25. Ruckstuhl, pp. 106 f.

more distinct stylistic features to the evangelist and leaving the rest, which are stylistically neutral and colorless, to the sources. Moreover, the characteristics of the evangelist are not uniquely his own, for they also appear in material Bultmann assigns to the sources, and to ascribe some hypothetical characteristic to the evangelist when one finds it in the midst of the "source," as Bultmann often does, is, according to Ruckstuhl, purely arbitrary.[26] Some of Bultmann's so-called stylistic characteristics are said to indicate only differences of content rather than separate authors or sources.[27]

In the course of his investigation, Ruckstuhl not only calls in question the validity of the stylistic characteristics adduced by Bultmann for the identification of sources but also argues against the other criteria, which in some cases are more important for his theory than the individual stylistic characteristics. In the case of the proposed Offenbarungsreden, he maintains that the criterion of rhythm, to which Bultmann attaches great importance, is not sufficiently defined to warrant its use in the separation of sources. Ruckstuhl proceeds to point out several cases in which either the proposed rhythm of the Offenbarungsreden is lacking in the material Bultmann assigns to the source or is more or less discernible in passages which Bultmann assigns to the evangelist.[28] He subsequently attempts to show that the recognition of what appear to be annotations and *Aporien* in the text does not really justify source separations.[29]

In investigating the evidence and arguments for the narrative sources—i.e. the semeia-source, the passion narrative, and smaller narrative fragments—

---

26. Cf. ibid., p. 62 n. 2. For example, the *wiederaufnehmende* οὖτος or ἐκεῖνος (αὐτός) occurs six times in material which Bultmann otherwise assigns to the Offenbarungsreden.

27. Ibid., pp. 104–06.

28. Ibid., pp. 43–54. Ruckstuhl contrasts the divergent rhythmic patterns found in 1:1 f.; 3:8; 3:12; 8:50; 8:54a; 12:47 f.; 15:2; 5:21; 15:4a; 15:5; 5:39 f.; 8:12; 11:9 f.; 12:49 f.; I John 1:6 f—all of which Bultmann assigns to the Offenbarungsreden. Remarkable differences are apparent. As we have seen, Käsemann and Jeremias had already pointed out that Bultmann is not able to trace the distinct rhythmic pattern of the prologue through the speeches of the Offenbarungsreden.

Ruckstuhl also refers to some eighty doublets in the style of the Offenbarungsreden which Bultmann assigns to the evangelist. As examples of these, he cites 4:32, 38; 8:47; 9:41; 13:20 (p. 48). While I agree that it is difficult to draw a line between the style of the evangelist and that of the Offenbarungsreden, the examples which Ruckstuhl adduces from the material assigned to the evangelist are not particularly well-chosen. Verse 13:20 is a synoptic variant which occurs in very similar form in Matthew 10:40 and Luke 10:16. Bultmann actually assigns 8:47a to the Offenbarungsreden, not to the evangelist (*Johannes*, p. 245 n. 4), and suggests that a tradition may lie behind 4:38 (ibid., p. 147 n. 4). 4:32 is so brief as to be unimpressive. Although 9:41 may be regarded as the evangelist's application of the Offenbarungswort of 9:39, it is the most clear-cut instance of the style of the source in the evangelist's compositions.

29. Ibid., pp. 54 ff. and 56 ff.

Ruckstuhl believes that he has discovered that Bultmann fails to produce adequate stylistic criteria to differentiate the various narrative sources from one another and from the work of the evangelist. Calling upon his own assessment of the stylistic evidence, he contends that the narratives of the gospel differ from those of the synoptics only as the gospel as a whole differs from the synoptics.[30] In particular Ruckstuhl argues that the contextual evidence set forth by Faure,[31] whose work Bultmann cites in support of the semeia-source, is not compelling. That 20:30 f. and 12:37 seem to stand out from their present context and to fit well together does not prove that they were originally the conclusion of a semeia-source. Moreover, the enumeration of the second sign in 4:54 does not, as Bultmann maintains, stand in contradiction to the references to other signs in 2:23 and 4:43. It is expressly qualified as the second sign done *in Cana.*[32] Ruckstuhl then takes up seriatim a number of passages which Bultmann assigns to the semeia-source or to another narrative source (1:35–51, 4:1–42, 6:1–26, 13:1–20, 13:21–30, 18:1–11, 18:12–27, 20:1–18) and attempts to demonstrate that the contextual and other grounds upon which he proposes such sources are inadequate.[33]

As a sort of coup de grâce, Ruckstuhl proposes to employ systematically the style-critical or style-statistical method and results of E. Schweizer (*Ego Eimi*) to test Bultmann's separation of sources.[34] As we have seen, this method had already been applied in a fragmentary way by Jeremias and Menoud. Since Ruckstuhl makes such extensive use of Schweizer's method, it is necessary to inquire what method Schweizer actually devised and what claims he makes for it.[35]

Schweizer first finds those characteristics of speech and style which occur principally or with great frequency in the Johannine literature. These he lists, giving the number of occurrences in the Gospel of John, in the Johannine epistles, in the rest of the New Testament, and in the synoptics, in that order. For each of these characteristics he has a formula which summarizes this information. For example, the formula for the occurrences of ἐκεῖνος as an independent personal singular (not a demonstrative adjective) is 44 + 6 / 11 + 0, meaning that the term occurs 44 times in the Fourth Gospel, 6 times in the Johannine epistles, 11 times in the rest of the New

30. Ibid., pp. 98–104.

31. A. Faure, "Die alttestamentlichen Zitate im 4. Evangelium und die Quellenscheidungshypothese," *ZNW, 21* (1922), 99–121.

32. Ruckstuhl, pp. 107–09.

33. Ibid., pp. 111–34.

34. Ibid., pp. 180–219, especially 212–16.

35. For Schweizer's investigation of the question of sources, see *Ego Eimi*, pp. 82–112.

Testament and not at all in the synoptics.[36] After having compiled a list of thirty-three such stylistic characteristics (*Eigentümlichkeiten*), Schweizer investigates the pattern of their occurrence to determine in how many cases two or more different characteristics occur close together in John. (He considers as common occurrences only those instances in which the same characteristics occur together at least twice.) If it should develop that in the laying out of these groupings of characteristics several separate groups of characteristics appear (i.e. if certain characteristics tend to occur with certain others, but none of the characteristics of the groups thus formed appears with other characteristics of similar groups) this stylistic evidence would indicate several independent sources or strata. When the pattern of occurrences is plotted, however, no such separate groups appear, although those characteristics associated with narrative style show more interrelations with each other than with those associated with discourse style, and vice versa.[37] This proves nothing about sources, since it is only a reflection of the different character of the material. Rather, a stylistic unity of the gospel seems to be indicated.

Schweizer tests the source or redaction theories of Spitta, Wendt, and Hirsch against his table of Johannine characteristics and discovers that none of them gains any stylistic support whatsoever.[38] The stylistic characteristics are found scattered throughout the proposed sources and redactions of all these scholars. Schweizer is careful not to claim that all the source theories are thereby disproved; he only asserts that for want of proper stylistic support they must remain hypothetical.[39] He does not attempt to pass judgment on Bultmann's source separations, since, at the time of writing, too little of the commentary had appeared.[40] According to Schweizer's general and admittedly provisional judgment, however, the Fourth Gospel is a stylistic unity, and this probability, while it does not preclude written sources, makes the task of separating them uncertain. Nevertheless, Schweizer himself believes that the gospel was probably no free creation of the evangelist and may well have been composed on the basis of written sources.[41] A definite and important result of Schweizer's study is the clarification of the fact that the unity of

36. *Ego Eimi*, pp. 88 ff.

37. Ibid., p. 101.

38. See his complete tabulations, ibid., pp. 103–05. Schweizer concludes: "Die Tabelle zeigt eindeutig, dass keine dieser Scheidungen stilistisch zu begründen ist, ja dass die Stileigentümlichkeiten bestimmt dagegen sprechen" (p. 105).

39. Ibid., p. 105.

40. Ibid., p. 105.

41. Ibid., p. 108: "Sehr wahrscheinlich ist das Evangelium keine vollständig freie Schöpfung, sondern ist geschrieben auf Grund von vermutlich schriftlicher Tradition . . . Diese Tradition ist aber sehr stark mit dem eigenen Stil des Evangelisten durchdrungen und in das Ganze hinein verarbeitet, sodass sie kaum mehr mit Sicherheit herauszulösen ist." Cf. also pp. 87, 107 f.

the gospel lies at the end, not at the beginning, of whatever process produced it. Henceforth all theories of a *Grundschrift* with extensive later additions by a redactor or redactors become highly questionable.[42] Interestingly enough, Schweizer's conclusions do not affect theories of displacement. Indeed, Schweizer suggests rearrangement as a possible means of resolving some of the difficulties of the Fourth Gospel.[43]

After pronouncing Schweizer's method a great step forward in scientific biblical study,[44] Ruckstuhl proceeds to examine, revise, and expand the list of stylistic criteria which Schweizer had gathered, and emerges with fifty [45]

42. Although he affirms the possibility of source analysis and assigns certain material to a redactor, Bultmann stands in essential agreement with this position (*RGG*, *3*, 842). It is the evangelist who imparts to his sources the impression of unity.

In a twofold reply to the work of both Schweizer (who had attempted to cast doubt on his redaction theory) and Bultmann, Hirsch attacks their understanding of the relation of style criticism to literary criticism and defends his own earlier work on the Fourth Gospel: "Stilkritik und Literaranalyse im vierten Evangelium," *ZNW*, *43* (1950–51), 129–43, actually completed in 1942. In *Das vierte Evangelium in seiner ursprünglichen Gestalt verdeutscht und erklärt* (Tübingen, J. C. B. Mohr, 1936), Hirsch had separated a stratum E (evangelist) from a later stratum R (redactor) on the basis of criteria which were primarily *sachlich* and only secondarily and dependently stylistic (i.e. the stylistic criteria resulted from the redactor's method of altering and correcting the Vorlage with various annotations and glosses). According to Hirsch, this attempt to recover E from R is the proper and profitable role of literary analysis, not the recovery of a Grundschrift (Wellhausen) or written sources (Bultmann). In this separation, the redactor's attempt to imitate the evangelist is *assumed*, and stylistic considerations are thereby relegated to a secondary role in the literary analysis. Hirsch raises pertinent questions about what Schweizer's Johannine characteristics really prove (e.g. such words as ὀψάριον and such constructions as the explanatory ἵνα-clause, while found exclusively or almost exclusively in John in the New Testament, are not actually uncommon in contemporary koine Greek, and therefore are not decisive stylistic criteria) and argues that they only "prove" what Schweizer has from the beginning assumed, namely, the stylistic unity of John. Despite many sharp observations, Hirsch does not succeed in overthrowing Schweizer's evidence against source theories. The greater the redactor's additions (Hirsch's redactions are much more extensive than Bultmann's), the more difficult it would have been for him to conform his own style to the gospel's. Moreover, while a degree of literary unity at the end of the composition process can be shown, the difficulty of objectively establishing an earlier stage at which such a unity existed is considerable. (On source-critical methodology cf. H. M. Teeple, "Methodology in Source Analysis of the Fourth Gospel," *JBL*, *81*, 1962, 279–86.)

43. *Ego Eimi*, pp. 109 ff.

44. Ruckstuhl, p. 181: "Das Vorgehen Schweizers ist nicht nur etwas Neues auf dem Gebiete der Stilkritik überhaupt, sondern so einfach wie zwingend und klar. Sein 'Ego Eimi' dürfte einmal um dieses Abschnittes willen als Einschnitt in der Geschichte der biblischen Literarkritik gelten."

45. Cf. ibid., pp. 203 ff. (Numbers in parentheses after each characteristic refer to Schweizer's tabulation): τότε οὖν (4); οὖν historicum (3); ἄν for ἐάν (if) (15); τὰ Ἱεροσόλυμα; ἵνα epexegeticum (2); asyndeton epicum (10); resumption (*Wiederaufnahme*) (11); possessive pronoun with the article following the noun it modifies (1); noun-substantive with the article used as attributive (7); unusual separations of words (12); substitution of the neuter singular for the

rather than thirty-three. A few of Schweizer's are dropped, and others are added. In his marshaling and evaluating of criteria Ruckstuhl proceeds with care and caution. His two criteria of selection are rarity of occurrence in the New Testament outside John and the unlikelihood that the characteristics in question would have been imitated.

In formulating the pattern of occurrence of the characteristics, Ruckstuhl appears to put himself under the greatest restrictions and limitations. After ranking his fifty Eigentümlichkeiten in general order of importance—the first nineteen being the most important, the next twelve of next importance, and the rest of least importance—he investigates first the "common occurrences" of the first nineteen. The object is to see whether these characteristics occur with one another in an indiscriminate way or whether they divide into several groups that appear only with one another and thus indicate the existence of sources. He counts as a common occurrence any place where more than one characteristic occurs within the same verse or within a verse and its preceding or following verse. He does not count as a common occurrence any instance in which the line of source division of any of the major source theories (Schwartz, Wellhausen, Wendt, Spitta, Hirsch, Bultmann) falls between two characteristics. Thus, in checking the occurrences of these characteristics with one another he cannot be accused of begging the question by assuming that any of the source theories is wrong. With a display of caution, he puts himself at a temporary disadvantage, since all of the source theories could not possibly be right.[46]

Ruckstuhl sets forth his results in diagram form, as Schweizer had done. The first of his three diagrams shows only the relationships among the first nineteen characteristics, and only those characteristics which occur together at least twice are counted. The next shows the relationships among the first nineteen, taking into consideration all those characteristics which occur together even once. The third and final diagram shows the relationships

---

plural number of persons; καθώς . . . καί (9); οὐ . . . ἀλλ' ἵνα (8); οὐχ ὅτι . . . ἀλλ' ὅτι; ὥρα ἵνα; ὥρα ὅτε; ἀπεκρίθη καὶ εἶπεν (Menoud); ἐκεῖνος (6); ὥρα with personal pronoun (Jeremias); παρρησία in the dative without a preposition (25); οὐ μὴ . . . εἰς τὸν αἰῶνα; παροιμία-riddle; σκοτία instead of σκότος (20); λαμβάνω τινά-to receive one who comes from God (23); Σίμων Πέτρος; τίθημι ψυχήν (28); μέντοι (17); γύναι used to address the mother of Jesus (Jeremias); φανερόω used reflexively; μεταβαίνω-to go out of the ungodly into the divine; μαρτυρέω περί τινος used personally; ἀφ' ἑαυτοῦ (21); (ἐν) τῇ ἐσχάτῃ ἡμέρᾳ (24); οὐ . . . πώποτε; μικρός used of extent of time; ἀνθρακιά; ἐκ τούτου; πάλιν + δεύτερος; ἑλκύω (26); ὀψάριον (27); ἀμὴν ἀμήν (Menoud); ὑπάγω + πορεύομαι meaning to go from the world into the beyond (22); πιστεύω εἰς τινα (Jeremias); μετὰ τοῦτο; οὐ . . . ἐὰν (εἰ) μή (16); ἐκ partitivum (13); εἶναι, γεννηθῆναι ἐκ (14); (ἐ)ὰν (μή) τις (15); ἐντεῦθεν; ὥρα ἐν ᾗ; πιάζω (29).

46. Ruckstuhl, p. 206. Cf. Schweizer, *Ego Eimi*, p. 100 n. 142.

among the first thirty-one characteristics, again taking into consideration all the characteristics which occur together even once.[47] The net result is that these diagrams reveal only a single grouping of stylistic characteristics and therefore bespeak the stylistic unity of the gospel. Had certain characteristics occurred only with certain others, separate groups would have appeared in the diagram. The appearance of several groups in one or more diagrams would have been taken as an indication of several stylistic, and presumably literary, strata in the gospel.

Having thus demonstrated anew the stylistic unity of the gospel, Ruckstuhl proceeds to test Bultmann's sources against these same characteristics as Schweizer had tested the theories of Spitta, Wendt, and Hirsch.[48] The result is as clear-cut as Schweizer's. By and large, the characteristics are scattered at random throughout Bultmann's sources. Hence his theory has as little stylistic support as theirs. Ruckstuhl concludes that "the list [showing the random distribution of characteristics in Bultmann's sources] clearly shows the incorrectness of Bultmann's literary critical dispositions and separations." [49]

So far Ruckstuhl and Schweizer have applied substantially the same method and have come to similar conclusions both as to the stylistic unity of the gospel and the stylistic support, or lack of it, for the source theories examined. In their further conclusions, however, a difference of emphasis appears. As we have already seen, Schweizer only claims to have proved a certain stylistic unity which lies at the end of the process of the development of the gospel and which he believes should be rather discouraging to future attempts to identify the sources, if any, behind it. Ruckstuhl goes a considerable distance beyond this, however, arguing in general and in specific cases not merely against Bultmann's source (and redaction) theory but against all such theories either undertaken or contemplated. According to Ruckstuhl, the possibility of written sources is scarcely worthy of further consideration. [50]

Despite its general impressiveness and many indications of the author's acumen, Ruckstuhl's work must be received with reservation. Schweizer's scientific study is enlisted in what seems in part to be an apologetically motivated, if not unscientifically executed, attempt to prove that Bultmann

47. Ruckstuhl, p. 210.
48. Ibid., pp. 212–16.
49. Ibid., p. 215.
50. Ibid., pp. 218 f., where Ruckstuhl summarizes his conclusions regarding the literary unit of the gospel. Cf. also p. 16, where, it seems to me, Ruckstuhl overstates the implications of his projected refutation of Bultmann's literary analysis: "Sollte sich herausstellen, dass B. nicht im Recht ist, dann dürfte allein schon diese Tatsache zeigen, dass jede literarkritische Arbeit am vierten Ev zum Scheitern verurteilt sein muss, dass dessen Einheit und Geschlossenheit jeder zersetzenden Aufteilung widersteht."

is wrong and, moreover, that because his most skillful attempt has failed, all thought of source criticism and written sources must be given up.[51] Now, this is almost certainly an exaggerated claim, although it has its measure of truth insofar as it suggests the probable futility of any such detailed source analysis as Bultmann attempts. Schweizer sensed the same thing but wisely limited his claims to the assertion that source criticism of John probably cannot be successful or profitable.[52] In addition, Ruckstuhl can scarcely be said to have attempted to do justice to Bultmann's reasons for undertaking source analysis in the first place. He quotes Bultmann at the places where he introduces, summarizes, or makes explicit his arguments, but does not suggest the added force which they acquire in the light of the many difficulties within the gospel and of Bultmann's assiduous gathering and organizing of the evidence in the total exegesis and interpretation of the text. It is not surprising that from his book one gets little idea of the cumulative effect of Bultmann's evidence and argument. Finally, Ruckstuhl's belief that the distribution of the Johannine characteristics guarantees the literary unity of the entire book, not simply in its present form but from its inception, is subject to doubt. Critics have rightly argued that the impressive demonstration of the overall unity of the book does not ipso facto make it impossible to distinguish more than one literary or traditional stratum at some points, although it may well make impossible the exact delineation of extensive sources. Rudolf Schnackenburg, another Catholic scholar, grants the effectiveness of Ruckstuhl's criticism of Bultmann but denies that it permits a categorical judgment about every passage in the gospel. Rather, he contends that the style-critical key must be used on specific passages to determine whether or not we may in certain cases distinguish between the hand of the evangelist and other material. Schnackenburg supports his contention with a style-critical examination of the prologue. His findings are striking. Verses 1, 3, 4, part of 9, 10, 11, part of 14, and 16 contain only one Johannine characteristic, the *Wiederaufnahme* or repetition of key words found in verses 1, 4, 10, and 11. [53] This is in agreement with his literary analysis, through which he had already found verses 6–8, 12c–13, 15, 17, and 18 to be secondary additions to the original composition.[54] Moreover, the results are surprisingly similar to those of Bultmann, whose prologue source includes all or part of verses 1–5, 9–12, 14, and 16. (For Schnackenburg, however, Johannine stylistic characteristics elimi-

---

51. Ibid., pp. 106 f. and 218 f.

52. He himself indicated the likelihood that written sources or traditions are embodied in the gospel. *Ego Eimi*, pp. 87 f., 107 f.

53. "Logos-Hymnus und johanneischer Prolog," *BZ, 1* (1957), 69–109, especially 77–82.

54. Ibid., p. 75.

nate verses 2, 5, and 12.) S. Schulz also feels the weight of Ruckstuhl's demonstration of the overall unity of the Fourth Gospel, but, like Schnackenburg,
he has found it possible to use the Johannine stylistic characteristics to isolate
traditional materials.[55] Significantly, in his analysis of the prologue, Schulz
discerns a source similar to Bultmann's and Schnackenburg's.[56]

Such reservations as these do not discredit Ruckstuhl's work, which does
in fact point unerringly to the difficulties Bultmann encounters in developing
a source theory out of his literary analysis. They are, however, indicative of
the fact that Ruckstuhl, like his opponent, attempts to arrive at too great a
degree of certainty in drawing conclusions on the basis of the literary and
stylistic evidence of the Fourth Gospel. If Bultmann goes too far in attempting to define extensive sources down to the most minute detail, perhaps
Ruckstuhl goes too far in concluding from a demonstrable stylistic unity of
the gospel that such sources not only cannot be proved, but, in fact, never
existed at all.

Three years after Ruckstuhl's volume appeared, a Scandinavian scholar,
Bent Noack, published a monograph dealing extensively with Bultmann's
literary analysis and source separations.[57] Noack wishes to argue that oral
traditions rather than written sources lie immediately behind the Fourth
Gospel. Before he can launch his own theory, however, he must come to
terms with literary analysis and source criticism. He selects Bultmann's work
for examination because, like Ruckstuhl, he regards it as the most comprehensive and methodologically sound example of such criticism. Significantly,
Noack explicitly dissociates himself from Ruckstuhl's judgment that all literary source analysis of the Gospel of John stands or falls with Bultmann.[58]

After a brief description of Bultmann's method, Noack examines a number
of the stylistic characteristics which Bultmann employs as criteria for the
identification of the hand of the evangelist in the gospel.[59] This examination
shows that in some significant cases the characteristics which Bultmann
ascribes to the evangelist also appear in his sources and are therefore of very
questionable value for source analysis. Where such characteristics occur in
material already assigned to the source, Bultmann sometimes views them as

55. See below pp. 88–96 for a discussion of Schulz' work. For Schulz' statement of the
role of *Stilstatistik* in isolating traditional materials see *Untersuchungen*, pp. 56, 58 ff. For an
implied criticism of Ruckstuhl see *Komposition und Herkunft der Johanneischen Reden*, p.
21 n. 79.

56. *Komposition und Herkunft*, pp. 7–28.

57. B. Noack, *Zur johanneischen Tradition*.

58. Ibid., p. 11: "Es kann zwar nicht von vornherein behauptet werden, dass alle literarkritische Arbeit am Johannesevangelium mit der Richtigkeit oder Unrichtigkeit dieser [Bultmann's] Analyse steht und fällt." Cf. also p. 11 n. 7.

59. Ibid., pp. 18–34.

additions of the evangelist, sometimes not. The resulting impression is one of considerable blurring between the style of the sources and that of the evangelist.[60] Furthermore, in order to account for the similarities between the evangelist and the Offenbarungsreden, Bultmann has recourse to the explanation that the evangelist has been influenced by the style and content of this source. Such an explanation can only mean that we are on very uncertain ground indeed in attempting to distinguish between the speech source and the hand of the evangelist.[61] The point—already suggested by Jeremias and Ruckstuhl—is well taken. If Bultmann maintains that the evangelist has both reworked and imitated his sources in order to make his source theory convincing, the proposal is not in itself impossible, but the necessity of continual recourse to it casts doubts on the feasibility of the sort of detailed source analysis Bultmann has undertaken.

Like Ruckstuhl, Noack points out that at points there are far greater disparities between different segments of the Offenbarungsreden source than between certain passages assigned to the Offenbarungsreden and others assigned to the evangelist. Again in agreement with Ruckstuhl, he observes that the stylistic characteristics of the evangelist are much more numerous and clearly defined than those of the speech source, and he notes that the absence of the characteristics of the evangelist serves in some cases to identify a passage as being from the source.[62] Neither stylistic distinctions nor distinctions of substance seem sufficient to justify the separation of a continuous Offenbarungsredequelle from the work of the evangelist. If Bultmann's separation of the Offenbarungsreden is not convincing to Noack, his attempt to reconstruct the original order of that document is even less so. Noack examines the reconstruction of the order of the Offenbarungsreden at several points and finds it unsatisfactory.[63]

In opposition to Bultmann, Noack develops his own theory of the origin

60. Ibid., p. 22: "Sätze die ein ἐκεῖνος enthalten, entfallen auf die Beiträge des Evangelisten, bezeichnen also eine Erweiterung oder Unterbrechung der Quelle; bisweilen kommt aber auch in den Quellen ein ἐκεῖνος vor (z.B. 5.11 Sem. und 8, 42.44 Offenb.), und die Analyse muss dann mit Hilfe einer Behauptung durchgeführt werden, 'das ἐκεῖνος wird der Evglist eingefügt haben,' oder mit Hilfe der Annahme, er habe seine Quelle nur benutzt und stark umgestaltet, nicht aber getreu wiedergegeben.

"Dann versagt also das Wort als Kriterium; und die Benutzung als solches wird denn auch nicht durchgeführt; in etliche Verse soll der Evangelist nicht eingegriffen haben, *obwohl* sie ein ἐκεῖνος enthalten: gegenüber 5:19 und 43 (die beide aus den Offenb. stammen sollen) hat Bultmann offensichtlich keine Bedenken. . . .—Danach dürfte es unmöglich sein, die Sätze nach Vorkommen oder Fehlen dieses Wortes auf den Evangelisten und die Quellen zu verteilen; man wird sich damit begnügen müssen, dass das gebrauchte Wort eine Eigentümlichkeit des vierten Evangelisten ist."

61. Ibid., p. 31; also pp. 31–34.

62. Ibid., p. 37 n. 98.

63. Ibid., pp. 36 ff.

of the gospel. This in itself is a distinct advance over Ruckstuhl, who is as vague in his positive suggestions about the origin of John and the resolution of the literary difficulties in the document as he is precise and positive in his criticism of Bultmann.[64] Beginning with an analysis of the Johannine tradition based on the principle of breaking up the material into its smallest possible components, Noack develops a theory according to which the entire gospel arose directly from oral tradition. The discourse as well as the narrative material is said to stem from this source.

According to Noack we find in the discourse material of the Fourth Gospel both synoptic-like sayings and sayings which are foreign to the synoptics, but which have close, if not antecedent, parallels in the Mandaean literature.[65] Bultmann is right in seeing this latter relationship. But there is not adequate reason to suppose, as he does, that the Mandaean-like tradition in John comes from a written source which the evangelist brought over from the Baptist sect at the time of his conversion. Such a theory makes the evangelist appear to be personally responsible for the introduction of this Gnostic-type material into the Christian tradition, i.e. for the translation of the Christian message into Gnostic or quasi-Gnostic terminology. But it is Noack's contention that this gnosticizing of the Christian message was the result of a traditional process, not the work of an individual. He is confident that his view is supported by the existence of a Johannine Gnostic logion in the synoptic tradition (Matt. 11:27, Luke 10:22) and by the fact that in the Fourth Gospel we find—in juxtaposition with the gnosticized or distinctly Johannine material—various narratives, the passion story, synoptic logia, Old Testament quotations, and certain traditional proverbs (e.g., 4:35–37, 6:63, 4:44, 21:18) which were already in use in the church when the gospel was composed. Further, the appearance of the solemn ἀμὴν ἀμήν before some sayings bespeaks their traditional and probably liturgical character.[66] As to the logia in John

---

64. Compare the judgment of W. Eltester, "Notizen," *ZNW*, *45* (1954), pp. 279 f. He rightly criticizes Ruckstuhl for not taking sufficiently seriously the actual difficulties in the text of the Fourth Gospel which give rise to such theories as Bultmann's. Eltester has praise for Noack's work and asserts that his thesis should be given the most serious consideration—granted that it may not solve all the riddles of the Fourth Gospel.

65. For this and the following assertions see Noack, pt. II ("Die Struktur des Stoffes"), pp. 43–125. On the Johannine logia see pp. 43–71.

66. Noack argues (ibid., pp. 70 f.) that the formula's occurrence with the synoptic as well as with the Gnostic-Johannine sayings—not to mention passages which have been ascribed to the evangelist or redactor—indicates that the evangelist had a tradition of sayings of Jesus which for him did not fall into our neat categories. Had he been conscious of the difference between the Johannine-Gnostic sayings and the synoptic, and had he thought that he was introducing a new set of sayings (i.e. the Johannine-Gnostic) along with the traditional synoptic type, he would have probably sown the ἀμὴν ἀμήν formulae in the one type or the

which are similar to or recall synoptic logia, Noack readily admits that they are related to the same synoptic tradition that appears in the first three gospels.[67] But he attempts to demonstrate by the examination of individual instances of such logia in John that it is much more likely that the evangelist drew them from an earlier source of synoptic tradition, very probably oral, than from the extant gospels. Both strands of the Johannine sayings tradition, the quasi-Gnostic and the quasi-synoptic, are viewed as stemming from oral tradition rather than from written sources. The speeches as a whole are said to be composed of individual sayings which give evidence of their original independence.[68] They are organized around certain key sentences or expressions so that one moves from one traditional segment to another without sensing conspicuous disharmony.[69] Nevertheless, it is still possible to recover the individual elements of the tradition from the amalgam which the author has produced.

Similarly, the narrative material[70] can best be accounted for by the hypothesis that the author drew it from the church's oral tradition rather than by supposing that he took it from any written source, be it one of the synoptic gospels or the proposed semeia-source. Noack's arguments against the semeia-source,[71] which in my opinion are not entirely decisive, are bolstered by the claim that it is highly unlikely that such a document, containing reports of the deeds of Jesus apart from any tradition of his words, ever circulated independently. It is unprecedented and improbable.

Thus, in both narrative and discourse sections, the Gospel of John represents the initial writing down of a stream or streams of tradition. The entire gospel was written down from memory and does not require, but rather

---

other—in the synoptic type, with which the ἀμήν formula is usually associated, or in the new type, in order that he might set them forth as genuine words of the Lord. That he sows them indiscriminately indicates he does not know the distinction of which we speak.

67. Ibid., pp. 89–109.

68. Ibid., p. 131: "Die Reden des Joh bestehen wie die der Synopse aus Aneinanderreihungen von Aussprüchen, die sich in manchen Fällen deutlich voneinander abheben und als selbständige Elemente der Überlieferung zu betrachten sind."

69. Ibid., pp. 151 ff.

70. For Noack's discussion of the *Erzählungsstoff*, ibid., pp. 109–25.

71. Ibid., pp. 112–14. He argues that Bultmann's semeia-source theory is weakened by his inability to ascribe all the narrative material of the gospel to it. Further, it is difficult (according to Noack) to imagine why the evangelist, if he were using a source in which the signs were numbered, indicated the number of the first and second sign but not of the rest. On the other hand, he himself might have numbered the first two miracles and designated them as signs in order to emphasize them and bring out their special character and significance. Bultmann's argument for a semeia-source on the basis of 20:30 f. is said to break down when one gives up the false distinction between Jesus as wonder-worker and Jesus as revealer and recognizes that the evangelist could perfectly well have written this conclusion.

forbids, the hypothesis of written sources.[72] It is true that there were gospels before John, that a variety of streams from the history of religions are encountered within the gospel, and that there are irregularities, instances of unevenness, or difficulties of one sort or another within the text. But none of these considerations demands the explanation that the gospel was composed out of written sources. Admittedly, problems such as the order of chapters 5 and 6 or 14–17 are scarcely solved by Noack's hypothesis, but he does not regard these as insurmountable difficulties. He deems it quite possible that the key to their resolution may be found in the proposal that the gospel was edited by a circle of disciples or by a single redactor. They do not disturb the thesis that the gospel represents the fixing in literary form of a tradition which stands side by side with the synoptic.[73]

In the course of developing his thesis, Noack devotes a significant chapter to the Fourth Evangelist's use of the Old Testament,[74] the only extant source which we are sure he used and which may possibly offer an insight into his use of sources in general. This line of investigation yields some interesting results. He discovers that the evangelist usually quotes the Old Testament so freely as to give the impression that he is quoting from memory and not from a text lying before him. The fact that many of the quotations serve as polemic against the Jews and that no tendency can be observed in the modifications of them makes it unlikely that John deliberately altered them. That the evangelist quoted directly from a testimony source is also unlikely, since such a source, designed to be used polemically against Jews, presumably would have adhered faithfully to some Old Testament text. But the Old Testament quotations in John are so aberrant that they could scarcely have come from any textual tradition. Neither can John's quotations be explained from the synoptics, although some synoptic quotations follow no known Old Testament text. The obvious conclusion is that John quotes the Old Testament from memory, and the implication is that if he quotes the Old Testament in this way it is unlikely that he would have been more meticulous in the use of other sources.

Coincidentally with Noack's book and without knowledge of his findings, Charles Goodwin published an article in which he examines the Old Testa-

---

72. "Das Joh ist ohne Benutzung irgendeiner schriftlichen Quelle geschrieben, sei es eines synoptischen oder eines unbekannten Evangeliums, sei es Aufzeichnungen einzelner Perikopen oder Logien, auch der sogenannten Offenbarungsreden. Der ganze Stoff ist aus dem Wissen und Gedächtnis des Verfassers (oder der Verfasser—darauf kommt es uns nicht an) niedergeschrieben" (ibid., p. 157).

73. Ibid., p. 162. Whether a tradition is written or oral does not necessarily have any bearing upon its validity or authenticity.

74. Ibid., pp. 71–89.

ment evidence in John[75] and also concludes that the evangelist quoted the Old Testament from memory.[76] He, too, derives the implication that he would have treated his other sources in the same manner. But whereas Noack uses this insight in support of his oral tradition theory, Goodwin attempts to interpret it to mean that one cannot deny knowledge of the synoptic gospels to John, since, if he had known them, he would have used their material quite freely, giving it from memory and often changing it. While it may take more than the analogy of the use of the Old Testament to prove John's knowledge and use of the synoptics, Goodwin's conclusion is certainly valid in principle; whatever sources John used, he may be suspected of having quoted them loosely and from memory, if this is in fact the way he quoted the Old Testament. Under such circumstances the recovery of such sources would be very difficult, if not impossible, as Goodwin has indicated.[77]

Bultmann lost no time before replying to Noack. In a review of his book [78] he strongly rejects the principle of criticism whereby Noack breaks the gospel into small fragments. This already suggests that the author did not get his material from written sources but from individual bits of oral tradition. Putting aside the objection that such a breaking up of a text into its smallest component parts does not prove that no written source lies behind it, Bultmann brands as absurd Noack's analytical method of approaching the Fourth Gospel, maintaining that it is impossible to apply to that document the principle that literary dissection must be carried through not only where it gives the best solution but wherever possible. Its discourses do not present themselves as a series of single units to which such a method is appropriate, as do the synoptic "discourses," for example. The discourses of the Fourth Gospel are an entirely different sort of literature, and it should be obvious from the outset that an analytical approach such as Noack attempts cannot legitimately be applied to them.

Bultmann grants that Noack has demonstrated that the Fourth Evangelist quotes the Old Testament from memory, but he will not concede that this has overwhelming significance for his possible use of other sources. He accepts Noack's contention that the evangelist did not use the synoptic gospels in their present form, but the fact that he was already strongly

75. "How Did John Treat His Sources?" *JBL, 73* (1954), pp. 61–75.

76. "He quoted . . . [the Old Testament] *rarely, loosely and confusedly,* often *conflating* two or more passages, *distorting* their *meaning* and *hiding their context.* . . . He appears to have quoted from memory . . ." (ibid., p. 73).

77. "It is reasonable to suppose that he would have treated his unacknowledged sources in the same manner [as he treated the Old Testament]." In that case wherever the sources are lost we must despair of any attempt to recover them from his text (ibid., p. 73).

78. "Zur johanneischen Tradition," *TL, 80* (1955), 521–26.

inclined toward that position is indication enough that he does not regard this as a hindrance to his own source theory. Moreover, Bultmann believes that Noack's analysis of the text has yielded many valuable insights into the Johannine narratives and discourses, but he firmly maintains that the evidence mustered by Noack, correct in many respects though it may be, does not demand the author's hypothesis that the gospel was composed directly out of oral tradition, but fits the hypothesis of written sources just as well.[79]

We must here point out at least one place where Bultmann seems to gloss over a valid objection to his position. It is true, as Bultmann indicates, that the evidence of the evangelist's practice of quoting the Old Testament from memory rather than from the written text does not necessarily mean that he did not use written sources at all. Noack cannot and does not claim this.[80] But it seems to me that this practice does imply that such written sources as he used were employed so freely that, barring some unforeseen manuscript discovery, their exact delineation within the gospel may be impossible.[81]

Against Noack's criticism, Bultmann attempts to stand his ground by asserting that while Noack tests his criteria individually (e.g., ἐκεῖνος) he, Bultmann, always uses them together in such a way that they offer mutual support and confirmation. Bultmann also continues to insist that characteristics of the evangelist which occur, for example, in the Offenbarungsreden can legitimately be accounted for by the fact that the evangelist imitates and annotates the source.[82] Nevertheless, the complete effectiveness of Bultmann's reply may be questioned. Although he employs his criteria in a remarkable way, so that he is seldom dependent on one criterion for the identification of any sizable section of the source, his case is certainly weakened when in a number of instances his individual stylistic characteristics are shown to be indecisive. This is particularly true in the light of his own earlier demand, pointed out by Ruckstuhl, that source criticism be based firmly on stylistic considerations. Perhaps Bultmann makes the best point in his own favor when he singles out places in the gospel where one passes from one world into another, so to speak, in moving from one section to another, e.g. from the

---

79. Haenchen, "Johanneische Probleme," *ZTK, 56* (1959), 19–54, also rejects Noack's theory that the gospel was written down directly from oral tradition (cf. pp. 20–22, 52 f.), but he does not subscribe to Bultmann's source hypothesis (p. 33 n. 2).

80. Noack, p. 72.

81. Goodwin, *JBL,* 73 (1954), 73.

82. *TL, 80* (1955), 522 f.: "Ich muss nur noch hinzufügen, dass gegen eine Quellenscheidung auch die Tatsache nicht angeführt werden kann, dass sich Charakteristika der von mir angenommenen Quelle der 'Offenbarungsreden' auch in dem Evangelisten zugeschriebenen Sätzen finden. Denn wenn er überhaupt diese Quelle verarbeitet hat, so doch deshalb, weil ihre Gedanken seiner Gedankenwelt entsprechen oder ihr verwandt sind. Dann ist es aber sehr begreiflich, dass er sie imitiert bzw. Wendungen aus ihr übernimmt."

prologue to the witness of the Baptist or from the farewell discourses to the passion account. Certainly such instances do admit of the possibility of different literary strata, and, as Bultmann points out, this conjecture is often supported by theological and stylistic considerations.[83]

That Bultmann continues to believe that there are sources behind the Fourth Gospel and that they are substantially what he declared them to be twenty years ago in his commentary is also attested by his criticisms of Dodd's *Interpretation of the Fourth Gospel*,[84] which passes over the problem of sources, by his encyclopedia article on the Gospel of John,[85] and by his publication of the late H. Becker's dissertation on the Johannine Offenbarungs-reden.[86]

Becker's monograph is, as the title implies, an attempt to confirm Bultmann's theory of the Offenbarungsreden source by showing that there is a characteristic style or form of the revelation discourse which can be documented from material drawn from the history of religions (part I) and that this same form of discourse appears in the Fourth Gospel (part II). In his view, the source analysis of the Fourth Gospel may not be undertaken solely on the basis of internal criteria.[87] The analyst must either presuppose the existence of an Offenbarungsreden source and distinguish it from the work of the evangelist by gathering and sifting stylistic evidence (Bultmann) or, with Becker, he must proceed from an external scheme, found in relevant sources, whose characteristics may then be discovered in the gospel as well. Becker expects to find that while this revelation discourse scheme occurs in John and manifests the typical style of the Offenbarungsreden, the clear-cut outlines of the source have been somewhat obscured by the fact that the evangelist has imitated his style; hence the overall impression of unity which Schweizer noted.

83. Ibid., col. 523.
84. *NTS*, 1 (1954–55), 77–91.
85. *RGG*, 3 (1959), 840–50.
86. Becker, *Die Reden des Johannesevangeliums*. Note especially Bultmann's foreword, in which he denies that the appearance of the commentaries of Hoskyns, Wikenhauser, and Barrett and the studies of Dodd and Noack have made Becker's work superfluous—"im Gegenteil!"
87. This, according to Becker, is Schweizer's error in the chapter on source criticism in *Ego Eimi*. Becker asserts that Schweizer's method could have produced no positive results: "Das methodische Vorgehen Schweizers . . . ist anfechtbar. Seine Argumentation bewegt sich in einem circulus vitiosus. . . . Angenommen, der Verfasser des Joh Evg.'s hat eine Quelle benutzt, die sich durch sein ganzes Werk hindurchzieht und die er selber mit Anmerkungen und Exkursen versehen hat, so entfällt jeder Anhaltspunkt, um auf Grund einer vergleichenden Untersuchungen des Stiles zu einer Quellenscheidung zu kommen. Denn dann werden selbstverständlich bestimmte Eigentümlichkeiten der Quelle für den Evangelisten gebucht; so kommt die Konstatierung eines 'durchgängig einheitlichen Stiles' zustande" (ibid., pp. 12 f.).

After examining many Gnostic, quasi-Gnostic and Jewish documents,[88] Becker discovers the following primary elements of the Offenbarungsreden-schema:

1. The self-predication of the revealer, often with a description of the situation of the world which has motivated his coming.

2. The invitation, or call to decision from without this Godless world, cast in personal or ethical terms (e.g. "turn to the Redeemer" or "turn from your sins").

3. The promise to those who respond to the call of the redeemer, often combined with threats of dire consequences for those who do not.[89]

This proclamation strikingly embodies the very essence of Gnosticism and can, as in the Hermetic tractate *Poimandres*, form the basis for the exposition of Gnostic doctrines. In most cases, however, the appearance of this scheme is marked by its kerygmatic, nonspeculative character. Two forms of proclamatory utterance are observed by Becker in the materials he examines: a western type, in which the stages follow one another in the above order and therefore evolve logically and progressively, and a more characteristically oriental form, in which the *telos* is present from the beginning and the various elements of the Gnostic proclamation do not appear in logical progression but arrange themselves in what Becker calls a spiraling pattern. The Johannine discourses are of this latter, oriental type.[90]

In the second part of his study,[91] which is devoted to the Johannine discourses proper, Becker first identifies those passages which conform most closely to the already established scheme of the Gnostic revelation discourse and moves from these to a thoroughgoing, if admittedly not entirely certain, identification of the Johannine Offenbarungsreden. This task is carried out in a long exegetical analysis of the Johannine speeches. The result substantially confirms the analysis of Bultmann, with certain minor modifications or corrections. Becker also attempts his own reconstruction of the Offenbarungs-

---

88. Celsus' version of the speech of Palestinian messianic prophets, reported by Origen (*Contra Celsum*, VII 8 f.); Odes of Solomon, 33; four Hermetic texts; two texts from the pseudo-Clementine literature; an example from the *Acta Archelai* of Hegemonius; examples from some of the apocryphal acts of the apostles; Clement of Alexandria, *Protreptikos*, XII, 120, 2 ff.; an example from the *Kitâb al-bâkoûrah;* above all, the Mandaean literature, the *John Book* and the *Right Ginza.*

89. *Reden des Johannesevangeliums*, pt. I and especially pp. 53 ff.

90. Against Karl Kundsin, *Charakter und Ursprung der johanneischen Reden* (Acta Universitatis Latviensis, *I*, 4, Riga, 1939), Becker denies that the Johannine discourses can be explained in terms of a spinning out of certain basic apocalyptic ideas. What we encounter in John is rather a typical example of Oriental Gnostic Offenbarungsreden in which the major elements are arranged together in a spiraling pattern (ibid., p. 56).

91. Ibid., pp. 60–120.

reden in its original order, and, in an appendix, he sets forth the recovered source.[92]

Becker is fully aware of the circularity of his argument.[93] He believes, however, that the existence of a discourse scheme or pattern in the Gnostic materials allows one to conjecture that the speeches in the Gospel of John which show this scheme have been worked into it by the evangelist, who took them from a written source. When, in the discourse sections, very clear-cut examples of this pattern are found, this conjecture receives confirmation.[94] Becker consciously takes as his presupposition what is properly only the result and postulates in advance an Offenbarungsredequelle for the Fourth Gospel. The starting points are the strikingly similar formulations of the scheme of the revelation discourses in the Gnostic or quasi-Gnostic literature and in John. The demonstration of the proposal, according to Becker, depends upon the outcome of the analysis of the gospel carried out on the basis of the newly attained knowledge of the form of the Gnostic Offenbarungs-reden.[95]

One need not dispute Bultmann's judgment about the significance of this study or the promise of its late author [96] to raise questions about what he has really demonstrated. In the painstaking examination of the Mandaean litera-ture, the Odes of Solomon, the Hermetica, the Wisdom literature of the Old Testament and Apocrypha, etc., the author has made an impressive and persuasive case for the view that the discourses of the Fourth Gospel belong to the same genre as the "revelation discourses" found in other documents of various religions. Its effect is to weaken considerably the arguments that the discourses were spun out from certain basic ideas common also to the Apocalypse (Kundsin) or that they were developed by the weaving together of single elements of a Christian tradition that had grown under Gnostic influence (Noack). In such cases we would be confronted with a phenom-enon that, while subject to outside influences, is fundamentally an inner

---

92. Ibid., pp. 129–36.

93. "Wir sind uns bewusst, dass wir eigentümlich zirkelförmig verfahren, indem wir das eigentlich erst Herauszustellende zur Voraussetzung machen und von vornherein für das Joh-Evg. eine Quelle von Offenbarungsreden postulieren" (ibid., p. 62).

94. "Schon die Existenz eines solchen ganzen Redeschemas, zu dem der soteriologische Satz als intergrierender Bestandteil hinzugehört, lässt auch für das Joh-Evg. vermuten, dass in ihm Reden, die dieses Schema aufweisen, verarbeitet worden sind; der Evangelist muss sie einer Quelle entnommen haben. Diese Vermutung wird noch dadurch bestärkt, dass wir in den Redestücken des Joh-Evg. ganz offensichtliche stilistische Gebilde analog denen des Offen-barungsreden-Schemas finden . . ." (ibid., p. 60).

95. Ibid., p. 62: "Doch kann natürlich erst das Ergebnis der Analyse Recht oder Unrecht unserer Methode erweisen."

96. Ibid., Bultmann's "Vorwort."

Christian development. But Becker views the Johannine discourses as a wide-spread phenomenon in the history of religion, here manifesting itself in Christian form.

All this may be granted without for a moment conceding that Becker has demonstrated the existence of an Offenbarungsredequelle of pre- or non-Christian origin behind the text of the Fourth Gospel.[97] It seems to me that there is in Becker's argument an unwarranted and precipitate leap from the demonstration of the kinship of the Johannine speeches and non-Christian revelation discourses to the hypothesis that the evangelist's use of this form and style can only be attributed to a written source, which he copied out in so meticulous a manner that it is now possible to recover it in detail. Becker's attempt to recover and reconstitute the Offenbarungsreden source of John consists of a literary analysis of the gospel with the use of the *religionsgeschichtlich* scheme reconstructed from other sources. While Becker makes use of Bultmann's earlier work, he goes beyond it in attempting to deduce and support the existence of the Offenbarungsreden source by show-ing the affinities of the Johannine discourses with the Offenbarungsreden scheme. Bultmann himself had already paved the way for such a systematic undertaking when he adduced as evidence for the existence and content of the Offenbarungsreden of John material from the Odes of Solomon, the Mandaean discourses, etc. That such parallels exist and that they can be shown to stand in close relationship to John's discourses does not, however, mean that John used such a non-Christian document (or a Christian one, for that matter) as the basis for his own gospel. What is more, such parallels do not give one the right, certainly they do not compel one, to hypothesize that John used such a written source, in the belief that such a hypothesis, once adopted, could be vindicated in the course of literary analysis. Once the hypothesis is made, the literary analysis is likely to produce a "source," i.e., a literary stratum, with one or another degree of success. And the degree of success with which such a source is produced cannot be uncritically accepted as the only criterion by which one may judge whether or not an independent literary source-document ever actually existed. The degree of success may only serve as an index of the cleverness of the scholar in execut-ing such a literary analysis and laying bare a literary form, but not neces-sarily a literary source, within a document.

One is compelled to ask whether the source hypothesis is really necessary to explain the evidence, or on what presuppositions the source hypothesis is necessary to explain the evidence and whether those presuppositions are the

97. After arriving at this position independently, I was encouraged to find that a similar judgment had already been advanced by W. Nauck, *Tradition und Charakter*, p. 11 n. 2.

only ones or the best ones. May one not suggest, with Käsemann,[98] that the evangelist himself speaks in the solemn manner of the revelation discourse, especially when he takes it upon himself to speak through the mouth of Jesus? The difficulties which give rise to the source hypothesis could be explained as the result of the illogical spiraling progression of the discourses (Becker) or as simply arising from the author's own sequence of thought, which is very different in kind from ours. Furthermore, in view of the evangelist's use of the Old Testament (cf. Noack and Goodwin) is it not reasonable to suppose that, if he had had access to such a document as the hypothetical revelation discourses, he would have quoted it from memory rather than have copied it verbatim? If this had been the case, would not Goodwin and Schweizer be justified in doubting that any attempt to recover and reconstruct such a source could ever be successful?

Finally, we are brought again to the question of the significance of Schweizer's style-critical work, which Becker wishes to set aside. I confess that I am perplexed by Becker's charge that Schweizer's argument moves in a vicious circle and his insistence that the proper approach to the source analysis of the Fourth Gospel is through external rather than internal criteria. He is not in possession of a source upon which direct literary dependence can be proved or even claimed. The kind of external evidence which he adduces, namely, the pattern of the revelation discourse, is relevant for an understanding of the milieu of the Johannine speeches, but it does not prove anything about sources. I find it difficult to see how such evidence can take precedence over the stylistic evidence which Schweizer and Ruckstuhl have presented. To attribute the phenomena which give the impression of the overall stylistic unity of the Fourth Gospel to the evangelist's imitation and reworking of his sources as Becker and Bultmann would apparently have us do, while it offers a way out of a difficult situation, becomes an increasingly suspect procedure the more it is utilized. If imitation and reworking have taken place on a large scale, is not skepticism of the possibility of the recovery of extensive sources justified even if one strongly suspects, as Schweizer himself does, that the evangelist used some written sources?

In dealing with the hypothetical Offenbarungsreden I have put the problem of pre-Christian Gnosticism to one side. That problem is still being vigorously investigated and debated, and I am in no position to decide it here. Few scholars any longer doubt that most of the so-called Gnostic motives are pre-Christian, but there is real disagreement about the existence of a pre-

---

98. *ZTK*, *48* (1951), 306 n. 2. Hirsch, *ZNW*, *43* (1950–51), 143, has also criticized Bultmann for failing to take into account the evangelist's own variations in style and manner of expression.

Christian Gnostic redeemer or revealer myth.[99] The problem is a complex one, and the questions involved are manifold. If such a Gnostic myth existed, what was its relation to New Testament and specifically Johannine Christology? Was it ever historicized outside Christianity and not merely applied to a mythical figure of the past or future? Is the case for a widespread pre-Christian belief in Gnostic revealers so solid that we can regard as viable Bultmann's suggestion that the Offenbarungsreden were originally attributed to the Baptist by the community which venerated him? Despite the fact that the best attestations of the redeemer myth are Christian or post-Christian, it must be granted, as Bultmann points out, that it is difficult to explain such evidence as the Mandaean literature on the basis of the Gospel of John, while it is easier to explain certain aspects of the Johannine Christology on the basis of the Mandaean literature.[100] An attractive, if not necessarily compelling, explanation is that adopted by Bultmann and others, namely, that an ancient and presumably pre-Christian myth of the redeemer lies behind both John and the Mandaean literature and that elements of it missing in John are explicit in the Mandaean materials.[101] Thus, they shed light on the gospel. Some recent research tends to support Bultmann's position that, regardless of the relatively late date of the Mandaean materials in their present form, their roots lie in the early Christian or pre-Christian era.[102] The view that the Mandaean

99. There is no reason to doubt that there were precursors of some of the conceptual forms of New Testament Christology in the ancient world, e.g. Philo's concept of ὁ λόγος ἔμψυχος. What is at issue here, however, is the peculiarly Gnostic myth proposed by scholars such as Reitzenstein and Bultmann.

100. *ZNW, 24* (1925), 100–46.

101. In altering his earlier views in the light of Lietzmann's research, Bultmann contends that Lietzmann has not disproved the existence of very old Gnostic material in the Mandaean literature. For example, even if the immediate origin of the Mandaean baptism ritual is Syrian Christianity, one must still account for the origins of the baptismal practices of this highly syncretistic branch of the church. Bultmann cannot regard Lietzmann's work as the last word on the Mandaean problem and its relation to early Christianity. See his review of *Ein Beitrag zur Mandäerfrage, TL, 56* (1931), 577–80.

102. K. Rudolph, *Die Mandäer*, Vol. I: *Prolegomena, Das Mandäerproblem* (Göttingen, Vandenhoeck & Ruprecht, 1960). Rudolph maintains that there was a pre-Christian, proto-Mandaean sect in Syria and Palestine. For an excellent summary and evaluation of recent research and discoveries in the field of Mandaean and other Gnosticism, see Schulz, *Komposition und Herkunft*, pp. 170–82, and his article "Die Bedeutung neuer Gnosisfunde für die neutestamentliche Wissenschaft," *TR*, new ser. *26* (1960), 209–66, 301–34. Cf. also O. Cullmann, *The Christology of the New Testament*, trans. S. C. Guthrie and C. A. M. Hall (Philadelphia, Westminster Press, 1959), p. 27 n. 1. R. P. Casey disputes the relevance of the Mandaean literature for the New Testament and rejects the whole concept of a pre-Christian Gnosticism; cf. "Gnosis, Gnosticism and the New Testament" in *The Background of the New Testament and Its Eschatology: In Honour of C. H. Dodd*, ed. W. D. Davies and D. Daube (Cambridge, Cambridge University Press, 1956), pp. 52–80.

Other English scholars (e.g. Dodd, Burkitt, and Howard) have long resisted interpreting

literature and traditions are entirely post-Christian [103] is no longer as attractive or tenable as it once seemed.

It cannot be claimed, without much investigation going beyond the scope of this study, that Bultmann's Offenbarungsreden source is impossible because his view of pre-Christian Gnosticism, and particularly his belief in the existence of a pre-Christian Gnostic redeemer myth, is erroneous. The whole Gnostic problem is more than ever in a state of flux. Perhaps the Nag Hammadi discoveries will prove to be of great value in resolving this problem, which has long perplexed students of Christian origins and antecedents. Even if Bultmann could be proved entirely right in his view of Gnosticism, however, the existence of the special Johannine speech source is only made possible, not demonstrated.

A POST-BULTMANNIAN ERA?

Bultmann's commentary marks a decisive point in the understanding and interpretation of John,[104] but his work has often been disregarded or rejected out of hand. In the introduction to this study I have given some indication of the neglect of Bultmann's work in some circles. Discussion and evaluation of the debate on his literary source analysis require more specifics.

In his important book on the Fourth Gospel, C. H. Dodd does not actually reject or dismiss Bultmann's work but disavows responsibility for taking it into account since the commentary as a whole did not come into his hands until his own book had been completed.[105] Hence, Dodd does not examine the source hypothesis of Bultmann at all, but his occasional references to the problem of sources indicate that he and Bultmann are poles apart. Although, like Bultmann, Dodd does not believe the Fourth Evangelist depended directly

---

John against a Gnostic, particularly a Mandaean Gnostic, background, because they believed that the existence of a pre-Christian Gnosticism could not be established. Recently, however, C. K. Barrett has asserted that John presupposes a Gnosticism and that he does not merely combat it. The evangelist sees the appropriateness of the Gnostic terminology that he uses: "The Theological Vocabulary of the Fourth Gospel and of the Gospel of Truth," *Current Issues in New Testament Interpretation, Essays in Honor of Otto A. Piper,* ed. W. Klassen and G. F. Snyder (New York, Harper, 1962), p. 223.

103. Cf. Dodd, *The Interpretation of the Fourth Gospel,* pp. 115–30.

104. F. M. Braun, "Conclusions" in *L'Évangile de Jean, études et problèmes,* Recherches Biblique, 3, Brouwer, Desclée, 1958, says that Bultmann's book marks the end of an era in Johannine scholarship, since here one finds the most rigorously worked out proposals for sources and textual transpositions—which Braun regards as already disproved (pp. 249, 250 f.).

105. *Interpretation,* p. 121 n. 2. Käsemann has deplored Dodd's failure to take Bultmann's book ("without which discussion of the gospel simply cannot be carried on") into consideration. Cf. *Gn, 28* (1956), 321. Bultmann's book was completed in 1941 and Dodd's in 1953, but the war intervened, and access to many German works was difficult for some time thereafter.

upon the synoptics, unlike Bultmann he believes that the whole problem of sources may be solved by supposing that the evangelist derived his material entirely or almost entirely from oral tradition.[106] Like Bultmann, however, he recognizes that there is evidence of disagreement with the synoptics which cannot be traced to the theological interests of the evangelist. Whether oral tradition is sufficient to account for this evidence, as Noack also thinks, is a real question. Haenchen, who cannot be accused of favoring Bultmann, has argued (against Noack) that the narratives were not composed directly out of oral tradition but had already been fixed in written form when the evangelist appropriated them.[107]

C. K. Barrett, in his commentary, does not engage in detailed debate with Bultmann on the general question of sources although he refers more than once to his proposals. Barrett believes that John knew Mark and probably Luke (or Lucan material), several nonsynoptic narratives drawn from one or more sources (written or oral), and a passion narrative. He thinks it is hardly possible to posit the existence of a discourse source, but he does not exclude the possibility that synoptic or other sayings of Jesus may underlie the discourses or that the discourses may have had some independent existence before the publication of the gospel: "The hypothesis that they were in the first place sermons delivered by the evangelist and subsequently (perhaps even after his death) arranged in the gospel has much to commend it . . . but this is very different from the hypothesis that the discourse material was derived by John from an earlier source." [108] Thus, while Barrett offers several credible suggestions on the problem of sources, he does not go on to develop them as genuine alternatives to Bultmann. His suggestion that the discourses were originally sermons is interesting in view of the statements in the first person ascribed to Jesus in the Apocalypse of John and in a second-century sermon attributed to Melito of Sardis.[109]

Oscar Cullmann has published widely on the Fourth Gospel [110] but has not

106. *Interpretation*, pp. 448 ff. This is a departure from his earlier opinion, if we may lay any weight on Dodd's remark in the introduction of *The Johannine Epistles*, The Moffatt New Testament Commentary (New York, Harper, 1946), p. lvi.

107. *ZTK*, *56* (1959), 50–54.

108. *St. John*, p. 17. Cf. M. Black, *An Aramaic Approach to the Gospels and Acts* (2d rev. ed. Oxford, Clarendon Press, 1954). Black thinks that Aramaic sources may lie behind the Johannine discourses.

109. The relevant passages from Melito are given in Robert M. Grant and David N. Freedman, *The Secret Sayings of Jesus* (Garden City, N. Y., Doubleday, 1960), p. 118.

110. Perhaps of greatest significance are his articles "Der johanneische Gebrauch doppeldeutiger Ausdrücke als Schlüssel zum Verständnis des vierten Evangeliums," *TZ*, *4* (1948), 360–72 and "L'Opposition contre le Temple de Jérusalem, motif commun de la théologie johannique et du monde ambiant," *NTS*, *5* (1958–59), pp. 157–73 and his monograph, *Les*

undertaken a direct discussion with Bultmann on the literary problem. Where it proves necessary for his own interpretation, Cullmann rejects with a minimum of argument Bultmann's assignment of certain passages to an ecclesiastical redactor.[111] Aside from the significant fact that both Cullmann and Bultmann look to esoteric oriental sects (especially the Mandaean sect or its progenitor) as the milieu of the Fourth Gospel,[112] there is little contact or agreement between them. Cullmann's interpretation of the Fourth Gospel, especially his sacramental emphasis, simply stands in opposition to Bultmann's. He has apparently not deemed it necessary to refute Bultmann's source hypothesis, which he ignores and presumably rejects in his presentation of the development and interpretation of John.[113]

Quite recently a number of scholars have taken cognizance of Bultmann's literary analysis and source theory only to reject it, often on the grounds that it has been refuted by Jeremias, Menoud, and, above all, Ruckstuhl and Noack. Typical of this kind of judgment are the remarks of the Roman Catholic scholar, P. Niewalda, who prefaces his study on the sacramental symbolism in John with the following:

Sacraments dans l'évangile johannique. Cullmann is planning commentaries on the Gospel, Epistles, and Apocalypse of John for the Commentaire du Nouveau Testament.

111. *Sacraments*, p. 62 n. 94.

112. Cullmann agrees with Bultmann in seeing a close relationship between the prologue of John and the Baptist sect. Cf. his *Christology*, pp. 277 ff.

113. Cullmann's sacramental interpretation of John has been taken up by certain Roman Catholic scholars, among others. Note Ruckstuhl's highly favorable comments in "Literarkritik am Johannesevangelium und eucharistische Rede Joh 6, 51c–58," *Divus Thomas, 23* (1945), 163 f. Basically sympathetic, but much more critical, is P. Niewalda, *Sakramentssymbolik im Johannesevangelium? Eine exegetisch-historische Studie* (Limburg, Lahn-Verlag, 1958), pp. 14–17. On the Protestant side, scholars such as R. Mehl "Zur Bedeutung von Kultus und Sakrament im 4. Evangelium," *ET, 15* (1955), 65–74 ("Die These von O. Cullmann als Ganzes erscheint uns richtig und Sorgfältig gestützt."), W. Nauck, *Tradition und Charakter*, and A. J. B. Higgins, *The Lord's Supper in the New Testament*, Studies in Biblical Theology, 6 (London, SCM, 1952), pp. 74–88, have given their general assent, with reservations in matters of detail. W. Michaelis, however, has argued extensively and not ineffectively against Cullmann in his monograph *Die Sakramente im Johannesevangelium*. See Cullmann's reply in *Les Sacraments dans l'évangile johannique* (a revised edition of the second part of *Urchristentum und Gottesdienst*, 1944, against which Michaelis had directed his attack), especially p. 20 n. 7. I cannot help feeling the weight of Michaelis' objections to Cullmann's exegesis, which is not lightened by Cullmann's protest that one must view the gospel as a whole in order to see the pervasive sacramental element and not concentrate, as Michaelis does, on each passage as a separate entity. But how can conclusions about the meaning and point of reference of a whole text precede the detailed examination and determination of individual texts? Cf. E. Lohse, "Wort und Sakrament in Johannesevangelium," *NTS, 7* (1960–61), 110–15. He argues that 6:51–58, 3:5, and 19:34 are the crucial passages for deciding the question about the sacraments in John and agrees with Bultmann that they are all secondary.

We need not go further into the source separations of R. Bultmann. The investigations of B. Noack and E. Ruckstuhl have arrived at the same conclusions independently of one another, namely that the style of the Gospel of John, the main support of Bultmann's separation, is uniform and that a separation into different stratifications is therefore not justified.[114]

J. A. T. Robinson, F.-M. Braun, Pierson Parker, S. Mendner, and Haenchen also agree that Bultmann's source criticism is unacceptable.[115]

But perhaps more significant is the fact that the latest monographs on the problem of the origin and structure of John do not make direct and positive use of Bultmann's source analysis. Siegfried Schulz and Wilhelm Wilkens [116] approach the problem in ways different from, although not altogether unrelated to, Bultmann's. Both take cognizance of Bultmann's work, but neither can be content with his solution. Wilkens voices his reservations about Bultmann's source criticism at the outset of his work, citing the criticisms of Jeremias, Menoud, Ruckstuhl, and Noack and quoting the remark of Käsemann that Bultmann's evidence for the separation of the Offenbarungsreden actually only proves the evangelist's close kinship to the style of the Gnostic Offenbarungsreden, not the existence of an independent written source.[117] Schulz' interpretation of the history of scholarship [118] and his own investigations represent a movement away from Bultmann's formulation and application of critical method, and from his results. It is not our purpose to offer here an extensive résumé and critique of these monographs but to indicate their nature and scope in order to see how they are related to Bultmann's theory of sources.

In his first book, Schulz undertakes a study of Johannine traditions by investigating the origins of the Son of Man christology in the Fourth Gospel. In a long prolegomenon he deals with the types of method which have been employed in the critical study of John. The sifting and evaluation of these

114. Niewalda, p. 2.

115. J. A. T. Robinson, "The New Look on the Fourth Gospel," *Studia Evangelica*, ed. K. Aland, F. L. Cross, J. Daniélou, H. Riesenfeld, and W. C. Van Unnik (Berlin, Akademie-Verlag, 1959), p. 341; F.-M. Braun, "Conclusions" in *L'Évangile de Jean*, pp. 249 f. and *Jean le théologien et son évangile dans l'église ancienne*, Études Bibliques (Paris, Gabalda, 1959), pp. 11 f.; Parker, "Two Editions of John," *JBL*, 75 (1956), 304; Mendner, "Johanneische Literarkritik," *TZ*, 8 (1952), 422; Haenchen, *ZTK*, 56 (1959), 53 n. 2.

116. Schulz, *Untersuchungen* and *Komposition und Herkunft*; Wilkens, *Die Entstehungsgeschichte des vierten Evangeliums*.

117. *Entstehungsgeschichte*, p. 6.

118. "Methodengeschichtlicher Überblick und Grundlegung der themageschichtlichen Methode," *Untersuchungen*, pp. 39–95.

methods lead to conclusions about their appropriateness, limitations, and further usefulness in the exploration of the Johannine materials.[119] The methods are first reduced from thirteen, the number originally described, to the nine which are still in common use. Of these, all except two are reconstruction or recovery methods and do not penetrate to the depths of the Johannine material. The remaining two methods, the study of the history of tradition and the study of the history of religion, are exposition or explanation methods and are of fundamental significance. While other methods (e.g. literary analysis) have yielded some results before running into dead ends, these two continue to have great promise for getting at the roots of the Johannine material. Via the study of the history of religion, one discovers the multiplicity of religious and cultural influences in the Fourth Gospel. Via the study of the history of tradition, one discovers the multiplicity and the relative independence and brevity of the various traditional segments. By a combination of these two methods, with certain other methods playing contributive roles, Schulz believes he will be able to identify the basal themes of the Fourth Gospel as isolable units of tradition and depositories of a multiplicity of identifiable elements from the history of religions. It is to be expected that this combined method, called the theme-history method (*Themageschichte*), will prove to be as appropriate to the analysis of John as form criticism has proved to be to the synoptics. It takes cognizance of and is competent to deal with the weaving together of traditions in John just as form criticism takes cognizance of and is competent to deal with the juxtaposition of different types of material in the synoptic gospels.[120] (Analogies to the Themageschichte method are found also in Noth's work on the Pentateuch and Lagrange's on Jewish apocalyptic.[121]) If Dibelius affirmed that in the beginning was the preaching, Schulz holds that in the beginning were the traditions in their multiplicity. This is his fundamental conclusion based on the methodological prolegomenon and the presupposition of his own analysis of Johannine texts:

> The point of departure and the goal of the Johannine history of method is, therefore, the fundamental recognition that the Johannine

119. For the summary presentation which follows, *Untersuchungen*, pp. 39–95.

120. *Untersuchungen*, pp. 85–87. Schulz describes the Themageschichte method succinctly as follows: "Die Themageschichte ist nämlich—methodengeschichtlich gesehen—in den übergreifenden Zusammenhang der überlieferungsgeschichtlichen Methode zu stellen. Damit wird zugleich ein gewisser, allgemeiner Methodenweg vorgezeichnet: Aufgabe und Ziel ist das Eindringen in das vorliterarische Stadium des Schriftwerkes, die Analyse der kleinen Traditionselemente und Überlieferungseinheiten und die grundsätzliche Unterscheidung zwischen Tradition und Komposition" (p. 91).

121. Ibid., p. 86.

proclamation is extensively defined by tradition. The consequent task, to comprehend and explain the παραδόσεις which are found scattered through the Gospel of John, is by no means discharged, but remains a further goal of investigation in the Fourth Gospel.[122]

Through his investigation of the Son of Man christology in John, Schulz sets out in pursuit of that goal. The Son of Man christology is not limited to the instances in the gospel where the Son of Man is explicitly mentioned. It can be understood historically only if the traditional Son of Man sayings are investigated along with three closely related traditions which embody the themes of the Son, the Paraclete, and the Coming Again of Jesus. These complete the field of investigation for the Son of Man Christology in John. The second part of Schulz' book is devoted to the exegesis of the passages in which these themes are found and an evaluation of the results.[123] Using statistics of style (Schweizer and Ruckstuhl)[124] and conventional literary analysis, Schulz attempts to sound out traditional materials, whose limits, traditional connections, and religio-historical relationships are then explored by means of his theme-history method.[125] The results of this investigation have some bearing on Bultmann's theory of redaction, since what Bultmann assigns to the redactor in 5:27–28 and 6:27, 53 as a throwback to primitive Christian eschatology, Schulz assigns to the earliest stage of tradition.[126]

Apropos of Bultmann's source theory, it is important to note that Schulz does not completely deny the possibility of sources in John. It is rather that the whole problem of sources must now be defined and resolved by recourse to the theme-history method, which breaks the gospel up into its component traditional units. Now, the question of sources may only be put forward in the light of the result of this analysis of tradition and ought to take the form of the question of whether certain elements were already joined together in traditional complexes, oral or written, before having been incorporated into

122. Ibid., p. 95.

123. Ibid., pp. 96–97.

124. "Die stilstatistische Methode in ihrer Anwendung auf das Joh-Ev. kann sowohl zum Erweis der literarischen Einheit als auch für den Nachweis der Existenz von Überlieferung dienen. Sie ist der stete Trabant—allgemein gesprochen—der überlieferungsgeschichtlichen Analyse und wird damit zu einem unentbehrlichen Hilfsmittel der sachgemässen Unterscheidung von Tradition und Komposition bzw. Interpretation, wenn ihre unübersteigbare Grenze auch darin beschlossen liegt, Traditionen in ihrem blossen Dasein nachzuweisen, ohne die Frage nach der Entstehung, religionsgeschichtlichen Struktur und theologischen Relevanz stellen zu können" (Untersuchungen, pp. 58 f.).

125. For the Son of Man theme Schulz investigates 1:51; 3:13–15; 5:27–29; 6:27, 53, 62; 8:28; 12:23, 34; 13:31 f.; for the Son 3:35 f.; 5:19–23, 25–26; 3:16; for the Paraclete 14:15–17, 25, 26; 15:26; 16:4b–11; 16:12–15; for the Coming Again 14:1–3, 18–23, 27–28; 16:16, 20–23a.

126. Komposition und Herkunft, pp. 145 ff.

the gospel.[127] Earlier attempts to identify on the basis of literary and stylistic analysis either a Grundschrift or continuous literary sources running throughout the gospel have come to grief on the hard fact of its stylistic unity.[128] The theme tradition research of Schulz does not, however, exclude the possibility of some sort of source for the Johannine speeches.[129]

Apparently because he believes that the stylistic unity precludes conventional source analysis, Schulz thinks that the most profitable procedure is to attempt to penetrate to the roots of the tradition and, instead of peeling off layers of literary strata in the manner of Bultmann, to lay hold of the traditional element in its original context, i.e. prior to incorporation into the gospel. In the case of the Son of Man complex of themes, the traditional Son of Man theme is located in its supposedly original setting in Jewish apocalypticism and is traced through a Gnostic reinterpretation in the primitive community to its resting place in the gospel. Bultmann's analysis of the various elements of the gospel is reversed—Gnosticism becoming secondary and apocalyptic primary—and so is his method. The separation of literary sources, which is fundamental to his critical procedure, is set to one side, and a tradition history or tradition analysis is put in its place.

Schulz has continued his investigation of the Johannine traditions in a monograph on the Johannine speeches published in 1960.[130] Observing that almost all exegetes now agree that the Fourth Evangelist used previously formed traditions in the composition of his gospel, he asserts that the present question is whether this traditional material is recoverable and whether its historic roots and relationships can be laid bare. This question raises in turn the problem of methodology, with which Schulz concerns himself briefly at the beginning of the book. Certain methods have proved indispensable in the study of the Fourth Gospel: the study of the history of religions, style-statistics, textual criticism and the history of tradition. Schulz intends to co-ordinate this multiplicity of methods in an approach that will be suited to the

127. *Untersuchungen*, p. 94: "Eine andere Frage ist es, ob diese Pluralität von Traditionen mit der Hypothese einer vorliegenden 'Quelle' zu vereinen ist. Diese Frage ist berechtigt, kann aber vorerst nur sekundären Charakter beanspruchen; da sie sachgemäss wohl immer erst nach den vollzogenen traditionsgeschichtlichen Analysen beantwortet zu werden vermag. Wichtig ist jedenfalls das methodengeschichtliche Ergebnis, dass man primär nicht von der Hypothese einer Quelle, sondern von Einzelüberlieferungen auszugehen hat, die dann allerdings, wenn der Nachweis möglich ist, zu Kollektionen und Kompositionen als einer Quelle zusammengeordnet werden können. Entscheidend ist allein der Ausgangspunkt; vor einer Blickpunkt- bzw. Perspektivenverschiebung ist zu warnen."

128. For the demonstration of this unity Schulz refers primarily to the style-statistical work of Schweizer; also to Ruckstuhl and others (ibid., pp. 51–59, especially p. 57 n. 7).

129. Ibid., p. 175.

130. *Komposition und Herkunft.*

multiple structure of the tradition in the Gospel of John.[131] He regards this
as an ideal time for an investigation of the Johannine tradition, for in the
period since World War II the discovery or publication of such documents
as the Dead Sea Scrolls, the Nag Hammadi Gnostic books, and certain less
heralded but nonetheless important Manichaean and Mandaean texts has
caused Johannine scholarship to enter a new phase whose consequences are
not yet clearly seen.[132]

In this study Schulz proposes to deal with the prologue and the predicative
ego eimi sayings. He hopes to shed some light on this material by investigating its traditional roots and their relations to other traditions. This, then, is
an investigation in the fields of the history of religion and tradition.

Schulz attempts first to discover whether the prologue contains a pre-
Johannine tradition and, if so, to ferret it out.[133] An established tradition
behind the prologue is already indicated by earlier study, whose results are
carefully brought forward, examined, and evaluated. This careful investigation and evaluation of previous scholarship forms the basis for Schulz' con-
structive conclusions. His own analysis of the history of tradition yields a
pre-Johannine hymn in 1:1–5, (9)–12ab, (16), (18).[134] This result is confirmed by the comparison of materials from the history of religion, which
discloses parallels to 1:1–5, 10–12ab, 14, and 7–18. The background of the
prologue is found to consist of late Hellenistic Jewish wisdom speculation,
Old Testament theophanies (especially Sinai), and Oriental Gnostic logos
speculation. The first two elements constitute the root of the tradition, which
is, so to speak, reinterpreted in terms of the Gnostic logos title.[135] Here we
have a tradition that is basically Jewish given a non-Jewish reinterpretation.
Thus, a pattern which Schulz had discovered in his study of the Son of Man
sayings is found to occur in the prologue as well. As we shall see, Schulz
will discover it again in the ego eimi sayings of the gospel.

The predictive ego eimi sayings, those that are accompanied by a *Bildwort*
or *Bildrede* (metaphorical word or discourse), are singled out for special investigation. Schulz inquires about the ego eimi sayings in the sixth, eighth,
tenth, eleventh, fourteenth, and fifteenth chapters of the gospel.[136] In each
case his investigation proceeds along lines similar to those followed in the

131. Ibid., pp. 1 f.
132. Ibid., pp. 2 ff.
133. Ibid., pp. 7–70.
134. Ibid., pp. 7–27, 68 f. Status of verses in parentheses is more or less uncertain.
135. Ibid., pp. 28–57, 68.
136. Ibid., pp. 70–131.

prologue. The initial objective is to demonstrate that these sayings go back to a tradition taken over by the evangelist.[137] The general result is the discovery that the ego eimi sayings exhibit similar characteristics of style and rhythm and are bound very loosely if at all to their contexts.[138] They also show a characteristic form of self-predication (including both the presentation formula, the ego eimi; and the Bildwort) and a subsequent soteriological statement consisting of an invitation and a promise or threat.[139] There are naturally some variations, but the general structure of the ego eimi sayings seems to be well fixed.

Having established the traditional character of the sayings, Schulz attempts to identify their historical roots and relationships.[140] Since previous attempts to do this have been one-sided in their emphasis on only one milieu (Gnostic, Rabbinic, or whatever), Schulz will deliberately hold open the possibility that the Johannine ego eimi sayings are the result of diverse influences. A distinction must be made between the ego eimi formula itself and the image that is connected with it. Schulz finds that the imagery is drawn mainly from late Judaism, while the ego eimi formula, together with the entire formal structure of the sayings (cf. Becker), is Gnostic. In chapters 10 and 15, however, where the ego eimi sayings cannot be disengaged from their context as easily as elsewhere, the imagery itself (the Shepherd and the Vine) seems to owe more to Gnosticism than to Judaism. The combination of the Gnostic ego eimi with the Jewish eschatological imagery in chapters 6, 8, 11, and 14 results in the affirmation of the present reality of Jewish hopes of salvation in Jesus. It is in a Christian context that this combination takes place, and it results in a distinctly Christian "realized eschatology."

Reviewing his earlier work on the Son of Man traditions and drawing together the results, Schulz reports that he has unearthed in the Johannine speeches six units of tradition centered around the themes Logos, Ego Eimi, Son of Man, Son, Paraclete, and the Coming Again of Jesus. Despite the variety of themes, there appears in all of them the same pattern of *Mutterboden-Neuauslegung*, that is, there appear traditional root concepts which have undergone reinterpretation in the Johannine or pre-Johannine Christian community.[141] Further examination of the pre-Christian roots of this Johannine speech tradition leads Schulz to locate its origin in three or four types of sec-

---

137. Ibid., p. 72.
138. Ibid., p. 84 f.
139. Ibid., pp. 86 ff.
140. Ibid., pp. 90–128.
141. Ibid., pp. 132–39, especially 138 f.

tarian Judaism: the Qumran community, certain apocalyptic circles (which overlap somewhat with the Qumran community), the proto-Mandaean gnosticizing sects that are supposed to have broken off from Judaism just prior to the advent of Christianity, and the syncretistic baptist circles in which John the Baptist arose. Schulz devotes a section of his work [142] to a discussion of Jewish groups such as these in order to elucidate the historical background of the Johannine speech traditions and to explain how they were brought together in what he calls a Johannine *Ḥabura*. In this *Ḥabura* the representatives of these various groups and their respective traditions, now Christian, saw their old traditions in the light of their new faith, amalgamated them, and subjected them to a radical reinterpretation.[143]

As to the problem of sources, Schulz' position remains essentially what it was in his initial monograph. He asks whether the traditional units which he has laid bare belonged to an oral or written source before their adoption by the evangelist, and he answers that this is a question which probably can never be decided with finality. If there was a source, it was not a continuous document with a purposeful progression of thought but a collection of traditions and sayings. Since the publication of his second monograph, the relationship of Schulz' work to Bultmann's source theory can be more clearly seen, but it is no different from what his first book led us to expect. As I have noted, some of the same instances of unevenness or difficulty which Bultmann attempts to resolve by his source and redaction theory serve as starting points for Schulz' identification of traditional units (e.g., 5:27–29). Beyond this, Schulz recognizes no less clearly than Bultmann, Becker, and Schweizer that the discourses of the Fourth Gospel did not emerge from a vacuum but from a distinct religious milieu and belong to a specific type of religious speech. He differs from Bultmann and Becker in his unwillingness to embark upon the task of identifying extensive hypothetical sources and in his insistence that the investigation of traditional units and their religious and historical roots is the initial task of Johannine study. His investigation really stops at the point where Bultmann's begins, with the analysis of the text in order to understand the purpose and perspective of the evangelist himself. Schulz specifically disavows as his immediate objective the task of attempting to understand the evangelist's use of his tradition.[144]

The manner in which Schulz has conceived and executed his investigation

142. Ibid., pp. 150–87.
143. Ibid., pp. 182–87. Schulz had already mentioned this Johannine *Ḥabura* in a preliminary article on the Johannine speeches, "Die Komposition des Johannesprologs und die Zusammensetzung des 4. Evangeliums," *Studia Evangelica*, pp. 351–62; note especially pp. 361 f.
144. *Komposition und Herkunft*, p. 144.

is not unassailable.[145] It is questionable, for example, whether an analysis of the tradition behind the gospel can be carried through with precision and certainty if literary analysis of the type of Bultmann's finally breaks down. Bultmann begins with the known (the text) and moves to the unknown (sources and tradition). Does Schulz actually increase the element of uncertainty when he begins with the relatively unknown (the tradition) and moves to the known?[146] An acute problem arises at the point of locating precisely the maternal soil (Mutterboden) of specific traditions whose concepts are to be found in the Old Testament, Jewish apocalyptic, Mandaean literature, and the Qumran Scrolls (the sources of tradition which Schulz thinks are most closely related to the Fourth Gospel). To complicate this problem, the affinity of the Fourth Gospel with, for example, the Hermetica, Hellenistic Jewish wisdom speculation, and Philo presents the possibility of other Mutterboden farther removed from the Oriental, Semitic context.

In his review of Schulz' study of the Son of Man traditions, Robinson has consequently reproved Schulz for sometimes labeling a concept Jewish apocalyptic without adequately demonstrating that the concept does not occur in other contexts.[147] The Old Testament and late Jewish apocalyptic texts with which Schulz paralleled Johannine passages in his first volume did not

145. Cf. Robinson, "Recent Research in the Fourth Gospel," *JBL, 78* (1959), 251: "The debate with Bultmann is carried on by the use of a procedure the reverse of his. Rather than working backwards from the present Johannine text to the immediate cultural context and from there back to the anterior context, the point of departure is the *Mutterboden*, from which one then moves forward until via reinterpretation one reaches the present form of the text. . . . The danger is that the postulated *Mutterboden* will provide such an adequate explanation that alternative origins will hardly be considered seriously. And as a matter of fact a logical fallacy does from time to time gain admission, namely the tacit argument that since apocalypticism normally uses a concept, the concept is apocalyptic. Such an inference would be legitimate only if it were shown that the concept were not normally used by alternate sources as well. Yet this is not demonstrated."

146. This is a fair question to pose, but it is not unanswerable. In the first place, contrary to Ruckstuhl's own opinion, his proof of a literary unity in the Fourth Gospel does not mean that there are no sources or traditions behind that document or that, if there were such, they could never be found. That sources or traditions can be identified at many points in the Fourth Gospel is quite possible. Much more doubtful, however, is the attempt to delineate such materials precisely and extensively. In the second place, Schulz does not abjure the results of literary analysis of the text, even though he believes that it can lead to no conclusive results by itself. His procedure, strictly speaking, is not really the reverse of Bultmann's. After all, a source critic such as Bultmann projects an hypothesis of a source or sources that runs ahead of his analysis and that is then tested by it. When Bultmann cites the Mandaean or other literature in connection with the discourse source, he is not arguing strictly from the text of John, but introducing external evidence that supports the source hypothesis. Perhaps the fundamental question is whether *Traditiongeschichte* can finally escape the limitations and uncertainties of source analysis.

147. See above n. 145.

always seem to provide the basis for a conclusive demonstration of the pre-dominantly apocalyptic rootage of the Johannine Son of Man traditions. This situation is somewhat ameliorated, however, by Schulz' second book, in which he considerably broadens his religio-historical perspective.

The possible positive relation of Schulz' work to Bultmann's is significant. Both believe that some form of Oriental, Semitic Gnosticism has influenced the language and formulation of the Johannine speeches. Schulz, however, sees a much more complex and intimate relation between John and sectarian Jewish thought. But the extent of the penetration of some Jewish circles by Hellenistic and Gnostic ways of thinking is even plainer now than it was twenty years ago when Bultmann wrote his commentary. The discovery of the Qumran scrolls, with their quasi-Gnostic dualism, and the Nag Hammadi Gnostic documents, some of which seem to be preoccupied with Judaism; the tendency of recent research to see a Syrian-Palestinian, if not Jewish, origin of the Mandaean traditions; the monumental collection and investigation of Jewish symbols by E. R. Goodenough[148]—these factors and others which have come to light since World War II have considerably altered our picture of Jewish thought and practice at the beginning of the Christian era. And we must not forget that Bultmann himself saw in the evangelist an erstwhile adherent of the John the Baptist sect who came over to Christianity bringing his traditions with him in just the manner that Schulz imagines that former Baptists, Qumraners, proto-Mandaeans and apocalyptists came over to Chris-tianity and reinterpreted their various traditions in the light of the new faith. Whatever the weaknesses or limitations of Schulz' work, he has done us a valuable service in pointing out how the Gospel of John as a whole and its various components (whatever their origin) may well be the result of the amalgamation of a number of influences from the history of religions.

Wilkens' book represents an entirely different species of criticism. Al-though Schulz could only regard it as a methodological throwback, it cer-tainly shows that literary criticism of the Fourth Gospel is not dead and has not exhausted all its possibilities. From first to last it is a thoroughgoing speci-men of such criticism in the grand tradition of a Wellhausen. Fittingly enough, Wilkens tells us that it is Wellhausen who has given us the key to the under-standing of the Entstehungsgeschichte of the Fourth Gospel with his theory of a Johannine Grundschrift. This theory has been adopted by Wilkens and adapted to bring it into line with the demonstration of stylistic unity in the gospel by Ruckstuhl and Schweizer.[149] Thus, instead of proposing a Grund-schrift modified by a later redactor, Wilkens suggests that a Grundschrift was

---

148. *Jewish Symbols in the Graeco-Roman Period*, Bollingen Series, 37 (8 vols. New York, Pantheon, 1953–58).

149. Wilkens, *Entstehungsgeschichte*, p. 7.

composed and then twice revised by the same author. He first wrote a relatively simple gospel consisting of a report of the signs of Jesus in Galilee, the
entry into Jerusalem, and events of the passion week and the passion narrative proper. At a later date he revised this document extensively, expanding
it and bringing into it several continuous discourses including a *Lichtrede*
similar to the one Bultmann had proposed for the original gospel.[150] Finally
he returned once again to the gospel, this time adding still more material and
rearranging the document as a Passover, and therefore a passion, gospel by
introducing into earlier parts of the gospel three pericopes which once stood
in the passion week: the cleansing of the temple (2:13–22), the institution of
the Eucharist (6:51c–58) [151] and the anointing at Bethany (12:1–11). In this
revision the several longer discourses were broken up and scattered throughout the gospel. In the process the gospel was made increasingly anti-Docetic.[152]

The insight that the present positions of all three of these events (along
with the Passover formulae of 2:13 and 6:4 and that portion of the passion
story which most clearly brings out the paschal character of the crucifixion,
19:14a, 13–37) are secondary in the present text leads Wilkens to his hypothesis of a revision of the gospel whereby it was transformed into a Passover gospel. Wilkens believes that this hypothesis is supported by the fact
that this revision can be shown to have resulted in the very striking differences
between the Johannine and synoptic chronological and geographical framework. If such a revision is to be confirmed, the existence of the earlier stage
of the gospel must be demonstrable. And, as it turns out, not one but two
such earlier stages can be shown, not in a general way but down to the last
half-verse!

We need not concern ourselves with the many details of Wilkens' theory.
He argues cogently and plausibly, and the broad outline of his proposal is
worthy of serious consideration. Whether his reconstruction is believable is
another matter. In reviews of Wilkens' book, both Robinson and Barrett have
indicated their strong reservations,[153] not because of any obvious error on the
part of Wilkens but mainly because of the immensely complex and entirely
hypothetical character of the proposal. One is compelled to concur with their
judgment. Few scholars will be able to follow Wilkens, if for no other reason

150. Ibid., pp. 108–11.

151. A synoptic-like account of the institution of the Lord's Supper gave way to the
Eucharistic discourse when this change of position was made (ibid., pp. 68, 75 f.).

152. Ibid., p. 171: "Das ganze Werk Jesu in Wort und Tat wird in die Passionsgeschichte
hineingenommen. Das geschieht offenbar in einem bewusst theologischen Akt, und zwar in
Auseinandersetzung mit dem Doketismus. Das Kreuz Jesu ist *die* Mitte des Evangeliums."
Cf. also p. 24 and "Das Abendmahlszeugnis im vierten Evangelium," *ET, 18* (1958), 369–70.

153. *JBL, 78* (1959), 242–46 and *TL, 84* (1959), 828–39 respectively.

than that he pushes an interesting and attractive theory to an impossible extreme.

Wilkens' proposal is not really a source theory at all in the usual sense. He expressly leaves open the question of sources in order to deal with the history of the gospel's development (Entstehungsgeschichte). His understanding of this process, however, takes into account much of the evidence that also serves as grist for the mill of source or tradition analysis (represented by Bultmann and Schulz respectively) and thus greatly reduces the need for developing other theories to account for the origin of the gospel.[154] The striking feature of Wilkens' work is his reliance on literary analysis as an almost infallible key to the separation of strata within the gospel.[155] Certainly exegetical insights are gained in the course of his analysis, whether or not reliable evidence for the development of the gospel can really be adduced on as grand a scale as Wilkens thinks. It is to Wilkens' credit, however, that he has sought to make positive use of major literary critical insights of modern scholarship. Not only does he take up and combine the achievements of Wellhausen, Schweizer, and Ruckstuhl, but he also takes into account the literary analysis of Bultmann and frequently employs his individual exegetical insights in a positive way. In its scrupulous concern for detail and its comprehensive consideration of earlier scholarship, his work constitutes a landmark in Johannine literary criticism.

Wilkens' sacramental interpretation of many parts of John (following Cullmann) has relatively little bearing on his central thesis. Nor is his opinion that the gospel was written by an eyewitness a genuine conclusion of his research—although given his hypothesis it cannot be called an impossibility. This opinion is perhaps related to Wilkens' forced attempt to answer the embarrassing question which his theory poses for him: why did the author rearrange and expand his original composition but never alter it by revision or rewriting? (For Wilkens to admit that he did would make his own reconstruction self-evidently impossible.) Wilkens replies that the evangelist considered his own earlier writing an inspired and authoritative witness and therefore felt he ought not change any of it.[156] Such a suggestion is so

---

154. Wilkens nevertheless works on the assumption that the evangelist composed his book out of traditions rather than out of his head (*Entstehungsgeschichte*, pp. 7 f.).

155. Of course, Wilkens cannot attempt to employ stylistic criteria in this analysis, since in his terms the entire gospel stems from the same hand.

156. Ibid., pp. 167–69. "Man muss hier ja vor allem in Rechnung stellen, dass der Evangelist Zeuge Jesu ist, durch dessen Mund der Paraklet die Gemeinde Jesu lehrt und sie an alles erinnert, was ihr Jesus gesagt hat (14, 26). Das Zeugnis des Evangelisten ist vollmächtiges Zeugnis, weil es gebunden ist an das Lehren und Erinnern des Heiligen Geistes, d.h. des erhöhten und bei seiner Gemeinde im gottesdienstlichen Geschehen gegenwärtigen Herrn.

dubious as to throw into sharp relief the difficulty of executing Wilkens'
proposal. Moreover, Wilkens does not succeed in accounting for all the difficulties of the present text and must finally resort to the explanation that for
some reason the evangelist left his work unfinished.[157] If after such exhausting
literary analysis we come to this conclusion, there is some question as to
whether the effort was worthwhile. Perhaps the unfinished state of the gospel
alone accounts for the most glaring incongruities in the text, as W. F. Howard
has suggested.[158]

The work of Schulz and Wilkens indicates the effect, if not the positive influence, which Bultmann has had on the study of John. Although neither
agrees with Bultmann, both stand in his shadow. Both are dealing with some
of the same problems and attempting to explain the same difficulties. In a
sense each goes to an extreme, Schulz turning away from source analysis to
an investigation of the tradition, and Wilkens accommodating an extensive
literary source analysis to the evidence of the literary unity of the gospel.
Although in principle their works are not mutually exclusive inasmuch as
they purport to deal with different periods in the history of the Johannine
material, in practice they represent the continued divided state of research.
At the same time, they show that there is a developing consensus as to the
problems and issues to be resolved.

The continuing vitality of the problem of the composition and order of
the Fourth Gospel among Anglo-Saxon as well as continental scholars is attested by the appearance in 1960 and 1961 respectively of works by three
British scholars, *The Fourth Gospel and Jewish Worship* by Aileen Guilding [159] and *The Structure of the Fourth Gospel* by A. Q. Morton and G. H.
C. Macgregor.[160] Neither of these works takes account of Bultmann's commentary, but both have some relevance for his literary theory. If either proved
to be right, Bultmann's position would have to be surrendered.

The book by Morton and Macgregor makes a novel approach to the problem of the structure of the gospel based on certain mathematical calculations.
According to Morton, the "enlargement" theory of Macgregor (i.e. the theory
that an original gospel has been expanded into the present one), first advanced
in his commentary on John in the Moffatt Series, can be substantially sup-

---

Solches Zeugnis ist gültig und, falls es geschrieben ist, geschrieben" (p. 169). Why could
the evangelist not have viewed his revision as the result of the inspiration of the Spirit and
the Exalted Lord?

157. Ibid., p. 172.
158. *The Fourth Gospel,* p. 119.
159. Oxford, Clarendon Press, 1960.
160. Edinburgh and London, Oliver and Boyd, 1961.

ported by statistical evidence.[161] Morton proposes to demonstrate the essential truth of Macgregor's proposal by calculations based on the peculiar problems involved in the art of ancient bookmaking. He believes it very likely that the *autographon* of the Gospel of John, like that of many New Testament books, was inscribed in a codex and was therefore of predetermined length (the length determined, of course, by the length of the codex). This proposal is said to be supported by the observation that there are "terminal difficulties" in at least five of the first eight New Testament books. Mark has no ending. John has a final chapter that is probably secondary. Acts breaks off abruptly. The final chapter of Romans is probably not a part of the original letter. Chapters 10–13 of II Corinthians are usually held to be of separate origin. All these terminal difficulties can be explained on the hypothesis that the original authors could not quite fit their books to the codices in which they wrote. The codex theory is, in a way, supported by early New Testament manuscript evidence. The vast majority of early New Testament manuscripts, particularly for the Gospel of John, are codices. Now, the fact that a book is of determinate length may tell us nothing of the book is homogeneous, but if it is composite, and especially if it is an enlargement of an earlier version, this fact may be of first importance. In order to decide whether John is composite or homogeneous, Morton examines its structure.[162] This examination centers about the paragraphing of the gospel, which while admittedly a later feature (Souter's text is used!), may be a good index of changes or new departures in the sequence of thought or action and thus of the units of narrative or discourse within the gospel. Souter begins a new paragraph with every change of scene or speaker.

Morton maintains that while transpositions in a text will result in short paragraphs, since units of thought or narrative are thereby broken up and scattered, conflation or expansion results in longer than normal paragraphs, since units are thereby expanded. John is discovered to have nine paragraphs that are decidedly longer than average. This suggests that the Gospel of John may be composite rather than homogeneous, and that it has been expanded at several points. When, at the request of Morton, Macgregor (the "Commentator" vis-à-vis Morton, who is called the "Analyst") then adds the adjacent material considered integral to these paragraphs (that is, inseparable from them), some of them combine, and the result is six "panels" (4:1–42, 6:22–71, 8:21–9:41, 11:1–53, 14:1–16:24, 17:1–26), which, Macgregor agrees, could come from the same separate source. These six panels are now referred to as J_2. The remainder of the gospel is called J_1, except passages assigned to the

161. Cf. *Structure*, p. 15.
162. Ibid., pp. 17–29.

redactor who conflated the sources that are called R. "The inquiry is now confronted by a direct challenge. Can it be shown that the condition of the text of the Fourth Gospel is the necessary consequence of the enlarging of J_1 by the addition of J_2?" [163]

Morton envisages the redactor "sitting with the components of the Fourth Gospel laid out before him. His major source is the short form of the Gospel, J_1. His minor source is J_2. He has chosen a book which is large enough to hold both sources; he will have some space to spare, but just how much, he has yet to see." [164] The book is to be both composite and of determinate length. Morton then shows in detail how the incorporation of J_1 and J_2, the rearrangements, and the redactional additions (which often coincide with the rearrangements) were determined by the redactor's calculated effort to conform the gospel to the length of his codex.[165] Then by a statistical study of paragraph length, sentence length, word length, and vocabulary, he attempts to show that there is a qualitative stylistic difference between J_1 and J_2.[166]

In a separate section of the book Macgregor sets forth his source, redaction, and rearrangement theories in the light of Morton's proposals.[167] It is perhaps significant that Macgregor stops short of accepting Morton's statistical confirmation of his own earlier suggestion: "The Commentator would not be willing to commit himself to agreement in detail with his colleague's analysis of the Gospel. He still finds it difficult to believe a scribe's mind would work in just this way [i.e. carefully calculating the interweaving of sources and redaction so as to fill, but not to exceed, his codex]." [168] This is an important reservations. Others may be mentioned. Morton's thesis demands the supposition that the autographon of John was written in a codex and that the author or editor was preoccupied with fitting his material to it. While our earliest manuscripts are codices or remnants of codices, we have no proof that the use of the codex antedates the early second century. The earliest manuscripts are probably official books for church use, but this is not necessarily the case with the autographon of the gospel. In fact, one may doubt whether a codex would have been used by the author or editor in the composition of the gospel and, if so, whether he would have at this stage committed himself to making the finished product conform so exactly to his book. Even if the autographon was composed for official use in the church, there is no guarantee that it would have been written upon a codex. If in Revelation chapters

163. Ibid., p. 39.
164. Ibid., p. 75.
165. Ibid., pp. 75–85.
166. Ibid., pp. 86–92.
167. Ibid., pp. 51–71.
168. Ibid., p. 51.

4 and 5 we have any reflection of the liturgical practices of the early church, we could conclude that the scroll, not the codex, was used in church worship. The evidence adduced by Morton concerning the use of codices for the New Testament manuscripts is pertinent but not conclusive. Furthermore, the source and redaction theory of Macgregor, which in its origin is the product of the imagination of a literary-historical critic, as Morton admits, and can only be confirmed by mathematical calculations, is just as vulnerable to the style-statistical demonstration of the unity of the gospel as the theories of Bultmann and others. Furthermore, one's inability to pass judgment on statistical arguments does not preclude some doubt that the composite character of the gospel can be ascertained from the length of paragraphs in a modern text. This is especially the case when there is a great deal of evidence, disregarded in this book, which supports the homogeneity of the gospel. I therefore feel justified in withholding assent to the thesis of this book, at least until it is subjected to more extensive examination and testing by those qualified to pass judgment upon its statistical and mathematical basis.

Guilding also attempts to solve the problem of the sources and structure of the Fourth Gospel with a comprehensive theory which, if true, explains everything. In this case it is not the problem of fitting a book to a codex that provides the key that unlocks the riddlesome gospel but the recognition of the dependence of the Fourth Evangelist on an ancient Jewish lectionary system. Although the evangelist drew on his imagination as well as on the tradition of Jesus' sayings, his primary purpose was to set forth Jesus as the fulfillment of the Jewish system of worship. To this end he took as the structural and substantial basis of his gospel the Old Testament readings as appointed by the Jewish lectionary system. The Johannine discourses, which are the heart of the gospel, are then really expositions of Old Testament texts. The gospel embodies three full annual lectionary cycles and a part of another (1:19–4:54; 6, 5, 7–12; 13–20 are the complete cycles). The evangelist naturally did not cover all the Jewish lectionary readings but was selective, placing particular emphasis on the readings for the great feasts. Indeed, the fact that the evangelist dates the discourses on the occasions of the great Jewish feasts seems to provide the starting point for Guilding's theory. Her thesis is presented and argued with the greatest care and erudition and deserves serious attention. The author recognizes that there are important implications not only for John but also for other New Testament documents, if the basic thesis is correct.[169] Since a really thorough evaluation of her work would require a monograph as ambitious as her own, I shall limit myself to some general observations and questions about it.

169. *Jewish Worship*, pp. 197 ff., 230 f.

As Guilding knows, the evidence for a first-century Jewish lectionary system is not overwhelming.[170] Since it is not possible to produce much in the way of direct evidence from the first century, she naturally looks elsewhere. Later evidence, from rabbinic sources and the Masoretic text, is of great value in reconstructing a lectionary system, but, for the demonstration of the existence and use of a triennial system in the first century A.D., Guilding relies largely upon what she regards as convincing evidence that the final edition of the Pentateuch was arranged by its editors to form a three-year lectionary cycle.[171] The Pentateuchal dates and the repetition of themes in the Pentateuch at what would be the proper points in the reconstructed lectionary calendar (given a three-year cycle) are taken to support the thesis. In addition, the apparent arrangement of the Psalter for lectionary purposes, as well as the appropriateness of the sections of the Pentateuch that would fall on the festival dates, afford evidence that the final edition of the Pentateuch was designed with a lectionary system in mind. If Guilding is right, an important contribution has been made to our understanding of the growth of the Pentateuch. Until her thesis is examined by qualified experts, however, few will be willing to accept her demonstration as final. And her thesis about the Gospel of John depends upon this attempt to prove, on the basis of the structure of the Pentateuch itself, that a more or less standard Jewish lectionary system existed in the first century A.D.

It is significant that according to her thesis the Gospel of John does not follow the triennial system which goes through the Pentateuch once in three years. John's first annual cycle, which corresponds to the Jewish liturgical year, does not necessarily draw from the readings for the first year of the triennial system, the second cycle from the second year, etc. Rather, a passage from any of the gospel's three annual cycles may have drawn from any one of three appropriate lections in the triennial Pentateuchal (or the accompanying prophetic) lectionary.[172] Thus, for every Johannine text there are three possible Pentateuchal *sedarim* with accompanying prophetic *haphtaroth*, not to mention lections from the Psalter. As a background for each Johannine passage, therefore, there are nine possible Old Testament readings. Add to this Guilding's willingness to look for the Old Testament background of a given

170. Cf. ibid., pp. 6–23 for Guilding's marshaling of first-century evidence from Ben Sirach, Philo, Josephus, the New Testament, and the later evidence of the rabbinic materials and the Masoretic text. Utilizing the work of other scholars, particularly A. Büchler, she attempts a reconstruction of a triennial cycle.

171. Ibid., pp. 24–44.

172. Ibid., p. 53; especially n. 1. Guilding's demonstration of the Jewish lectionary system applies not only to the Pentateuchal *sedarim* but also to the accompanying prophetic reading (*haphtaroth*), which by the first century were supposedly already regularized.

Johannine text in more than one sabbath's lections, and one sees how the number of possible Old Testament readings available for the interpretation of a single Johannine text begins to increase. For example, for the sixth chapter of John, which obviously contains many allusions to the Exodus, Guilding considers the lections for the second half of Nisan, even though 6:4 expressly dates the feeding, the miracle of Jesus' walking on the water, and the accompanying discourse shortly before Passover: "although the miracles recorded in verses 1–21 took place shortly *before* the Passover, and the discourse was given next day, yet the lections on which Jesus' sermon is based are those that would be read towards the *end* of Nisan." [173] Most appropriate of all are the readings for the last Sunday in Nisan. Apparently the author has examined the numerous readings for Sabbaths before Passover and has found them less adaptable to John than the later Nisan readings. Now, the more lections considered—from which those that seem to relate to the Gospel of John are singled out for special consideration—the more Guilding's method seems to have a certain arbitrariness about it and the more vulnerable it becomes to the suggestion that the relations between John and the Old Testament are merely coincidental, or at least that they have grounds other than a dependence on a lectionary system whose divisions, and even existence, in the first century A.D. are presumably still subject to doubt.

Moreover, John's use of the Old Testament has been examined by Goodwin and Noack, who independently arrive at the conclusion that John's Old Testament quotations are from no known Old Testament text but give every indication of having been dredged up from his memory. This conclusion does not adapt well to the thesis that John's gospel is based upon a Jewish lectionary system.

Finally, the many Old Testament texts adduced by Guilding as the background of the "preaching" of the Fourth Gospel are not all equally impressive. Sometimes the Johannine discourses do not seem to be related to the Old Testament lections in any significant way. To observe that the meaning of a Johannine passage in question seldom has any close relation to the meaning of the Old Testament lection is not a devastating criticism, since ancient exegetes did not follow the canons of historical interpretation and did not differentiate between the original meaning of the text and the meaning which they saw in it. It is of some significance, however, that no distinguishing principles of interpretation, such as are found in Philo, can be discerned in the Johannine treatment of the lections. Indeed, John's references or allusions to the Old Testament are often vague, and one is hard put to find any principle or pattern in them. In fact, the allusive character of the alleged Old

173. Ibid., p. 61. Guilding's italics.

Testament references in John is a factor not to be taken lightly. One might reasonably ask (if John bases himself so firmly upon the Old Testament and, indeed, on a lectionary system) why the Old Testament foundation of the discourses is not more apparent. Old Testament references and allusions in the Gospel of John are clear enough, but the kind of elaborate substructure for which Guilding argues is not.[174] The comparative study of the history of religions has shown the possibility of a multiplicity of extra-biblical and extra-Jewish influences on the formation of the Johannine discourses. Unfortunately, the author gives no attention, or even recognition, to this large area of research.

Like the monograph of Morton and Macgregor, this work suffers because it ignores the many other viable possibilities for explaining the composition and order of the Fourth Gospel. The thesis of neither of these books can stand or fall on its own merits. In this shadowy area of research, in which we speak of probability rather than proof, a thesis must be seen in relation to the other possibilities at hand. If an author gives such possibilities no consideration, even to refute them, this does not relieve us of our responsibility. Despite the ingenuity and erudition involved in both works, and especially the significance of much of the evidence brought forth by Guilding, I am not convinced that the theses which they present offer better options than had been available. As the works of Bultmann and Dodd show, and as Schulz has explicitly stated, the origins and form of the Fourth Gospel are to be accounted for by a multiplicity of factors. There is good reason to doubt that there is any single key such as the ones offered us by Morton and Macgregor and Guilding.

Two other recent efforts to unlock all the mysteries of the Johannine literature involve still greater difficulties and, in my opinion, do not encourage hope for any early solution of vexing Johannine problems. They rather exemplify the confusing diversity of much research and publication in this field.

174. C. W. F. Smith, "Tabernacles in the Fourth Gospel and Mark," *NTS, 9* (1962–63), 130–46, accepts Guilding's thesis as substantially correct, but in recent reviews E. Haenchen, *TL, 86* (1961), 670–72, and M.-É. Boismard, *RB, 68* (1961), 599–602, do not. Nevertheless, the Old Testament or Old Testament tradition is often seen as a structuring element in the Gospel of John. Cf. R. H. Smith, "Exodus Typology in the Fourth Gospel," *JBL, 81* (1962), 329–42, and the literature cited there.

G. Ziener, "Johannesevangelium und urchristliche Passafeier," *BZ, 2* (1958), 263–74, traces a relationship between the Book of Wisdom 10:1–19:22 and the miracles of John's gospel that he attributes to a common dependence upon a Jewish Passover haggada. This haggada, which the Christian church had already appropriated and applied to Jesus, is said to have formed the basis of a collection of miracle stories which John incorporated into his gospel. Despite its similarities to his own proposal, Ziener explicitly repudiates Bultmann's semeia-source theory (p. 272).

K. A. Eckhardt advances the rather daring thesis that the original author of the Fourth Gospel was John the son of Zebedee, whose resurrection from the dead is recounted in chapter 11.[175] This same John was also the author of the Book of Revelation, which contains the revelations granted to him through that experience. Eckhardt contends that word of Jesus ("if it is my will that he remain until I come . . .") reported in John 21:22 arose out of the literal understanding of his words in 11:23 ff. (especially verses 25 f.) as a promise that the resurrected disciple would never die. When in fact he died, a redactor corrected Jesus' promise in 21:23 and substituted the name of Lazarus in chapters 11 and 12 so as to hide the actual identity of the man to whom the promise was originally said to have been made. The gospel then underwent several redactions before reaching its present form. Before A.D. 100 it was edited by Ignatius of Antioch. In this edited form it was translated from the original Aramaic into Greek by John the Elder in Ephesus (A.D. 100 or a little later). Still later, an Interpolator, Papias, further complicated matters by adding synoptic material (e.g., 14:31). Eckhardt promises another volume in which he will attack the problem of interpolation and rearrangement by making calculations, based on manuscript evidence, of the number of lines per page and words per line in the original Johannine corpus. The many genuine exegetical and methodological insights in this work do not, in my opinion, enhance the credibility of the general thesis.

An even more intensive analysis has been published by W. Hartke, who regards the literary-historical problem of the Fourth Gospel as crucial for the understanding of Christian origins.[176] The first volume of his two-volume work is devoted to the problem of Johannine sources and the relation of John to the synoptic gospels. Within the Gospel of John he finds three literary strata, which he calls Z, V, and H. Z corresponds rather closely to Bultmann's semeia-source. It is the work of John, the son of Zebedee, who incorporated into it an even earlier sign book, *Urmarkus*. The latter contains Peter's witness as it was recorded by John Mark. John Mark in turn revised and augmented the Z document, bringing into it the Passion and certain discourse material. He turns out to be both the Mark of the gospel of that name and the elder of the Johannine epistles. Finally, H, the last redactional layer, is the work of Judas Barsabbas (John 14:22) an apocalypticist and erstwhile Jewish sectarian. The author of the Book of Revelation, he introduced into

175. *Der Tod des Johannes, als Schlüssel zum Verständnis der Johanneischen Schriften*, Studien zur Rechts und Religionsgeschichte, III (Berlin, Walter de Gruyter, 1961).

176. *Vier urchristliche Parteien und ihre Vereinigung zur apostolischen Kirche*, Deutsche Akademie der Wissenschaften zu Berlin, Schriften der Sektion für Altertumswissenschaft, 24 (2 vols. Berlin, Akademie-Verlag, 1961).

the gospel the eschatological material and the theological concept of predes-
tination. In Hartke's view, Judas was responsible for the publication of the
Fourth Gospel, and also for its blemishes. Hartke's work is governed by his
conviction, expressed in the preface, that not only the essential, but also the
earliest, element in the New Testament has to do with the overthrow of the
diabolical Lordship of Mammon and the erection of the kingdom of bound-
less, divine love on earth, which was the essential thing in the word and work
of Jesus. The way in which this criterion is applied to the Gospel of John and
the extensive imaginative constructions of the relations of persons and parties,
introduced on the basis of little clear evidence, scarcely commend this solution
of the Johannine problem to the critical reader.

The review of more recent attempts to analyse the text of the Fourth
Gospel in order to lay bare the process of composition shows that a suitable
alternative to Bultmann's proposals has not appeared. In some cases credible
suggestions and comprehensive efforts have been made. Yet there has been
no proposal which, in comprehensiveness and the completeness and cogency
of its execution, can stand alongside Bultmann's. It may well be that this is
almost inevitable because of the difficulty of the problem, and that the reluc-
tance of some scholars to commit themselves one way or the other is justifiable. Instead of simply ending on such a diffident note, however, let us see
whether the extensive examination of Bultmann's work and the criticism and
discussion of it admits of any more substantial or firmer conclusions, positive or negative.

First of all, it is fair to say that the air of dubiety cast by Schweizer upon
attempts to separate continous sources in the Fourth Gospel has not been
removed. Indeed, Ruckstuhl's elaboration of Schweizer's style-statistical
method and his application of it to Bultmann's separation of sources have
raised serious questions about Bultmann's procedure and results. Ruckstuhl's
investigation has certainly shown that the stylistic basis of Bultmann's source
theory is far from unassailable, although it may be doubted whether it is as
destructive of it and all other attempts to impugn the unity of the gospel
as he desires to believe. While it is true, as Ruckstuhl notes, that in 1927 Bultmann called for a thorough style-critical investigation of the gospel (and I
John) as the basis for the separation of sources,[177] the source separation actually carried out in his commentary is not grounded upon stylistic evidence
alone. As I have already shown in my exposition of Bultmann's method, many
considerations are involved. The source theory uses criteria so various that
when it is attacked at one point its defenders can retreat to another, or, if it
is a matter of detail, surrender the point in question but hold to the theory.

177. Ruckstuhl, *Einheit*, p. 39 f.; Bultmann, *CW, 41* (1927), 502 f.

Against any stylistic counter-argument it can always be said, with whatever degree of plausibility, that the evangelist imitated and reworked his sources. Nevertheless, the judgment that the criticism of Ruckstuhl has materially weakened Bultmann's case cannot be avoided. It presents serious obstacles for his theory which, as far as I know, have not yet been removed.

It is worth noticing, however, that stylistic evidence can be made to point in different directions, depending on what stylistic evidence is used, whether it is set forth in statistical tables (Schweizer and Ruckstuhl) or in the context of actual exegesis (Bultmann), and what presuppositions or hypotheses govern its use and interpretation. A real question may be raised as to whether stylistic evidence is as unambiguous as is sometimes assumed,[178] especially when the issue is whether one or more styles can be discerned in a document and, if so, how they are to be accounted for. Ruckstuhl sees an overarching stylistic unity (which Bultmann is ready to grant) with variations attributable to the type of material involved—discourse, dialogue, or narrative. For Bultmann the stylistic variations are not merely indicative of the nature of the material but, when taken with other evidence, indicate different sources. The evidence as a whole, set forth in the context of the exegesis and interpretation of the gospel, gives rise to and illumines the theory. Such unity as the gospel manifests may be accounted for by supposing that the evangelist imitated and worked over his material. The interpretation of the stylistic evidence is a matter of great importance, and the crucial question at issue between Ruckstuhl and Bultmann concerns the extent to which the evangelist could have imposed his own style upon the source material or imitated the stylistic characteristics of the sources. That the evangelist could have imitated and reworked his sources cannot be denied. It is less likely, but possible, that the process should have resulted in a random distribution throughout the sources of stylistic characteristics such as Ruckstuhl and Schweizer have adduced. But if the evangelist so assimilated the sources to his own style, then the task of source criticism becomes highly problematic, and any results must be regarded as highly questionable.

If Bultmann's source theory has been received with considerable criticism

178. Hirsch, ZNW, 43 (1950–51), 129–43; above p. 68 n. 42. It is possible that common stylistic features could be shared within a school or circle of tradition. While important stylistic similarities between I John and the Fourth Gospel cannot be denied, there is impressive evidence that the two documents are not from the same author but only from the same school or circle. Cf. C. H. Dodd, *The Johannine Epistles*, pp. xlvii–lvi; H. Conzelmann, *Neutestamentliche Studien für Rudolf Bultmann*, 194–201; F.-M. Braun, *Jean le théologien*, pp. 39 ff. In contrast with Conzelmann and Dodd, Braun believes that the Fourth Gospel is later than the First Epistle.

and opposition, the grounds for wariness are real and are not limited to ob-jections based on stylistic evidence. There are other objections rooted in in-tangible but indispensable considerations of historical probability. One of the first to raise such objections against Bultmann was Käsemann, who doubted that a Christian evangelist would have employed as the vehicle of his theological thought a pre-Christian Gnostic document (the Offenbarungs-reden) which he had, so to speak, emptied of its old mythical meaning. Käse-mann maintained that what Bultmann assigns to this source is better accounted for on the assumption that it was written by the evangelist himself,[179] and he has raised doubts about the theological sophistication and subtlety of the evangelist and the quasi-kenotic character of his Christology. If the evan-gelist's basic theological position and intention must be re-evaluated in the direction of ascribing to him less theological sophistication, as Käsemann thinks, the tension between his perspective and the miraculous and mythical elements in the gospel does not stand in such great need of resolution. The hypothetical semeia-source and Offenbarungsreden, which served Bultmann so well in his total exposition of the gospel by allowing him to maintain that the crassly miraculous and the speculative, mythical elements were not un-derstood literally by the evangelist, are no longer so vital to exegesis. If the evangelist did not commend a crass miracle faith, he probably did accept the miracle stories as accounts of what actually happened. This does not mean, of course, that the affirmation of their historicity was his principal purpose in narrating them. But it was probably an important part of his purpose. (If so, then the equation of sign and word in John needs some qualification. While the evangelist occasionally equates the two, the signs have a peculiar efficacy of their own, which lends authority to, or heightens the offense of, the word. The signs without the words are meaningless, but the words without the signs are empty.) If the evangelist had no interest in the Gnostic imagery, he at least believed this to be the most adequate vehicle for his message and was not, so to speak, one step away from it, using it to express a point of view that it had not been originally intended to convey. Add to this Bultmann's own recognition that the evangelist and the Offenbarungsreden are closely

179. Käsemann's view finds some confirmation in Schweizer's earlier judgment (*Ego Eimi*, p. 107 f.) that the speeches are either the evangelist's own composition or have been thor-oughly impressed with his style. It is further strengthened by Ruckstuhl's observations about the different rhythmic styles within the source and the similarity of many passages assigned to the evangelist to the rhythmic style(s) of the source (above p. 65). Bultmann himself holds that the evangelist imitates his source and concedes that the style of the evangelist and that of the Offenbarungsreden cannot always be distinguished (*Johannes*, p. 409 n. 2, 301 n. 4).

related in Denkweise,[180] and one becomes increasingly doubtful that such a source actually existed and, if it did, whether it can be separated from the redactional work of the evangelist, with which it is now mixed, and reconstructed with any certainty at all.

These considerations do not and are not intended to discredit Bultmann's entire source theory. Certainly something positive may be said for the semeia-source.[181] The case for it is intrinsically stronger than the case for the Gnostic discourse source, since obviously the evangelist used some miracle tradition about Jesus, unless, as I think unlikely, he either made up the stories or was an eyewitness to the events themselves. The apparent relation of some of his narrative material to the synoptics precludes the evangelist's having composed it himself, while the picture of Jesus presented in his gospel is not—if

180. The Gnosticism of the Offenbarungsreden is not purely pagan or Hellenistic but manifests Old Testament and Jewish influences (*Johannes*, pp. 13 ff.). Käsemann believes that the evangelist himself was a genuinely Christian Gnostic. Cf. "Ketzer und Zeuge," *ZTK, 48* (1951), 306 n. 2.

181. Haenchen's recent analysis of the Johannine narrative material is intended to show that it belongs to an advanced stage of literary development and, against Noack, that it does not represent the initial commitment to writing of a stream of oral tradition (*ZTK, 56,* 1959, 19–54). Although Haenchen rejects Bultmann's semeia-source hypothesis, his own understanding of the way in which the evangelist employs narrative material is, after all, not so different from Bultmann's ("Der Vater, der mich gesandt hat," *NTS, 9,* 1962–63, 208–16). Against Haenchen's attempt to separate a pre-Johannine literary form of the tradition see Wilkens, "Evangelist und Tradition im Johannesevangelium," *TZ, 16* (1960), 81–90. The relationship of John to the sources of tradition is an important and fascinating problem and one I cannot treat here. A few observations, however, may not be out of order. Bultmann, in an article on the relation of John to the Mandaean literature (*ZNW, 24,* 1925, 100–46), suggested (pp. 142 f.) that the Johannine form of Christianity was more closely related to the Baptist sect and was older than that represented by the synoptic gospels. In the light of Lietzmann's research in the Mandaean materials, Bultmann later gave up his initial view that the Mandaeans and their literature sprang directly from the John the Baptist sect, which he believes had a significant relation to the origins of the Fourth Gospel (cf. his review of Lietzmann's work, *TL, 56,* 1931, 577–80). Perhaps for this reason, and because of the results of his literary analysis, Bultmann has never carried further his early suggestion about the antiquity of Johannine Christianity. Yet in his commentary he suggests that the Fourth Evangelist was a convert from the Baptist sect (*Johannes,* p. 5). His earlier proposal has recently been revived by A. Gyllenberg ("Die Anfänge der johanneischen tradition," *Neutestamentliche Studien für Rudolf Bultmann,* 144–47), who draws upon the evidence of the Qumran scrolls. Cullmann has also been persuaded by the scrolls that the Christianity of John is fully as old as that of the other gospels (*NTS, 5,* 1958–59, 157–73). W. F. Albright has probably gone as far as anyone in drawing conclusions about the origin and antiquity of the Fourth Gospel on the basis of the scrolls: "we may rest assured that it contains the memories of the Apostle John . . ." ("Recent Discoveries in Palestine and the Gospel of St. John," *The Background of the New Testament and its Eschatology,* p. 171). With no desire to rest assured in the gospel's essential apostolicity, E. R. Goodenough ("John a Primitive Gospel," *JBL, 64,* 1945, 145–82) had already argued for a Jewish origin and possible early date before the discovery of the scrolls.

we can at all trust the synoptics—that of an eyewitness. The suggestion of a semeia-source or something like it is supported also by the consideration that the proposed relationship of the evangelist to this source—especially his way of using the source—is somewhat more plausible than in the case of the discourse source. In the semeia-source we have miracle stories which have been commented upon and altered by the evangelist, but without any of the stories having lost their essential character or individuality. Neither has the source lost its essential order. In the Offenbarungsreden we have poetic discourses made up of doublets which the evangelist broke into small sections and rearranged, interlarding them with his own annotations which interrupt, expand, or imitate the source in such a fashion that even Bultmann can scarcely distinguish one from the other.[182] It is, then, more probable that the evangelist used a traditional narrative source, annotating it freely, but partially preserving its character and outline, than that he used a discourse source to set forth a theological position, especially since such a source needed to be broken up into small pieces and interlarded with notations in order to be useful to him.[183]

182. Cf. Noack, *Tradition*, p. 13.

183. Yet there are substantial reasons for being somewhat skeptical about the semeia-source proposal. In the first place, although Bultmann cites Faure's original proposal (*ZNW*, 21, 1922, 107–12), he does not follow the clue which Faure thought decisive, namely, that the Old Testament is cited differently in the first twelve chapters from the remainder of the gospel. We usually find ἔστιν γεγραμμένος or something similar in chapters 1–12 and ἵνα ἡ γραφὴ πληρωθῇ or the like from 12:38 on. None of the Old Testament passages in chapters 1–12 is ascribed by Bultmann to the semeia-source, but rather to the evangelist, the redactor, and other traditions or source fragments. If, then, the Old Testament quotations in chapters 1–12 do not support the semeia-source theory, the prospects for convincingly demonstrating the existence of such a source distributed throughout the first part of the gospel become questionable. It is probable that 2:11 and 4:54 indicate that the stories to which they belong stem from a common source (E. Schweizer, "Die Heilung des Königlichen: Joh 4, 46–54," *ET*, 11, 1951, 387). This, however, does not necessarily bespeak the existence of a more extensive source. For evidence of this one may perhaps turn to 12:37 f. and 20:30 f., where the entire work of Jesus appears to be brought under the category of "signs." But it is at least arguable that these passages were written by the evangelist, and if they were not they only suggest that he used a "Book of Signs" in the composition of his gospel without helping to define its extent. Stylistic evidence is really not conclusive, and other unambiguous evidence is not to be found. Interestingly enough, there is no mention of signs in several of the narratives which Bultmann would like to ascribe to the semeia-source: 1:35–52; 4:1–42; chapter 5; 6:1–26, where references to signs in 6:2, 14, and 26 are assigned to the evangelist; 7:1–13, where in verse 3 Jesus' miracles are called "works" rather than signs; chapter 9, where reference to signs in verse 16 is again from the evangelist; 11:1–44. The absence of any mention of signs from 12:37 to 20:30 has little to do with the source question. Since the evangelist himself speaks frequently of signs in the earlier part of the gospel, the absence of the term here does not need to be construed to mean that he has now left his semeia-source behind. Rather, in substantial agreement with the synoptic tradition, he recounts no signs during the Passion week.

That the Fourth Evangelist did not rely upon, use, or probably even know the synoptics in the form in which we have them is now generally agreed by such scholars as Dodd,[184] Noack, and Haenchen, as well as Bultmann.[185] If he used an entirely oral tradition, as Noack claims, it seems to have been appropriated in highly developed form. Both Bultmann and Haenchen [186] point to the developed form of the Johannine narrative tradition in support of the contention that the evangelist relied upon written source materials. While the possibility that the evangelist used some oral tradition ought never to be excluded,[187] neither can the evidence indicating the use of written sources be disregarded.[188]

It is certainly not impossible that the evangelist had access to both written narrative sources—perhaps Johannine sources—and oral tradition. Of course, this does not mean that he used a semeia-source along with other narrative tradition of the type described by Bultmann. Apart from the many important and detailed arguments against the semeia-source offered by Ruckstuhl and others, there is further cause for misgivings.[189] Noack expressed doubt that a narrative tradition would have been circulated without a tradition of Jesus' words. More doubtful still is the possibility of a narrative tradition being circulated without a passion and resurrection story. If there had been such a document, designed to evoke belief on the basis of Jesus' miraculous signs, would it have omitted the greatest sign of all, namely Jesus' resurrection? A

184. *Interpretation*, p. 449. Cf. Dodd, "Some Johannine 'Herrnworte' with Parallels in the Synoptic Gospels," *NTS*, 2 (1955–56), 75–86. For the view that John is independent of the synoptics, Dodd cites P. Gardner-Smith's *Saint John and the Synoptic Gospels* (Cambridge, Cambridge University Press, 1938). Like Dodd, I find Gardner-Smith's book convincing. A good earlier statement of the case for John's use of the synoptics, especially Mark and Luke, is to be found in B. H. Streeter, *The Four Gospels*, pp. 393–426. Citing Streeter, Barrett cautiously opts for John's knowledge of Mark and Lucan material (*St. John*, p. 34), but concedes that John in no sense used Mark as Matthew did.

185. Noack, *Tradition*, pp. 89–109, especially 108 f. Haenchen, *ZTK*, 56 (1959), 19–54, especially 51 f. Bultmann, *Johannes*, p. 151 and passim; see above, p. 77; also *TL*, 80 (1955), 524.

186. On the developed, and therefore secondary, character of certain Johannine narratives in comparison with the synoptics, see, for example, *Johannes*, p. 151 (4:46–54); p. 178 n. 4 (5:2–15); p. 250 (9:1–41); p. 316 n. 8 (12:1–8); also Haenchen, *ZTK*, 56 (1959), especially p. 52 f.

187. Bultmann does not exclude it completely, e.g. *Johannes*, p. 122 (3:23).

188. It is true that Wilkens has contested Haenchen's analysis of the narrative tradition. But he is only interested in arguing that one cannot distinguish between Johannine and non-Johannine material in the way in which Haenchen does. While he has attempted to show the Johannine character of various literary strata in the gospel narratives, he does not deny that the stories have a traditional base. Wilkens' own view of the origin of the Fourth Gospel does not in principle exclude the possibility of written sources. Cf. "Die Erweckung des Lazarus," *TZ*, 15 (1959), 22–39; also *TZ*, 16 (1960), 81–90 and *Entstehungsgeschichte*, xi.

189. See also above, n. 183.

resurrection account would have demanded a passion story also. It is difficult to imagine a Christian mission tract, which is what Bultmann believes the source to have been, containing no mention of the event that stands at the center of New Testament proclamation. It could be suggested that the narrative source included a passion-resurrection report, in which case it would be more appropriately styled an *Urevangelium* (Wellhausen, Wilkens, and Haenchen) than a semeia-source. Such a proposal might adequately explain the evidence that Faure and Bultmann cite in support of the semeia-source. On the other hand, it is possible that the evangelist worked with a diasporate collection of narratives, none of them very extensive, upon which he impressed his own style and terminology. To decide among these and other alternatives, however, is beyond the scope of this study.

That the evangelist relied on some tradition for the passion narrative is certain. Bultmann has made it appear most probable that he did not use any of the synoptic passion stories but relied upon a different, although related, strand of tradition.[190] He discerns a single written narrative source underlying the passion and Easter accounts, which he isolates in much the same fashion as the semeia and other narrative sources. Once it is granted that John did not use the synoptics, Bultmann's proposed passion source becomes entirely credible. If John had any tradition at all he must have had a passion narrative, inasmuch as this story was almost surely written down and circulated, probably in various forms, at a relatively early date. Ironically enough, however, at the point where Bultmann's source proposal is most convincing by virtue of its intrinsic historical probability, he has the greatest difficulty separating the source with precision, and the least success in finding stylistic evidence to undergird his proposal.

To summarize briefly, Bultmann's hypothesis of a pre-Christian Offenbarungsreden source presents the greatest problems, not only because of the difficulty in separating it from the evangelist's work, but also because of its lack of intrinsic probability. That some tradition lies behind the discourse of Jesus, however, need not be denied. The prima facie possibility of something approximating Bultmann's semeia-source is to be granted, although the characterization and delineation of that source remain doubtful. That the evangelist used other narrative tradition as Bultmann proposes is quite

190. P. Borgen's suggestion ("John and the Synoptics in the Passion Narrative," *NTS*, 5, 1958–59, 246–59) that at several points John's account represents an assimilation of synoptic reports seems quite unnecessary. The dependence of John upon a related but independent tradition—which Borgen himself grants—is sufficient to account for all the evidence he wants to explain by this proposal. (Borgen's footnotes are, however, an excellent index to the literature on this problem.) Cf. S. I. Buse's convincing demurral, "St. John and the Passion Narratives of St. Matthew and St. Luke," *NTS*, 7 (1960–61), 65–76.

possible and, indeed, one of the factors that makes the identification of a semeia-source or other Grundschrift difficult. A traditional, probably written, passion narrative was very likely employed, even if, in attempting to trace such a narrative, Bultmann is plagued by lack of unambiguous stylistic evidence.

In conclusion, it is illuminating to compare the positions of Bultmann and Schweizer (*Ego Eimi*), since they are not as far apart as might have been supposed. Their respective works appeared at approximately the same time and have proved to be basic to this discussion. Schweizer, like Bultmann, favors the possibility of written sources behind the gospel and even believes it possible that the evangelist has reworked and utilized a collection of narratives and discourses.[191] Schweizer also suggests that the origin of the possible speech source lay very near the Mandaean community and its literature, although in contrast to Bultmann he speaks of a Christian speech source and even suggests that the evangelist may have composed it.[192] Bultmann, like Schweizer, recognizes that a stylistic unity stands at the end of the process of development[193] and that the task of source criticism is therefore a difficult and delicate one. He does not claim certainty for all of his results.[194] There is, of course, an obvious difference. Bultmann has undertaken source separations in the gospel, while Schweizer has maintained, with a suitable openness, that such an undertaking cannot yield sufficiently certain results to make it worthwhile. Perhaps the key to this sharp divergence is to be found in Schweizer's belief, in view of the demonstrable stylistic unity of the gospel, that the author so thoroughly reworked any sources he may have used that the source question can no longer be decisive for exegesis.[195] We have already seen how crucial a role the assignment of material to various sources, especially

191. *Ego Eimi*, p. 107: "Es ist also denkbar, dass der Evangelist eine Sammlung von Erzählungen oder (resp. und) eine von Reden benutzt und verarbeitet hat." Since the publication of *Ego Eimi* and the appearance of Bultmann's commentary, Schweizer has indicated his rejection of Bultmann's source analysis: "Ich die von Bultmann vertretene weitgehende Annahme von Quellen (insbesondere auch bei den Reden) nicht für richtig halte." *ET, 11* (1951–52), 65 n. 5.

192. *Ego Eimi*, p. 108: "Es ist uns daher sehr wahrscheinlich, dass der Evangelist entweder an eine christliche Redequelle gebunden ist, deren Verfasser der 'mand.' Religionsgemeinschaft und ihren Texten sehr nahe stand resp. gestanden hatte, oder . . . , dass er selber dieser Verfasser ist . . ."

193. *RGG, 3* (1959), 842.

194. Cf. the bracketed material in the reconstructed sources in Chapter 1 above.

195. *Ego Eimi*, p. 88: "Es ist dabei denkbar, dass dieser endgültige Verfasser (a) seine Vorlage mit dem eigenen Stil durchdringt, (b) ihre Eigentümlichkeiten umgekehrt in seinen Stil aufnimmt. Sollte dies beides aber in stärkerem Mass der Fall sein, dann müssen wir auf Scheidungen verzichten, dann wird aber auch die Einheitlichkeit schon so stark sein, dass die Quellenfrage exegetisch nicht mehr so entscheidend ist."

the semeia-source and the Offenbarungsreden, plays in Bultmann's exegesis. If we believe Schweizer's caution to be commendable, even after Bultmann's prodigious work, we recognize that we have not advanced but have had to fall back in the exegesis and interpretation of John. If a new beginning must be made in the exegesis of the gospel with no final resolution of the source problem in sight, the prospect is far from hopeless. No better guiding principle could be adopted than the one contained in Haenchen's observation that the most important question is what the evangelist wanted to say to his readers, and that the source problem, while relevant to that question, is secondary and does not have a claim to priority in exegesis.[196]

196. "Jesus vor Pilatus (Joh 18:28–19:15)," *TL, 85* (1960), 100.

3

The Displacement of the Text, Its
Rearrangement and Redaction

THE DISRUPTION OF THE TEXT AND ITS RESTORATION
BY THE ECCLESIASTICAL REDACTOR

Bultmann's rearrangement of the Fourth Gospel, although original in many respects, is not unprecedented. A number of scholars have attempted to resolve certain difficulties in the gospel by recourse to theories of rearrangement.[1] The premise of such theories is that the present order of the gospel is not original. Since the original order has been lost, critical scholarship must try to restore it. As Bultmann himself has said, the rearrangement of the text of the Fourth Gospel raises two distinct questions: first, whether the rearrangements themselves can be justified and, second, whether the existence

---

1. The displacement theories of F. W. Lewis, J. Moffatt, G. H. C. Macgregor, J. H. Bernard, and G. P. Lewis are outlined in W. F. Howard, *The Fourth Gospel*, p. 303. Worthy of special mention is the rearrangement carried out by Hirsch, *Das vierte Evangelium in seiner ursprünglichen Gestalt*. See pp. 5–57 for Hirsch's presentation of the gospel in its original form. He makes a number of rearrangements with which Bultmann agrees (Bultmann, "Hirsch's Auslegung des Johannes-Evangeliums," *ET*, 4, 1937, 115–42; also his *Johannes*, passim), although Bultmann thinks he fundamentally misunderstands the gospel.

of the wrong order in the present text can be explained.[2] The establishment of a system of rearrangements demands that both questions be satisfactorily answered. In his commentary, Bultmann justifies the rearrangements exegetically in their new contexts, having shown that the passages involved offer insurmountable difficulties in their present positions. For him, the most glaring examples of disorder in the gospel are the position of chapter 6 after chapter 5, the order of chapter 10, 12:44–50 in its present isolated position, and the "obvious" disorder of chapters 13–17 (e.g., 14:30 f. leads directly into chapter 18).[3] He ascribes the present order of the text to an ecclesiastical redactor (or redaction) who attempted to bring order out of a text which came to him in pieces as the result of an external, mechanical disruption.[4] He does not attempt to show how this destruction of the original textual order could have occurred; indeed, he has asserted that we cannot now know this.[5] From the rearrangements Bultmann proposes, it is evident that the destruction was fairly complete and involved a mangling of the text as well as the displacement of individual pages.[6] The devastation was particularly heavy at the center of the gospel.[7] It presumably occurred before the gospel was copied and circulated, inasmuch as no manuscript evidence for the hypothetical original order has come down to us. Nevertheless, the restoration of the text by the ecclesiastical redactor, and its publication, presumably took place at a time somewhat later than the original composition of the book.[8]

2. *ET*, *4* (1937), 117.

3. *RGG*, *3* (1959), 840–41; *ET*, *4* (1937), 117.

4. *Johannes*, p. 162, p. 269 n. 1. *ET*, *4* (1937), 117: the function of the redactor was "ein noch nicht veröffentlichtes und durch äussere Gründe aus der Ordnung geratenes Werk in Ordnung zu bringen . . ."

5. See above, p. 3; *RGG*, *3* (1959), 841.

6. Bultmann believes that the displacement of pages would account in part for the disorder of John. The nearly equal size of some of the larger displacements indicates this. "Indessen kommt man nicht überall mit der Annahme einer Versetzung eines Blattes (bzw. meherer Blätter) aus; die Zerstörung muss, wenigstens teilweise, weitergegangen sein, wie die m. E. innerhalb Kap. 6 und Kap. 10 bestehende Unordnung zeigt.

"Es ist klar, dass die kritische Arbeit eine ausserordentlich schwierige ist; und es ist sehr die Frage, wieweit der Diskussion der Forscher zu einem einheitlichen Ergebnis führen kann. Immerhin ist die Aufgabe gestellt, und in die Feststellung der Aporien besteht weithin Übereinstimmung" (*ET*, *4*, 1937, 119). Therefore the attempt to rearrange the text must be made. (Cf. *Johannes*, p. 163: "Kann die ursprüngliche Ordnung auch nicht mit Sicherheit wiederhergestellt werden, so muss doch der Versuch dazu gemacht werden.") Against Dodd, who abjures all rearrangements, Bultmann again makes the point that scholarship has reached some consensus of opinion on the necessity of rearrangement at some places in the gospel (*NTS*, *1*, 1954, 86).

7. *Johannes*, p. 164 n. 2: "Der Text des Evg muss dem Red. gerade in den mittleren Partien stark zerbrochen und wohl auch verstümmelt vorgelegen haben."

8. Hirsch suggested 100 as the date of composition in Syria, and 130–140 as the date of

In Bultmann's view, the redactor's purpose in reworking the gospel was to bring it into intelligible order and then to publish it in a form that would be accepted as authoritative in a church which was already becoming more and more conscious of a distinction between orthodoxy and heresy.[9] As a means to the latter end, he added chapter 21, which is intended to establish the Beloved Disciple, to whom he ascribes the gospel, as a witness from the earliest times.[10] The fact that chapter 21 seems to be a later appendix is taken as an important indication that the gospel as a whole has been edited.[11] It is, of course, the same editing or redaction which produced the gospel in its present order that is also responsible for most of the secondary material—indeed all that is theologically significant—in the extant edition.

There is no way to consider Bultmann's displacement theory seriously without carefully examining his arguments, which, while they have a certain basic similarity, differ in individual cases. There are no criteria susceptible to summary treatment and categorization as was the case with his source criticism. Bultmann gives his main arguments for displacements and rearrangement in the discussion of matters of literary criticism which precede his commentary on each section of the gospel. Instead of simply quoting at length from these discussions, I have attempted to distill from them the essence of Bultmann's arguments and to combine this with other evidence and assertions made elsewhere in the text and footnotes. To follow the argument closely, it is necessary to refer constantly to the text of the New Testament, which I have not frequently quoted at length, since this would have enormously increased the length of this study. Having set forth Bultmann's own arguments, I shall point out the questions raised by each of his rearrangements and by his general theory. There has been a surprising lack of such discussion, although many scholars have rejected or registered strong reservations about Bultmann's rearrangements.[12] Such rejections and reservations

redaction and publication in Asia Minor. Rylands Papyrus 457 (the Roberts Papyrus containing a few verses from John and dating from the first half of the second century) damages Hirsch's theory—at least as regards his dates—since it shows that the gospel was circulating in Egypt in the first half of the second century. Since Bultmann does not attempt to set dates and fix places of origin (see above, p. 3 and n. 12), his theory is less vulnerable to such manuscript discoveries.

9. NTS, 1 (1954–55), 90.
10. Johannes, p. 554.
11. RGG, 3 (1959), 841.
12. J. Jeremias, TB, 20 (1941), 42; M. Dibelius, TL, 67 (1942), 261; E. Käsemann, VF, 3 (1942–46), 185; Wilkens, Entstehungsgeschichte, pp. 6, 7; W. Michaelis, Einleitung in das Neue Testament (Bern, BEG-Verlag, 1946), pp. 109 f.; W. Grossouw, "Three Books on the Fourth Gospel," NT, 1 (1956), 42 f.; H. van den Bussche, "La Structure de Jean I–XII," L'Évangile de Jean, pp. 62 f. A positive approach to the question of the structure of John is

have involved general principles and presuppositions, and, for the most part, have only indicated an unwillingness to become committed to such a far-reaching rearrangement of the text. Although there has been relatively little discussion of Bultmann's specific proposals,[13] P. Niewalda has nevertheless felt justified in asserting that "Bultmann's rearrangements are unfounded," citing Barrett's declaration that "none of them is to be regarded as proven." [14] But although Barrett takes Bultmann's rearrangements seriously enough to consider and reject them individually, his arguments are usually very brief and do not deal with Bultmann's reasons for undertaking the rearrangements in the first place. In the following discussion we intend to ask whether there are convincing reasons for following Bultmann's proposals. This will doubtless lead us into an examination of the reasons behind Bultmann's rearrangements and to some judgments about their validity.

BULTMANN'S REARRANGEMENT OF THE TEXT: EXPOSITION AND CRITICISM

1:19–34 [15]

Bultmann finds the first evidence of displacements and redactional additions in 1:19–34. He designates 1:22–24 an addition of the ecclesiastical redactor following the synoptic tradition and rearranges the remaining verses of the section. With the removal of verses 22–24, verses 19–21 and 25–26 fit together well enough and are left in that order. Verse 27 is also called an addition from the synoptic tradition and is assigned to the redactor. Verse 28 is a concluding formulation to be likened to the concluding sentences in 6:59, 8:20, and 12:36. Bultmann decides that it is the conclusion of the sec-

---

found in W. Grundmann's *Zeugnis und Gestalt des Johannes-Evangeliums, eine Studie zur denkerischen und gestalterischen Leistung des vierten Evangelisten,* Arbeiten zur Theologie, 7 (Stuttgart, Calwer Verlag, 1961).

13. The most significant defense of the traditional order of the text against the rearrangements of Bultmann is found in a series of articles by J. Schneider: "Zur Frage der Komposition von Joh 6:27–58 (59) (*Die Himmelsbrotrede*)," in *In Memoriam Ernst Lohmeyer,* ed. W. Schmauch (Stuttgart, Evangelisches Verlagswerk, 1951), 132–42; "Zur Komposition von John 10," *Coniectanea Neotestamentica XI, in honorem Antonii Fridrichsen sexagenarii,* edenda curavit Seminarium Neotestamenticum Upsaliense (Lund und Köpenhamn, Gleerup and Ejnar Munksgaard, 1947), pp. 220–25; "Zur Komposition von Joh 7," *ZNW,* 45 (1954), 108–19; "Die Abschiedsreden Jesu, ein Beitrag zur Frage der Komposition von Joh 13, 31–17, 26," *Gott und die Götter, Festgabe für Erich Fascher zum 60. Geburtstag* (Berlin, Evangelische Verlagsanstalt, 1958), pp. 103–12.

14. *Sakramentalssymbolik im Johannesevangelium?* p. 2 n. 5; Barrett, *St. John,* p. 19.

15. For Bultmann's principal discussion of the redaction and rearrangement of this section see *Johannes,* p. 58.

tion under consideration, and it is therefore placed at the end along with verses 29–30, which cannot be separated from it. Verse 31 then follows directly upon verse 26, while verse 32 is said to be still another addition of the redactor from the synoptic tradition. Verses 33–34 follow verse 31, after which comes the conclusion, verses 28–30.[16]

But how, we may ask, does Bultmann come to such conclusions about the text? He first observes that verses 22–24 break the connection between 21 and 25 (which is restored by the removal of the intruding passage). Then he contends that the evangelist, from whom most of the passage is said to stem, understood the Baptist as a witness, and a witness only, and therefore could scarcely have written the characterization of him found in verses 22–24, which does not contain this idea and stands in no clear relation to his assertions in verse 21. Bultmann finds the characteristic style of the evangelist as well as his distinctive idea of Jesus as the "prophet" in other parts of this section (verses 19–34), and this strengthens his belief that verses 22–24 were interpolated by the redactor in order to harmonize the Johannine account with the synoptic. Similar considerations are employed to show that verses 27 and 32 are from this redactor.

We have here what is fundamentally an instance of content-criticism. Stylistic considerations are mentioned, but they are at best supporting criteria and in themselves indecisive. Neither here nor elsewhere does Bultmann attempt to prove that the style of the redactor's work stands out distinctly from that of the evangelist or his sources.[17] The really decisive considerations are that verses 22–24 interrupt the connection between verses 21 and 25, and that they (along with verses 27 and 32) express traditional synoptic notions about the Baptist which do not conform to the evangelist's understanding of him as witness and witness only. Moreover, in verse 21 the Baptist declares that he is not Elijah, but in verse 23 he identifies himself by reference to the famous Isaiah 40:3 passage. According to Bultmann, in some Jewish traditions this identification of the Baptist would be tantamount to calling him Elijah. Mark and Matthew, who initially identify John by reference to this Isaiah passage, later definitely imply that he is to be interpreted as Elijah.[18] Thus, verse 23 is said to contain an implicit contradiction of verse 21.

The "I baptize in water" of verse 26a is assigned to the redactor because

16. For this and all of Bultmann's other rearrangements of the text see pp. 179–212.

17. In fact, verses 22–24 seem to show some of the Semitic characteristics of the semeia-source or the passion narrative: placing of the verb first, asyndeta, $οὖν$-connective, use of $καί$, etc. Although the subordinate clause and the participle appear here, their use is not at all un-Semitic.

18. *Johannes*, p. 62 n. 6.

it has no connection, intrinsic or syntactical, with the following statement about the one standing "in the midst of you." The "I baptize in water" would ordinarily be expected to precede a counterbalancing statement about "another" who will baptize in the Holy Spirit, but such a statement does not occur. One would expect at least a μέν . . . δέ construction tying the "I baptize with water" to the rest of the sentence,[19] but none is to be found. Furthermore, the phrase "in water" in verses 31 and 33 is also without doubt an addition by the redactor from the synoptic tradition, so its occurrence cannot be cited to support the originality of 26a. The ἐν ὕδατι of verse 31 is classified as redactional because the question at issue in the context (see verse 25), is *why* John baptized. That he baptized with water (which seems to underscore the provisional character of his baptism in contrast to that of the one who comes after, baptizing in the Spirit) is irrelevant.[20] The "he who baptizes in the Holy Spirit" of verse 33, as well as the "in water" of the same verse, are assigned to the redactor as harmonizations with the synoptic tradition. The original form of verse 33 was "Upon whom you see the Spirit descend and remain upon him, this is he." The "and I did not know him" of verse 33a is simply a repetition of verse 31a by which the redactor makes connection again with the evangelist's text.

Bultmann's rearrangements within the section 1:19–34 and his assignment of material to the redactor raise as many questions as they resolve.[21] Perhaps the fundamental criticism of Bultmann's assignment of material to the redactor has to do with his circular method of argument. At some points in the gospel, where an apparent theological contradiction is involved, he can argue impressively for the excision of a passage which allegedly cannot be integrated into a theological perspective otherwise quite clearly defined. Here, this sort of tension or contradiction cannot be clearly established.

Bultmann claims that verses 22–24 interrupt the original immediate connection between the threefold questions and answers of verse 21 and the obvious reference to them in verse 25. It must be remembered, however, that this original immediate connection of verses 21 and 25 is a pure hypothesis without textual evidence. It is questionable whether one ought to argue that because an excision results in a smoother connection between the remaining elements that the original form of the passage is to be recovered

19. Ibid., p. 63 n. 1.
20. Ibid., p. 63 n. 6.
21. Against Bultmann's assignment of verses 22–24 and other portions of this section to a redactor, see Ruckstuhl, *Einheit,* pp. 149–59; he presents detailed and, in large measure, convincing counter-arguments. My own criticisms have been confirmed and expanded by the use of Ruckstuhl's, but were formulated independently.

by such an excision. One must admit that verse 24, which identifies the questioners as having been sent by the Pharisees,[22] is very awkward. But it is possible to excise it and nothing else.[23] If, however, verses 22 and 23 are excised, the Baptist never actually answers the question "Who are you?" which was originally put to him in verse 20. Moreover, it is only to be expected that after the possibilities raised by the questioners in verse 21 are rejected they should again ask (verse 22), "Who are you?" That verses 22–24 agree with the synoptic idea of the Baptist as forerunner does not necessarily mean they are not original and indicate, as Bultmann believes, that here we are dealing with a harmonization which makes the Baptist a forerunner in order to bring the Johannine concept into line with the synoptic.[24] The idea of the Baptist as forerunner found in verses 22–24 is not really contradictory to his role as witness, and even Bultmann admits that the redactor who added verses 22–24 may have thought of the forerunner as a witness.[25] We seem to be dealing with ideas that are complementary rather than mutually exclusive. What is more, in verse 15 (cf. also verse 30) the Baptist characterizes Jesus as ὁ ὀπίσω μου ἐρχόμενος, thus recognizing him as forerunner. In 3:28 John explicitly says αὐτοὶ ὑμεῖς μοι μαρτυρεῖτε ὅτι εἶπον . οὐκ εἰμὶ ἐγὼ ὁ χριστός, ἀλλ' ὅτι ἀπεσταλμένος εἰμὶ ἔμπροσθεν ἐκείνου, and Bultmann assigns this verse to the evangelist! What could be more explicit? Not only is the Baptist here designated the forerunner, but, most significantly, this passage apparently refers back to what he has said in *1:20 and 1:23* (cf. 1:27). If this is the case, 1:23 could scarcely be redactional. It is apparent that the evangelist knows the tradition of the Baptist as forerunner (cf. Mark 1:2, Matt. 11:10) even though he may emphasize his role as witness. That the Baptist explicitly denies he is Elijah (verse 21), the forerunner in some Jewish tradition taken over by Christians (cf. Mark 9:11–13, Matt. 11:14), does not necessarily mean, as Bultmann assumes,[26] that the evangelist did not think of him as forerunner

22. If verse 24 could be understood as introducing a new group of questioners and therefore a new section, it would not be objectionable, but the lack of an article before the participle ἀπεσταλμένοι makes such an understanding highly inappropriate.

23. Cf. the conjecture of Schmiedel, noted in Nestle's apparatus.

24. Ruckstuhl, *Einheit*, pp. 155 f., points out that the redactor appears to have done a poor job of bringing the account into line with the synoptics if that was his intention. For example, why did he not introduce in verse 27 a reference to Jesus' baptizing in the Spirit to parallel the Baptist's baptism in water, thus setting the two baptisms over against one another in the manner of the synoptics? Furthermore, even after Bultmann's excisions (or "before the redactor's work"), the account of the Baptist in John shows some affinities to the synoptics.

25. Cf. Ruckstuhl, *Einheit*, p. 152; Bultmann, *Johannes*, p. 62 n. 6.

26. *Johannes*, p. 61. Because in some Jewish circles Elijah was the forerunner of the Messiah and some Christians apparently took over this tradition and applied it to the Baptist, Bultmann assumes that any Christian understanding of the Baptist as forerunner is tantamount to the

at all or that he could not have used the Old Testament testimonia which were presumably, but not certainly, originally used to identify the Baptist as Elijah.

Bultmann also wants to assign the quasi-synoptic elements which he identifies in verses 26, 27, 31, 32, and 33 to the redactor rather than to the evangelist or his source. In each case he points out the alleged incongruity of such elements. They are not to the point ($\dot{\epsilon}\nu$ $\ddot{\upsilon}\delta\alpha\tau\iota$ in verses 31, 33),[27] merely repetitive (verse 32), contain a grammatical construction found nowhere else in the gospel (verse 27),[28] or do not speak to the question just asked (the $\dot{\epsilon}\gamma\grave{\omega}$ $\beta\alpha\pi\tau\dot{\iota}\zeta\omega$ $\dot{\epsilon}\nu$ $\ddot{\upsilon}\delta\alpha\tau\iota$ of verse 26). We may doubt whether these are sufficient grounds for assigning material to the redactor. One should not approach texts of the Fourth Gospel with too fixed an idea of what the evangelist would have thought or written or with the supposition that he never wrote anything or used any source in a manner that was not perfectly clear and obviously relevant to his theological purpose. The evangelist's use of traditional material in the passion, which Bultmann observes so acutely, should make one wary of such an assumption. It may well be that tradition rather than redaction accounts best for the seeming difficulties of verses 19–34.[29]

---

identification of him as Elijah. This is at best a questionable assumption. Since in verse 23 the Baptist is not explicitly identified as Elijah, this verse does not contradict the Baptist's previous denial that he is Elijah (v. 21). Perhaps the Baptist is denying that he is the Christ, Elijah, or the Prophet in order to dissociate the inbreaking dispensation of which he is a part from various forms of Jewish expectation.

27. Verse 31 follows immediately upon verse 26 in Bultmann's order, and is thus part of the answer to the question "Why do you baptize?" The $\dot{\epsilon}\nu$ $\ddot{\upsilon}\delta\alpha\tau\iota$ of verse 31 then becomes rather pointless, especially since Bultmann also strikes out as redactional the "I baptize in water" of verse 26. But after verse 30 ($\dot{o}\pi\dot{\iota}\sigma\omega$ $\mu o \upsilon$ $\ddot{\epsilon}\rho\chi\epsilon\tau\alpha\iota$ $\dot{\alpha}\nu\dot{\eta}\rho$ $\ddot{o}\varsigma$ $\ddot{\epsilon}\mu\pi\rho o\sigma\theta\dot{\epsilon}\nu$ $\mu o \upsilon$ $\gamma\dot{\epsilon}\gamma o\nu\epsilon\nu\cdot$) the $\dot{\epsilon}\nu$ $\ddot{\upsilon}\delta\alpha\tau\iota$ of verse 31 is less objectionable. Moreover, if verses 25–27 are left in their present order, verses 26 f. answer after a fashion the question of verse 25, especially if some familiarity with the synoptic tradition on the part of the reader is assumed (as knowledge of Jesus' baptism by John the Baptist seems to be assumed). If the answer is somewhat obscure, compare Jesus' rejoinder in 3:3, his "answers" in 3:5, 4:10, and 6:26, and the evangelist's summary in 2:23–25.

28. The relative taken up again by a pronoun is a somewhat awkward construction, suggesting that verse 27 is a gloss. Even if it were, this would not mean that verses 22–24 (or other phrases excised by Bultmann) are the work of a redactor. Indeed, the presence of verses 22–24 could have inspired a redactor to add other synoptic material such as verse 27.

29. B. M. F. van Iersel, "Tradition und Redaktion in Joh. I 19–36," *NT*, 5 (1962), 245–67 (especially 250), recognizes that Bultmann's explanation of the present order as the result of a redactor's rearrangement of a disordered text is inadequate. He also rejects—rightly, in my opinion—the proposal of H. Sahlin, "Zwei Abschnitte aus Joh 1 rekonstruiert," *ZNW*, 51 (1960), 64–69, that the present text is the result of two almost identical scribal errors. Following Bultmann's lead in separating an original account from secondary additions, he produces a reconstruction that is even smoother than Bultmann's. He refrains from attributing the secondary material to an ecclesiastical redactor, leaving open the possibility that the

Moreover, it is difficult to understand why a redactor would have interpolated material from the synoptic tradition into this section and not into certain others where John differs significantly from the synoptics, e.g. the Last Supper. Granted that the Baptist holds an important position in the gospels, and perhaps in the pre-gospel primitive kerygma, what apologetic interest could lead a redactor to bring the account of the Baptist into closer conformity with the synoptics? Perhaps conformity to the synoptics was an end in itself. But if this were the case, why did the redactor not introduce the baptism of Jesus into the account? Its omission is certainly one of the more striking departures from the synoptic reports.

Finally, Bultmann's analysis does not gain in credibility from the fact that the rearrangement of the text is necessitated by the excisions. In answer to the question of why he baptizes if he is not Christ, Elijah, or the prophet (verse 25), the Baptist indicates that he is the forerunner (verses 26 f.). This seems clear enough if we accept the extant order, although the answer is given by way of allusion rather than by direct statement. If Bultmann's excision of verse 27 is accepted, however, the reply of verse 26 makes no sense at all as an answer to the question of verse 25. In that case something more is required before the statement of place in verse 28. So Bultmann places verses 31(32)–34 between verse 26 and verses 28–30. If the excision of part of verse 26 (ἐγὼ βαπτίζω ἐν ὕδατι) and of verse 27 is not allowed, this rearrangement becomes unnecessary, although verses 31 ff. could still follow verse 27, and verses 28 ff. could follow verse 34 if none of Bultmann's excisions were accepted. While the excisions demand the rearrangements, the obverse is not true. That is, while the present text will not accommodate excisions without rearrangements (so that the redactor could not have made his additions to an original text in the present order), the restored, original text will accommodate the redactor's additions as well or better than the present one. The redactor, then, must not have known the original order, but rather found the text in disorder and tried to restore it. Such a disordering of bits of text may

---

elements of the text are the evangelist's source and his own additions to it. Furthermore, van Iersel rightly recognizes that the validity of his reconstruction depends upon whether he can explain how and why the present text was constructed. He regards it as the result of a purposeful conflation of the Johannine and synoptic accounts, with the awkwardness of the narrative resulting from the redactor's attempt to introduce a somewhat artificial structuring or division of the text while preserving intact as much of both traditions as possible, and he describes in detail how this took place.

Even more complex is M.-É. Boismard's suggestion that the Baptist material in chapters 1 and 3 consists of several versions of the same account, which the evangelist wrote and rewrote. Luke, whom Boismard regards as the redactor of the Fourth Gospel, is said to have combined two versions in chapter 1 and to have put a third in chapter 3 ("Les Traditions johannique concernant le Baptist," *RB*, 70, 1963, 5–42).

not be accounted for by the simple hypothesis of the shuffling of pages. The text itself must have been preserved in fragments. This is admittedly not impossible, unlikely as it may seem, but it presents a difficulty for Bultmann's rearrangement theory which we shall deal with at the end of the chapter. Moreover, rearrangement is not so urgently demanded if verses 26b and 27 are not set aside as redactional.

Chapter 3 [30]

This chapter has always caused some perplexity among exegetes. The Nicodemus story and the discourse of Jesus which grows out of it are followed abruptly—indeed, one might almost say interrupted—by a section dealing once again with the witness of John the Baptist (3:22–30). In 3:31 ff. there is another abrupt shift, and while the Baptist may be presumed to be still speaking if the text is left in its present order, his tone changes completely. There is no more talk about the relation of Jesus and the Baptist, but, instead, we hear of "he who comes from above" and "he who is of the earth." Like others before him, Bultmann decides that it is necessary to rearrange the sections of this chapter (verses 1–21, 22–30, 31–36). He puts the section containing the witness of the Baptist at the end and lets verses 31–36 follow immediately upon 3:21 where it forms the continuation of the speech of Jesus. As such, its language and form appear to be quite appropriate. According to Bultmann, verses 31–36 cannot be understood as the word of the Baptist. While the Baptist says, "That one must increase while I must decrease" (verse 30), the implied contrast between Jesus as the one from heaven and John as the one of the earth who speaks earthly things (verses 31 ff.) is hardly appropriate, since John fills the positive role of witness to Jesus and as such does not speak only of what is earthly. Not only does its content bespeak the fact that 3:31–36 belongs after verses 1–21 and before verses 22–30, but "no one receives his witness" (verse 32b) is impossible after "everyone is going to him" (verse 26b). The new arrangement works out well. The main section (3:1–21, 31–36) may now be divided into three clearly defined sectons: 3:1–8, the grounding of the coming of the revealer in the necessity of rebirth; 3:9–21, the coming of the revealer as the *krisis* of the world; and 3:31–36, the authoritative witness of the revealer. In verse 13 Jesus begins speaking of the revealer in the third person and (if 31–36 is placed immediately after verse 21) continues to do so until the end of the discourse, whereas if the verses are left in their present order there is a sudden and unexplained shift from the first to the third person as one moves from

30. For Bultmann's principal discussion of the problems of this section see *Johannes*, pp. 92 f.

verse 30 to verse 31. After the discourse of Jesus is completed, the witness of John the Baptist (verses 22–30) is introduced.

Bultmann has conjectured that the size of the displacement allows one to think that the page on which 3:31–36 was originally written may have been misplaced.[31] Apparently the redactor must have either left it in the wrong place or been unable to find the right place for it. Although Bultmann finds traces of the work of the redactor in chapter 3, his additions to the text here are not, as in 1:19–34, directly involved in the problem of the rearrangement of the order.[32]

Bultmann's arguments for rearranging chapter 3 are somewhat stronger than those for 1:19–34. There is no involvement with the problem of redaction, and the size of the displacements and the space between them suggests the possibility of a shuffling of pages. The new connections effected by placing verses 31–36 between verses 21 and 22 have much to commend them.[33]

Dodd, however, suggests that if verses 31–36 were found between verses 21 and 22 in the original text of the gospel (as Bultmann proposes), critics would still suspect that a displacement had occurred.[34] Verse 31 immediately following verse 21 produces an abrupt and unaccountable shift in the train of thought. Although, as Dodd observes, verses 31–36 may from the standpoint of content and theme follow very well upon verses 9–21, there is no connection at all between verses 21 and 31; instead, there is an obvious break. Formal and substantial reasons may be adduced for keeping verses 1–21, 22–30, and 31–36 in their present sequence. Both verses 13–21 and 31–36 are discourses which bring to a climax and conclusion preceding conversations between Jesus and John and between John and certain disciples. Both may be understood as commentary of the evangelist rather than words of Jesus and John the Baptist respectively.[35] Neither connects smoothly with

31. *ET, 4* (1937), 119. Such an explanation of the hypothetical dislocations in the Gospel of John is, of course, not original with Bultmann.

32. In making this rearrangement Bultmann is in exact agreement with Bernard and, to a lesser degree, with F. W. Lewis, Moffatt, and Macgregor, who also believe that 3:31–36 cannot follow 3:22–30 (*Johannes*, p. 92 n. 6; cf. Howard, p. 303).

33. Barrett's assertion (*St. John*, p. 183) that "it does not seem necessary to adopt these conjectures. The whole paragraph is a unity," does not quite speak to the problem.

34. *Interpretation*, p. 309.

35. Cf. R. Schnackenburg, "Die 'situationlösten' Redestücke in Joh 3," *ZNW, 49* (1958), 88–89. While agreeing with and learning much from many of Schnackenburg's shrewd observations on the analogies between the two passages, I remain skeptical of his somewhat speculative thesis that verses 31–36, 13–21 (in that order) originally composed a separate homily which the evangelist "filed" at this point among the leaves of his gospel, and which was later

what goes before. The break between verses 30 and 31 finds a parallel in the sudden change of person between verses 12 and 13. Further, after Jesus' questioning of Nicodemus' ability to understand τὰ ἐπουράνια in verse 12, there follows immediately the disclosure of just such heavenly things (verses 13–21). Jesus no longer seems to be speaking to Nicodemus, but the evangelist to his readers. There is a somewhat similar situation in the relation of verses 31–36 to 22–30. But while ὁ ἄνωθεν ἐρχόμενος (verse 31) is clearly Jesus, one hesitates to identify ὁ ὢν ἐκ τῆς γῆς (verse 31) with the Baptist. Hence the frequently noticed difficulty. But if one maintained with Bultmann that chapters 1 and 3 are heavily freighted with polemic against the Baptist sect, this bold contrasting of Jesus with the Baptist would not seem so strange.[36] Furthermore, verse 31 follows verse 30 (ἐκεῖνον δεῖ αὐξάνειν, ἐμὲ δὲ ἐλλατοῦσθαι) very well indeed. In verses 31 ff. it is not John who debases himself. Rather, the evangelist again takes up the discourse, not merely with the intention of disparaging the Baptist, but primarily in order to say something about "he who comes from above."

That verse 32b is contradictory and therefore impossible after verse 26, as Bultmann claims, would be a more impressive argument if verse 33 did not also contradict verse 32b—and Bultmann leaves these verses in the extant order. Besides, it is not clear that the complaint of the Baptist's followers that everyone is going to Jesus (verse 26), occurring as it does in a narrative, is really contradicted by the assertion of Jesus that no one receives his witness, which may well mean something quite different. (Bultmann himself assigns the statements to different sources, a circumstance which is often sufficient in his eyes to account for such a contradiction.) Possibly in the Fourth Evangelist's view all men may go to Jesus and yet none receive his witness. The assertion that everyone goes to Jesus serves only to emphasize the contrast which the evangelist makes between Jesus and John.

---

split and incorporated in the present order by a redactor who reversed the sequence of the two halves.

36. That primitive Christianity pointed to the Baptist as witness and forerunner of Jesus is clear enough. It is also true that John was given a distinct but subsidiary status. Note especially Matthew 11:11: "among those born of women there has risen no one greater than John the Baptist, yet he who is least in the kingdom of heaven is greater than he." The placing of the Baptist in the age before and outside the kingdom in the synoptic tradition finds its Johannine equivalent in 3:31, where the Baptist is placed among those of the earth. This corresponds to the difference between the eschatological dualism of the synoptics and the cosmological dualism of John.

W. Wilkens, in *Entstehungsgeschichte*, p. 134 n. 492, indicates that verses 31–36 cannot be linked directly to verse 21, although in content the section is closely related to verses 11 ff. Wilkens suggests that verses 31–36 may have constituted an originally independent meditation later joined to verses 22–30 by the evangelist.

Chapters 4, 5, 6, 7 [37]

According to Bultmann, "The traditional sequence of chapters 5 and 6 cannot be original." If in 6:1 Jesus is said to have gone across the Sea of Galilee, he must have been on one or the other side of the sea immediately beforehand, not in Jerusalem as the present order of the text would have it. From the geographic standpoint of Jerusalem, says Bultmann, it is senseless to designate any point on the Sea of Galilee as "on the other side." Although chapter 6 has no point of connection with chapter 5, it makes good connection with chapter 4. Moreover, in 7:1 it is presupposed that Jesus had been in Judea up to that point, as would be the case if chapter 5 rather than chapter 6 immediately preceded it. Bultmann therefore maintains that chapter 6 originally preceded chapter 5. This revised order is said to be confirmed by several considerations. Verse 4:44 demands that chapter 6 follow immediately, since in this chapter and not in chapter 5 is the truth of the word about a prophet not being without honor except in his own country fulfilled and illustrated.[38] Verse 6:2 is intended as a reference to what has taken place immediately before in 4:46–54 (i.e. the healing). The chronological order which the evangelist had in mind is clear: 6:4 speaks of the nearness of Passover, which is the feast already at hand in 5:1; 7:1 can appropriately refer to 5:18 (as it clearly does) only if chapter 7 follows immediately upon chapter 5; Jesus' withdrawal to Galilee (7:1) is the direct result of the Jews' seeking to kill him. The reversed sequence of chapter 6 and chapter 5 is also appropriate to the themes taken up in each. In chapter 6 revelation appears as the judgment of man's natural desires of life and in chapter 5 as the judgment of his religion. Correspondingly in chapter 6 there is a discussion with the people and in chapter 5 a discussion with their leaders.

The reasons adduced by Bultmann and other scholars for placing chapter 6 before chapter 5 are so substantial and impressive that they cannot easily be set aside. That John is not interested in writing good historical narrative in the modern sense does not necessarily mean that the evidence for disarrangement which Bultmann finds is all beside the point. Not all of it is based on the assumption that the evangelist meant to write good historical or quasi-historical narrative.[39] Neither does it hang by a single thread, but, as

37. *Johannes*, pp. 154 f. The transposition of chapters 5 and 6 is quite common; cf. Howard, p. 303; also Guilding, *Jewish Worship*, pp. 45 f., and Grundmann, pp. 10, 39 ff., 43 ff.

38. *Johannes*, p. 150. In addition, 4:44 is said to be a variant of Mark 6:4, and 6:41 ff. a variant of Mark 6:1–6.

39. As is implied by Barrett, *St. John*, p. 227. The evidence has been conveniently summarized by Wilkens (*Entstehungsgeschichte*, p. 10 n. 30), who believes that chapter 6 origi-

we have seen, depends upon a number of factors, theological and thematic as well as geographical and chronological. The size of the rearranged sections is sufficient to permit the conjecture that pages were misplaced,[40] and this enhances the plausibility of the proposal. Therefore I do not intend to argue that Bultmann is demonstrably wrong in placing chapter 6 before chapter 5 but shall only make one or two positive suggestions in support of the traditional order.

Noack has argued that the discussion and discourse of 5:10 ff. develop from the miracle story of 4:46, which has no discourse of its own, as well as from the healing at the pool of Siloam (5:1–9). If so, the apparent lack of the characteristic Johannine pattern of miracle leading into discourse in chapter 4 is accounted for, and the discussion and discourse of 5:10 ff. are understood as the development of both miracle stories.[41] This is a plausible but not compelling argument. The discussion and discourse following the healing at the pool relate primarily, if not exclusively, to that miracle. Yet we must not overlook the fact that in one account (4:46–54) a Gentile is the principal figure and in the other (5:1 ff.) a Jew. Is it significant that the Gentile believes and sees a miracle, while the Jew sees a miracle and apparently does not believe? If this is not coincidental, it indicates that the evangelist has purposefully paired these miracles off.

It is also arguable that the theme of the work of the Father and the Son (5:17; cf. 5:19)—namely, the raising of the dead, the giving of life, and judgment (5:22)—is logically prior to the question about the work of God (meaning man's work in response to God's demands) in 6:28.[42] Since the work of God, or the work of the Father and the Son, is the eschatological and therefore final work of resurrection and judgment, the works of God in the sense of the work demanded by God (cf. 6:28) can only be belief— belief in the one who, having seen the work of God and having been given authority to execute this work, is then sent into the world (6:29). That a legitimating sign should be demanded of him indicates a thorough misunder-

nally preceded chapter 5 and that the evangelist himself reversed the order for the sake of his passion framework (pp. 165 f.).

40. I have determined the approximate size of each of the fragments involved in Bultmann's displacement proposals by counting the lines and fractions thereof in the Nestle text and have found that these fragments are of virtually every conceivable length. This important fact means that while some of the proposed displacements could be accounted for by the shuffling of pages, by no means all of them could be. Bultmann recognizes this and is forced to fall back on the conjecture that the manuscript of John was in a state of chaos, with pages damaged as well as shuffled, when it came into the hand of the redactor. But does this conjecture make his proposal less or more difficult?

41. Noack, *Tradition*, pp. 118 f., 129 f. Cf. Dodd, *Interpretation*, p. 318.

42. For this suggestion I am indebted to Professor Paul Schubert of Yale University.

standing of the final and self-authenticating nature of his eschatological work
and of the faith which relates itself to him in acceptance of it. Since Bultmann cannot interpret 6:28 ff. (which deals with "work") in its present
context and cannot find a place for it elsewhere in the gospel,[43] perhaps this
supports the contention that chapter 5 should precede chapter 6 and that the
discussion of the works of the Father and the Son in chapter 5 forms the
proper background for the interpretation of 6:28 f. The question about the
works of God takes on a peculiar irony for the reader in view of the preceding discourse of chapter 5.

Although one must still deal with the difficulties cited by Bultmann,[44]
these considerations of geography, itinerary, smooth connection of narrative,
and theme are not compelling if it can be shown, in the manner just indicated, that the present textual order possesses an intrinsic validity. The burden of proof in this matter is upon whoever rearranges the text, and he must
not only show that his order is preferable but also that the present one is so
exceedingly difficult as to be virtually impossible. There may be at least some
doubt that this has been demonstrated.

5:1–47, 7:15–24, 8:13–20 [45]

Bultmann not only reverses the order of chapters 5 and 6 but places 7:15–24
and 8:13–20 in that order at the end of chapter 5 in order to restore the sup-

43. See below pp. 135 ff.

44. The saying in 4:44 about the prophet being without honor in his own country, the
reference to previous signs worked upon the sick in 6:2, and the mention of an attempt to
kill Jesus in 7:1 (cf. 5:18) support, but do not in themselves demand the reversal of chapters
5 and 6. It is by no means certain that the saying of 4:44 is fulfilled in the Galilean scene
of chapter 6, as Bultmann thinks. Here, as in the whole gospel, Jesus' "own country" seems
to be Judea, not Galilee (against Bultmann, *Johannes*, p. 150 n. 6), as may be inferred from
verse 45. Nowhere does Jesus refer to Galilee as his homeland although others mention his
Galilean origin (e.g., 1:46; 7:41, 52). If I am correct, chapter 5 affords an excellent illustration
of Jesus' saying in 4:44. In his own country Jesus is rejected, while among the Samaritans
(chapter 4) and Galileans (chapter 6) he finds wide acceptance. (Cf. E. C. Hoskyns, *The
Fourth Gospel*, ed. F. N. Davey, London, Faber, 1947, p. 260.) Verse 6:2 refers to signs
(plural) upon the sick, which would if anything demand more than the report of one
previous healing (4:46 ff.); this demand is satisfied if chapter 5 also precedes. The statement
at the beginning of chapter 7 that "after these things" Jesus traveled about in Galilee but not
in Judea because the Jews sought to kill him does not necessarily demand that the incident
reported in 5:18 or any event in Judea should immediately precede. In view of his brothers'
urging him to perform his works in the public eye in Judea (7:3 f.), it would be rather odd
if Jesus' most recent previous sign had been performed in Jerusalem (5:1–9). If we accept
the traditional order, we must concede that for one reason or other the evangelist's narrative
interests or instincts did not always succeed in asserting themselves, although more can be
said for the narrative sequence of the present order than has been supposed.

45. *Johannes*, pp. 177 f. F. W. Lewis, Moffatt, Macgregor, and Bernard agree with Bultmann in moving 7:15–24 from its present position (Howard, *The Fourth Gospel*, p. 303).

posedly original connection with what follows. According to his initial insight, 7:15–24 is impossible in its present place but makes good connection with chapter 5. Clearly, 7:19–23 takes up the themes of the healing on the Sabbath and the murderous intention of the Jews (cf. 5:1–18); also, 7:16 f. refers directly back to 5:19, 30 and 7:18 to 5:41–44. Verse 7:15 makes a very good continuation of 5:45–47, the astonishment of the Jews at Jesus' ability to argue from scripture (7:15) thus receiving its proper motivation. Finally, the appeal of Jesus for righteous judgment (7:24) clearly refers back to the beginning of the discussion and is directed to the Jews who have set themselves up as the judges of Jesus (5:9 ff.). Since the scene would have no closing formulation if it ended with 7:24, Bultmann suggests that 8:13–20 be added to round off the complex. This is accomplished easily enough, since, according to Bultmann's reckoning, chapter 8 is merely a collection of fragments that have been lumped together in their present position by the redactor.[46] Also, 8:20 is similar to 6:59, which is clearly a stylized concluding formulation. The catchwords μαρτυρία and κρίσις from 5:30–47 and 7:15–24 recur in 8:13–19, and the ironic calling upon the Mosaic law (5:45–47, 7:19–23) reaches its climax in the persiflage of 8:17.

There is also a solution to the problem of why and how the redactor arranged the text in its present order. He placed 7:15–24 where it now stands because it seemed to him to be a good illustration of Jesus' teaching in the temple (7:14); 7:15 ff. deals explicitly with Jesus' διδαχή (verse 16). Moreover, the catchword ζητεῖν ἀποκτεῖναι (7:19) seemed to prepare the way for 7:25. Such a clear explanation for the present position of 8:13–20 is regrettably not to be found, but it is understandable how 8:13 could be regarded as the continuation of 8:12.[47]

To the contextual evidence so far adduced, Bultmann adds material considerations which confirm the rearrangements. The theme of 5:19–30 is the identity of the work of Jesus as judge with the work of God. The theme of 5:31–47 and 7:15–24 is the justification of Jesus' claims or the question of μαρτυρία. In the conclusion, 8:13–20, the questions of μαρτυρία and κρίσις are appropriately brought together.[48] If 8:13–20 did not find its proper place as the conclusion of this complex, one might suppose 8:15 f. (which speak of judgment) to be an interpolation, since these verses have no connection with their immediate context.[49] There is little question that the placing of 7:15–24 and 8:13–20 immediately after 5:47 produces a smoother and more coherent

46. Ibid., p. 178 n. 2.
47. Ibid., p. 178 n. 3.
48. Ibid., pp. 185, 209.
49. Ibid., p. 211 n. 3.

text. Bultmann here relies more on the substance of passages involved in his rearrangements than on considerations of chronology and geography such as figured in the transposition of chapters 5 and 6. Although his judgment that 7:15–24 (or a part of it) is impossible in its present position is shared by a number of scholars,[50] the removal of 8:13–20 to this particular position is apparently a novel arrangement.

Despite the inner coherence of this proposal, there are several legitimate grounds for reservation. The accusation of Jesus' interlocutors that he bears witness to himself (8:13) already seems to fit perfectly well after the statement of Jesus in verse 12 ("I am the light of the world"), as Bultmann himself admits. It is certainly true that there are difficulties in connecting 7:52 and what precedes with 8:12 ff. Perhaps the story of the woman taken in adultery was inserted in manuscripts of the gospel at this point to fill the apparent lacuna in the text. But to remove 8:13–20 from the other side of 8:12 as Bultmann does leaves that verse hanging in midair. Although 8:12 is then made the opening statement of the hypothetical Lichtrede following chapter 9, which Bultmann reconstructs from various parts of the gospel,[51] this reconstruction itself involves further and more extensive rearrangements of material that in turn raise new difficulties while resolving others.[52]

As to the relation between 7:15–24 and 5:1–47, one must agree that, by the ἐν ἔργον of 7:21, Jesus refers to the miracle at the Sheep Gate Pool (5:1–9). But on close examination we discover that Jesus' question, "Why do you seek to kill me?" (7:19) is still abrupt and unmotivated even if Bultmann's juxtaposing of 7:15–24 and chapter 5 is allowed. If Bultmann's order is followed, this question occurs in the course of a single scene in which it has already been pointed out that the Jews were seeking to kill Jesus and in which he has addressed himself to that situation (5:18 f.). It would be rather awkward for him to raise the matter afresh in the very same scene—as happens if Bultmann's order is followed. Moreover, that the Jews,[53] in wounded inno-

50. Cf. ibid., p. 178 n. 1.

51. See below pp. 156 f.

52. If considerations of theme and content are to play a role in the rearrangements, 8:13 f., which interrupts the discussion of judgment in 7:24 and 8:15 ff., ought perhaps to be placed after 8:19, where, after Jesus' assertion, "If you had known me, you would know my Father also," the accusation that Jesus bears witness to himself is most appropriate. Becker, who usually follows Bultmann, in this case suggests placing 8:13 ff. between 5:30 and 31 (*Reden des Johannesevangeliums*, p. 118).

53. The ὄχλος replies in verse 20, but that they are the same as οἱ Ἰουδαῖοι is clear from verse 15. In 5:18 it is the Jews who seek to kill Jesus. It should be noted that the word ὄχλος does not appear in chapter 5 except in verse 13, where Jesus leaves the crowd. Only subsequently does he engage the Jews in debate. Thus while "crowd" and "Jews" are identified in chapter 7, they seem to be distinguished in chapter 5.

cence at his question, should then accuse him of insanity and ask, "Who seeks to kill you?" (7:20) would be somewhat incongruous.[54] Both the way Jesus puts the question and the way the Jews respond seem to indicate that the matter is being raised for the first time in the particular scene to which 7:19 ff. belongs. If the present textual order is accepted, it is not an insurmountable difficulty that the evangelist should let the matter of the Jews' murderous intent drop in one place (5:18 f.) only to bring it up again in another (7:19 ff.). Jesus' question in 7:19 then becomes something of a prophecy, whose truth is attested by the question of the Jerusalemites, "Is this not he whom they seek to kill?" (7:25), and the subsequent machinations and intrigues of the Jewish authorities and their agents (7:25–52).

It is not unthinkable that 7:16 f. should have been originally separated from 5:19, 30 or 7:18 from 5:41–44 by chapter 6. There is no need to bring the passages in question into close proximity, for in the Fourth Gospel significant themes tend to recur at scattered points. Nor is it incredible that the evangelist should have mentioned (7:21) a miracle worked on one Jerusalem journey (5:1–9) in connection with a subsequent journey described in a later chapter. It could be that the reference to the miracle is related to the sudden re-emergence of the Jewish intention to kill Jesus, first mentioned in connection with it. Jesus' appeal for righteous judgment (7:24) may refer back to the beginning of the discussion (5:9 ff.) and be directed against those Jews who set themselves up as judges of Jesus (Bultmann), but it should be remembered that the idea of the Jews judging Jesus appears in chapter 5 only by implication. This consideration does not afford strong support for a rearrangement of the textual order. One might also observe that 7:15 already follows 7:14 well enough, as Bultmann himself concedes when he says that it is easy to understand why the redactor arranged the text in this order. Could it have been the evangelist instead of a redactor?

We must admit that the thematic considerations having to do with the recurrence of the ideas of κρίσις and μαρτυρία in 8:13–20 and the references to Moses and the law in 5:30–47 and 7:15–24 lend substantial support to Bultmann's placing of 7:15–24 and 8:13–20 after chapter 5. On the other hand, it is not entirely clear that the Jews of 7:15–24 are the same group as the Jews of chapter 5, as Bultmann's rearrangement would require. In chapter 5 the Jews are obviously hostile (verses 16, 18), but this is not so clearly the case in chapter 7 as a whole or in 7:15–24. In chapter 7 the Jews and the people of Jerusalem stand over against the chief priests and Pharisees, who are the representatives of patent hostility. This latter group plays the same

54. Bultmann recognizes this difficulty (*Johannes,* p. 209 n. 2) and suggests that 7:20 may be redactional.

hostile role as that of the Jews of chapter 5. The "Jews" of 7:15, however, are called the "crowd" in verse 20 and are thus linked with the "crowd" (verses 31 f.) that is said by the Pharisees to be ignorant of the law and therefore accursed (verse 49). They appear to be the same as the τινες ἐκ τῶν Ἱεροσολυμιτῶν of verse 25. Thus, the interlocutors of 7:15–24 can hardly be distinguished from those in the rest of the chapter in order to be identified with the hostile Jews of chapter 5. They express amazement (7:15) and shock (7:20) at the words of Jesus, but they are not unequivocally hostile. Jesus' question, "Why do you seek to kill me?" (verse 19), indicates the outcome of his relationship to them and to all the people, not the conscious intention of those to whom he is speaking. Although he may say that they seek to kill him and imply that they are angry with him (verse 23), they actually seem to be divided in judgment (verses 12, 30 f.), unlike the Jews of 5:16, 18, whose opposition is unambiguous.

Aside from the considerations mentioned above, or perhaps on the basis of them, one must make a general judgment about whether John's thought moved in orderly progression without sometimes, or even frequently, skipping from one incident to another or from one theme to another. Bultmann presupposes the orderliness, indeed the logical consistency, of the evangelist's mind. This presupposition needs to be questioned. If the evangelist himself wrote the material which Bultmann attributes to the Offenbarungsreden, their somewhat circular pattern of thought and manner of expression permit us to suppose that he allowed himself the same circularity and lack of logical progression in the total structure of the gospel.[55]

6:27–59 [56]

Having reversed the order of chapters 5 and 6, Bultmann makes far-reaching changes within chapter 6 itself. Immediately, 6:51c–58 [57] comes under suspicion as being a secondary addition. The previous assertions about Jesus as the bread of life are here interpreted in terms of the sacramental meal understood as φάρμακον ἀθανασίας. According to Bultmann, such an interpretation is not only contrary to the general theological perspective of the evangelist but also contradicts what has just been said in the discourse on the

55. The question of whether, in its present order, the gospel shows an intelligible, not to say logical, structure (particularly in those parts rearranged by Bultmann) remains of utmost importance. On the structure of chapter 7 see the excellent article by Schneider, *ZNW, 45* (1954), 108–19.

Barrett carries on an extensive and profitable discussion with Bultmann over the position of 7:15–24 (*St. John*, p. 261 f.).

56. Bultmann, *Johannes*, pp. 161 ff.; also pp. 174 ff.

57. Bultmann refers to 6:51b–58, but verse 51 falls into three clearly defined parts, and the redactional element begins with the third (ibid., pp. 161, 174).

bread of life. There, Jesus himself is the bread of life as well as the one who distributes it to all who come to him. There is no mention of a sacramental act.[58] But it is precisely this sacramental act which is demanded in 6:51c–58. Hence 6:51c–58 must stem from a different realm of thought. Bultmann believes that this section has been added by the ecclesiastical redactor, whose typical churchly, sacramental interests and apocalyptic eschatological it embodies. To this redactor one must also assign the phrase ἀναστήσω αὐτὸν ἐν τῇ ἐσχάτῃ ἡμέρᾳ, which stands at the conclusion of verses 39, 40, and 44. In verse 54 this phrase fits into the context well enough, but, in the other cases, especially in verse 44, it is disruptive. The redactor has attempted to subsume the meaning of the whole speech under the viewpoint presented in 6:51c–58.[59] As he missed a reference to baptism in chapter 3 in connection with the idea of being reborn of the spirit, and therefore added one himself, so here in chapter 6 he adds the missing, and for him appropriate, reference to the Lord's Supper. Indeed, he makes it the culmination of the entire discussion. Bultmann therefore excises 6:51c–58.

When this is done, no clear train of thought immediately appears. The text remains in what he judges to be disorder, or at best very broken order, which can only be explained on the supposition that the redactor was working with fragments and attempting, albeit with little success, to bring them into order. The question in verse 28 about working the works of God, and its answer in verse 29, do not follow from the injunction of verse 27 not to work for the bread which perishes but for that which abides. According to Bultmann, to maintain the connection of verses 28 f. with verse 27 one must suppose that Jesus' hearers at least partially understand him and then make a word-play with the concept of ἐργάζεσθαι, which in verse 27 means "create" or "effect for yourselves," but in verses 28 f. would have to mean simply "work." This is difficult to believe in the light of the usual procedure in Johannine dialogues, in which the hearers prove themselves to be completely without understanding, as in verse 34.[60] Would it not be more natural to

58. Ibid., p. 162. "Das [6:51c–58] befremdet nicht nur angesichts der Gesamtanschauung des Evglisten, speziell seiner Eschatologie, sondern es steht auch in Widerspruch zu den vorausgehenden Worten. Denn in diesen ist unter dem Lebensbrot, das der Vater gibt, indem er den Sohn vom Himmel sendet (v. 32 f.), er selbst, der Offenbarer verstanden. Er spendet (v. 27) und ist (v. 35, 48, 51) das Lebensbrot, wie er das Lebenswasser spendet (4:10), wie er das Licht der Welt ist (8:12), als der Offenbarer, der Welt Leben gibt (v. 33, vgl. 10:28; 17:2),—denen nämlich, die zu ihm 'kommen' (v. 35, vgl. 3:20 f. 5:40), d.h. die an ihn glauben (v. 35; und vgl. 3:20 f. mit 3:18), ohne dass es noch eines sakramentalen Aktes bedürfte, durch den sich der Glaubende das Leben aneignet."

59. In assigning this passage to the redactor, Bultmann agrees with M. Dibelius, W. Bousset, and A. Faure among earlier exegetes (ibid., p. 162 n. 6).

60. Bultmann rejects Odeberg's suggestion that the identification of the "abiding bread" and the works of God is understandable, since the Torah was identified with spiritual nourish-

suppose that verse 34 ("give us this bread always"), which makes a request
that would be altogether appropriate after the imperative of verse 27, actually followed verse 27 originally? Just as verses 28 f. do not really connect
with verse 27, so the connection to verse 30 is only apparent, since in verse
30 it is presupposed that Jesus has demanded, "Believe in me," and such a
demand is not found in the preceding verses. Verses 30–33 form a continuous section, but verse 34 cannot be the continuation of verses 32 f. The request "Give us this bread" (verse 34) wrongly assumes that the living bread
is a miraculous food, but this misunderstanding would be impossible after
verses 32 f., where Jesus defines this bread as "*he* who comes down from
heaven." [61] The conjecture that verse 34 should follow immediately after
verse 27 is thus confirmed. Verses 34–35 form a unity. In the face of the
mistaken request of verse 34 Jesus identifies himself as the bread of life and
promises life to those who believe. Verses 36–40 seem somewhat inappropriate if left in their present place, since Jesus would then be scolding his
hearers for their unbelief at the beginning of the discussion (verse 36), before
there has been any opportunity for an expression of unbelief on their part
and before the certainty of salvation for believers (verses 37–40) is mentioned. According to Bultmann, verses 36 ff. can scarcely be the continuation
of verses 34 f., and in any case the murmuring of the Jews in verse 41 after
verse 40 is completely uncalled for. It presupposes a preceding statement such
as is found in verse 33 or, better, verse 51a, in which Jesus explicitly speaks
of himself as the bread of life who has come down from heaven. Hence,
verses 36–40 are detached from their context, and verses 30–33, which deal
with the question of legitimation, are placed after verses 34 f., forming a
suitable continuation after the claim of Jesus in verse 35. Thematic grounds
warrant keeping verses 41–46 together, although not after verse 40. In verses
41–46 the unbelief of the Jews is traced back to its metaphysical ground.
When the unbelief of the Jews has been accounted for, verses 36–40 become
appropriate. Verses 41–46 should therefore immediately precede verses 36–
40.[62] Verses 47–51a could follow verses 36–40, but they fit even better after
verse 33, where Bultmann accordingly places them.

ment (*Johannes*, p. 162 n. 8). If accepted, this explanation would make verses 28 f. intelligible after verse 27.

61. Bultmann insists on this translation, which takes the participle as a substantive. He admits
that the ὁ καταβαίνων ἐκ τοῦ οὐρανοῦ could be translated adjectivally but maintains that this
would be senselessly redundant after verse 32 and that verses 41, 50, 51a (58), which refer or
allude to an assertion by Jesus that he is the Bread come down from heaven, prevent an
understanding of verse 33 in an adjectival sense.

62. Bultmann thinks that the με of verse 36 is probably not original (several notable witnesses lack it) if, as he supposes, verse 36 ought to follow verse 46. (Ibid., p. 173 n. 3.)

While admitting that the original order cannot be restored with certainty, Bultmann insists that the attempt must be made. Taking verse 27 as the beginning point of the dialogue and placing verse 34 immediately after it as its continuation, he arrives at the following order: verses 27, 34–35, 30–33, 47–51a, 41–46, 36–40, 59.

What, then, is to become of verses 28–29? These verses constituted a fragment which the redactor inserted after verse 27 because of the occurrence of the verb ἐργάζεσθαι in both places. Using the erroneous insertion of verse 28 f. as his clue, Bultmann attempts to explain why the redactor arranged the fragmented text in its present order. With the insertion of verses 28 f. after verse 27, verses 34 f. (the request of the Jews for bread) could no longer follow, but the question of Jesus' legitimation, which is raised and answered in verses 30–33, doubtless seemed the appropriate continuation after Jesus' assertion (verse 29) that the work of God is to believe in the one whom he has sent. Since verses 30–33 take up the theme of the bread of God, verses 34–35, which begin with the crowd's demanding that Jesus give them that bread, could have easily been thought to be the proper continuation. Verses 47–51a, which originally followed verses 34–35, were placed by the redactor at the end where they could form a transition to the redactor's own composition in verses 51c–58, which presents the solution of what heretofore has been the mystery of the living bread, and hence must be the conclusion and high point of the discourse. Verses 41–46 were placed after verses 35–40 so that the parts of Jesus' speech before and after the interruption of his listeners (verses 41–42) would be approximately the same length.[63] The extant order of the text is explained, but a place in the original order has not yet been found for verses 28 f. These verses are genuine, for they appear to embody the characteristic Johannine motif of misunderstanding. They could very easily stem from a dialogue having to do with the works (or "work") of God, but there is nothing else to be found of this dialogue in the gospel. Bultmann suggests that perhaps 6:28 f. belongs with one or more of the other "fragments" strung together in chapters 7 and 8.[64]

There are no substantial stylistic grounds for denying 6:51c–58 to the evangelist,[65] but it is said to stand out sharply from its context because of its interpretation of the bread of life as the bread of the Eucharist. In verse 51c the mention of Jesus' giving his flesh for (ὑπέρ) the life of the world is an allusion to his giving of himself in death, which in early Christian thinking is death ὑπέρ . . . etc. That Jesus gives up his flesh (instead of his ψυχή, which

63. Ibid., p. 163 n. 4.
64. Ibid., p. 164 n. 2.
65. Ibid., p. 174 n. 8.

would have been the characteristically Johannine way of putting it) is an allusion to the Eucharist,[66] which he established through his giving of himself in death. Furthermore, Jesus' answer to the question of the Jews in verse 52 ("How is he able to give us his flesh to eat?"), in which he emphasizes not only the necessity of eating the flesh but also of drinking the blood, clearly refers to the Eucharist.

Bultmann adduces reasons other than the presence of the idea of salvation through the sacramental meal for supposing that this passage is redactional. The hearers' misunderstanding (verse 52) is an imitation of Johannine style, and only an imitation, since, unlike the genuine instances of misunderstanding, it is not founded upon the Johannine dualism. Also, "Son of Man" in verse 53 seems simply to be used in place of the first person singular (verses 52, 54–56) in such a way as to lead one to believe that the identity of the exalted Jesus, who gives himself as the abiding bread in the Lord's Supper, with the Son of Man is unreflectively presupposed. Probably verse 53 stems from the liturgical language of the church. The evangelist uses this title for Jesus in his role as the revealer walking upon earth, the revealer who is already judge but who must be lifted up upon the cross. He does not use it of the pre-existent logos or the exalted cultic lord. But in the passages under consideration and in 6:27b, which Bultmann also assigns to the redactor, the title is used of the exalted one.[67]

Bultmann attempts to distinguish very precisely between the Eucharistic and eschatological thought of verses 51c–58 and the position of the evangelist himself. In verse 54 Jesus promises life to the one who eats his flesh and drinks his blood—a clear indication of an understanding of the Eucharist as $\phi\acute{\alpha}\rho\mu\alpha\kappa\sigma\nu$ $\mathring{\alpha}\theta\alpha\nu\alpha\sigma\acute{\iota}\alpha\varsigma$, an idea also presupposed in the expression $\mathring{\epsilon}\chi\epsilon\iota\nu$ $\zeta\omega\mathring{\eta}\nu$ $\mathring{\epsilon}\nu$ $\mathring{\epsilon}\alpha\upsilon\tauo\mathring{\iota}\varsigma$ of verse 53. The evangelist says simply $\mathring{\epsilon}\chi\epsilon\iota\nu$ $\zeta\omega\mathring{\eta}\nu$ $\alpha\mathring{\iota}\acute{\omega}\nu\iota\sigma\nu$ (verses 40, 47). According to Bultmann, the expression "to have life in one's self" means that "the partaker of the sacramental meal carries in himself the power which guarantees for him the resurrection." [68] What is more, the explanation of "life" as resurrection at the last day (verse 54) is wholly foreign to the Johannine outlook (3.18 f., 5:24 f., 11:25 f.). The use of the verb $\tau\rho\acute{\omega}\gamma\epsilon\iota\nu$ instead of $\phi\alpha\gamma\epsilon\mathring{\iota}\nu$ in verse 54 underscores the "scandal" of what is said, and makes a spiritualizing of the passage impossible. Verse 55, "For my flesh is true ($\mathring{\alpha}\lambda\eta\theta\acute{\eta}\varsigma$) bread, and my blood is true ($\mathring{\alpha}\lambda\eta\theta\acute{\eta}\varsigma$) drink," only serves to emphasize this. For Bultmann, sacramental union (cf. verse 56) is the key to the understanding of verse 53 f. Whoever drinks the flesh and blood of Jesus in the

66. Note the words of institution in Mark 14:22–25 par.; I Cor. 11:23–25.
67. *Johannes*, p. 166 n. 10.
68. Ibid., p. 175.

Lord's Supper is united with him mystically so that he possesses his life in himself, a guarantee of his future resurrection. "He in me and I in him" (verse 56) is admittedly a Johannine expression, but in 15:4 and 17:21–23, where it is genuine, it describes the faith relationship of the believer to Christ and, according to Bultmann, does not have the sacramental and mystical connotations that are found here. In verse 57 the redactor applies the evangelist's distinctive idea of the mediation of the power of life from the Father through the Son (5:21, 26) to the sacramental appropriation of life. Verse 58 recapitulates the whole section and brings it to a close, taking up again from verses 31 f., 49 the comparison of the bread from heaven (cf. verses 51a, 33, 50) with the manna which the fathers ate in the wilderness. The living bread, which has been the main subject of discussion, is, by means of the οὖτός ἐστιν, identified with the sacrament, and the one who eats it is promised eternal life, in contrast with the fathers, who ate manna and died.

Bultmann maintains that the redactor understood the σκληρὸς λόγος of verse 60 as the natural response of the hearers to verses 51c–58, since for him the offense (verse 61) was the historical Jesus' designating his flesh and blood as sacramental food in his own lifetime. Of course, his hearers could scarcely comprehend this and hence were "scandalized." Thus the idea of *skandalon* or offense is misunderstood and externalized by the redactor. It is no longer an inevitable consequence of revelation as incarnation but is made into a literary motif.

8:30–40, 6:60–71 [69]

Bultmann indicates that 6:60–71 does not rightly belong with the rest of the chapter by deferring consideration of it in his analysis of chapter 6. In his judgment there are at least three possibilities for the original location of this section: (1) in its present position as the close of the complex (of chapter 6), (2) immediately after chapter 5 and before the complex beginning with 7:1 ff., (3) at another place.

The first possibility is immediately eliminated. Verse 59 concludes 6:1–59. The number of disciples presupposed as the hearers of Jesus in 6:60 ff. is not limited to the Twelve but includes others. The disciples mentioned throughout 6:1–59 are, however, the Twelve (verse 24) who, as in the source of 6:1–26, are understood to be the constant companions of Jesus. In addition, 6:60–71 marks an important turning point in the work of Jesus, when the twelve genuine disciples are separated from a much larger group. In Bultmann's judgment, this turning point cannot be placed at the end of chapter 6 since it cannot separate chapters 6 and 5, which belong together because

69. For Bultmann's discussion of this section, ibid., pp. 214 f.

they deal with related themes: revelation as judgment upon the natural desires of life and revelation as judgment upon man's religion.[70] Furthermore,
6:60–71 presupposes a public ministry which is inadequately represented by
the events which precede it if it is placed at this point. Against the removal
of these verses from their present context, it may be objected that Jesus' reference to a previous statement that "no one is able to come to me except it
be given him of the Father" (verse 65) is a direct reference to verses 44 ("No
one is able to come to me except the Father who sent me draw him"). Bultmann counters this objection by asking why the word of verse 44 is cited so
loosely when in other places the citations of preceding words of Jesus are
much stricter.[71] In addition, the word of Jesus in verse 44 is directed to the
crowd, while the word of verse 65 is directed to Jesus' disciples. The reference in 6:62 to the Son of Man ascending "where he was before," while it
corresponds outwardly to what is said in verses 33, 38, and 50 f., does not
necessarily presuppose these passages, since an adequate basis has been laid
for such an assertion elsewhere. That 6:62 does not refer back to verses 33,
38, and 50 f. is shown by the fact that the catchword of those verses ($\check{\alpha}\rho\tau os$)
does not appear in verse 62. In addition, the Son of Man is not mentioned in
verses 27–59 except in the redactional additions of verses 27b and 53.

If one places verses 60–71 before 7:1 ff., one must suppose that the section
immediately preceding it has been lost, since 6:60–71 cannot follow the complex of chapter 5 (5:1–47, 7:15–24, 8:13–20) for several reasons: (1) that
complex already has its conclusion in 8:20; (2) the Twelve, who are presupposed in 6:60–71, are not encountered there; (3) the crucial turning point
of the gospel would still be somewhat early.[72] The small section cannot stand
by itself, since, according to the analogy of the structure of Johannine narratives, it requires a preceding setting of the scene and a speech of Jesus
(and/or discussion) of which it would form the conclusion and high point.
It is possible that in chapter 8 a portion of the complex which stood before
6:60–71 may be found; 8:30–40 may well have immediately preceded it.[73]
This does not solve the problem, however, since 8:30–40 cannot be the beginning of a scene but only its continuation. If 8:30–40 and 6:60–71 originally stood before 7:1 ff., as is possible, it must be supposed that a section
has fallen out between the end of the complex of chapter 5 (8:20) and 8:30.

70. Ibid., p. 155.

71. Ibid., p. 214 n. 7.

72. Bultmann notes (ibid., p. 215 n. 1) that he has long attempted to keep 6:60–70 after the
complex of chapter 5 as the conclusion of both chapters 6 and 5. The result of the judgment
of man's natural desires of life and of his religion would then be shown in concrete form
in the sundering of the true from the false disciples which takes place here (p. 149). Nevertheless, he has been forced to abandon this attempt.

73. On the position of 8:30–40, see below pp. 157 f.

Bultmann cannot commend this solution, however, since 7:1 ff. already fits well enough immediately after the complex of chapter 5.

Only the third possibility remains, namely that of seeking the original position of 6:60–71 (with 8:30–40 immediately preceding) in another place. On the basis of content, one would judge the original position of this fragment to be between chapters 12 and 13, since this is the turning point of the gospel, and 6:60–71 is certainly intended to mark a crucial point in the history of Jesus. Through chapter 12 Jesus' ministry is public; after chapter 12 he appears only before his disciples until the crucifixion. This major division of the gospel is symbolic of the fact that the coming of Jesus is the judgment of the world, and this scene (6:60–71) serves admirably as the concrete historical sign of this κρίσις. But when we have placed 8:30–40 and 6:60–71 at the end of chapter 12 and before chapter 13, we must still reckon with the possibility of the loss of a portion of the text which stood before this section. Bultmann nevertheless deems it advisable to explain 8:30–40 and 6:60–71 in connection with chapter 12, and from the complex of chapter 5 to pass directly over to 7:1 ff.

One may then ask how the redactor happened to place the scattered sheets containing 8:30–40 and 6:60–71 in their present positions. He must have thought that "the characterization of the speech of Jesus as a σκληρὸς λόγος and likewise the expression about the πνεῦμα and the σάρξ in 6:63 fit well in connection with the section 6:51b–58, which he had added to the speech on the bread of life. Thus he placed 6:60–71 in its present position." [74] And 8:30–40 was combined with 8:41–47 because in both sections the Jews were designated as children of the devil—although in 8:30–40 in antithesis to Abraham's children and in 8:41–47 in antithesis to God's children.

John 6 is a chapter beset with problems, including its location in the text and its original content and order. Bultmann has pointed out the difficulties of this chapter in a necessary and thoroughgoing way. I do not now propose to take up all the questions raised by chapter 6 or to present a complete exegesis of it. That would require a sizable monograph or dissertation.[75] I shall

74. Ibid., p. 215.

75. Since the appearance of Bultmann's commentary there has been a steady stream of articles and other works dealing with John 6, especially with the position of 6:51c–58 and the problem of its originality. This is, of course, the key passage for understanding John's position with regard to the Lord's Supper. By removing it as redactional, Bultmann is able to give the evangelist's views an interpretation that would be otherwise difficult if not impossible. My own approach to this problem has naturally been influenced by this discussion, but I have attempted to attack it in what seems to me a new and different way, i.e. an extensive running conversation or discussion with Bultmann.

On John 6, note especially Ruckstuhl, *Einheit*, pp. 169–71, 243–71 (debate with Bultmann and extensive criticism of Jeremias' stylistic evidence against the originality of John 6:51–58);

simply focus upon the problems and issues related to Bultmann's handling of this chapter.

In attempting to assess Bultmann's analysis of chapter 6, I have concluded that another interpretation, which takes the redactional material to be original, is preferable, because this material is really necessary to complete the train of thought begun earlier in the chapter. Therefore I shall first briefly set forth this alternative approach.

In chapter 6 we have a literary and thematic unit, especially if chapter 5 precedes and chapter 7 follows. In any event, chapter 6 stands apart from its context. Within chapter 6 as it is presently constituted, the feeding, which begins the chapter, does not simply function as a narrative introduction contributing little of substantial nature to the ensuing discourse, but begins a line of thought that only finds its fulfillment in the emphasis on eating and drinking at the end of this discourse. This fulfillment is provided principally by the controversial Eucharistic discourse of 6:51c–58, which Bultmann regards as redactional. The miraculous distribution of the five loaves and two fish and their consumption at the beginning of the chapter foreshadow the dispensation of the heavenly bread and the emphatic insistence that it be consumed at the end. At the center of the chapter—that is, at the beginning of the discourse—the two parts are related by Jesus' admonition to work not for the food which perishes ($\dot{\alpha}\pi\acute{o}\lambda\lambda\upsilon\mu\iota$), a reference to the loaves and fish of 6:1–21, but for the food which abides unto eternal life, "which the Son of Man will give to you" (verse 27b), an allusion to the bread of the subsequent discourse. As we have noted, Bultmann regards verse 27bc as redactional mainly because of the way the Son of Man title is used. But is this a sufficient reason for excising verse 27bc? The contention that the differing conceptions of the Son of Man indicate different writers is in itself questionable, and Bultmann's arguments are not overwhelming.[76] If there is not sufficient reason

---

Schneider, *In Memoriam Ernst Lohmeyer*, pp. 132–42; E. Schweizer, "Das johanneische Zeugnis von Herrenmahl," *ET*, *12* (1952–53), 341–63, especially pp. 353 ff.; Jeremias, *ZNW*, *44* (1952–53), 256–57 (In the light of Ruckstuhl's arguments both Schweizer and Jeremias repudiate their earlier assessment of 6:51–58 as redactional.); Bornkamm, "Die eucharistische Rede im Johannes-Evangelium," *ZNW*, *47* (1956), 161–69; Wilkens, *ET*, *18* (1958), 354–70; H. Schürmann, "Joh 6:51c ein Schlüssel zur grossen johanneischen Brotrede," *BZ*, *n.s. 2* (1958), 244–62 and "Die Eucharistie als Repräsentation und Applikation des Heilsgeschehens nach Joh 6, 53–58," *TTZ, 68* (1959), 30–45, 108–18; P. Borgen, "The Unity of the Discourse in John 6," *ZNW, 50* (1959), 277–78; B. Gärtner, *John 6 and the Jewish Passover, Coniectanea Neotestamentica, XVII*, Lund, Gleerup, 1959; Lohse, *NTS, 7* (1960–61), 110–25; R. E. Brown, "The Johannine Sacramentary Reconsidered," *TS, 23* (1962), 183–206 (seen only in abstract, *NTA*, 7, 1962, 52); Grundmann, pp. 41 f. While not accepting Bultmann's redaction theory, both Brown and Grundmann believe that the sacramental section of the bread discourse, 6:51(53)–58, may be secondary.

76. Cf. *Johannes*, p. 166 n. 10. Bultmann says that verse 27bc presupposes that the hearers

for excising verse 27bc as redactional, Bultmann's arguments against verses 51c–58 are dealt a serious blow. Clearly verse 27bc looks forward to, and almost demands, the Eucharistic discourse. (This holds true even if verse 27c is set aside as redactional on account of the sacramental allusion seen in σφραγίζειν and verse 27b is said to have originally read "which I shall give you," as Bultmann himself thinks possible.)

After the command of verse 27, the word-play on work (τὸ ἔργον, ἐργάζεσθαι) in verses 28 f. forms a transitional section, leading into the extended discussion of the living, heavenly bread. The Jews understand that, in Jesus' admonition in verse 27, the demand of obedience to God is implied. Therefore, they ask how they may work the works (τὰ ἔργα) of God. Jesus responds by bringing all "work" (τὸ ἔργον) of man under one head. Man can only believe in the one whom God has sent (verse 29), who works his life-giving work (5:17 ff. and 6:33 ff.). The quest for a sign (verse 30) is certainly strange after the feeding miracle, but not necessarily pointless. The subject of the discussion has been changed from earthly to heavenly bread in verse 27. The crowd perhaps expects a sign accompanying the distribution of heavenly bread comparable to that which it has just experienced with earthly bread. In any case the request for a sign serves as the occasion for introducing the fact that the fathers ate manna in the wilderness and, therefore, the scripture quotation (Ps. 78:24; cf. Exod. 16:4, 13–15), "He gave them bread (ἄρτον) from heaven to eat (φαγεῖν)." It is precisely this scripture which henceforth serves as the center of the discussion and especially of Jesus' contribution to it. The theme of the whole discussion and discourse is alluded to in verse 27, but the key term or phrase ἄρτον ἐκ τοῦ οὐρανοῦ is only introduced in this thematic quotation, this "text," from Ps. 78:24 (or Exod. 16:4).[77] Verse 26 points back to the eating of the loaves (ἐφάγετε ἐκ τῶν ἄρτων . . .) while verse 27 mentions the food (βρῶσις) which abides unto (εἰς) eternal life, but this idea is not immediately taken up and developed. Only after the question about the works of God (verses 28 f.) and the demand for a sign (verse 30)

would be able immediately to identify Jesus as the Son of Man (unlikely in view of the question of 12:34); also, the concept of the Son of Man as the exalted Lord, implicit in this passage, diverges from the evangelist's use of the title. But the fact that the interlocutors of 12:34 ask "Who is this Son of Man?" does not necessarily have any bearing on 6:27. That the evangelist intended this to be the same group as in 6:27 or that he would have been conscious of so subtle an inconsistency in the narrative seem to me to be gratuitous assumptions. The argument from the supposedly different concepts of the Son of Man is not beyond question, since this distinction is not simply the result of literary analysis but of the *Sachkritik*, which is logically prior to such analysis (below, p. 151 n. 94). Moreover, Schulz, *Untersuchungen*, p. 115, finds two Johannine *Stileigentümlichkeiten* in verse 27c. Like Bultmann, Schulz sees that verse 27bc clearly points ahead to verses 51c–58.

77. P. Borgen, *ZNW*, 50 (1959), 277–78, indicates the midraschic or homiletic nature of this whole section as an exposition of the Old Testament text of verse 31.

does the crowd recall the manna in the wilderness and identify it as the bread from heaven (verse 31). At this point the rather vague allusion to the food which abides unto eternal life is taken up and developed in terms of this bread, and the discussion which follows concerns the identity of the true bread from heaven. Is it the Old Testament manna or Jesus?

Throughout the entire discourse and discussion as well as the feeding narrative, there is recurring reference to the act of eating. Harking back to the miraculous distribution of food, Jesus declares, "You seek me not because you saw signs, but because you ate (φαγεῖν) of the loaves and were filled" (verse 26). The Jews declare, "Our fathers ate (φαγεῖν) manna in the wilderness, as it is written, 'he gave them bread of heaven to eat'" (verse 37). Jesus says, "I am the living bread which has come down from heaven, if anyone eats (φαγεῖν) of this bread he shall live forever (verse 51). If 6:51c–58 is excised, the discourse finds its conclusion in 6:50, 51ab; he who eats the living bread, which is Jesus himself, will never die, but will live forever. As far as it goes, this is an appropriate conclusion, taking up as it does the theme of eating the living bread, which was set forth in the thematic Old Testament quotation in verse 31. (Bultmann's removal of these verses to another position in the order is therefore highly questionable.) One must then ask whether the evangelist expanded and interpreted this eating of the bread as the eating of Jesus' flesh (6:51c–58), with the obvious allusion to the Lord's Supper. There are at least two reasons for believing that the evangelist himself may have done so. First, for New Testament Christianity the eating of bread, indeed, the presentation of Jesus under the image of bread, would have almost certainly called to mind the Lord's table, so that a Eucharistic allusion is to be suspected quite apart from our controversial passage.[78] Second, it is characteristic of the Fourth Gospel that Jesus' enigmatic sayings evoke from interlocutors a specific question about their meaning. In 3:4 Nicodemus asks how rebirth is possible and in 4:11 f. the Samaritan woman asks how the living water is accessible to Jesus and whether he is greater than Jacob. Jesus really ignores the specific questions of both Nicodemus and the woman and continues by reiterating and expanding upon his initial statement (3:5 ff.; 4:13 f.). In 6:52 f. a very similar question is raised, and Jesus responds to it in much

78. Köster, "Geschichte und Kultus im Johanneserangelium und bei Ignatius von Antiochen," ZTK, 54 (1957), 56–69. Köster, one of Bultmann's former students, agrees with Bultmann in assigning 6:51c–58 to the redactor but recognizes that the preceding discourse, with its references to ἄρτος and manna, is fraught with eucharistic allusions (pp. 62 ff.). Köster, however, thinks that the cultic categories have been transformed into historical categories. Revelation is appropriated through the historic word, not through cultic rites. I wonder whether these alternatives would have appeared to the evangelist to be mutually exclusive. Is not the historic word proclaimed in and from the cultus, and is not the cultic rite the embodiment of the historic word?

the same way by expatiating on what he has already said without directly answering the question. In all three cases the interlocutor's question involves a misunderstanding. Bultmann's objection, that the misunderstanding of 6:52 is atypical because it does not involve the Johannine dualism, is only valid if 6:51–58 is interpreted in terms of the medicine of immortality. Then the misunderstanding is due to the belief that flesh means the physical substance of his bodily flesh, when actually flesh means the physical substance of the Eucharist. Precisely this interpretation needs to be questioned.

If one tentatively accepts 6:51c–58 as a genuine part of the chapter, it is not entirely clear that it presumes such a sacramental understanding of salvation and thus contradicts the evangelist's own position, as both Bultmann and Bornkamm believe.[79] The transitional statement of verse 51c, καὶ ὁ ἄρτος δὲ ὃν ἐγὼ δώσω ἡ σάρξ μού ἐστιν ὑπὲρ τῆς τοῦ κόσμου ζωῆς, is ascribed by Bultmann to the redactor as the begining point of his interpolation.[80] It is not at all difficult, however, to view this statement as the culmination of the preceding discourse, since in alluding to Jesus' death it ties the dispensation of the heavenly bread to a definite historical event. The bread of heaven is Jesus' flesh given for the life of the world in his death. (The ἣν ἐγὼ δώσω modifying σάρξ in some manuscripts is an essentially correct scribal gloss.) For John as for Paul the death is the culminating salvific event. While the whole manifestation of the glory in the ministry is already the eschatological event in John, in contrast to Paul, the death retains a peculiar significance.[81] The revelation of the glory is always anticipatory of the final glorification of the Son of Man in his elevation upon the cross. It is clear from the entire gospel that only through Jesus' departure,

---

79. Bornkamm, ZNW, 47 (1956), 161–69, especially 169. Cf. Cullmann, Sacraments, pp. 62 f. n. 94: "Bultmann souligne, oeuvr. cité [Johannes], p. 166, justement en ce qui concerne le monde d'alors: 'sakramentaler Glaube und Glaube an das Offenbarungswort sind oft verbunden.' Il se réfère également à Ignace, et surtout aux Odes de Salomon."

80. "Stilistisch angesehen könnte der Satz vom Evangelisten stammen, der auch die Erläuterung eines Begriffes liebt, die mit καί angefügt ist." (Bultmann, Johannes, p. 174 n. 8).

81. Johannes, p. 175. The whole gospel is written from the standpoint of the death of Jesus, which is inseparable from his exaltation, as Bultmann would certainly agree. But it is arguable that the death in itself has an essential and very important place in the thought of the evangelist, and that this is set forth in such sections as the parable of the Good Shepherd (10:1–18) and the foot-washing (13:1–30). Cf. Paul W. Meyer, "The Eschatology of the Fourth Gospel: A Study in Early Christian Reinterpretation" (unpublished Th.D. dissertation, Union Theological Seminary, New York, 1955), pp. 292–305, 315–20; also Meyer, "A Note on John 10:1–18," JBL, 75 (1956), 232–35.

If this is the case, then a reference to the death of Jesus with subsequent allusions to the Lord's Supper is not surprising at this point in the discourse. If Jesus' death is the prerequisite of the fulfillment of the promise of eschatological life which he brings, as is clear from the farewell discourses alone, it is not surprising to find it mentioned in this discussion of life under the image of bread.

i.e. his death, do his disciples really receive the eschatological blessedness which he brings (cf. especially the farewell discourses). In this connection the evangelist does not hesitate to employ traditional early Christian ideas (1:29, 36), and even the ἔδωκεν of 3:16 contains an allusion to Jesus' death, as Bultmann acknowledges.

Thus it seems that 6:51c is not just an appendage, or a transition to the introduction of an alien sacramental idea, but rather a fitting culmination to what has preceded. In fact, if the allusion to Jesus' death were omitted, the preceding discourse would be deprived of a very important historical point of reference.[82] In death, Jesus becomes the bread of life (conversely, for raising Lazarus to life he is condemned to death). In no other relationship can the heavenly bread be understood or received. In the following question (verse 52), the Jews misunderstand because they do not catch the reference to his death. They think he is speaking of his physical flesh; he is actually speaking of the benefits of his passion—something which no one save Jesus himself really understands.

This does not mean that there is no reference to the Eucharist in what follows; such allusions are to be seen in the preceding discourse. But now the Eucharist itself is to be understood in relation to Christ's death. Bultmann and Bornkamm see this relationship in the redactor's work, but they regard it as somewhat external or superficial, since, in the sacramental section of the redactor, emphasis is said to fall upon the role of the elements themselves as the medicine of immortality. But E. Schweizer [83] makes a valid point when he maintains that the intention of this passage is to lay heavier stress upon the act of eating—and, therefore, on the importance of participation in the Eucharist—than upon the potency of the physical elements themselves.[84]

82. On the importance of verse 51c as the key to the preceding discussion and discourse, see Schürmann, *BZ, 2* (1958), 244–62.

83. *ET, 12* (1952–53), 361.

84. Wilkens, *ET, 18* (1958), 359 ff., argues against interpreting the passage in terms of φάρμακον ἀθανασίας. Bultmann himself never seems to question whether this is the only possible interpretation of the passage. Actually, if one does not assume that, because of similar terminology, the background of the passage is the sacramental theology represented by Ignatius, this interpretation is not so obviously the only one possible. Moreover, although Ignatius may refer to the Eucharistic bread as the medicine of immortality (Eph. 20:2), he does not simply equate this bread with the flesh of Jesus Christ. Romans 7 is most interesting in this regard. In 7:1, 2, Ignatius speaks of renunciation of the world and desire for death. In 7:2b, he says his lust has been crucified and that there is in him no "fire of love for material things" (presumably anything in this world). There is only water "living and speaking in me, and saying to me from within, 'Come to the Father.'" (This water is scarcely the sacramental water of baptism; rather it is the water of life from Christ himself.) Then in 7:3 Ignatius once again disavows any pleasure in this life (in the light of the foregoing, I cannot believe that he is merely forswearing sensual pleasures), after which he declares, "I desire the 'bread

In verse 58, which refers back to the "text" of 6:31 and rounds off the discourse very nicely, it is not the potency of the manna and of the bread (i.e. Jesus' flesh) that are contrasted, but the effects of eating the manna and eating the bread.[85]

According to the line of interpretation here being pursued, Jesus does not insist upon the eating of sacramental elements as containing a magical potency. Rather he insists upon the eating of his flesh and the drinking of his blood by way of alluding to his death as the historical point at which the living, heavenly bread, identical with himself, is dispensed. That there is also here an allusion to the Lord's Supper understood as a participation in Christ's death and its benefits is not to be denied. It is entirely possible that the evangelist is insisting that participation in the Lord's Supper be understood in this way. Denial of the Lord's real death, or its significance, and neglect of the Eucharist seem to have gone hand in hand among some Docetists (Ignatius, Smyrnaeans, 7:1). It may well be that in this passage the evangelist is opposing just this sort of heresy.[86] It would then be entirely understandable that this section (6:1–59), which begins with a miraculous feeding story common also to the synoptics and reminiscent of the Lord's Supper, and which dwells on the eating of the bread, identifying the living and life-giving bread from heaven with Jesus' giving of himself in death (verse 51c), should finally relate the whole to participation in the Lord's Supper.

Furthermore, it is significant that the term βρῶσις (food), which appears in the introduction to the discourse (verse 27) but is then dropped in favor of

---

of God,' which is the flesh of Jesus Christ, who was 'of the seed of David,' and for drink I desire his blood, which is incorruptible love." Does this mean he desires the Eucharist? Without denying any Eucharistic allusion at all, it seems that Ignatius is referring primarily to his own death as a recapitulation of Christ's death. This interpretation is supported by chapter 8, in which he continues to speak only of his desire for martyrdom.

85. It is necessary to note the unique use of the term τρώγειν in 6:54, 56, 57, 58. It is doubtless correct that the evangelist here wishes to emphasize the act of eating. This may influence his choice of the almost coarse word, which occurs nowhere else in the chapter and only in 13:18 in the rest of the gospel. However, it is important to observe that "up to this point he has used the aorist stem √φαγ. He now requires a present participle, and instead of using ἐσθίειν, the usual supplement of the defective √φαγ, he uses τρώγειν. ἐσθίειν is never used in John, though √φαγ is quite common. τρώγειν occurs four times in this paragraph, and in v. 13:18 (where it is substituted for the ἐσθίειν of Ps. 41:10)": Barrett, St. John, p. 247. Every occurrence of τρώγειν in John (including v. 13:18) is the nominative singular present participle. Is it a technical designation for the participant in the Lord's Supper?

86. Wilkens, ET, 18 (1958), 358. Schweizer, ET, 12 (1952–53), 361, maintains that in this context the significance of the Lord's Supper is to secure against all Gnostic spiritualizing the reality of the incarnation culminating in the death upon the cross. Both anti-Docetic and sacramental interests may be at work in 19:35 also. The anti-Docetic character of I John has long been recognized. Bornkamm, ZNW, 47 (1956), 169, while assigning 6:51c–58 to the redactor, agrees that it is anti-Docetic.

ἄρτος (bread, loaf), does not reappear if verses 51c–58 are excised. If, however, this section is allowed to stand, we find that the term βρῶσις reappears at the end (verse 55). Appropriately enough, the flesh of Christ—understood anti-Docetically as well as sacramentally—is called βρῶσις: "My flesh is true *food.*" This is the βρῶσις which abides forever (verse 27) and which the Son of Man gives to his own. Are we to say that the redactor is responsible for reintroducing this key term with which the evangelist began his discourse? It is much easier to suppose that the evangelist has done it himself.

The more one ponders Bultmann's suggestion that the evangelist had an ambivalent attitude toward the Lord's Supper, the more one wonders why he should have written and incorporated into his gospel chapter 6, which, even without Bultmann's redactions, has so many possible allusions to the Lord's Supper. On the other hand, if a redactor had wanted to bring the Gospel of John into line with the Eucharistic teaching of the church, it is difficult to understand why he did not simply add to the gospel an account of the institution of the Lord's Supper. There is an account of Jesus' last supper with the disciples into which it could have been interpolated, and it is precisely this sort of harmonization with the synoptics which Bultmann finds in the redactor's handling of the account of the Baptist (1:19–34).[87]

Now that I have allowed myself to be led from a discussion of the structure of chapter 6 into an exploration of the possibility that 6:51–58 occupies an integral place in it, I turn again to the question of the proposed rearrangements in 6:27–51.

Bultmann's placing of verses 34–35 immediately after verse 27 presents a very real difficulty, since in verse 27 Jesus admonishes his hearers, "Do not work for the βρῶσιν which perishes, but for the βρῶσιν which abides unto eternal life," whereupon the crowd replies, "Lord, give us this ἄρτον always." This obviously will not do. Verse 34 presupposes verse 31, where ἄρτος is first introduced into this discussion, and cannot follow verse 27 directly. Since verses 31–33 belong together, as Bultmann also believes, the earliest point at which verses 34 f. could occur is immediately after verse 33, where they stand in the present text. Against this connection, Bultmann argues that the ὁ καταβαίνων of verse 33 must be understood substantively, as referring to Jesus

---

87. It is possible that John did not relate the story of Jesus' institution of the Lord's Supper at the Last Supper because he simply did not know it. E. R. Goodenough, *Jewish Symbols in the Graeco-Roman Period*, Vol. V: *Fish, Bread, and Wine* (1957), pp. 52 f., suggests that the evangelist's Eucharist was rooted in the tradition of the Jewish liturgical meal. The closest he comes to an account of its "institution" is the story of the feeding and the related discourse in chapter 6. Bultmann's redactor, however, is presumed to have known the synoptic tradition, if not our synoptic gospels, and thus would have known the institution narrative. It is therefore very much to the point to ask why he did not use it.

("he who comes down"), instead of adjectivally, as referring to bread ("that which comes down"), because verses 41, 50, 51a (58) forbid an adjectival understanding, which in any case would be "ein sinnloser Identitätsatz":[88]

> (32) . . . my Father gives to you the true bread from heaven. (33) For the bread of God is that which comes down from heaven and gives life to the world. (34) They said to him, "Lord, always give us this bread." (35) He said to them, I am the bread of life . . .

A substantival understanding, on the other hand, is supposedly forbidden by the request of verse 34, which presupposes a miraculous bread, not a redeemer already described as "he who comes down from heaven." Therefore, it is asserted that verse 34 cannot follow verse 33.

This argument lacks persuasiveness. In the first place, the adjectival understanding of verse 33 is not, in fact, forbidden by verses 41, 50, and 51a (58).[89] In the second place, it is not clear that with verse 32 this understanding results in a meaningless redundant clause. The point of verse 33 seems to be the life-giving effect of the bread. That verse 33 repeats the last part of verse 32 is no real objection. Is this not typical Johannine style? But the most important point, which Bultmann overlooks, is that verse 33 itself is an ambiguous Greek sentence and that its hearers or readers could have taken the participle adjectivally or substantively. With this ambiguity, the evangelist intends to hold the *reader* in suspense while in verse 34 the *hearers* understand the ὁ καταβαίνων adjectivally.[90] In reply to their uncomprehending request (verse 34) for the bread of which he has spoken in verse 33, Jesus informs them that he is the bread of life (verse 35). Probably the hearers should have recognized this from verse 33 (understood substantively!), but, in any case, because of the ambiguity, the evangelist is able to reiterate the point.

Verses 34 f. are thus understandable as the continuation of verses 30–33 and should not be placed immediately after verse 27. If just this much of the traditional order is accepted, verses 28 f. then form the only available, and thoroughly appropriate, bridge between verses 27 and 30. It is no longer necessary to regard them as a lost fragment that cannot be placed in the present edition of the gospel. With verses 34 f. now following verse 33,

---

88. *Johannes*, p. 163 n. 1.

89. These passages, especially verse 41, presuppose that Jesus has already identified himself as the bread of life who has come down from heaven, but this identification of Jesus as the bread of life is clear enough in chapter 6 without a substantival understanding of the participle in verse 33. Cf. verses 33–35 as a whole.

90. After arriving at this understanding of the text, I discovered a similar resolution of the problem in Barrett, *St. John*, p. 24. Both the RSV and the NEB translators understand the participle to be adjectival referring to bread.

verses 47 ff., which Bultmann had placed there, must be placed somewhere else (and these verses cannot very well follow verse 35). With the removal of these passages from their place in Bultmann's order—that is, with the vindication of the traditional order of verses 27–35—his entire reconstruction is undermined. Either a new reconstruction must be attempted, or we must fall back upon the extant order of the text.[91]

The rearrangement of 6:27–51 combined with the excision of verses 51c–58 necessitates the removal of verses 60–71 to another context, although Bultmann claims that the statement of place (verse 59) already makes this necessary. Verse 59 does bring the discourse to a close, but whether it separates it from verses 60–71 so that the two are completely independent of each other is another matter. Verse 59 may only indicate a change in scene or dramatis personae. Before verse 59, the interlocutors are the crowd (or the Jews), after it, the disciples. Actually, there is real continuity between verses 27–58 and 60–71. Bornkamm, who argues for the excision of verses 51c–58 as redactional, nevertheless keeps the order of verses 27–59 intact and allows verses 60–71 to follow immediately.[92] This seems to be the wiser course, whether or not verses 51c–58 are excised, since it avoids cutting 6:60–71 loose from its moorings in chapter 6. We have seen that when Bultmann places 8:30–40 and 6:60–71 after 12:33 he is forced to reckon with the possi-

91. For a defense and exposition of the present order, cf. J. Schneider, *In Memoriam Ernst Lohmeyer*, pp. 132–42. Schneider presents in explicit opposition to Bultmann his own analysis and interpretation of the structure of 6:27–58. Fundamental to his argument is the observation that the entire *Himmelsbrotrede* divides into three sections, each of which is marked off at the beginning by an objection or question of the Jews (verses 28, 41, 52). All three sections are said to express the same basic thoughts but with varying emphasis, thus corresponding fully to the style of the Offenbarungsreden in John. The expressions vary only in form. In all three there is mention of the fathers in the wilderness and the perishable bread, of the living bread which is Christ himself (and eternal life), and of the resurrection which guarantees eternal life beyond death. In all three parts the high point is the self-predication of Jesus (verses 35, 48, 51, 58; with οὗτός ἐστιν instead of ἐγώ εἰμι in verse 58). In the entire discourse and discussion, the following significant theological points are made: (1) in his earthly appearance Christ is the bread of life which has come down from heaven, (2) in his sacrificial death he will give his flesh for the life of the world, (3) as the crucified and exalted he distributes his flesh and blood as true food and true drink (p. 134).

Verses 37–40 and 44–46, which sit loosely in their present context or even interrupt it, Schneider believes to be later, explanatory glosses added by the evangelist himself. The present order is said to be meaningful and to correspond to the laws of composition illustrated elsewhere in the gospel, that is, to the threefold pattern which is decisive for Schneider's analysis. The argument for the existence of this pattern at the base of the discourse of chapter 6 is supported by the threefold ἀμὴν ἀμὴν λέγω ὑμῖν, which in each part introduces the central assertions of Jesus.

92. *ZNW*, 47 (1956), 166, 168. Bornkamm is not explicit on the question of textual order, but only the traditional order seems to satisfy his interpretation.

bility that a section of the text has been lost, since the transition from 12:33 to 8:30 ff. is not good. But if 6:60–71 can be kept in chapter 6, the conjecture of textual loss becomes unnecessary. While 8:30–40 and 6:60–71 do not really fit together very well,[93] there are patent allusions to 6:27–51 in 6:62, 65.[94] Also, verse 60 indicates the disciples' offense at the allusion to the death of Jesus (verse 51) and its relation to the Lord's Supper (verses 52–58). In verse 63 Jesus warns against any interpretation of verse 51c–58 in strictly materialistic terms (as φάρμακον ἀθανασίας).[95] The assertion that the flesh profits nothing

93. The scenes described are not clearly identical. If anyone should object that we do not have the same people in 6:60–71 as in 6:27–59, it may be replied that this is just as true for 6:60–71 and 8:30–40. Verse 6:63, with its antithesis of flesh and spirit (σάρξ and πνεῦμα), can refer to nothing in 8:30–40, while it could allude to the eucharistic speech (6:51c–58) or to the entire discourse of chapter 6. Moreover, 6:65 does not refer to anything in 8:30–40, although in the context of chapter 6 it is clearly a backward reference to and, indeed, a conflation of 6:37 and 44 (Bornkamm, ZNW, 47, 1956, 168; Noack, Tradition, p. 144). Bultmann notwithstanding, Noack has convincingly argued that the evangelist's "quotations" which take up earlier assertions, especially Jesus' references to what he has already said, are, like the Old Testament quotations of John, remarkably free and loose (Tradition, pp. 144–50). The passage (6:60–71) ends on an ominous note with a direct reference to one of the Twelve, Judas Simon Iscariot, as the betrayer. This clear allusion to the death of Jesus fits well after the passage about Jesus' giving his flesh for the life of the world in 6:51c. There are, then, quite a few difficulties in going from 8:30–40 to 6:60–71 (not to mention the difficulty of finding something to immediately precede these two sections if they are placed together) and some good reasons for keeping the traditional order as it stands.

94. Aside from the fact that 6:65 contains a clear reference to verses 37 and 44 (see preceding note), verse 62 presupposes verses 33, 38, and 50. Bultmann's argument that Jesus' ἀναβαίνειν in verse 62 does not really presuppose his καταβαίνειν in verse 33 is based on two considerations: (1) that ἄρτος does not occur in verse 62 as it does in verse 33 (and 50) and (2) that "Son of Man," which occurs in 6:62, does not occur in chapter 6 except in the redactional passages verses 27b and 53. I have, however, shown the questionableness of considering these passages redactional. Here, one hypothesis stands upon the not too stable shoulders of another. Significantly, in 6:51c–58 the Son of Man is identified with the bread from heaven (cf. especially verses 53 and 51), thus providing the proper link between 6:62 and verses 33, 38, and 50. Ἄρτος does not occur in 6:62 because it would be inappropriate there, for the Son of Man is comprehended under the image of ἄρτος only as he gives himself for and to man, not as he ascends to the Father.

The argument that the evangelist never speaks of the Son of Man except as the revealer sent from God walking upon earth and fulfilling a revelatory mission culminating in his death depends upon a literary analysis and the excision of redactions—and vice versa. Furthermore, the references to the Son of Man in 6:62 and 1:51 (assigned by Bultmann to the evangelist) do not really fit this characterization, since they concern the exaltation of the Son of Man with no mention of the earthly ministry or crucifixion, except insofar as the exaltation in John always implies the crucifixion. More closely related to the crucifixion itself are 6:27b, 53. Is not the Son of Man in these two passages the Lord exalted upon the cross, who gives his flesh and blood as food which abides forever?

95. Bornkamm, ZNW, 47 (1956), 161–69 argues that nothing in 6:60–71 refers back to verses 51c–58 but that this concluding section makes good connection with verses 27–51. H. Schürmann agrees with Bornkamm that verses 60–71 are devoted primarily to the ex-

is as Johannine as the assertion that the spirit gives life. For the evangelist, the historical per se is without meaning; the trans-historical gives meaning. But as the evangelist will not dispense with the historical, so will he not dispense with the fleshly or material, especially when, as in the case of the Lord's Supper, the material is so intimately related to Jesus' death.[96]

I naturally do not claim to have solved all the problems of this perplexing chapter, but I think I have shown that Bultmann's attempts to solve them through rearrangement and excision involve him in problems of equal, if not greater difficulty. It is my view that the text may be interpreted with sufficient clarity and coherence to warrant leaving it as it is. Its incongruities or inconsistencies may be attributed to the evangelist as easily as to the redactor. They are perhaps a sign of the gulf that separates our ways of thinking from his.

7:1–14, 25–52; 8:48–50, 54–55 [97]

Bultmann regards 7:1–13 as the introductory section of a new complex which prepares the way for the appearance of Jesus in Jerusalem; 7:14, 25–52 is the continuation of this complex. He divides 7:25–52 into four scenes: 7:14, 25 f.; 7:31–36; 7:37–44; and 7:45–52. Although the present order of these scenes has something to commend it, it is not really original. According to this order, the events of the second and fourth scenes (7:31–36 and 7:45–52), in which the servants of the chief priests and Pharisees are sent forth and return, are separated by several days. Hence, these servants appear to make their report to the chief priests and Pharisees only after an inexplicable lapse of time. In the third scene we are already in the last day of the feast (verse 37), and, according to the present order, the servants report only on or after that day. For Bultmann this constitutes a real difficulty; the servants should have reported back on the same day they were sent forth. The section 7:37–44 breaks the original connection between 7:31–36 and 45–52 (the theme of the crowds' belief in Jesus). If 7:37–44 is removed, the difficulty is remedied, and the two events, the dispatching of the servants

---

planation of verses 26–51 but nevertheless believes that verses 51c–58 (or 53–58) are an integral part of chapter 6. He regards verse 51c as the culmination of the *Lebensbrotrede* rather than the beginning of the *Abendmahlsrede*. Thus verse 51c must be genuine. If so, verses 52 (53)–58 are genuine too, since they indicate how one appropriates the flesh of Jesus given for the life of the world (verse 51c). Cf. *BZ*, n.s. 2 (1958), 244–62 and *TTZ*, *68* (1959), 30–45, 108–18.

96. On the interpretation of verse 63 in relation to verses 51c–58, cf. Schweizer, *ET*, *12* (1952–53), 356–58; Wilkens, *ET*, *18* (1958), 362 ff. Interestingly enough, Bultmann (*Johannes*, p. 215) believes that the redactor put verses 60–71 in their present position partly because he thought 6:63 fit well after the sacramental discourse which he had interpolated. But if so, should verses 51c–58 then be construed strictly in terms of the "medicine of immortality," even if they are secondary?

97. *Johannes*, p. 216.

and their return, are narrated as having occurred on the same day. The section 7:37–44 is then placed between verses 30 and 31, or after the first scene. Now, while verse 31 did not fit well as the continuation of verse 30 (opposite reactions to Jesus are thereby juxtaposed), it follows very well after verse 44. The two sides of the σχίσμα mentioned in verse 43 would then be described in verses 44 and 31 respectively. The difficulty occasioned by the fact that after the uprising of verse 30 Jesus continues speaking in verse 33 as if nothing at all had happened is also removed, since the action of verse 33 is now separated from that of verse 30 by several days. The scene described in verses 31–36 now finds a proper conclusion, which it did not have in the traditional order, in verses 45–52. So 7:1–13 and 45–52 remain the introductory and concluding scenes of the appearance of Jesus in Jerusalem, while the other scenes are now arranged in the order 7:14, 25–30; 37–44; and 31–36. The first of these (7:14, 25–30) appears to be rather brief and without much content. Moreover, it is hard to see how the few words of Jesus in verses 28 f. could lead to such anger on the part of his hearers as is displayed in verse 30. The resolution of this difficulty appears when one discovers that there is in chapter 8 a fragment (8:48–50, 54–55) which fits poorly into its present context but would serve very well here. Admitting that certainty is impossible, Bultmann feels justified in inserting 8:48–50, 54–55 between 7:29 and 30, where, in his judgment, it fits admirably and supplies the motivation heretofore missing for 7:30.[98]

One must admit that the order which Bultmann produces in chapter 7 makes for a better motivated narrative than the order of the traditional text of the Fourth Gospel. There are, however, two questions which we must continually raise with Bultmann. Has the impossibility of the present order been adequately demonstrated? Is a better order attainable? Unless the first can be answered affirmatively, a positive answer to the second can scarcely justify, or serve as the criterion for, the rearrangement of a text. In addition, the critic ought to be able to give a plausible suggestion to account for the present disrupted order. The categories involved in both the argument against the old order and that in favor of the new must also be appropriate to the text in question. The categories Bultmann employs in the criticism

---

98. Bultmann indicates that there would be some justification for removing 8:21–29 from its present position to a place immediately following 7:31–36, where these additional words of Jesus would supply what he feels is a deficiency and would afford a better motivation for the words of the servants in 7:46. He does not make this transposition, however; 8:21–29 will serve better as a section in the discourse on light which begins with 8:12 (ibid., p. 216 n. 4).

and rearrangement of the order of chapter 7 and the material related to it are, first, chronological succession and, second, cause and effect.

The present succession of 7:31–36, 37–44, and 45–52 is supposed to create a difficulty because it separates by several days the dispatch (verse 32) and return (verse 45) of the servants of the high priest and Pharisees. One should ask whether, in fact, the dispatch and return must be understood as having been separated by several days, whether the evangelist had temporal sequence in mind at all when he reported this matter, and, if he did, whether it presents as great a difficulty as Bultmann thinks. It may be that verses 37–44 were placed before the return of the servants so that it could be viewed by the reader of the gospel in the light of a more complete account of the words of Jesus on that occasion and in the light of an account of the discussion with and about him, without consideration as to whether their return took place on the same day as the action of verses 31–36 or on the last day, after the action of verses 37–44. Moreover, even if one assumes that the evangelist was aware of chronology, it is not difficult to conceive of agents being sent out on the first day of a feast with orders to arrest Jesus at the opportune moment (7:45). They would *not* have reported back until the last day had they been unsuccessful, as they were, in arresting him.

Bultmann justifies the placing of 8:48–50, 54, 55 between 7:29 and 30 through two factors, the alleged difficulty in the present context and the necessity of supplying a better motivation for the attempt by Jesus' opponents to seize him in verse 30. Looking at 7:28–30 alone, however, one sees no compelling reason for making such an interpolation. The verses make perfectly good sense as they stand. It is hazardously subjective for a modern exegete to propose rearrangements of material in order to improve the causal sequence, which is what Bultmann is doing here. One can argue that there is already ample cause in verses 28 f. for the outbreak of violence against Jesus reported in verse 30, and, even if there is not, the hostility of the Jews has already been well established. At any rate, one has no criterion for what would constitute efficient causality in the immediate context.[99] We must beware of imputing a modern mode of thought to the evangelist and of creating a difficulty thereby. That the scene is relatively brief and limited in content is scarcely an argument for supplementing the text. Moreover, it is not so brief and limited in content if one allows 7:15–24 to stand in its

99. It must be remembered, also, that we are dealing here with what is presumably—and particularly in Bultmann's terms—an author's composition rather than historical fact. While it may be true that, if a question of historical probability with respect to an actual event had been involved, more provocation than that which 7:28 f. describes would have been necessary to motivate verse 30 properly, the question of what might have been sufficient to motivate an actual uprising against Jesus is here beside the point.

present position and does not, with Bultmann, remove it to another context!

That 7:31–36 has no formal conclusion is not an overpowering argument against leaving it in its present position, since there are other pericopes without such conclusions. In these cases, however, Bultmann often conjectures, as he does here, that there has been a displacement and moves the passages to other contexts or begins looking for the proper conclusions.[100] That Jesus continues his discourse without perturbation in 7:33, as if the outburst of verse 30 had never taken place, is hardly out of keeping with the thought of the evangelist, for whom nothing in the human sphere stands in the way of Jesus' execution of his mission.

Since the traditional order of chapter 7 is quite intelligible, there is no need to make a critical examination of Bultmann's reconstruction. The reconstruction is unnecessary.[101]

Chapters 8, 9, and 10 [102]

All semblance of the traditional order in chapters 6, 7, and 8 has now disappeared. As a consequence of the rearrangements already discussed, further rearrangements are not only possible but necessary. The passages 8:13–20, 30–40, 48–50, and 54–55 have been removed from their traditional places, and, if chapter 8 were not, as Bultmann supposes, a collection of fragments to begin with, it certainly is at this point in the analysis.

No consideration is given to 7:53–8:11, since "the textual tradition shows it did not belong to the Gospel of John either in its original or in its churchly, redacted form." [103] In 10:19–21 Bultmann finds a clue which indicates to him a further extensive disruption of the original order. Impossible in its present place, 10:19–21 must have originally formed the conclusion of a complex which included the story of the healing of a blind man and a speech of Jesus. What is more, the discourse about the Good Shepherd (10:1–18) cannot be understood as the continuation of, or as following from, the story of the healing of the blind man in chapter 9. The passage 10:22–39 is not the continuation of verses 1–18 but the beginning of some new section or complex. The verses 10:27 ff. contain the same shepherd-sheep imagery as in 10:1–18

100. The example closest to hand is 7:15–24, which, according to Bultmann, can scarcely end the complex of chapter 5 since it has no conclusion (above, p. 131 and *Johannes*, p. 178). A section with a proper conclusion is then found in 8:13–20. (Note also 6:60–71.)

101. Barrett notes Bultmann's rearrangement of chapter 7 and comments that it is only justifiable if the material is unintelligible as it stands (*St. John*, p. 273). For a defense of the traditional order against Bultmann's rearrangements, I again cite an article by Schneider, *ZNW, 45* (1954), 108–19.

102. Bultmann, *Johannes*, pp. 236 ff.

103. Ibid., p. 236 n. 2.

and cannot, as in the traditional order, be separated from it. This separation is not merely a matter of a few lines of text but, in view of the interposition of a new date in 10:22, involves a temporal separation of several days or even weeks, since, if the present order of 10:1–18 following immediately upon chapter 9 is maintained, 10:1–18 must be assumed to be a speech of Jesus on the occasion of the event reported in chapter 9, while all that follows verse 22 must have occurred later. Actually, 10:1–18 belongs in the scene beginning with verses 22 ff. and stands somewhere after it. Bultmann decides that it is best inserted after verse 26. Before he can go farther, he must find the original place of the detached conclusion of 10:19–21.

The miraculous healing of a blind man which is referred to in 10:21 is to be found in chapter 9, but 10:19–21 cannot follow directly upon chapter 9, since it presupposes a longer speech or discussion than the brief encounter reported in 9:39–41. What is to be placed between? The clue is found in 9:39–41, which Bultmann thinks was originally a transition from the preceding miracle story to a discourse of Jesus on the theme of light. Light per se is not mentioned in 9:39–41, but seeing is. There is also the mention of "day" in contrast with "night" in 9:4, which is construed as an allusion to light. But where is the discourse about light? It can be found in no one place, but has been broken up, and fragments of it are scattered through the extant text of the Fourth Gospel. Bultmann finds the beginning of the Lichtrede in 8:12, which has no connection with 7:52 or with what follows, for 8:13–20 is not the continuation of 8:12, and it could scarcely be, since it has already been placed in another context (as the conclusion of the complex of chapter 5). It could not be part of the Lichtrede, because it already contains a concluding formulation in verse 20 while the conclusion of the Lichtrede is to be found in 10:19–21, which, although out of place in its traditional position, fits into this new situation admirably. The passage 12:44–50 is identified as a "situationless segment," apparently a separated fragment of the Lichtrede which originally followed 8:12. Bultmann is so confident of this transposition that he forgoes any attempt to interpret 12:44–50 in its present context.

Next, 8:21–29, which admittedly is not prima facie recognizable as a section from the Lichtrede—neither φῶς nor any of its related forms occurs in it—is brought under consideration, together with 12:34–36. The passage 12:34–36 is declared to be out of place and is said to have been attracted to its traditional position only because it contains the word ὑψοῦν, which also occurs in 12:32. But it does not fit there, since the question of the crowd in verse 34 presupposes that Jesus has already spoken in the third person of the "lifting up" of the Son of Man, whereas he actually speaks of his own ὑψοῦν in the first person in the immediate context (12:32).[104] Indicating his agreement with E. Hirsch, Bultmann attaches 12:34–36 to 8:28 f., where Jesus speaks of the "lifting up" (ὑψοῦν) of the Son of Man in the third person. Establishing the connection between these two segments is the first step in assigning them both to the Lichtrede. Because 12:34–36 contains ample references to φῶς, the temporary embarrassment occasioned by the complete lack of that term, or even of the idea, in 8:21–29 is overcome. Since 10:19–21 follows 12:34–36 well and makes a good conclusion for the entire complex, there is no need to look further for material for the Lichtrede. The order of the entire complex is 9:1–41, 8:12, 12:44–50, 8:21–29, 12:34–36, and 10:19–21. The shepherd discourse then immediately follows.

Having further riddled chapter 8 in the reconstruction of this complex, Bultmann turns to the task of disposing of the remaining fragments. He begins at the end, which is virtually all that is left and, as he says, tries to pick up a thread and trace it backward. In 8:48–59 two themes are discerned which have no organic or original relationship: the δόξα of Jesus (verses 48–50, 54–55) and Jesus and Abraham (verses 51–53, 56–59). As verse 54 joins 50 well, so 56 joins 53. Apparently verses 48–50 and 51–53 have been placed together by the redactor because of the use of δαιμόνιον ἔχεις. Verses 54–55 could then be placed next because 54 seems to continue 53. Verses 56–59 were then added mechanically because of the mention of Abraham. Verses 51–53 and 56–59 form the close of a discussion into which the other verses have been erroneously interpolated from another context. All of this is further justification for placing 8:48–50, 54–55 between 7:29 and 30.[105]

Now, 8:30–47 falls into two parts, 8:30–40 and 8:41–47. In the former the question is whether the Jews are truly children of Abraham, and in the latter whether they are children of God. Because these are related themes, the redactor placed the two sections together here; but they are not integrally related. The conjunction of verses 40 and 41 is very harsh, and the theme of ἐλευθερία found in the section on kinship to Abraham is not continued in verses 41–47, where the dominant antithesis is not ἐλεύθερος-δοῦλος but ἀλήθεια-ψεῦδος.[106] Verses 30–40 are directed to those who have heard the words of Jesus and

104. Bultmann heads off a possible objection by pointing out that although Jesus does speak of the Son of Man in the third person in verse 23, this has no bearing on the question at issue, since it is too far removed from the immediate context and says nothing at all about the ὑψωθῆναι of the Son of Man. Only his δοξασθῆναι is spoken of.

105. See above, p. 153 for the justification of this transposition from the standpoint of 7:29, 30.

106. Although the concepts of ἀλήθεια and ἐλευθερία actually belong together, as verse 32 shows, "ein ursprünglicher literarischer Zusammenhang wird aber durch die sachliche Zusammengehörigkeit nicht bewiesen" (Bultmann, *Johannes*, p. 238.)!

have believed (although with a false faith), while verses 41–47 are directed to those who have not believed at all. Different motivations are at work in the two passages. The accusation in verses 41–47 that the Jews are children of Satan and the impugning of their claim to be children of God indicate the basis of their unbelief (verses 46 f.), while in verses 30–40 the indirect accusation of kinship with the devil and the contesting of their claim to be children of Abraham are the basis of the assertion that Jesus' word leads to freedom. Bultmann places 8:41–47 immediately before the conclusion, which he has found in 8:51–53, 56–59. Verse 51 is said to follow very well after verse 47. In both sections the same polemical tone is dominant. The removal of 8:30–40 from this context to its new position with 6:60–71, between chapters 12 and 13—a rearrangement previously proposed [107]—now receives further justification.

Although Bultmann has now determined to his own satisfaction that 8:41–47, 51–53, and 56–59 belong together and in that order, the section preceding them has not been located. It would not be surprising in view of the destruction of the original text if parts of it have become lost. The loss of portions of the text may be confirmed by pairing off the formalized concluding and introductory passages. This reveals that there are more conclusions than introductions (6:71 and 8:59, which are conclusions, have no corresponding introductions). The verses of 8:41–47, 51–53, and 56–59 seem to be a fragment which, since it has a conclusion and no introduction, should follow a break in the text. Presumably the passage follows the discernible break after 7:52, which is apparently the result of a textual loss. The lost section preceding 8:41 probably had to do with the theme of ἔργα, judging from the content of verses 41 ff. If this is the case, 6:28 f. may very well be a fragment from this lost section of text.

In support of his reconstruction, Bultmann points to the similarity of the structure of his complex to that of the complex of chapter 5, which is also to some extent his construction. In both there is a healing miracle leading to a discussion between Jesus and his opponents which involves the man just healed. In both cases the complex concludes with a long discourse of Jesus.[108] That 12:44 ff. should follow 8:12 is supported by Bultmann's theory of the structure and order of the Offenbarungsreden. The ἐγώ εἰμι . . . saying of 8:12 appropriately precedes the ὁ πιστεύων . . . of 12:44, as, in the source, the self-predication of the revealer must precede the promise to the believer. Thus, the original order of the source as well as of the gospel is restored.[109]

107. Ibid., p. 215.
108. Ibid., p. 249.
109. Ibid., p. 262 n. 1.

The passage 8:25–28 presents a problem. There is a digression between the question of verse 25 and Jesus' answer in verse 28.[110] Verses 26 f. are therefore taken to be a misplaced fragment which the redactor placed in this position because of the occurrence of ταῦτα λαλῶ. In verse 26 the adversative ἀλλά and the clause which follows give the entire verse the improbable meaning that Jesus had many things to say and to judge but that he would forgo these things in order to say to the world what he had heard from the Father. Elsewhere, if Jesus speaks and judges at all, he conveys what he has heard from the Father. Only if the assertion that Jesus did not speak of himself (i.e. from his own resources and authority) had preceded the ἀλλά-clause would verse 26 have had the proper sense. As things now stand, it yields the somewhat perplexing meaning which we have indicated. Also, the evangelist's comment (verse 27) that the Jews did not know that Jesus spoke of the Father ("He who sent me," verse 26) is not to the point, and while in verses 26 f. the possibility of falsely understanding someone other than the Father to be "He who sent me" is presupposed, in verses 28 f. their identity is assumed. As to the original location of verses 26 f., Bultmann conjectures that perhaps the passage could have been somehow connected with 8:13–20. Here, as in the case of 6:28 f., we have a fragment for which Bultmann finds no definite place in his reconstruction of the text. Although Bultmann insists upon the removal of verses 26 f. from this context, he acknowledges that the problem of the text at this point is not thereby completely solved. The transition from verse 25 to verse 28 is still not easy. The difficulty lies in Jesus' reply to the question "Who are you?" (verse 25b), τὴν ἀρχὴν ὅτι καὶ λαλῶ ὑμῖν, which Bultmann, after surveying the possibilities of translation, decides is textually corrupt. (Bodmer Papyrus II or p66 reads ειπον υμιν την αρχην οτι και λαλω υμιν, but Bodmer XV or p75 has the same more difficult reading as the rest of the manuscripts; so the new textual evidence probably does not take us beyond Bultmann's *non liquet*.) That may be the problem of the whole section (verses 25–28). If so, it would obviate the necessity of explaining 8:26 f. as a fragment that has fallen out of the text somewhere else and fallen in here. At any rate, the intrinsic difficulty of verse 26 would not be solved by moving it to another place.

In the rearrangements under consideration, much depends on the judgment that chapter 8 is a collection of fragments. Whether or not the judgment is correct is a question with important implications for Bultmann's entire theory.

It is significant that the fragments of this chapter present their own pe-

110. For Bultmann's discussion of this problem, ibid., pp. 266–67.

culiar problems when Bultmann removes them to other contexts. Verse 8:12 becomes the opening, thematic statement of the Lichtrede ("I am the light of the world") and is placed immediately after 9:1–41. Aside from the difficulty of imagining how a fragment so small as to contain only 8:12 became detached from its original position, its proposed relation to 9:39–41 is not beyond question, for the theme of the latter is "seeing" rather than light. Bultmann himself admits that 8:12 does not fit badly with 8:13 ff. If one objects that 8:12 does not take up where 7:52 leaves off, it may be replied that even after he has made all his rearrangements Bultmann must conjecture that there has been an irrecoverable textual loss after 7:52, so that even on his terms the problem of what should follow 7:52 remains unsolved.

Bultmann has placed 8:13–20 as the conclusion after 4:43–54; 6; 5; and 7:15–24, because its themes, μαρτυρία and κρίσις, are apropos and because 8:20 is an appropriate concluding statement. The passage 8:21–29 has been removed from its present position and placed in the Lichtrede on the strength of its supposed relationship to 12:34–36, which is also removed to the Lichtrede. There is, however, nothing about light in 8:21–29. Furthermore, it is doubtful that 12:34–36 ought to be removed from its traditional place in the text in order to be placed after 8:21–29 (cf. the saying about the raising up of the Son of Man in verse 28). In 12:34 the crowd asks πῶς λέγεις σὺ ὅτι δεῖ ὑψωθῆναι τὸν υἱὸν τοῦ ἀνθρώπου; but in 8:28 nothing is said of the necessity of the lifting up of the Son of Man. This, however, is precisely the theme of 12:22 ff., which therefore forms the appropriate basis for the question about the necessity of the raising up of the Son of Man in 12:34. (That verse 34 has ὑψοῦν while verse 23 has δοξάζειν is no objection; they both refer to the crucifixion.) Bultmann foresees this criticism of his rearrangement and rejects it, claiming that in 12:34 the evangelist has merely taken a Christian confessional formula (δεῖ ὑψωθῆναι τὸν υἱὸν τοῦ ἀνθρώπου) and placed it in the mouth of Jesus' opponents.[111] He regards the absence of any mention of the Son of Man in the immediately preceding verses as a sufficiently weighty objection to the present order to warrant its abandonment. But is not the better explanation that the order of the extant manuscripts is the evangelist's and that he has in 12:34 introduced the term "Son of Man," which both he and his readers know means Jesus and which has just been used in verse 23, on the lips of Jesus' opponents? Is it not somewhat pedantic to insist that the term "Son of Man" must have been used by Jesus just previously if his opponents are to employ it in verse 34? Is the evangelist describing a historical encounter in which it would be necessary for the interlocutors to take their cue

111. *Johannes*, p. 269 n. 7.

from the phrase which had already been used?[112] It is clear to the evangelist and to the perceptive reader that 12:22–32 concerns the necessity of the exaltation of Jesus, and the *evangelist* certainly knows that it is precisely as Son of Man that Jesus is exalted. (The crowd shows its characteristic ignorance by asking not only why Jesus says the Son of Man must be lifted up, but also, "Who is this Son of Man?"[113]) What the evangelist knows, what he assumes his readers know, or what he intends to convey is more important for interpretation than what, by the canons of narrative prose, one supposes he should have permitted his dramatis personae to know. In all probability the evangelist was not half so clever as Bultmann in noting what the interlocutors would have already known and what they would have occasion to ask on the basis of a dialogue just transpired. As Bultmann himself makes clear elsewhere, the evangelist cannot be understood primarily as a dramatist.[114]

Bultmann concedes that 8:21–29 is not immediately recognizable as the continuation of 12:44–50, which it follows in his reconstructed Lichtrede.[115] In fact, the connection is no more obvious than that between 8:12–20 and 8:21–29, but 8:13–20 has already been removed to another context. Thus, the connection of 8:21–29 with the section which precedes it in Bultmann's order (12:44–50) as well as the section which follows it (12:34–36) is subject to some doubt. New problems are generated when 8:21–29 is removed from its present position to a new one.

We have already observed the difficulties involved in the transposition of 8:30–40 in combination with 6:60–71 to a position near the end of the first major portion of the gospel. There is also substantial reason for maintaining the connection between 8:30–40 and 8:41 ff. As Becker has pointed out, the

112. The evangelist does not introduce the term out of the blue, so to speak, since it has already been used in verse 23. Even if the αὐτοῖς of verse 23 are Philip and Andrew, verse 29 probably indicates that the crowd (the same crowd as in verse 34) has heard Jesus' entire discourse.

113. The question τίς ἐστιν οὗτος ὁ υἱὸς τοῦ ἀνθρώπου; (verse 34) presents a difficulty, since, if the crowd has asked about the lifting up of the Son of Man just previously (verse 34a) in a question that can only refer to Jesus (cf. verse 32), how can they now ask, "Who is this Son of Man?" as if they did not know that Jesus is the Son of Man? Presumably the question has to do with the role and office of Son of Man, not with his identity. "Son of Man" is set against "Christ," (verse 34). The crowd is familiar with doctrines and speculations about the Messiah, but "who is this Son of Man?" Had the crowd been seeking identification, it would have more likely asked, "Who is the Son of Man?" If this question means, "What person is the Son of Man?" it is as inappropriate after 8:28 as it is after 12:32; in 8:28 Jesus says, "When you have lifted up the Son of Man, then you will know that ἐγώ εἰμι."

114. *ET*, 4 (1937), 128.

115. *Johannes*, p. 264: "Dass der Evglist Jesus dieses Wort in der Folge auf 12:44–50 sprechen lässt, könnte zunächst als unmotiviert erscheinen."

theme of sonship to Abraham occurs throughout the section 8:30–59, and its juxtaposition with the theme of sonship to the devil gives no ground for literary separations.[116] While it is to be admitted that 8:48–59 presents an alternation of motifs, the passage is not incoherent. For example, the word of Jesus in verse 51 is an interjection which does not evolve directly out of the preceding discussion, but this does not necessarily mean that it has its original position elsewhere. Jesus here injects a new thought into the discussion, seemingly breaking the connection but also introducing a point which must be made or reiterated. On the other hand, verse 54 follows verse 53 well enough, as Bultmann himself points out, and this connection offers little occasion for rearrangement. The contention that 8:56–59 was added mechanically because of the Abraham theme does not in itself prove that it does not come from the evangelist, who might have been perfectly capable of making such a connection. After the removal of 8:48–50 and 54–55, 8:41–47 and 8:51–53, 56–59 join together well enough, but this in itself does not justify the rearrangements. Against the rearrangements which Bultmann makes in connection with the fragmentation and dispersal of chapter 8, we may assert his own dictum: "An original literary connection is not proved through a relationship of content."[117]

When Bultmann assembles the remains of chapter 8 (verses 41–47, 51–53, 56–59) he finds that there is no reason to suppose that the complex of which these verses form the conclusion did not originally stand immediately before chapter 9, but he can find no trace of the rest of this complex—unless 6:28 f. is a fragment of it—and must suppose that there has been a textual loss between 7:52 and 8:41. The theory of textual loss is not necessarily an arbitrary device, although it is perhaps significant that this is not the only point at which Bultmann is forced to speculate about such a possibility in connection with his rearrangements. It is indicative of the difficulty chapter 8 gives Bultmann—it is a difficult chapter in any case—that despite his redistribution of it he cannot avoid proposing such a loss. He has not been able to improve on the already poor connection between chapters 7 and 8. (If the gap between 7:52 and 8:12 must be regarded as intolerable, one could simply suppose that there has been a textual loss, without resorting to any rearrangements at all.) If chapter 8 is retained intact, it may be considered a possible, if awkward, continuation or summary of the utterances of Jesus on the occasion of the feast of chapter 7.[118] Chapter 8 may be a collection of

116. *Reden*, pp. 115 f.

117. *Johannes*, p. 238. Bultmann enunciates this principle, however, in rejecting the original connection of two passages standing side by side in the text!

118. Dodd, *Interpretation*, pp. 347–48.

Jesus' discourses which the evangelist set forth at this point to illustrate further the preaching of Jesus and the growing opposition to him.[119] It is perhaps not insignificant that the threefold structure discerned by J. Schneider in the discourses of the gospel is also found in chapter 8 (8:12–20, 21–30, 30–59).[120] If chapter 8 can be understood as a unity stemming from the evangelist, Bultmann's theory of rearrangement has been dealt a severe blow, since the fragments which he takes from this chapter are indispensable for his reconstruction of other parts of the gospel.

10:1–39 [121]

According to Bultmann, the shepherd discourse of chapter 10 has its introduction in 10:22–25(26) and its concluding scene in 10:31–39.[122] The metaphorical reference to sheep in verse 26 leads smoothly into the discourse about the Good Shepherd, confirming this reconstruction.[123] The passage 10:27–30 is identified as the conclusion of the discourse proper. Jesus' claim that he and the Father are one (verse 30) affords the motivation of the Jews' desire to stone him in 10:31. The restoration of the original order is not to be attained, however, by simply inserting 10:1–18 between verses 26 and 27, for verse 1 will not fit well after verse 26, or verse 27 after verse 18. Verses 1–18 fall into separate sections which must be rearranged. Verse 6 is taken to be the conclusion of the παροιμία (verses 1–5), of which it speaks. The point of this παροιμία is the antithesis between the Good Shepherd and the thieves and robbers. This antithesis becomes clear in that the Good Shepherd goes into the fold through the door, while the thief takes another, and illegitimate, way. Insofar as 10:1–5 deals with the person of Jesus, it presents him as the one whom the sheep follow as their rightful shepherd. Bultmann recognizes that the identification of Jesus with the Good Shepherd is not made explicit, but he attributes this to the fact that we are here dealing with a "pure parabolic image."

In 10:7–10 we have another parable or allegory, in which Jesus appears in the image of the door (verses 7, 9). But in verses 8 and 10 there is again

---

119. 8:12–20 contains a denial of Jesus' claims on the part of his opponents and his own refutation of the denial. 8:21–30 represents the opponents as standing perplexed before Jesus. In 8:31–59 their opposition crystallizes so that they finally take up stones against him. In 8:59 Jesus hides himself and comes out of the Temple—not an unfitting conclusion of the scene which begins in chapter 7.

120. See above, n. 119 and p. 150 n. 91.

121. *Johannes*, pp. 272 ff.

122. See above, pp. 155 f.

123. Compare the similar technique of the evangelist in 6:27 and 9:39–41. The latter example depends, of course, on Bultmann's reconstruction of the textual order.

the opposition between the Good Shepherd and the thieves and robbers that we found in verses 1–5. Apparently verses 7 and 9 confuse the imagery, since Jesus cannot at the same time be the door and the shepherd. Bultmann thinks this discrepancy is not to be explained by displacement but arises out of the evangelist's method of annotating his source. Verses 7 and 9 are glosses of the evangelist on the Offenbarungsreden source, which, in verses 8 and 10, continue the image of verses 1–5.

In 10:11 Bultmann discerns what he takes to be the beginning of another new section in Jesus' declaration, "I am the Good (καλός) Shepherd" (10:11). Jesus appears as the Good Shepherd over against the "hireling," and neither the door nor the thieves and robbers plays a role. Like verses 1–5, verses 11–13 are said to have the character of a pure parable or figure, apart from the initial clause that makes the reference to Jesus explicit. This clause (verse 11) is an appropriate beginning for the discourse proper. In addition, verses 11–13 fit very well after the opening scene (verses 22–26) and form a fitting response to the demand in verse 24, "If you are the Christ, tell us plainly." Jesus does not in fact tell them plainly but, employing the image of the Good Shepherd, he speaks to them in figurative language (verses 11–13). Since verses 1–5 continue this parabolic or allegorical description of the Good Shepherd, it may be proposed that this section originally followed verses 11–13.

In verse 14 we have again a new beginning with the repetition of the ἐγώ εἰμι. But Bultmann finds that verses 14–18 are not a unity; no parable follows the ἐγώ εἰμι of verse 14, and no imagery is used to describe the relation between Jesus and his own. The idea of sheep knowing the shepherd and vice versa in verses 14 f. recalls verses 1–5, where the sheep hear and know the master's voice. The last clause of verse 15 initiates another motif, that of the shepherd laying down his life for his sheep, which recalls verses 11–13. This motif is developed in verses 17 f. [124] Since verses 14–18 take up the motifs of both parables, the verses may be placed after the parables and understood as a sort of editorial explanation of them. According to Bultmann, the following order is original with the evangelist: 10:22–26, 11–13, 1–10, 14–18, 27–39.

Given Bultmann's order and the interpretation based upon it, we can bring no compelling objections to his rearrangement of chapter 10. But

124. In verse 16 there appears a completely new and strange idea, that of the one shepherd and one flock. According to Bultmann this interest in ecclesiastical unity betrays the hand of the redactor (*Johannes*, p. 292).

while commentators have found difficulties in this chapter as it appears in all manuscripts and have disagreed on its interpretation, they have not been confounded by it. Its present form may be difficult, but it is not impossible.[125] In opposition to Bultmann, Schneider has attempted with some success to show that chapter 10 already has an intelligible structure and makes perfectly good sense.[126] Such rearrangements as Bultmann's presuppose a certain understanding of the evangelist's processes of thought and his method of composition, but this does not necessarily mean that they may be dismissed as arbitrary. There are, however, many dangers inherent in Bultmann's procedure of moving from a thoroughly assured grasp of the evangelist's mind and method—which after all can only be derived from this text—to a reconstruction of the textual order. This procedure is nowhere more evident than in chapter 10, where the discoveries of what appear to be a misplaced introduction (10:22–26), the proper beginning of a discourse (10:11 ff.), the conclusion of a discourse (10:27–30), and a concluding scene (10:31–39) form the basis for the confident rearrangement of the text.

Aside from this general consideration, several specific objections to Bultmann's order ought to be noted. There is between verses 26 and 11 an abrupt shift from the mention of sheep to the idea of the Good Shepherd. Sheep and shepherd are related thoughts, but here the jump from one to the other is rather sudden and without preparation. One would expect more to be said of sheep before attention focuses on shepherd. Between verses 18 and 27 there is a more serious break; Jesus' attention turns suddenly and inexplicably from his own laying down of his life to the sheep. Also, if Bultmann's order is followed, the demand of the Jews (verse 24), εἶπον ἡμῖν παρρησίᾳ, precedes the παροιμία of verses 1–5 and 11–13. This is not unthinkable, but would it not be better if the demand that Jesus speak plainly followed rather than preceded the παροιμία, as in the traditional order? In commenting on 10:24, Bultmann says that all preceding revelations of Jesus had been παροιμίαι

125. Among recent interpretations, note especially Paul W. Meyer, *JBL*, 75 (1956), 232–35. He declares: "The exegetical analyst has a right, and even a certain obligation, to adopt as a working hypothesis, until the text forces him to abandon it, the view that a passage under consideration possesses literary unity and integrity. Difficulties in the thought of a text which does not otherwise present irregularities of style, vocabulary and syntax ought not to be taken as reason for at once abandoning this hypothesis, but should occasion first of all a re-examination of the author's arguments and possible intentions" (p. 232).

126. *Coniectanea Neotestamentica XI*, pp. 220–25. Schneider's fundamental contention is that 10:1–5 is a Bildrede which is basic for the rest of the discussion and cannot be placed in another position. There are three thematic words in this Bildrede, each of which comes up for further treatment in the course of the discussion: θύρα (verses 7–10), ποιμήν (verses 11–18), and πρόβατα (verses 27–30).

for the Jews and thus recognizes the relationship of παροιμία and παρρησία (cf. 16:25 ff.).[127] But only the discourse of 10:1–5 is explicitly called a παροιμία (10:6). The word does not occur earlier in the gospel either in reference to the revelation of Jesus or anything else. Moreover, in Bultmann's order, the speech about the Good Shepherd laying down his life for his sheep comes at the very beginning of the discourse. Would it not be more appropriate at a later and climactic point, as in the traditional order?

These objections to Bultmann's reconstruction may not be as numerous or as serious as those which he brings against the present order. The point is, however, that the same kind of questions and criticisms can be raised against his reconstruction. The reason for this may well be the nature of the material itself, which resists the effort to order it in what appears to us to be a more natural sequence. Even when rearrangements are skillfully executed, typically Johannine perplexities nevertheless appear.

10:40–12:33, 8:30–40, 6:60–71 [128]

Since parts of chapter 12 have already been placed elsewhere and 8:30–40 and 6:60–71 have been provisionally assigned to the conclusion of the first major part of the gospel, the rearrangements in this section are in part already determined. This portion of the gospel centers around two events, the raising of Lazarus and the final entry of Jesus into Jerusalem, which Bultmann allows to remain in this order. His analysis begins with the observation that 12:20–50 does not appear to be in its original form. The passage 12:37–43, with its backward glance over the whole public ministry of Jesus and succinct summary of its result (verse 37: οὐκ ἐπίστευον εἰς αὐτόν), is recognizably the close of the whole first part of the gospel (chapter 3–12). The passages 12:34–36 and 44–50 are separated fragments, which have already been restored to their original place in the Lichtrede. When these sections are removed, it is questionable whether 12:33 forms the original conclusion of the complex that precedes 12:37–43. Bultmann has already assigned 8:30–40 and 6:60–71 to the end of the first part of the gospel (between 12:33 and 12:37) where it would become the conclusion of this complex.[129] Even with this done, one still may suspect that there is something missing between 12:33 and 12:37, but Bultmann nevertheless cautiously proceeds to interpret the reconstructed complex as it stands.

---

127. *Johannes*, p. 275.

128. For Bultmann's discussion, upon which my assertions are based, *Johannes*, pp. 298 f. and especially p. 321.

129. See above, pp. 139–41. The formulation πεπιστεύκαμεν καὶ ἐγνώκαμεν in 6:69 is taken as support for the proposed sequence of 8:30–40; 6:60–71 (*Johannes*, p. 344 n. 1).

The difficulties in 12:20–33 may be solved by insight into the manner in which the evangelist employed his sources and without recourse to the rearrangement of the text. There still remains, however, the problem of 12:20–22. The Greeks come to Philip seeking Jesus; Philip goes to Andrew, and together they go to Jesus. From this point on Philip, Andrew, and the Greeks disappear completely, and Jesus does not seem to take cognizance of the incident in any way (cf. verses 23 ff.). Bultmann admits it is possible that a section has fallen out here and been lost, since not only is there no direct answer to the request of the Greeks but, whereas in verse 29 the crowd seems to be standing in direct contact with Jesus, in verses 20–22 the Greeks have to approach him through the disciples, which implies that they are not in a position to address him directly. Yet Bultmann attempts to interpret the entire passage (12:20–33) as it stands and assumes that the evangelist either used a source-fragment in verses 20–22 or that he composed the incident himself, but that, in any case, he used it deliberately as the introduction to what follows. In support of this position, Bultmann suggests that if one takes verses 20–26 as a unity, the question concerning access to Jesus is dealt with by referring whoever asks for the historical Jesus to the Exalted One.[130]

Inasmuch as Bultmann is here only drawing out the implications of re-arrangements already proposed and upon which I have already commented, it is not necessary to dwell at length on this section. His reconstruction of the complex of chapter 12 (as the conclusion of the first half of the gospel) is not noticeably superior to chapter 12 in its present form. Is not this reconstruction really the inevitable consequence of his treatment of chapters 6 and 8 and his reconstruction of the Lichtrede? The former involves the removal of 8:30–40 and 6:60–71 from their usual positions and finding a new place for them. Chapter 12, already decimated by the removal of verses 34–36 and 44–50 to the Lichtrede, becomes the likeliest general location, since it forms the end of the first half of the gospel, and 8:30–40 and 6:60–71 are best qualified for a position here because of their thematic and theological content. Nevertheless, they do not connect very well with 12:1–33, and this prompts Bultmann himself to suggest the possibility of a textual loss. If we assume Bultmann's order, the transition from 6:71 to 12:37 is questionable. The section 6:60–71 ends with the confession of Peter on behalf of the Twelve and Jesus' prophecy of Judas' betrayal. If 12:37 ff. follows, it seems to describe the Twelve as unbelievers. This may be true in a sense, but it

---

130. Ibid., p. 326. "Wer nach dem Zugang zum historischen Jesus fragt, wird auf dem Weg zum Erhöhten gewiesen."

does not take account of Peter's genuine confession and does not fit well after it. Moreover, 12:37 ff. seems to apply to the Jews (cf. verse 42) rather than to the Twelve, as does 8:30–40. This inconsistency is most confusing and doubtfully original. Moreover, if 12:34–36, 12:44–50, and 6:60–71 are retained in their respective places, Bultmann's somewhat unsatisfactory reconstruction of the complex of chapter 12 becomes unnecessary. Chapter 12 retained intact forms an appropriate conclusion from the first half of the gospel and does not need to be supplemented by 8:30–40 and 6:60–71, even if—as I scarcely believe—it is necessary to remove those sections from their contexts.

13:1–17:26 [131]

The question about the textual order of chapters 13–17 arises from the observation that 14:25–31 is almost certainly the conclusion of the farewell discourses, as is shown by the following considerations: (1) the ταῦτα λελάληκα ὑμῖν of 14:25 is distinguished from the same phrase in 16:1, 4, 25, and 33 by the addition of the παρ᾽ ὑμῖν μένων which brings under one head all that has preceded and indicates that the discourse is drawing to a close. (The πολλά of verse 30a, which gives leeway for further remarks of Jesus, is said to be an interpolation.[132]) (2) Verses 26–28 provide a brief concluding summary of what has preceded. (3) The εἰρήνην ἀφίημι ὑμῖν is a departing wish. (4) Verses 30 f. form a transition to the narrative of the arrest. The statement "For the ruler of the world is coming" (14:30) clearly anticipates the arrival upon the scene of Judas and those who are going to arrest Jesus (18:1 ff.), and the imperative "Arise, let us go hence" (14:31) expressly brings the discourses to an end, setting the stage for the unfolding of the passion story, which begins in 18:1. Therefore, chapter 14 is said to belong immediately before chapter 18.

But if one moves directly from 14:31 to chapter 18, chapters 15–17 are left without a setting, and there is the problem of finding a suitable place for them. That chapters 15–17 were spoken after the disciples had arisen and were on the way is, according to Bultmann, an absurd proposal unwarranted by anything in the text. There are then only two alternatives: either chapters 15–17 are a secondary addition or they now stand in the wrong place. The first possibility raises serious difficulties because of the fully Johannine character of these chapters. It is difficult to comprehend how a redactor who could have imitated the style and spirit of the evangelist so well would have introduced a redactional addition at such an awkward

131. *Johannes*, pp. 349–51.
132. Ibid., p. 487 n. 7.

place rather than, for example, between 14:24 and 25. For Bultmann, the only plausible solution is that these chapters are the composition of the evangelist but are now in the wrong place, a situation attributable partly to chance and partly to the embarrassed attempts of the redactor to bring a disordered text into order. If one asks why the redactor could not have found a better position for this long section (e.g. between 14:24 and 25), Bultmann can only answer that this question wrongly presupposes that the redactor worked as an independent editor. But the present state of the text is best understood as the result of an undertaking forced upon the redactor, like it or not, by the chaotic state in which he found the gospel.[133] Bultmann sets aside the view of some scholars that 13:31–14:31 and 15:1–16:33 are separate recensions of the farewell discourses (which were both composed by the evangelist, who for some reason left his work incomplete) on the ground that the two sections do not deal with the same themes and are not parallel.[134]

In spite of some uncertainty, an attempt to restore the original order must be made. Like not a few scholars before him, Bultmann places chapter 15 (in fact, 15:1–16:33) after 13:35. The passage 15:1–17 is then understood as a direct commentary on the commandment of love in 13:35. Also, 13:36 ff. forms a good continuation of 16:33, since by this rearrangement the traditional sequence (cf. Mark and Matthew) of the prophecy of the flight of the disciples followed by Peter's denial is restored.[135] The one difficulty in placing chapters 15 and 16 before chapter 14 is that the Paraclete appears to be introduced for the first time in 14:16 but, in the rearrangement, would already have been spoken of in 15:26, 16:7 ff., and 12 ff. For Bultmann this is not an insurmountable difficulty, because 14:16 did introduce the Paraclete sayings in the *Offenbarungsreden*,[136] but the evangelist has changed the original order of the sayings. Bultmann also argues that the theme of μικρόν ("a little while") is handled in 16:16 ff. so as to indicate that it should precede the mention of the same idea in 14:19, since in 16:16 ff. the idea is discussed and explained, while in 14:19 it is mentioned as some-

133. "Indessen ist die vorliegende Ordnung als Ergebnis einer wohl oder übel infolge des trümmerhaften Zustandes des Manuskriptes notwendigen Redaktion leichter verständlich denn als das Ergebnis einer selbständigen Bearbeitung, wie sie die erste Hypothese voraussetzt" (ibid., p. 350 n. 1).

134. Ibid., p. 350 (*Ergänzungsheft*).

135. According to Bultmann, 13:36 ("Lord, where are you going?") only appears to follow 13:33 ("where I go you are not able to come"). Actually the question "Where are you going?" (13:36) cannot precede Jesus' assertion that no one has asked him this question (16:5), but the redactor was misled by this seeming connection into placing 13:36 f. in its present position (ibid., p. 350 n. 3).

136. Ibid., p. 425 n. 4.

thing known and understood. There still remains the problem of placing
chapter 17, since chapter 14 must now immediately precede chapter 18.
Bultmann thinks that chapter 17 cannot be placed within the discourse proper
but must be given a new position at the beginning. It cannot be argued
that 17:8, a petition for those who have received the word which Jesus has
given them and know that he has come from God, presupposes the "confession" of the disciples in 16:30, since 17:8 is a general petition of the revealer
for the church which he leaves behind on earth and has no reference to a
specific event. One may suspect that chapter 17 originally preceded chapters
13–16. The turning point of the gospel, which occurs at the end of chapter 12,
would be fittingly marked by this prayer. It would afford a sort of pause
or interlude before the beginning of the passion drama.

The prayer anticipates the situation of the farewell discourses, in which
Jesus, as he turns homeward in his glory, takes leave of his own. Therefore
its most appropriate position, according to Bultmann, is after 13:30. This
indeed appears to be the correct and original position; the "Now is the
Son of Man glorified" of 13:31 fits exceedingly well immediately after the
prayer, indicating the fulfillment of the petition "Father . . . glorify thy
Son" (17:1). Jesus can now say to his own what he says in the subsequent
speeches as one who is already glorified. Indeed, the discourses may be
regarded as a commentary upon what has been said in the prayer. The
position of the prayer at the beginning of the discourses helps explain why
John omits the institution of the Lord's Supper. He substitutes the prayer
for it.

One may regard 13:31a, ὅτε οὖν ἐξῆλθεν, as having been originally intended
to introduce the prayer. The λέγει Ἰησοῦς (verse 31) is to be dropped as a
formulation of the redactor along with the ταῦτα ἐλάλησεν Ἰησοῦς of 17:1. So,
in moving from 13:31 to 17:1, one could read ὅτε οὖν ἐξῆλθεν Ἰησοῦς ἐπάρας τοὺς
ὀφθαλμοὺς . . . εἶπεν. But Bultmann finds a special introduction to the prayer
in 13:1–3, where the many corrections of the manuscripts and the controversy
of the exegetes confirm the impossibility of the present text. This introduction, which is actually composed of parts of 13:31a, 13:1, and 17:1, reads
as follows: ὅτε οὖν ἐξῆλθεν, εἰδὼς ὁ Ἰησοῦς ὅτι ἦλθεν αὐτοῦ ἡ ὥρα ἵνα μεταβῇ ἐκ τοῦ
κόσμου τούτου πρὸς τὸν πατέρα, ἀγαπήσας τοὺς ἰδίους τοὺς ἐν τῷ κόσμῳ εἰς τέλος, ἐγείρεται
ἐκ τοῦ δείπνου καὶ ἐπάρας τοὺς ὀφθαλμοὺς αὐτοῦ εἰς τὸν οὐρανὸν εἶπεν . . . In attempting
to restore the text to order, the redactor placed the central portion of the
introduction (now 13:1) at the beginning of the heavily edited section
13:1–3, where, according to Bultmann, it only introduces confusion.[137] While

137. The complex analysis (ibid., pp. 352 f.) by which Bultmann proves the impossibility
of 13:1–3 may be summarized as follows: "Before the feast of the Passover" (verse 1) is in-

apparently recognizing that his reconstruction must remain hypothetical, Bultmann insists that in any case the εἰδὼς ὁ Ἰησοῦς . . . κτλ of 13:1 is outstandingly suitable as an introduction for the prayer. In accord with the motifs of 13:1 the prayer is uttered in the hour of Jesus' departure as the proof of his love.

The following reconstruction of the entire complex is proposed by Bultmann and followed in the exposition of the text: 13:1–30 (the last meal of Jesus with his disciples), 17:1–26 (the departing prayer), and 13:31–35, 15–16:33, 13:36–14:31 (the farewell discourses).

Bultmann carefully points out how his rearrangement of the text is supported by theological and related considerations. In itself, 16:33 could be the end of the farewell discourses, as the redactor obviously believed. But 14:25–31 excludes this possibility. Leading so beautifully into the passion, it is obviously the original ending of the discourse. Moreover, 14:25 f. summarizes the promise of 16:12–15, and verse 27 the motifs of 15:18–16:7 and, above all, of 16:16–24.[138] There are other intrinsic reasons for placing 13:36–14:31 after chapter 16. The sections 13:31–35 and 15:1–16:33 deal with the unity of the disciples with Jesus in this world and this life, while 13:36–14:31 deals

tended to date only the εἰδώς, not the whole clause, since to date the statement "having loved his own . . . etc." would be senseless. To say this, however, does not solve the problem. The εἰδώς can scarcely be understood causally with the phrase "before the feast of the Passover" ("Since before the feast the Passover Jesus knew . . . "). But to regard the εἰδώς as simply temporal again results in a meaningless dating of Jesus' love for his disciples. To attempt to understand "before the feast" as a statement of date independent of the participle ("It was before the feast of the Passover") is possible but awkward. The εἰδώς of verse 1 is in form and function suspiciously like that of verse 3. Bultmann conjectures that the first εἰδώς-clause, with the rest of verse 1, is an interpolation. It is not, however, a redactional gloss but a fragment from the disrupted original text which the redactor has introduced at this point. It is the original introduction of chapter 17. This being the case, the ἠγάπησεν αὐτούς is secondary, since, if the εἰδώς clause originally followed the ὅτε οὖν ἐξῆλθεν of 13:31a, it would again be senselessly dated. Bultmann thinks that the εἰς τέλος originally belonged with the ἀγαπήσας τοὺς ἰδίους τοὺς ἐν τῷ κόσμῳ and that the statement ἐγείρεται ἐκ τοῦ δείπνου originally stood in place of the ἠγάπησεν. Since a statement about Jesus arising from the dinner occurs in verse 4, the redactor dropped it here when he placed 13:1 in its present position. He did not see that in reality he was producing a meaningless text. From verse 1, only the πρὸ δὲ τῆς ἑορτῆς τοῦ πάσχα is original, and, from verse 2, only the words καὶ δείπνου γινομένου. Both define the ἐγείρεται of verse 4 and precede verse 3 which is original and in the right place.

Although from the standpoint of form the redactor made an awkward arrangement in 13:1–3, Bultmann points out that he did not make a mistake by putting the ἀγάπη-motif here at the beginning of chapter 13, thus indicating its theme (ibid., p. 353 n. 1). Bultmann also cautions that one must not suppose that the formulation of 13:27–29 should be understood as a reference to verse 2, so that verse 2 would be proved an original part of the text (ibid., p. 353 n. 3).

138. Ibid., p. 485.

with the promise to the disciples that this unity is not limited to their earthly existence but encompasses the future that lies beyond it. It is obvious that the rearrangement of these sections of the farewell discourses produces a better structural and theological sequence, whose correctness is supported by the occurrence of the same succession of themes in the prayer of chapter 17.[139]

The reasons for placing 14:25–31 near the end of the discourse are indeed persuasive,[140] especially in view of the "Arise let us go hence" of 14:31, which, in the present order, is followed by two more chapters of dialogue and Jesus' prayer! Bultmann's rearrangement proposals, although not unprecedented, are in some respects unique. His removal of the prayer of Jesus to the beginning of the farewell discourses is, as far as I know, a fresh suggestion. It is certainly the most ingenious and probably the most questionable of the rearrangements he has proposed for this section and for that reason will serve as a focal point for our discussion.

The juggling of the text whereby Bultmann introduces chapter 17 between 13:31a and the rest of the verse—bringing in as the introduction of the prayer a conjecturally revised version of 13:1—is unwarranted. Had the redactor actually reconstructed 13:1–3 out of the misplaced introduction to the prayer plus a couple of phrases original in the context—as seems extremely unlikely—the task of recovering the original bits of the text would be virtually impossible. When Bultmann proposes such a rearrangement as this, he assumes an exceedingly heavy burden of proof. Admittedly the Greek of the passage is difficult, but its burden—the love of Jesus toward his disciples εἰς τέλος (the ambiguity may be intentional!) which was on this occasion made particularly clear—is not obscure.

Aside from this, there are several factors in favor of the position of Jesus' prayer at the end of the discourses. It is true that if the prayer preceded the discourses the latter could be regarded as a commentary upon it, but, assuming that the prayer follows, it can just as well be viewed as a summary and reiteration of the discourses' themes. While 17:6–8 may be regarded as the prayer of the revealer for his church apart from any particular historical situation (Bultmann), it nevertheless seems to me to presuppose the dis-

139. Ibid., p. 459; cf. 17:15 and 24.

140. Other scholars have suggested that rearrangements are necessary in the farewell discourses. Moffatt rearranges as follows: 13:1–13a, 15, 16, 13:31b–38, 14, 17. Macgregor: 13:1–35 (13:36–38), 15, 16, 14, 17. Bernard: 13:1–31a, 15, 16, 13:31b–38, 14, 17. F. W. Lewis: 13:1–32, 15, 16, 13:33–38, 14, 17 (Howard, *The Fourth Gospel*, p. 303). But the traditional order continues to have its defenders, e.g. Dodd, *Interpretation*, pp. 406–9; Barrett, *St. John*, p. 379; and especially Schneider's essay in *Gott und die Götter*, pp. 103–12.

courses. According to Bultmann, the prayer is spoken before the disciples have received the love commandment (13:34) and the promises and assurances of chapter 14–16, which even at this late stage they do not comprehend completely. But the prayer itself seems to indicate a later stage and the comprehension attained in the course of, or as a result of, the farewell discourses (cf. 16:29 f.). The claims made in 17:6–8 by the revealer on behalf of his own are decidedly inappropriate before the farewell discourses. Conversely, after 17:6–8, the demand for belief in 14:11 is a little strange.[141] On formal grounds a greal deal may be said for keeping the prayer at the end of the farewell discourses and immediately before the passion. Is not the prayer of the revealer in which he commends his own to the Father the fitting culmination of his ministry to the world and to them? Should not the revealer's ministry be terminated by prayer rather than theological discussion?[142] It seems to me that the prayer of Jesus properly stands at the end of his witness before the disciples, and from that perspective presumes their reception of his word and their witness to him. The assertion of Jesus in 17:4 ("I glorified thee upon earth, having brought to completion [τελειώσας] the work which thou hast given me to do.") is really appropriate only at the conclusion of all Jesus' words and work, including the discourses, and 17:5 ("And now, Father, glorify thou me . . .") is only appropriate if Jesus turns immediately to the cross.

I shall forgo further discussion of Bultmann's overall exegetical grounds for the rearrangement of chapters 13–17. Such a posteriori evidence cannot be accepted as determinative of rearrangement, and to discuss it would take me beyond the range of this study. With regard to the rearrangement of the farewell discourse as a whole, a few observations will suffice. Bultmann admits that in 14:16 the Paraclete seems to be mentioned for the first time, but, having assigned the Paraclete sayings to the speech source, he is able to argue that this particular saying was first only in the source, not in the gospel itself. If there were no such source, however, and 14:16 were from the evangelist, this argument would collapse, and we should have here an important bit of

141. While the disciples may also be representative of the later church, the evangelist has a conception of their historical role and relation to Jesus which comes to expression in the discourses and prayer. The fact that Jesus pointedly distinguishes the later church is an indication of this (17:20; cf. W. Wrede, *Das Messiasgeheimnis in den Evangelien*, Göttingen, Vandenhoeck und Ruprecht, 1963, pp. 188 ff.).

142. Dodd, *Interpretation*, p. 420, points out that in the Hermetic Tractates, particularly *Poimandres* and *De regeneratione*, the dialogue is concluded by a hymn or prayer which is the climax of the process of initiation. Becker, *Reden*, pp. 119 f., 136, whose investigation and results stand in close agreement with Bultmann, nevertheless places the prayer at the conclusion of the discourse.

evidence in favor of the originality of the traditional order in the farewell discourses. That the μικρόν motif in 16:16 ff. is explained, while in 14:19 it is only mentioned, as if the hearers or readers would understand without explanation, is not, as Bultmann suggests, another indication that chapter 14 should follow 16. There are already enigmatic and unexplained μικρόν sayings at 7:33 f. and 12:35.

Moreover, 13:36 ff. does not follow well after chapter 16. The connection is not smooth, and the content is not consistent. In 16:33 Jesus tells his disciples that in the world they will have trouble but that he has overcome the world. Whereupon Simon Peter asks Jesus where he is going (13:36). Jesus has not just said that he is *going* anywhere. True, in 16:28 he says he leaves the world and goes to the Father, but this statement is very clear and, if anything, obviates the necessity for Peter's question in 13:36. If 13:36 is kept in its present position, Peter's question arises naturally out of Jesus' enigmatic statement in verse 33 ("You shall seek me, and as I told the Jews, 'Where I go you are not able to come,' so also I now tell you."). That in 16:5 Jesus says νῦν δὲ ὑπάγω πρὸς τὸν πέμψαντά με, καὶ οὐδεὶς ἐξ ὑμῶν ἐρωτᾷ με . ποῦ ὑπάγεις; does not mean that the question of 13:36 (14:5) cannot have preceded. The ἐρωτᾷ of 16:5 is present tense and presumably refers only to the immediate context, not back to 13:36. Besides, in 13:36 Peter asks where Jesus is going, thinking only of a dangerous place or encounter, not knowing that Jesus' previous assertion (verse 33) referred to his going to his death. In 16:5 Jesus wishes to call forth a question about the ultimate goal of his journeying, namely, a question that can elicit the response that he is going to the Father.

If it is necessary to rearrange the farewell discourses in order to eliminate the most flagrant offense—the ill-placed injunction to arise and go hence in 14:31—we may simply remove 14:25–31 (which might pass for a manuscript page) to the end of chapter 17. Chapter 15 then follows 14:24 well enough. While the allegory of the vine and its interpretation (15:1–17) may be understood as a commentary on the love commandment of 13:34 f. (Bultmann), it does not have to follow it but fits equally well after 14:15–24, the theme of which is also love. The section 14:25–31 would be appropriate as the conclusion of the discourses after chapter 17, although it has no immediate connection with the prayer of Jesus. The introductory ταῦτα εἰπών of 18:1 passes better as a reference to the farewell words of Jesus in 14:25–31 than to the prayer of chapter 17. I leave this question open, however, for my purpose is to examine Bultmann's proposed rearrangements, not to introduce my own.

Bultmann finds no displacements and hence makes no rearrangements in the passion and Easter narratives. Ironically, in the single instance where manuscript support is found for the rearrangement of the order of the text (18:12–27, the hearings of Jesus before Annas and Caiaphas), Bultmann rejects the variant order of the Sinaitic Syriac as a later attempt to make the account more coherent by shuffling the verses. He solves the problem of this section by distinguishing between the traditional source and the redactional work of the evangelist and by showing how the latter has introduced confusion into the report.[143]

We have seen that Bultmann's rearrangement of the text of the Fourth Gospel is not without its objectionable features. Whether it or the traditional order is better, I have not attempted to decide. Judgments on such a question are bound to be subjective. Any attempt to weigh the number and seriousness of Bultmann's objections to the present order against those that I have raised to his reconstruction would be difficult or impossible, and fruitless. One thing, however, can never be forgotten, namely the total lack of manuscript evidence for theories or rearrangements such as Bultmann's. The lack of such tangible evidence throws the burden of proof very heavily upon him. Choosing between his critically reconstructed original order and the present one, we are not choosing between two equally possible alternatives. The two rival textual orders do not have the same status, as if we really had tangible and unambiguous evidence of a stage in which the Fourth Gospel was a series of fragments of which the traditional order is merely one possible reconstruction. In cases where there is reasonable doubt, prudence will always prefer as original the order universally attested by the manuscripts to that constituted by the critical scholar, unless the impossibility of the traditional order and the superiority of the new order can be clearly shown. When, however, the reconstructed order offers its own distinct problems we are certainly not obliged to commit ourselves to it in the name of critical scholarship.

This does not mean that all the various rearrangements proposed by Bultmann or anyone else are necessarily wrong or possess the same degree of probability or improbability. Some have more to commend them than others. For example, there is still much to be said for the reversal of chapters 5 and 6 and some rearrangements within the farewell discourses, although one may adduce some more or less significant evidence against such proposals.

143. *Johannes*, p. 498. Schneider, "Zur Komposition von Joh 18, 12–27, Kaiaphas und Hannas," *ZNW, 48* (1957), 11–19, suggests the attractively simple solution of placing verse 24 immediately after verse 13 (as actually occurs in Sy^s, 225, and as Luther conjectured). There remains, however, the problem of explaining how so awkward a dislocation occurred in the vast majority of manuscripts.

Other rearrangements, particularly those suggested by Bultmann within chapters 1, 6, 7, 8, and 10 and at the beginning of the prayer of Jesus (chapter 17), raise their own distinct difficulties apart from the exegetical considerations noted above. There are, in fact, several facets of Bultmann's displacement theory which place a rather heavy strain upon the historical imagination, and it will be useful to spell them out here in some detail.

(1) The state of the gospel as it apparently came into the hands of the redactor is difficult to account for. As Bultmann indicates, there must have been a destruction of the manuscript. Remarkably enough, this destruction seems to have taken place in such a way as never to have broken up words and smaller syntactical units, and seldom even complete statements. Small as they may have been, the fragments were always syntactically complete. Such a destruction of the text is difficult to conceive. Of course, it is possible—but I do not think very likely—that the destruction of the text did involve the breaking up of words and phrases but that in every case the redactor was able to fit the appropriate pieces back together.

(2) Bultmann's theory also requires us to believe that there was no destruction of the passion and resurrection accounts in John, or that the redactor succeeded in getting the text of those sections restored completely to the proper order. Furthermore, inept as this redactor was in some respects, he preserved intact the integrity of the two major sections of the gospel (chapters 3–12 and 13–20), allowing nothing from either section to spill over into the other. This is, of course, not impossible, but it is again a singular and surprising consequence of Bultmann's theory.

(3) In Bultmann's terms, we are to believe that the hypothetical destruction of the text occurred when there was only one extant manuscript. Presumably the *autographon* itself suffered this destruction. The other alternative is to suppose that all manuscripts save one were destroyed, lost, or suppressed and that this one survived to come into the hand of the redactor. The mutilation of the surviving text must have occurred before the gospel had been copied and circulated, otherwise it is extremely unlikely that we should have no manuscript, versional, or patristic evidence for the original order. The mutilation apparently occurred soon after the composition of the gospel, since from 20:30 f. we may infer that the gospel was intended for wide circulation and was not a private, esoteric document that existed for 25 to 50 years without being copied. If, then, as seems likely, the destruction or mutilation of the text took place at an early date and probably affected the autographon itself, how did it come about? There was not enough time to allow for the decay of the manuscript. If the enemies of the church had confiscated it, they would have surely destroyed it completely or carried it off.

Bultmann seems to assume that the redactor was a generation or so removed from the evangelist. Now, if the destruction of the manuscript took place almost immediately after its composition, probably accidentally, then it must be supposed that the gospel survived for some years in fragmentary form until the redactor chanced upon it. This is not impossible. It is, therefore, not direct evidence against Bultmann's theory, but it is still another factor adding to the increasingly bizarre picture of the manuscript history of the Fourth Gospel implied by the literary theory.

(4) If the redactor came into possession of this lone fragmented manuscript of the gospel, which had somehow been violently mishandled and mutilated (as Bultmann himself seems to believe) and had not simply crumbled of old age, would he not have received the fragments in such form that it would have still been possible to reconstitute the manuscript by fitting the edges together in the manner of a jigsaw puzzle? If this is the case, the marvel is not that the redactor did as well as he did, not confusing the major divisions, but that he did so poorly. Is it not likely that an ancient or modern scholar, attempting to bring order out of a fragmented text would try to fit the pieces together by sight and shape as well as by analysis of the content? But Bultmann seems to assume that he everywhere employed only the latter method, which is, of course, the only method available to the modern critic!

I have suggested that if, in the fragmented text assumed by Bultmann, there had been breaks in words or syntactical units, the evangelist apparently was able to make the correct restoration at every, or almost every, point. For him to have done this would have been virtually impossible had the edges of the manuscript crumbled. But this crumbling apparently did not take place, since Bultmann finds no evidence that the redactor patched together parts of words or clauses by improvisation or that the sense of any grammatical unit has been destroyed by textual loss.[144] If it is claimed that the edges of the manuscript fragments had perhaps crumbled but not so extensively as to prevent the redactor from making the proper restorations, then the fragments would not have been so extensively deteriorated as to have prevented him from fitting them together by size and shape. If he did not follow such an easy lead in bringing the manuscript into order, we must suppose, against Bultmann, that he was to some degree an independent editor consciously and intentionally rearranging the text.

Finally, Bultmann's elaborately developed proposal that the Gospel of John stems from a Gnostic milieu suggests that it might be possible to gain from

144. The few instances in which something like this may have occurred (e.g., 2:23, 8:25) do not help Bultmann's theory.

this source some idea of the kind of order and structure which the evangelist himself might have given it. But in almost all the Gnostic documents which Bultmann cites as distant or immediate background of the Gospel of John,[145] there is a deficiency in just the qualities of historical narration and logical discourse which Bultmann ascribes to the evangelist. Especially does his revised order attest for the evangelist a keen historical sensitivity, a quality notably lacking among the Gnostics and those influenced by them. Yet Bultmann holds that the evangelist, as well as his speech source, stems from a Gnostic milieu. Is it justifiable to impute to an author with such a background and conceptuality a keen historical sense when it is not readily apparent in the text as it is presently structured? In the degree to which John is a church (or Christian sectarian) and traditional document as well as an individual theological treatise and literary composition, the attribution of a keen sense of historical sequence becomes even more questionable. At this point also the insights of Bultmann into the evangelist's method of composition are integrally related to his treatment of the problem of order and rearrangement. If the evangelist actually worked as skillfully and self-consciously over sources as Bultmann supposes, treating them in a highly sophisticated way, it is not very difficult to imagine that he could have brought his materials into the kind of sensitively structured order which Bultmann attributes to him. But that the evangelist actually did work in this way is at least questionable and cannot be regarded as demonstrated. It is at best a hypothesis, not a fact which may be adduced in support of the originality of Bultmann's reconstructed order.

All of my objections and questions do not remove certain literary difficulties in the Fourth Gospel whose existence is not to be denied. Bultmann has made these difficulties stand out in sharp relief, but his explanation and resolution of them is not completely convincing.[146] Moreover, I have tried to show that Bultmann's theory itself creates other and equally difficult historical and literary problems for which he does not seem to offer any solution. Perhaps he can solve them. Perhaps he believes that when the picture is seen in its

145. Especially the Mandaean literature, the Hermetica, the Odes of Solomon; also Philo and Ignatius of Antioch. One might mention, too, the many Gnostic books of the New Testament apocrypha, including the newly discovered Gospel of Thomas and Gospel of Truth.

146. Although I have not subscribed to Wilken's detailed proposals regarding the Entstehungsgeschichte of the Fourth Gospel (see above, pp. 96-99), I believe that the general outline of his theory is not incredible and perhaps most enlightening. Quite possibly the evangelist himself intentionally rearranged portions of his work and added to it before its publication. This would account for the existence in the text of evidence both for and against the coherence and originality of the traditional textual order, and would also explain why there is no evidence for any order but the traditional one in extant manuscript witnesses.

entirety there are really no problems at all. In any case there are historical questions raised by Bultmann's primarily literary theory which cannot be dismissed as inconsequential but which must be treated with the literary problem. It is unsatisfactory for the literary critic to advance his theories without thorough and constant questioning of their historical probability. History is admittedly full of the improbable, but when improbabilities are piled one atop the other, they at least demand a full explanation. It is striking that Bultmann, who is characteristically so willing to advance detailed historical explanations and interpretations, should seem so reluctant to become involved in these matters in the commentary on John. Here the problem of weighing literary evidence against historical probability is acute, and it is unresolved.

The Hypothetical Original Text of the Fourth Gospel [1]

ΚΑΤΑ ΙΩΑΝΝΗΝ

1:

1 Εν αρχη ην ο λογος, και ο λογος ην προς τον θεον, και θεος

2.3 ην ο λογος. ουτος ην εν αρχη προς τον θεον. παντα δι αυτου

4 εγενετο, και χωρις αυτου εγενετο ουδε εν ο γεγονεν. εν αυτω

5 ζωη ην, και η ζωη ην το φως των ανθρωπων· και το φως εν τη

6 σκοτια φαινει, και η σκοτια αυτο ου κατελαβεν. Εγενετο

7 ανθρωπος, απεσταλμενος παρα θεου, ονομα αυτω Ιωαννης· ουτος

ηλθεν εις μαρτυριαν, ινα μαρτυρηση περι του φωτος, ινα παντες

8 πιστευσωσιν δι αυτου. ουκ ην εκεινος το φως, αλλ ινα μαρτυρηση

9 περι του φωτος. Ην το φως το αληθινον, ο φωτιζει παντα

10 ανθρωπον, ερχομενον εις τον κοσμον. εν τω κοσμω ην, και ο

12 κοσμος δι αυτου εγενετο, και ο κοσμος αυτον ουκ εγνω. εις τα

ιδια ηλθεν, και οι ιδιοι αυτον ου παρελαβον. οσοι δε ελαβον

αυτον, εδωκεν αυτοις εξουσιαν τεκνα θεου γενεσθαι, τοις πιστευ-

13 ουσιν εις το ονομα αυτου, οι ουκ εξ αιματων ουδε εκ θεληματος

σαρκος ουδε εκ θεληματος ανδρος αλλ εκ θεου εγεννηθησαν.

14 Και ο λογος σαρξ εγενετο και εσκηνωσεν εν ημιν, και εθεασαμεθα

την δοξαν αυτου. δοξαν ως μονογενους παρα πατρος, πληρης

---

[1] This section of text displays the Gospel of John in the form in which Bultmann believes the evangelist composed it. Once again, page numbers in the righthand margin refer to Bultmann's commentary (see p. 23 n. 1). Since the redactional material which Bultmann identifies was not added to the Gospel in this form (which the redactor never saw) but was incorporated into his substantially reconstructed and reordered text, I have made no indication of it here. Passages which may be redactional are included in brackets. (The question of ecclesiastical redaction is dealt with in Chapter 4.)

15 χαριτος και αληθειας. Ιωαννης μαρτυρει περι αυτου και κεκραγεν
   λεγων· ουτος ην ον ειπον· ο οπισω μου ερχομενος εμπροσθεν μου
16 γεγονεν, οτι πρωτος μου ην. οτι εκ του πληρωματος αυτου ημεις
17 παντες ελαβομεν, και χαριν αντι χαριτος· οτι ο νομος δια Μωυσεως εδοθη, η χαρις και η αληθεια δια Ιησου Χριστου εγενετο.
18 Θεον ουδεις εωρακεν πωποτε· μονογενης θεος ο ων εις τον κολπον
   του πατρος, εκεινος εξηγησατο.

19   Και αυτη εστιν η μαρτυρια του Ιωαννου, οτε απεστειλαν   57 f.
   προς αυτον οι Ιουδαιοι εξ Ιεροσολυμων ιερεις και Λευιτας ινα
20 ερωτησωσιν αυτον· συ τις ει; και ωμολογησεν και ουκ ηρνησατο,
21 και ωμολογησεν οτι εγω ουκ ειμι ο χριστος. και ηρωτησαν αυτον·
   τι ουν; Ηλιας ει συ; και λεγει· ουκ ειμι. ο προφητης ει συ; και
25 απεκριθη· ου. και ηρωτησαν αυτον και ειπαν αυτω· τι ουν
   βαπτιζεις ει συ· ουκ ει ο χριστος ουδε Ηλιας ουδε ο προφητης;
26 απεκριθη αυτοις ο Ιωαννης λεγων· μεσος υμων στηκει ον υμεις
31 ουκ οιδατε. καγω ουκ ηδειν αυτον, αλλ ινα φανερωθη τω Ισραηλ,
33 δια τουτο ηλθον εγω βαπτιζων. και ο πεμψας με βαπτιζειν.
   εκεινος μοι ειπεν· εφ ον αν, ιδης το πνευμα καταβαινον και μενον επ
34 αυτον, ουτος εστιν. καγω εωρακα, και μεμαρτυρηκα οτι ουτος
28 εστιν ο υιος του θεου. Ταυτα εν Βηθανια εγενετο περαν του Ιορδα-
29 νου οπου ην ο Ιωαννης βαπτιζων. Τη επαυριον βλεπει τον Ιησουν
   ερχομενον προς αυτον, και λεγει· ιδε ο αμνος του θεου ο αιρων
30 την αμαρτιαν του κοσμου. ουτος εστιν υπερου εγω ειπον· οπισω μου
   ερχεται ανηρ ος εμπροσθεν μου γεγονεν, οτι πρωτος μου ην.
35   Τη επαυριον παλιν ειστηκει ο Ιωαννης και εκ των μαθητων
36 αυτου δυο, και εμβλεψας τω Ιησου περιπατουντι λεγει· ιδε ο
37 αμνος του θεου. και ηκουσαν οι δυο μαθηται αυτου λαλουντος και
38 ηκολουθησαν τω Ιησου. στραφεις δε ο Ιησους και θεασαμενος
   αυτους ακολουθουντας λεγει αυτοις· τι ζητειτε; οι δε ειπαν αυτω·
   ρ α β β ι (ο λεγεται μεθερμηνευομενον διδασκαλε), που μενεις;
39 λεγει αυτοις· ερχεσθε και οψεσθε. ηλθαν ουν και ειδαν που
   μενει, και παρ αυτω εμειναν την ημεραν εκεινην· ωρα ην ως
40 δεκατη. Ην Ανδρεας ο αδελφος Σιμωνος Πετρου εις εκ των δυο
   των ακουσαντων παρα Ιωαννου και ακολουθησαντων αυτω·
41 ευρισκει ουτος πρωτον τον αδελφον τον ιδιον Σιμωνα και λεγει
   αυτω· ευρηκαμεν τον Μ ε σ σ ι α ν (ο εστιν μεθερμηνευομενον
42 χριστος). ηγαγεν αυτον προς τον Ιησουν. εμβλεψας αυτω ο
   Ιησους ειπεν· συ ει Σιμων ο υιος Ιωαννου, συ κληθηση Κ η φ α ς
43 (ο ερμηνευεται Πετρος). Τη επαυριον ηθελησεν εξελθειν εις την
   Γαλιλαιαν, και ευρισκει Φιλιππον. και λεγει αυτω ο Ιησους·
44 ακολουθει μοι. ην δε ο Φιλιππος απο Βηθσαιδα, εκ της πολεως
45 Ανδρεου και Πετρου. ευρισκει Φιλιππος τον Ναθαναηλ και λεγει
   αυτω· ον εγραψεν Μωυσης εν τω νομω και οι προφηται ευρηκαμεν,

46 Ιησουν υιον του Ιωσηφ τον απο Ναζαρεθ. και ειπεν αυτω Ναθα-
ναηλ· εκ Ναζαρεθ δυναται τι αγαθον ειναι; λεγει αυτω ο
47 Φιλιππος· ερχου και ιδε. ειδεν Ιησους τον Ναθαναηλ ερχομενον
προς αυτον και λεγει περι αυτου· ιδε αληθως Ισραηλιτης, εν ω
48 δολος ουκ εστιν. λεγει αυτω Ναθαναηλ· ποθεν με γινωσκεις;
απεκριθη Ιησους και ειπεν αυτω· προ του σε Φιλιππον φωνησαι
49 οντα υπο την συκην ειδον σε. απεκριθη αυτω Ναθαναηλ·
ρ α β β ι, συ ει ο υιος του θεου, συ βασιλευς ει του Ισραηλ.
50 απεκριθη Ιησους και ειπεν αυτω· οτι ειπον σοι οτι ειδον σε υπο-
51 κατω της συκης, πιστευεις; μειζω τουτων οψη. και λεγει αυτω·
αμην αμην λεγω υμιν, οψεσθε τον ουρανον ανεωγοτα και τους
αγγελους του θεου αναβαινοντας και καταβαινοντας επι τον
υιον του ανθρωπου.

2:

1 Και τη ημερα τη τριτη γαμος εγενετο εν Κανα της Γαλιλαιας,
2 και ην η μητηρ του Ιησου εκει· εκληθη δε και ο Ιησους και οι
3 μαθηται αυτου εις τον γαμον. και υστερησαντος οινου λεγει η
4 μητηρ του Ιησου προς αυτον· οινον ουκ εχουσιν. και λεγει αυτη
5 ο Ιησους· τι εμοι και σοι, γυναι; ουπω ηκει η ωρα μου. λεγει η
6 μητηρ αυτου τοις διακονοις· ο τι αν λεγη υμιν ποιησατε. ησαν
δε εκει λιθιναι υδριαι εξ κατα τον καθαρισμον των Ιουδαιων
7 κειμεναι, χωρουσαι ανα μετρητας δυο η τρεις. λεγει αυτοις ο
Ιησους· γεμισατε τας υδριας υδατος. και εγεμισαν αυτας εως
8 ανω. και λεγει αυτοις· αντλησατε νυν και φερετε τω αρχιτρικλινω.
9 οι δε ηνεγκαν. ως δε εγευσατο ο αρχιτρικλινος το υδωρ οινον
γεγενημενον, και ουκ ηδει ποθεν εστιν, οι δε διακονοι ηδεισαν οι
ηντληκοτες το υδωρ, φωνει τον νυμφιον ο αρχιτρικλινος και λεγει
10 αυτω· πας ανθρωπος πρωτον τον καλον οινον τιθησιν, και οταν
μεθυσθωσιν τον ελασσω· συ τετηρηκας τον καλον οινον εως αρτι.
11 Ταυτην εποιησεν αρχην των σημειων ο Ιησους εν Κανα της
Γαλιλαιας και εφανερωσεν την δοξαν αυτου, και επιστευσαν εις
αυτον [οι μαθηται αυτου].
12 Μετα τουτο κατεβη εις Καφαρναουμ αυτος και η μητηρ αυτου
και οι αδελφοι, και εκει εμειναν ου πολλας ημερας.
13 Και εγγυς ην το πασχα των Ιουδαιων, και ανεβη εις Ιεροσολυμα
14 ο Ιησους. και ευρεν εν τω ιερω τους πωλουντας βοας και προβατα
15 και περιστερας και τους κερματιστας καθημενους, και ποιησας
φραγελλιον εκ σχοινιων παντας εξεβαλεν εκ του ιερου, [τα τε
προβατα και τους βοας, και των κολλυβιστων εξεχεεν τα κερματα
16 και τας τραπεζας ανετρεψεν,] και [τοις τας περιστερας πωλουσιν]
ειπεν· αρατε ταυτα εντευθεν, μη ποιειτε τον οικον του πατρος
17 μου οικον εμποριου. [εμνησθησαν οι μαθηται αυτου οτι γεγραμ-

18 μενον εστιν· ο ζηλος του οικου σου καταφαγεται με.] απεκριθησαν ουν οι Ιουδαιοι και ειπαν αυτω· τι σημειον δεικνυεις ημιν,
19 οτι ταυτα ποιεις; απεκριθη Ιησους και ειπεν αυτοις· λυσατε τον
20 ναον τουτον, και εν τρισιν ημεραις εγερω αυτον. ειπαν ουν οι
Ιουδαιοι· τεσσερακοντα και εξ ετεσιν οικοδομηθη ο ναος ουτος,
21 και συ εν τρισιν ημεραις εγερεις αυτον; εκεινος δε ελεγεν περι
22 του ναου του σωματος αυτου. [οτε ουν ηγερθη εκ νεκρων, εμνησθησαν οι μαθηται αυτου οτι τουτο ελεγεν, και επιστευσαν τη
γραφη και τω λογω ον ειπεν ο Ιησους.]
23   Ως δε ην τοις Ιεροσολυμοις [εν τω πασχα] εν τη εορτη, πολλοι
επιστευσαν εις το ονομα αυτου, θεωρουντες αυτου τα σημεια α
24 εποιει· αυτος δε Ιησους ουκ επιστευεν αυτον αυτοις δια το αυτον
25 γινωσκειν παντας, και οτι ου χρειαν ειχεν ινα τις μαρτυρηση
περι του ανθρωπου· αυτος γαρ εγινωσκεν τι ην εν τω ανθρωπω.

3:

1 Ην δε ανθρωπος εκ των Φαρισαιων, Νικοδημος ονομα αυτω,
2 αρχων των Ιουδαιων· ουτος ηλθεν προς αυτον νυκτος και ειπεν
αυτω· ρ α β β ι, οιδαμεν οτι απο θεου εληλυθας διδασκαλος·
ουδεις γαρ δυναται ταυτα τα σημεια ποιειν α συ ποιεις, εαν μη η
3 ο θεος μετ αυτου. απεκριθη Ιησους και ειπεν αυτω· αμην αμην
λεγω σοι, εαν μη τις γεννηθη ανωθεν, ου δυναται ιδειν την βασι-
4 λειαν του θεου. λεγει προς αυτον ο Νικοδημος· πως δυναται
ανθρωπος γεννηθηναι γερων ων; μη δυναται εις την κοιλιαν της
5 μητρος αυτου δευτερον εισελθειν και γεννηθηναι; απεκριθη
Ιησους· αμην αμην λεγω σοι, εαν μη τις γεννηθη εξ πνευματος,
6 ου δυναται εισελθειν εις την βασιλειαν του θεου. το γεγεννημενον εκ της σαρκος σαρξ εστιν, και το γεγεννημενος εκ του
7 πνευματος πνευμα εστιν. μη θαυμασης οτι ειπον σοι· δει υμας
8 γεννηθηναι ανωθεν. το πνευμα οπου θελει πνει, και την φωνην
αυτου ακουεις, αλλ ουκ οιδας ποθεν ερχεται και που υπαγει·
9 ουτως εστιν πας ο γεγεννημενος εκ του πνευματος. απεκριθη
Νικοδημος και ειπεν αυτω· πως δυναται ταυτα γενεσθαι;
10 απεκριθη Ιησους και ειπεν αυτω· συ ει ο διδασκαλος του Ισραηλ
11 και ταυτα ου γινωσκεις; αμην αμην λεγω σοι οτι ο οιδαμεν
λαλουμεν και ο εωρακαμεν μαρτυρουμεν, και την μαρτυριαν
12 ημων ου λαμβανετε. ει τα επιγεια ειπον υμιν και ου πιστευετε,
13 πως εαν ειπω υμιν τα επουρανια πιστευσετε; και ουδεις αναβεβηκεν
εις τον ουρανον ει μη ο εκ του ουρανου καταβας, ο υιος του ανθρω-
14 που. Και καθως Μωυσης υψωσεν τον οφιν εν τη ερημω, ουτως
15 υψωθηναι δει τον υιον του ανθρωπου, ινα πας ο πιστευων εν
16 αυτω εχη ζωην αιωνιον. ουτως γαρ ηγαπησεν ο θεος τον κοσμον,
ωστε τον υιον τον μονογενη εδωκεν, ινα πας ο πιστευων εις αυτον

17 μη αποληται αλλ εχη ζωην αιωνιον. ου γαρ απεστειλεν ο θεος
τον υιον εις τον κοσμον ινα κρινη τον κοσμον, αλλ ινα σωθη ο
18 κοσμος δι αυτου. ο πιστευων εις αυτον ου κρινεται· ο μη πιστευων
ηδη κεκριται, οτι μη πεπιστευκεν εις το ονομα του μονογενους
19 υιου του θεου. αυτη δε εστιν η κρισις, οτι το φως εληλυθεν εις
τον κοσμον και ηγαπησαν οι ανθρωποι μαλλον το σκοτος η το
20 φως· ην γαρ αυτων πονηρα τα εργα. πας γαρ ο φαυλα πρασσων
μισει το φως και ουκ ερχεται προς το φως, ινα μη ελεγχθη τα
21 εργα αυτου. ο δε ποιων την αληθειαν ερχεται προς το φως, ινα
31 φανερωθη αυτου τα εργα οτι εν θεω εστιν ειργασμενα. Ο ανωθεν
ερχομενος επανω παντων εστιν· ο ων εκ της γης εκ της γης εστιν
και εκ της γης λαλει. ο εκ του ουρανου ερχομενος επανω παντων
32 εστιν· ο εωρακεν και ηκουσεν, τουτο μαρτυρει, και την μαρτυριαν
33 αυτου ουδεις λαμβανει. ο λαβων αυτου την μαρτυριαν εσφραγισεν
34 οτι ο θεος αληθης εστιν. ον γαρ απεστειλεν ο θεος τα ρηματα
35 του θεου λαλει· ου γαρ εκ μετρου διδωσιν. ο πατηρ αγαπα τον
36 υιον, και παντα δεδωκεν εν τη χειρι αυτου. ο πιστευων εις τον
υιον εχει ζωην αιωνιον· ο δε απειθων τω υιω ουκ οψεται ζωην,
αλλ η οργη του θεου μενει επ αυτον.

22 Μετα ταυτα ηλθεν ο Ιησους και οι μαθηται αυτου εις την
23 Ιουδαιαν γην, και εκει διετριβεν μετ αυτων και εβαπτιζεν. ην δε
και Ιωαννης βαπτιζων εν Αινων εγγυς του Σαλιμ, οτι υδατα
25 πολλα ην εκει, και παρεγινοντο και εβαπτιζοντο· Εγενετο ουν
ζητησις εκ των μαθητων Ιωαννου μετα Ιουδαιου περι καθαρισμου.
26 και ηλθον προς τον Ιωαννην και ειπαν αυτω· ρ α β β ι, ος ην μετα
σου περαν του Ιορδανου, ω συ μεμαρτυρηκας, ιδε ουτος βαπτιζει
27 και παντες ερχονται προς αυτον. απεκριθη Ιωαννης και ειπεν·
ου δυναται ανθρωπος λαμβανειν ουδεν εαν μη η δεδομενον αυτω
28 εκ του ουρανου. αυτοι υμεις μοι μαρτυρειτε οτι ειπον· ουκ ειμι
εγω ο χριστος, αλλ οτι απεσταλμενος ειμι εμπροσθεν εκεινου.
29 ο εχων την νυμφην νυμφιος εστιν· ο δε φιλος του νυμφιου, ο
εστηκως και ακουων αυτου, χαρα χαιρει δια την φωνην του νυμφιου.
30 αυτη ουν η χαρα η εμη πεπληρωται. εκεινον δει αυξανειν, εμε δε
ελαττουσθαι.

4: 1 Ως ουν ηκουσαν οι Φαρισαιοι οτι Ιησους πλειονας μαθητας
3 ποιει και βαπτιζει ο Ιωαννης, αφηκεν την Ιουδαιαν και απηλθεν
4 παλιν εις την Γαλιλαιαν. Εδει δε αυτον διερχεσθαι δια της
5 Σαμαρειας. ερχεται ουν εις πολιν της Σαμαρειας λεγομενην
Συχαρ, πλησιον του χωριου ο εδωκεν Ιακωβ [τω] Ιωσηφ τω υιω
6 αυτου· ην δε εκει πηγη του Ιακωβ. ο ουν Ιησους κεκοπιακως εκ
της οδοιποριας εκαθεζετο ουτως επι τη πηγη· ωρα ην ως εκτη.

92 f.

7 ερχεται γυνη εκ της Σαμαρειας αντλησαι υδωρ. λεγει αυτη ο
8 Ιησους· δος μοι πειν. οι γαρ μαθηται αυτου απεληλυθεισαν εις
9 την πολιν. ινα τροφας αγορασωσιν. λεγει ουν αυτω η γυνη η
Σαμαριτις· πως συ Ιουδαιος ων παρ εμου πειν αιτεις γυναικος
Σαμαριτιδος ουσης. [ου γαρ συγχρωνται Ιουδαιοι Σαμαριταις.]
10 απεκριθη Ιησους και ειπεν αυτη· ει ηδεις την δωρεαν του θεου,
και τις εστιν ο λεγων σοι· δος μοι πειν, συ αν ητησας αυτον και
11 εδωκεν αν σοι υδωρ ζων. λεγει αυτω. κυριε, ποθεν ουν εχεις
12 το υδωρ το ζων; μη συ μειζων ει του πατρος ημων Ιακωβ. ος
εδωκεν ημιν το φρεαρ, και αυτος εξ αυτου επιεν και οι υιοι αυτου
13 και τα θρεμματα αυτου; απεκριθη Ιησους και ειπεν αυτη· πας
14 ο πινων εκ του υδατος τουτου διψησει παλιν· ος δ αν πιη εκ του
υδατος ου εγω δωσω αυτω, ου μη διψησει εις τον αιωνα, αλλα το
υδωρ ο δωσω αυτω γενησεται εν αυτω πηγη υδατος αλλομενου εις
15 ζωην αιωνιον. λεγει προς αυτον η γυνη· κυριε, δος μοι τουτο το
16 υδωρ, ινα μη διψω μηδε διερχωμαι ενθαδε αντλειν. λεγει αυτη
17 υπαγε φωνησον τον ανδρα σου και ελθε ενθαδε. απεκριθη η γυνη
και ειπεν· ουκ εχω ανδρα. λεγει αυτη ο Ιησους· καλως ειπες οτι
18 ανδρα ουκ εχω· πεντε γαρ ανδρας εσχες, και νυν ον εχεις ουκ εστιν
19 σου ανηρ· τουτο αληθες ειρηκας. λεγει αυτω η γυνη· κυριε,
20 θεωρω οτι προφητης ει συ. οι πατερες ημων εν τω ορει τουτω
προσεκυνησαν· και υμεις λεγετε οτι εν Ιεροσολυμοις εστιν ο τοπος
21 οπου προσκυνειν δει. λεγει αυτη ο Ιησους· πιστευε μοι, γυναι,
οτι ερχεται ωρα οτε ουτε εν τω ορει τουτω ουτε εν Ιεροσολυμοις
22 προσκυνησετε τω πατρι. [υμεις προσκυνειτε ο ουκ οιδατε, ημεις
23 προσκυνουμεν ο οιδαμεν], αλλα ερχεται ωρα και νυν εστιν. οτε
οι αληθινοι προσκυνηται προσκυνησουσιν τω πατρι εν πνευματι
και αληθεια· και γαρ ο πατηρ τοιουτους ζητει τους προσκυνουντας
24 αυτον· πνευμα ο θεος, και τους προσκυνουντας εν πνευματι και
25 αληθεια δει προσκυνειν. λεγει αυτω η γυνη· οιδα οτι Μ ε σ σ ι α ς
ερχεται, ο λεγομενος χριστος· οταν ελθη εκεινος, αναγγελει
26, 27 ημιν απαντα. λεγει αυτη ο Ιησους· εγω ειμι, ο λαλων σοι. Και
επι τουτω ηλθαν οι μαθηται αυτου, και εθαυμαζον οτι μετα
γυναικος ελαλει· ουδεις μεντοι ειπεν· τι ζητεις η τι λαλεις μετ
28 αυτης; αφηκεν ουν την υδριαν αυτης η γυνη και απηλθεν εις την
29 πολιν, και λεγει τοις ανθρωποις· δευτε ιδετε ανθρωπον ος ειπεν μοι
30 παντα α εποιησα· μητι ουτος εστιν ο χριστος; εξηλθον εκ της
31 πολεως και ηρχοντο προς αυτον. Εν τω μεταξυ ηρωτων αυτον
32 οι μαθηται λεγοντες· ρ α β β ι, φαγε. ο δε ειπεν αυτοις· εγω
33 βρωσιν εχω φαγειν ην υμεις ουκ οιδατε. ελεγον ουν οι μαθηται
34 προς αλληλους· μη τις ηνεγκεν αυτω φαγειν; λεγει αυτοις ο
Ιησους· εμον βρωμα εστιν ινα ποιω το θελημα του πεμψαντος με
35 και τελειωσω αυτου το εργον. ουχ υμεις ελετε οτι ετι τετραμηνος

εστιν και ο θερισμος ερχεται; ιδου λεγω υμιν, επαρατε τους
οφθαλμους υμων και θεασασθε τας χωρας, οτι λευκαι εισιν προς

36 θερισμον. ηδη ο θεριζων μισθον λαμβανει και συναγει καρπον
37 εις ζωην αιωνιον, ινα ο σπειρων ομου χαιρη και ο θεριζων. εν γαρ
τουτω ο λογος εστιν αληθινος οτι αλλος εστιν ο σπειρων και
38 αλλος ο θεριζων. εγω απεστειλα υμας θεριζειν ο ουχ υμεις
κεκοπιακατε· αλλοι κεκοπιακασιν. και υμεις εις τον κοπον αυτων
39 εισεληλυθατε. Εκ δε της πολεως εκεινης πολλοι επιστευσαν εις
αυτον των Σαμαριτων δια τον λογον της γυναικος μαρτυρουσης
40 οτι ειπεν μοι παντα α εποιησα. ως ουν ηλθον προς αυτον οι
Σαμαριται, ηρωτων αυτον μειναι παρ αυτοις· και εμεινεν εκει δυο
41 ημερας. και πολλω πλειους επιστευσαν δια τον λογον αυτου.
42 τη τε γυναικι ελεγον οτι ουκετι δια την σην λαλιαν πιστευομεν·
αυτοι γαρ ακηκοαμεν, και οιδαμεν οτι ουτος εστιν αληθως ο σωτηρ
του κοσμου.

43   Μετα δε τας δυο ημερας εξηλθεν εκειθεν εις την Γαλιλαιαν.   149
44 αυτος γαρ Ιησους εμαρτυρησεν οτι προφητης εν τη ιδια πατριδι
45 τιμην ουκ εχει. οτε ουν ηλθεν εις την Γαλιλαιαν, εδεξαντο αυτον
οι Γαλιλαιοι, παντα εωρακοτες οσα εποιησεν εν Ιεροσολυμοις εν
46 τη εορτη· και αυτοι γαρ ηλθον εις την εορτην. Ηλθεν ουν παλιν
εις την Κανα της Γαλιλαιας, οπου εποιησεν το υδωρ οινον. και
47 ην τις βασιλικος ου ο υιος ησθενει εν Καφαρναουμ· ουτος ακουσας
οτι Ιησους ηκει εκ της Ιουδαιας εις την Γαλιλαιαν, απηλθεν προς
αυτον και ηρωτα ινα καταβη και ιασηται αυτου τον υιον· ημελλεν
48 γαρ αποθνησκειν. ειπεν ουν ο Ιησους προς αυτον· εαν μη σημεια
49 και τερατα ιδητε, ου μη πιστευσητε. λεγει προς αυτον ο βασιλικος·
50 κυριε, καταβηθι πριν αποθανειν το παιδιον μου. λεγει αυτω ο
Ιησους· πορευου. ο υιος σου ζη. επιστευσεν ο ανθρωπος τω λογω
51 ον ειπεν αυτω ο Ιησους, και επορευετο. ηδη δε αυτου καταβαινοντος
52 οι δουλοι υπηντησαν αυτω λεγοντες οτι ο παις αυτου ζη. επυθετο
ουν την ωραν παρ αυτων εν η κομψοτερον εσχεν· ειπαν ουν αυτω
53 οτι εχθες ωραν εβδομην αφηκεν αυτον ο πυρετος. εγνω ουν ο
πατηρ οτι εκεινη τη ωρα εν η ειπεν αυτω ο Ιησους· ο υιος σου ζη·
54 και επιστευσεν αυτος και η οικια αυτου ολη. Τουτο [δε] παλιν
δευτερον σημειον εποιησεν ο Ιησους ελθων εκ της Ιουδαιας εις την
Γαλιλαιαν.

6:

1   Μετα ταυτα απηλθεν ο Ιησους περαν της θαλασσης της   154 f.
2 Γαλιλαιας [της Τιβεριαδος]. ηκολουθει δε αυτω οχλος πολυς,
3 οτι εωρων τα σημεια α εποιει επι των ασθενουντων. ανηλθεν
δε εις το ορος Ιησους, και εκει εκαθητο μετα των μαθητων αυτου.
4, 5 ην δε εγγυς το πασχα, η εορτη των Ιουδαιων. επαρας ουν τους

οφθαλμους ο Ιησους και θεασαμενος οτι πολυς οχλος ερχεται
προς αυτον, λεγει προς Φιλιππον· ποθεν αγορασωμεν αρτους
6 ινα φαγωσιν ουτοι; τουτο δε ελεγεν πειραζων αυτον· αυτος
7 γαρ ηδει τι εμελλεν ποιειν. απεκριθη αυτω ο Φιλιππος· διακοσιων
δηναριων αρτοι ουκ αρκουσιν αυτοις, ινα εκαστος βραχυ τι λαβη.
8 λεγει αυτω εις εκ των μαθητων αυτου, Ανδρεας ο αδελφος Σιμωνος
9 Πετρου· εστιν παιδαριον ωδε ος εχει πεντε αρτους κριθινους και
10 δυο οψαρια· αλλα ταυτα τι εστιν εις τοσουτους; ειπεν ο Ιησους·
ποιησατε τους ανθρωπους αναπεσειν. ην δε χορτος πολυς εν τω
τοπω. ανεπεσαν ουν οι ανδρες τον αριθμον ως πεντακισχιλιοι.
11 ελαβεν ουν τους αρτους ο Ιησους και ευχαριστησας διεδωκεν τοις
12 ανακειμενοις, ομοιως και εκ των οψαριων οσον ηθελον. ως δε
ενεπλησθησαν. λεγει τοις μαθηταις αυτου· συναγαγετε τα
13 περισσευσαντα κλασματα, ινα μη τι αποληται. συνηγαγον ουν,
και εγεμισαν δωδεκα κοφινους κλασματων εκ των πεντε αρτων των
14 κριθινων α επερισσευσαν τοις βεβρωκοσιν. Οι ουν ανθρωποι
ιδοντες ο εποιησεν σημειον ελεγου οτι ουτος εστιν αληθως ο
15 προφητης ο ερχομενος εις τον κοσμον. Ιησους ουν γνους οτι μελ-
λουσιν ερχεσθαι και αρπαζειν αυτον ινα ποιησωσιν βασιλεα.
16 ανεχωρησεν παλιν εις το ορος αυτος μονος. Ως δε οψια εγενετο,
17 κατεβησαν οι μαθηται αυτου επι την θαλασσαν, και εμβαντες
εις πλοιον ηρχοντο περαν της θαλασσης εις Καφαρναουμ. και
σκοτια ηδη εγεγονει και ουπω εληλυθει προς αυτους ο Ιησους,
19 εληλακοτες ουν ως σταδιους εικοσι πεντε η τριακοντα θεωρουσιν
τον Ιησουν περιπατουντα επι της θαλασσης και εγγυς του πλοιου
20 γινομενον, και εφοβηθησαν. ο δε λεγει αυτοις· εγω ειμι· μη
21 φοβεισθε. ηθελον ουν λαβειν αυτον εις το πλοιον, και ευθεως
εγενετο το πλοιον επι της γης εις ην υπηγον.
22   Τη επαυριον ο οχλος ο εστηκως περαν της θαλασσης ειδον οτι
πλοιαριον αλλο ουκ ην εκει ει μη εν, και οτι ου συνεισηλθεν τοις
μαθηταις αυτου ο Ιησους εις το πλοιον αλλα μονοι οι μαθηται
23 αυτου απηλθον· αλλα ηλθεν πλοιαρια εκ Τιβεριαδος εγγυς του
24 τοπου οπου εφαγον τον αρτον. οτε ουν ειδεν ο οχλος οτι Ιησους ουκ
εστιν εκει ουδε οι μαθηται αυτου. ενεβησαν αυτοι εις τα πλοιαρια
25 και ηλθον εις Καφαρναουμ ζητουντες τον Ιησουν. και ευροντες
αυτον περαν της θαλασσης ειπον αυτω· ρ α β β ι, ποτε ωδε
26 γεγονας; απεκριθη αυτοις ο Ιησους και ειπεν· αμην αμην λεγω
υμιν, ζητειτε με ουχ οτι ειδετε σημεια, αλλ οτι εφαγετε εκ των
27 αρτων και εχορτασθητε. εργαζεσθε μη την βρωσιν την απολλυ-   161–64
34 μενην, αλλα την βρωσιν την μενουσαν εις ζωην αιωνιον. ειπον
35 ουν προς αυτον· κυριε, παντοτε δος ημιν τον αρτον τουτον. ειπεν
αυτοις ο Ιησους· εγω ειμι ο αρτος της ζωης· ο ερχομενος προς εμε
ου μη πειναση και ο πιστευων εις εμε ου μη διψησει πωποτε.

30 ειπον ουν αυτω· τι ουν ποιεις συ σημειον, ινα ιδωμεν και πιστευ-

31 σωμεν σοι; τι εργαζη; οι πατερες ημων το μαννα εφαγον εν τη
ερημω, καθως εστιν γεγραμμενον· αρτον εκ του ουρανου εδωκεν

32 αυτοις φαγειν. Ειπεν ουν αυτοις ο Ιησους· αμην αμην λεγω υμιν,
ου Μωυσης δεδωκεν υμιν τον αρτον εκ του ουρανου, αλλ ο πατηρ

33 μου διδωσιν υμιν τον αρτον εκ του ουρανου τον αληθινον· ο γαρ
αρτος του θεου εστιν ο καταβαινων εκ του ουρανου και ζωην διδους

47 τω κοσμω. αμην αμην λεγω υμιν, ο πιστευων εχει ζωην αιωνιον.

48, 49 Εγω ειμι ο αρτος της ζωης. οι πατερες υμων εφαγον εν τη ερημω

50 το μαννα και απεθανον· ουτος εστιν ο αρτος ο εκ του ουρανου

51 καταβαινων, ινα τις εξ αυτου φαγη και μη αποθανη. εγω ειμι ο
αρτος ο ζων ο εκ του ουρανου καταβας· εαν τις φανη εκ τουτου

41 του αρτου, ζησει εις τον αιωνα· Εγογγυζον ουν οι Ιουδαιοι περι

42 αυτου οτι ειπεν· εγω ειμι ο αρτος ο καταβας εκ του ουρανου. και
ελεγον· ουχ ουτος εστιν Ιησους ο υιος Ιωσηφ, ου ημεις οιδαμεν τον
πατερα και την μητερα; πως νυν λεγει οτι εκ του ουρανου

43 καταβεβηκα; απεκριθη Ιησους και ειπεν αυτοις· μη γογγυζετε μετ

44 αλληλων. Ουδεις δυναται ελθειν προς με εαν μη ο πατηρ ο

45 πεμψας με ελκυση αυτον. εστιν γεγραμμενον εν τοις προφηταις·
και εσονται παντες διδακτοι θεου· πας ο ακουσας παρα του

46 πατρος και μαθων ερχεται προς εμε. ουχ οτι τον πατερα εωρακεν

36 τις, ει μη ο ων παρα του θεου. ουτος εωρακεν τον πατερα. Αλλ

37 ειπον υμιν οτι και εωρακατε [με] και ου πιστευετε. παν ο διδωσιν
μοι ο πατηρ προς εμε ηξει, και τον ερχομενον προς με ου μη

38 εκβαλω εξω, οτι καταβεβηκα απο του ουρανου ουχ ινα ποιω το

39 θελημα το εμον αλλα το θελημα του πεμψαντος με. τουτο δε
εστιν το θελημα του πεμψαντος με, ινα παν ο δεδωκεν μοι μη

40 απολεσω εξ αυτου. τουτο γαρ εστιν το θελημα του πατρος μου,
ινα πας ο θεωρων τον υιον και πιστευων εις αυτον εχη ζωην

59 αιωνιον. Ταυτα ειπεν εν συναγωγη διδασκων εν Καφαρναουμ.

5:

1 Μετα ταυτα ην εορτη των Ιουδαιων, και ανεβη Ιησους εις   177

2 Ιεροσολυμα. εστιν δε εν τοις Ιεροσολυμοις επι τη προβατικη
κολυμβηθρα. η επιλεγομενη Εβραιστι Βηθζαθα, πεντε στοας

3 εχουσα. εν ταυταις κατεκειτο πληθος των ασθενουντων,

5[1] τυφλων, χωλων, ξηρων. ην δε τις ανθρωπος εκει τριακοντα και

6 οκτω ετη εχων εν τη ασθενεια αυτου· τουτον ιδων ο Ιησους κατακειμενον, και γνους οτι πολυν ηδη χρονον εχει, λεγει αυτω· θελεις

7 υγιης γενεσθαι; απεκριθη αυτω ο ασθενων· κυριε, ανθρωπον ουκ
εχω, ινα οταν ταραχθη το υδωρ βαλη με εις την κολυμβηθραν·

8 εν ω δε ερχομαι εγω, αλλος προ εμου καταβαινει. λεγει αυτω

---

[1] V. 4 is not attested by the best manuscripts and is relegated to the
apparatus in the Nestle text.

9 ο Ιησους· εγειρε αρον τον κραβατον σου και περιπατει. και ευθεως
εγενετο υγιης ο ανθρωπος, και ηρεν τον κραβατον αυτου και
10 περιεπατει. Ην δε σαββατον εν εκεινη τη ημερα. ελεγον ουν οι
Ιουδαιοι τω τεθεραπευμενω· σαββατον εστιν, και ουκ εξεστιν σοι
11 αραι τον κραβατον. ος δε απεκριθη αυτοις· ο ποιησας με υγιη,
12 εκεινος μοι ειπεν· αρον τον κραβατον σου και περιπατει. ηρωτησαν
αυτον· τις εστιν ο ανθρωπος ο ειπων σοι· αρον και περιπατει;
13 ο δε ιαθεις ουκ ηδει τις εστιν· ο γαρ Ιησους εξενευσεν οχλου οντος εν
14 τω τοπω. μετα ταυτα ευρισκει αυτον ο Ιησους εν τω ιερω και
ειπεν αυτω· ιδε υγιης γεγονας· μηκετι αμαρτανε, ινα μη χειρον
15 σοι τι γενηται. απηλθεν ο ανθρωπος και ειπεν τοις Ιουδαιοις
16 οτι Ιησους εστιν ο ποιησας αυτον υγιη. και δια τουτο εδιωκον οι
17 Ιουδαιοι τον Ιησουν, οτι ταυτα εποιει εν σαββατω. ο δε απεκρινατο
18 αυτοις· ο πατηρ μου εως αρτι εργαζεται, καγω εργαζομαι· δια
τουτο ουν μαλλον εζητουν αυτον οι Ιουδαιοι αποκτειναι, οτι ου
μονον ελυεν το σαββατον, αλλα και πατερα ιδιον ελεγεν τον
19 θεον, ισον εαυτον ποιων τω θεω. Απεκρινατο ουν ο Ιησους και
ελεγεν αυτοις· αμην αμην λεγω υμιν, ου δυναται ο υιος ποιειν αφ
εαυτου ουδεν, αν μη τι βλεπη τον πατερα ποιουντα· α γαρ αν
20 εκεινος ποιη, ταυτα και ο υιος ομοιως ποιει. ο γαρ πατηρ φιλει
τον υιον και παντα δεικνυσιν αυτω α αυτος ποιει, και μειζονα
21 τουτων δειξει αυτω εργα, ινα υμεις θαυμαζητε. ωσπερ γαρ ο
πατηρ εγειρει τους νεκρους και ζωοποιει, ουτως και ο υιος ους
22 θελει ζωοποιει. ουδε γαρ ο πατηρ κρινει ουδενα, αλλα την κρισιν
23 πασαν δεδωκεν τω υιω, ινα παντες τιμωσι τον υιον καθως τιμωσι
τον πατερα. ο μη τιμων τον υιον ου τιμα τον πατερα τον πεμψαντα
24 αυτον. Αμην αμην λεγω υμιν οτι ο τον λογον μου ακουων και
πιστευων τω πεμψαντι με εχει ζωην αιωνιον, και εις κρισιν ουκ
25 ερχεται αλλα μεταβεβηκεν εκ του θανατου εις την ζωην. αμην
αμην λεγω υμιν οτι ερχεται ωρα και νυν εστιν οτε οι νεκροι
ακουσουσιν της φωνης του υιου του θεου και οι ακουσαντες ζησου-
26 σιν. ωσπερ γαρ ο πατηρ εχει ζωην εν εαυτω, ουτως και τω υιω
27 εδωκεν ζωην εχειν εν εαυτω. [και εξουσιαν εδωκεν αυτω κρισιν
30 ποιειν. οτι υιος (ανθρωπου) εστιν.] Ου δυναμαι εγω ποιειν
απ εμαυτου ουδεν· καθως ακουω κρινω, και η κρισις η εμη δικαια
εστιν, οτι ου ζητω το θελημα το εμον αλλα το θελημα του πεμ-
31 ψαντος με. Εαν εγω μαρτυρω περι εμαυτου, η μαρτυρια μου ουκ
32 εστιν αληθης· αλλος εστιν ο μαρτυρων περι εμου. και οιδα οτι
33 αληθης εστιν η μαρτυρια ην μαρτυρει περι εμου. υμεις απεσταλ-
34 κατε προς Ιωαννην, και μεμαρτυρηκεν τη αληθεια· εγω δε ου παρα
ανθρωπου την μαρτυριαν λαμβανω, αλλα ταυτα λεγω ινα υμεις
35 σωθητε. εκεινος ην ο λυχνος ο καιομενος και φαινων, υμεις δε

36 ηθελησατε αγαλλιαθηναι προς ωραν εν τω φωτι αυτου. Εγω δε
εχω την μαρτυριαν μειζω του Ιωαννου· τα γαρ εργα α δεδωκεν
μοι ο πατηρ ινα τελειωσω αυτα, αυτα τα εργα α ποιω μαρτυρει
37 περι εμου οτι ο πατηρ με απεσταλκεν. και ο πεμψας με πατηρ,
εκεινος μεμαρτυρηκεν περι εμου. ουτε φωνην αυτου πωποτε
38 ακηκοατε ουτε ειδος αυτου εωρακατε, και τον λογον αυτου ουκ
εχετε εν υμιν μενοντα, οτι ον απεστειλεν εκεινος, τουτω υμεις ου
39 πιστευετε. ερευνατε τας γραφας, οτι υμεις δοκειτε εν αυταις ζωην
40 αιωνιον εχειν· και εκειναι εισιν αι μαρτυρουσαι περι εμου· και
41 ου θελετε ελθειν προς με ινα ζωην εχητε. Δοξαν παρα ανθρωπων
42 ου λαμβανω, αλλα εγνωκα υμας οτι την αγαπην του θεου ουκ
43 εχετε εν εαυτοις. εγω εληλυθα εν τω ονοματι του πατρος μου,
και ου λαμβανετε με· εαν αλλος ελθη εν τω ονοματι τω ιδιω,
44 εκεινον λημψεσθε. πως δυνασθε υμεις πιστευσαι, δοξαν παρα
αλληλων λαμβανοντες, και την δοξαν την παρα του μονου θεου ου
45 ζητειτε; μη δοκειτε οτι εγω κατηγορησω υμων προς τον πατερα·
46 εστιν ο κατηγορων υμων Μωυσης, εις ον υμεις ηλπικατε. ει γαρ
επιστευετε Μωυσει, επιστευετε αν εμοι· περι γαρ εμου εκεινος
47 εγραψεν. ει δε τοις εκεινου γραμμασιν ου πιστευετε, πως τοις

7:
15 εμοις ρημασιν πιστευσετε; εθαυμαζον ουν οι Ιουδαιοι λεγοντες·   177 f.
16 πως ουτος γραμματα οιδεν μη μεμαθηκως; απεκριθη ουν αυτοις
Ιησους και ειπεν· η εμη διδαχη ουκ εστιν εμη αλλα του πεμψαντος
17 με· εαν τις θελη το θελημα αυτου ποιειν, γνωσεται περι της
18 διδαχης, ποτερον εκ του θεου εστιν η εγω απ εμαυτου λαλω. ο αφ
εαυτου λαλων την δοξαν την ιδιαν ζητει· ο δε ζητων την δοξαν του
πεμψαντος αυτον, ουτος αληθης εστιν και αδικια εν αυτω ουκ εστιν.
19 ου Μωυσης εδωκεν υμιν τον νομον; και ουδεις εξ υμων ποιει τον
20 νομον. τι με ζητειτε αποκτειναι; απεκριθη ο οχλος· δαιμονιον
21 εχεις· τις σε ζητει αποκτειναι; απεκριθη Ιησους και ειπεν αυτοις·
22 εν εργον εποιησα και παντες θαυμαζετε. δια τουτο Μωυσης δεδωκεν υμιν την περιτομην, — ουχ οτι εκ του Μωυσεως εστιν αλλ εκ
23 των πατερων, — και εν σαββατω περιτεμνετε ανθρωπον. ει
περιτομην λαμβανει [ο] ανθρωπος εν σαββατω ινα μη λυθη ο
νομος Μωυσεως, εμοι χολατε οτι ολον ανθρωπον υγιη εποιησα εν
24 σαββατω; μη κρινετε κατ οψιν, αλλα την δικαιαν κρισιν κρινατε.

8:
13 ειπον ουν αυτω οι Φαρισαιοι· συ περι σεαυτου μαρτυρεις· η μαρ-   178
14 τυρια σου ουκ εστιν αληθης. απεκριθη Ιησους και ειπεν αυτοις· καν
εγω μαρτυρω περι εμαυτου, αληθης εστιν η μαρτυρια μου, οτι
οιδα ποθεν ηλθον και που υπαγω· υμεις δε ουκ οιδατε ποθεν ερχομαι
15 η που υπαγω. υμεις κατα την σαρκα κρινετε, εγω ου κρινω ουδενα.
16 και εαν κρινω δε εγω, η κρισις η εμη αληθινη εστιν, οτι μονος ουκ
17 ειμι, αλλ εγω και ο πεμψας με. και εν τω νομω δε τω υμετερω

18 γεγραπται οτι δυο ανθρωπων η μαρτυρια αληθης εστιν. εγω

εμι ο μαρτυρων περι εμαυτου, και μαρτυρει περι εμου ο πεμψας

19 με πατηρ, ελεγον ουν αυτω· που εστιν ο πατηρ σου; απεκριθη

Ιησους· ουτε εμε οιδατε ουτε τον πατερα μου· ει εμε ηδειτε, και

20 τον πατερα μου αν ηδειτε. Ταυτα τα ρηματα ελαλησεν εν τω

γαζοφυλακειω διδασκων εν τω ιερω· και ουδεις επιασεν αυτον,

οτι ουπω εληλυθει η ωρα αυτου.

7: 1   Και μετα ταυτα περιεπατει ο Ιησους εν τη Γαλιλαια· ου γαρ   216

ηθελεν εν τη Ιουδαια περιπατειν, οτι εζητουν αυτον οι Ιουδαιοι

2 αποκτειναι. ην δε εγγυς η εορτη των Ιουδαιων η σκηνοπηγια.

3 ειπον ουν προς αυτον οι αδελφοι αυτου· μεταβηθι εντευθεν και

υπαγε εις την Ιουδαιαν, ινα και οι μαθηται σου θεωρησουσιν τα

4 εργα σου α ποιεις· ουδεις γαρ τι εν κρυπτω ποιει και ζητει αυτος

5 εν παρρησια ειναι. ει ταυτα ποιεις, φανερωσον σεαυτον τω κοσμω.

5, 6 ουδε γαρ οι αδελφοι αυτου επιστευον εις αυτον. λεγει ουν αυτοις

ο Ιησους· ο καιρος ο εμος ουπω παρεστιν, ο δε καιρος ο υμετερος

7 παντοτε εστιν ετοιμος. ου δυναται ο κοσμος μισειν υμας, εμε δε

μισει, οτι εγω μαρτυρω περι αυτου οτι τα εργα αυτου πονηρα

8 εστιν. υμεις αναβητε εις την εορτην· εγω ουκ αναβαινω εις την

9 εορτην ταυτην, οτι ο εμος καιρος ουπω πεπληρωται. ταυτα δε ειπων

10 αυτοις εμεινεν εν τη Γαλιλαια. Ως δε ανεβησαν οι αδελφοι αυτου

εις την εορτην, τοτε και αυτος ανεβη, ου φανερως αλλα ως εν

11 κρυπτω. οι ουν Ιουδαιοι εζητουν αυτον εν τη εορτη και ελεγον·

12 που εστιν εκεινος; και γογγυσμος περι αυτου ην πολυς εν τοις

οχλοις· οι μεν ελεγον οτι αγαθος εστιν· αλλοι [δε] ελεγον· ου,

13 αλλα πλανα τον οχλον. ουδεις μεντοι παρρησια ελαλει περι

αυτου δια τον φοβον των Ιουδαιων.

14   Ηδη δε της εορτης μεσουσης ανεβη Ιησους εις το ιερον και

25 εδιδασκεν. Ελεγον ουν τινες εκ των Ιεροσολυμιτων· ουχ ουτος

26 εστιν ον ζητουσιν αποκτειναι; και ιδε παρρησια λαλει. και ουδεν

αυτω λεγουσιν. μηποτε αληθως εγνωσαν οι αρχοντες οτι ουτος

27 εστιν ο χριστος; αλλα τουτον οιδαμεν ποθεν εστιν· ο δε χριστος

28 οταν ερχηται, ουδεις γινωσκει ποθεν εστιν. εκραξεν ουν εν τω ιερω

διδασκων ο Ιησους και λεγων· καμε οιδατε και οιδατε ποθεν ειμι·

και απ εμαυτου ουκ εληλυθα, αλλ εστιν αληθινος ο πεμψας με,

29 ον υμεις ουκ οιδατε· εγω οιδα αυτον, οτι παρ αυτου ειμι κακεινος με

8: 48 απεστειλεν. Απεκριθησαν οι Ιουδαιοι και ειπαν αυτω· ου καλως

49 λεγομεν ημεις οτι Σαμαριτης ει συ και δαιμονιον εχεις; απεκριθη

Ιησους· εγω δαιμονιον ουκ εχω, αλλα τιμω τον πατερα μου, και

50 υμεις ατιμαζετε με. εγω δε ου ζητω δοξαν μου· εστιν ο ζητων και

54 κρινων. εαν εγω δοξασω εμαυτον, η δοξα μου ουδεν εστιν· εστιν ο

πατηρ μου ο δοξαζων με, ον υμεις λεγετε οτι θεος ημων εστιν,

7:

55 και ουκ εγνωκατε αυτον, εγω δε οιδα αυτον. καν ειπω οτι ουκ
οιδα αυτον, εσομαι ομοιος υμιν ψευστης· αλλα οιδα αυτον και τον
30 λογον αυτου τηρω. Εξητουν ουν αυτον πιασαι, και ουδεις επεβαλεν
επ αυτον την χειρα, οτι ουπω εληλυθει η ωρα αυτου.

37   Εν δε τη εσχατη ημερα τη μεγαλη της εορτης ειστηκει ο
Ιησους και εκραξεν λεγων· εαν τις διψα, ερχεσθω προς με και
38, 39 πινετω. ο πιστευων εις εμε, τουτο δε ειπεν περι του πνευματος ου
εμελλον λαμβανειν οι πιστευσαντες εις αυτον· [ουπω γαρ ην
40 πνευμα, οτι Ιησους ουδεπω εδοξασθη.] Εκ του οχλου ουν ακουσαντες των λογων τουτων ελεγον [οτι]· ουτος εστιν αληθως ο
41 προφητης· αλλοι ελεγον· ουτος εστιν ο χριστος· οι δε ελεγον·
42 μη γαρ εκ της Γαλιλαιας ο χριστος ερχεται; ουχ η γραφη ειπεν
οτι εκ του σπερματος Δαυιδ, και απο Βηθλεεμ της κωμης οπου
43 ην Δαυιδ. ερχεται ο χριστος; σχισμα ουν εγενετο εν τω οχλω
44 δι αυτον· τινες δε ηθελον εξ αυτων πιασαι αυτον. αλλ ουδεις
31 επεβαλεν επ αυτον τας χειρας. Εκ του οχλου δε πολλοι επιστευσαν εις αυτον, και ελεγον· ο χριστος οταν ελθη, μη πλειονα
32 σημεια ποιησει ων ουτος εποιησεν; ηκουσαν οι Φαρισαιοι του
οχλου γογγυζοντος περι αυτου ταυτα και απεστειλαν οι αρχιερεις
33 και οι Φαρισαιοι υπηρετας ινα πιασωσιν αυτον. ειπεν ουν ο
Ιησους· ετι χρονον μικρον μεθ υμων ειμι και υπαγω προς τον
34 πεμψαντα με. ζητησετε με και ουχ ευρησετε, και οπου ειμι εγω
35 υμεις ου δυνασθε ελθειν. ειπον ουν οι Ιουδαιοι προς εαυτους·
που ουτος μελλει πορευεσθαι, οτι ημεις ουχ ευρησομεν αυτον;
μη εις την διασποραν των Ελληνων μελλει πορευεσθαι και
36 διδασκειν τους Ελληνας; τις εστιν ο λογος ουτος ον ειπεν· ζητησετε
με και ουχ ευρησετε, και οπου ειμι εγω υμεις ου δυνασθε ελθειν;
45 Ηλθον ουν οι υπηρεται προς τους αρχιερεις και Φαρισαιους, και
46 ειπον αυτοις εκεινοι. δια τι ουκ ηγαγετε αυτον; απεκριθησαν οι
υπηρεται· ουδεποτε ελαλησεν ουτως ανθρωπος. ως ουτος λαλει ο
47 ανθρωπος. απεκριθησαν ουν αυτοις οι Φαρισαιοι· μη και υμεις
48 πεπλανησθε; μη τις εκ των αρχοντων επιστευσεν εις αυτον η εκ
49 των Φαρισαιων: αλλα ο οχλος ουτος ο μη γινωσκων τον νομον
50 επαρατοι εισιν. λεγει Νικοδημος προς αυτους, ο ελθων προς
51 αυτον προτερον, εις ων εξ αυτων· μη ο νομος ημων κρινει τον
ανθρωπον εαν μη ακουση πρωτον παρ αυτου και γνω τι ποιει,
52 απεκριθησαν και ειπαν αυτω· μη και συ εκ της Γαλιλαιας ει;
ερευνησον και ιδε οτι εκ της Γαλιλαιας προφητης ουκ εγειρεται.

(textual loss)

236–38

8:

41 υμεις ποιειτε τα εργα του πατρος υμων. ειπαν αυτω· ημεις εκ
42 πορνειας ουκ εγεννηθημεν, ενα πατερα εχομεν τον θεον. ειπεν

αυτοις ο Ιησους· ει ο θεος πατηρ υμων ην, ηγαπατε αν εμε· εγω
γαρ εκ του θεου εξηλθον και ηκω· ουδε γαρ απ εμαντου εληλυθα.
43 αλλ εκεινος με απεστειλεν. δια τι την λαλιαν την εμην ου
44 γινωσκετε; οτι ου δυνασθε ακουειν τον λογον τον εμον. υμεις εκ
του πατρος του διαβολου εστε και τας επιθυμιας του πατρος υμων
θελετε ποιειν. εκεινος ανθρωποκτονος ην απ αρχης, και εν τη
αληθεια ουκ εστηκεν, οτι ουκ εστιν αληθεια εν αυτω. οταν λαλη το
ψευδος, εκ των ιδιων λαλει, οτι ψευστης εστιν και ο πατηρ αυτου.
45, 46 εγω δε οτι την αληθειαν λεγω, ου πιστευετε μοι. τις εξ υμων
ελεγχει με περι αμαρτιας; ει αληθειαν λεγω, δια τι υμεις ου
47 πιστευετε μοι; ο ων εκ του θεου τα ρηματα του θεου ακουει· δια
51 τουτο υμεις ουκ ακουετε, οτι εκ του θεου ουκ εστε. αμην αμην
λεγω υμιν. εαν τις τον εμον λογον τηρηση, θανατον ου μη
52 θεωρηση εις τον αιωνα. ειπαν αυτω οι Ιουδαιοι· νυν εγνωκαμεν
οτι δαιμονιον εχεις. Αβρααμ απεθανεν και οι προφηται, και συ
λεγεις· εαν τις τον λογον μου τηρηση. ου μη γευσηται θανατου
53 εις τον αιωνα. μη συ μειζων ει του πατρος ημων Αβρααμ, οστις
απεθανεν; και οι προφηται απεθανον· τινα σεαυτον ποιεις;
56 απεκριθη Ιησους· Αβρααμ ο πατηρ υμων ηγαλλιασατο ινα ιδη
57 την ημεραν την εμην, και ειδεν και εχαρη. ειπαν ουν οι Ιουδαιοι
προς αυτον· πεντηκοντα ετη ουπω εχεις και Αβρααμ εωρακας;
58 ειπεν αυτοις Ιησους· αμην αμην λεγω υμιν, πριν Αβρααμ γενεσθαι
59 εγω ειμι. ηραν ουν λιθους ινα βαλωσιν επ αυτον· Ιησους δε
εκρυβη και εξηλθεν εκ του ιερου.

9: 1, 2   Και παραγων ειδεν ανθρωπον τυφλον εκ γενετης. και ηρωτησαν
αυτον οι μαθηται αυτου λεγοντες· ρ α β β ι, τις ημαρτεν,
3 ουτος η οι γονεις αυτου, ινα τυφλος γεννηθη; απεκριθη Ιησους·
ουτε ουτος ημαρτεν ουτε οι γονεις αυτου, αλλ ινα φανερωθη τα
4 εργα του θεου εν αυτω. ημας δει εργαζεσθαι τα εργα του πεμψαντος με εως ημερα εστιν· ερχεται νυξ οτε ουδεις δυναται εργα-
5, 6 ζεσθαι. οταν εν τω κοσμω ω, φως ειμι του κοσμου. ταυτα ειπων
επτυσεν χαμαι και εποιησεν πηλον εκ του πτυσματος, και επεθηκεν
7 αυτου τον πηλον επι τους οφθαλμους, και ειπεν αυτω· υπαγε
νιψαι εις την κολυμβηθραν του Σιλωαμ [ο ερμηνευεται απεσταλ-
8 μενος]. απηλθεν ουν και ενιψατο, και ηλθεν βλεπων. Οι ουν
γειτονες και οι θεωρουντες αυτον το προτερον, οτι προσαιτης
9 ην, ελεγον· ουχ ουτος εστιν ο καθημενος και προσαιτων; αλλοι
ελεγον οτι ουτος εστιν· αλλοι ελεγον· ουχι, αλλα ομοιος αυτω
10 εστιν. εκεινος ελεγεν οτι εγω ειμι. ελεγον ουν αυτω· πως [ουν]
11 ηνεωχθησαν σου οι οφθαλμοι; απεκριθη εκεινος· ο ανθρωπος ο
λεγομενος Ιησους πηλον εποιησεν και επεχρισεν μου τους οφθαλμους και ειπεν μοι οτι υπαγε εις τον Σιλωαμ και νιψαι· απελθων
12 ουν και νιψαμενος ανεβλεψα. και ειπαν αυτω· που εστιν εκεινος;

13 λεγει· ουκ οιδα. Αγουσιν αυτον προς τους Φαρισαιους, τον ποτε
14 τυφλον. ην δε σαββατον εν η ημερα τον πηλον εποιησεν ο Ιησους
15 και ανεωξεν αυτου τους οφθαλμους. παλιν ουν ηρωτων αυτον και
   οι Φαρισαιοι πως ανεβλεψεν. ο δε ειπεν αυτοις· πηλον επεθηκεν
16 μου επι τους οφθαλμους, και ενιψαμην, και βλεπω. ελεγον ουν
   εκ των Φαρισαιων τινες· ουκ εστιν ουτος παρα θεου ο ανθρωπος,
   οτι το σαββατον ου τηρει. αλλοι [δε] ελεγον· πως δυναται ανθρωπος αμαρτωλος τοιαυτα σημεια ποιειν; και σχισμα ην εν αυτοις.
17 λεγουσιν ουν τω τυφλω παλιν· τι συ λεγεις περι αυτου, οτι
   ηνεωξεν σου τους οφθαλμους; ο δε ειπεν οτι προφητης εστιν.
18 ουκ επιστευσαν ουν οι Ιουδαιοι περι αυτου οτι ην τυφλος και
   ανεβλεψεν, εως οτου εφωνησαν τους γονεις αυτου του αναβλεψαντος
19 και ηρωτησαν αυτους λεγοντες· ουτος εστιν ο υιος υμων, ον υμεις
20 λεγετε οτι τυφλος εγεννηθη; πως ουν βλεπει αρτι απεκριθησαν
   ουν οι γονεις αυτου και ειπαν. οιδαμεν οτι ουτος εστιν ο υιος ημων
21 και οτι τυφλος εγεννηθη· πως δε νυν βλεπει ουκ οιδαμεν, η τις
   ηνοιξεν αυτου τους οφθαλμους ημεις ουκ οιδαμεν· αυτον ερωτησατε,
22 ηλικιαν εχει, αυτος περι εαυτου λαλησει. ταυτα ειπαν οι γονεις
   αυτου οτι εφοβουντο τους Ιουδαιους· ηδη γαρ συνετεθειντο οι
   Ιουδαιοι ινα εαν τις αυτον ομολογηση χριστον, αποσυναγωγος
23 γενηται. δια τουτο οι γονεις αυτου ειπαν οτι ηλικιαν εχει. αυτον
24 επερωτησατε. Εφωνησαν ουν τον ανθρωπον εκ δευτερου ος
   ην τυφλος, και ειπαν αυτω· δος δοξαν τω θεω· ημεις οιδαμεν οτι
25 ουτος ο ανθρωπος αμαρτωλος εστιν. απεκριθη ουν εκεινος· ει
   αμαρτωλος εστιν ουκ οιδα· εν οιδα, οτι τυφλος ων αρτι βλεπω.
26 ειπαν ουν αυτω· τι εποιησεν σοι; πως ηνοιξεν σου τους οφθαλμους;
27 απεκριθη αυτοις· ειπον υμιν ηδη και ουκ ηκουσατε· τι παλιν
28 θελετε ακουειν; μη και υμεις θελετε αυτου μαθηται γενεσθαι; και
   ελοιδορησαν αυτον και ειπαν· συ μαθητης ει εκεινου, ημεις δε
29 του Μωυσεως εσμεν μαθηται· ημεις οιδαμεν οτι Μωυσει λελα-
30 ληκεν ο θεος, τουτον δε ουκ οιδαμεν ποθεν εστιν. απεκριθη ο
   ανθρωπος και ειπεν αυτοις· εν τουτω γαρ το θαυμαστον εστιν,
   οτι υμεις ουκ οιδατε ποθεν εστιν, και ηνοιξεν μου τους οφθαλμους.
31 οιδαμεν οτι ο θεος αμαρτωλων ουκ ακουει, αλλ εαν τις θεοσεβης
32 η και το θελημα αυτου ποιη, τουτου ακουει. εκ του αιωνος ουκ
33 ηκουσθη οτι ηνεωξεν τις οφθαλμους τυφλου γεγεννημενου· ει
34 μη ην ουτος παρα θεου, ουκ ηδυνατο ποιειν ουδεν. απεκριθησαν
   και ειπαν αυτω· εν αμαρτιαις συ εγεννηθης ολος, και συ διδασκεις
35 ημας; και εξεβαλον αυτον εξω. Ηκουσεν Ιησους οτι εξεβαλον
   αυτον εξω, και ευρων αυτον ειπεν· συ πιστευεις εις τον υιον του
36 ανθρωπου; απεκριθη εκεινος και ειπεν· και τις εστιν, κυριε, ινα
37 πιστευσω εις αυτον; ειπεν αυτω ο Ιησους· και εωρακας αυτον
38 και ο λαλων μετα σου εκεινος εστιν. ο δε εφη· πιστευω, κυριε·

39 και προσεκυνησεν αυτω. και ειπεν ο Ιησους· εις κριμα εγω εις
τον κοσμον τουτον ηλθον, ινα οι μη βλεποντες βλεπωσιν και οι
βλεποντες τυφλοι γενωνται.

40   Ηκουσαν εκ των Φαρισαιων ταυτα οι μετ αυτου οντες, και
41 ειπαν αυτω· μη και ημεις τυφλοι εσμεν; ειπεν αυτοις ο Ιησους· ει
τυφλοι ητε, ουκ αν ειχετε αμαρτιαν· νυν δε λεγετε οτι βλεπομεν·
η αμαρτια υμων μενει.

8:
12:

12 [Παλιν ουν αυτοις ελαλησεν ο Ιησους λεγων·] εγω ειμι το φως
του κοσμου· ο ακολουθων μοι ου μη περιπατηση εν τη σκοτια.
44 αλλ εξει το φως της ζωης. ο πιστευων εις εμε ου πιστευει εις εμε
45 αλλα εις τον πεμψαντα με, και ο θεωρων εμε θεωρει τον πεμψαντα
46 με. εγω φως εις τον κοσμον εληλυθα, ινα πας ο πιστευων εις εμε
47 εν τη σκοτια μη μεινη. και εαν τις μου ακουση των ρηματων και
μη φυλαξη, εγω ου κρινω αυτον· ου γαρ ηλθον ινα κρινω τον
48 κοσμον, αλλ ινα σωσω τον κοσμον. ο αθετων εμε και μη λαμβανων
τα ρηματα μου εχει τον κρινοντα αυτον· ο λογος ον ελαλησα,
49 εκεινος κρινει αυτον. οτι εγω εξ εμαυτου ουκ ελαλησα, αλλ ο
πεμψας με πατηρ αυτος μοι εντολην δεδωκεν τι ειπω και τι λαλησω.
50 και οιδα οτι η εντολη αυτου ζωη αιωνιος εστιν. α ουν εγω λαλω,
καθως ειρηκεν μοι ο πατηρ, ουτως λαλω.

8:

21   Ειπεν ουν παλιν αυτοις· εγω υπαγω και ζητησετε με, και
22 εν τη αμαρτια υμων αποθανεισθε· οπου εγω υπαγω υμεις ου
22 δυνασθε ελθειν. ελεγον ουν οι Ιουδαιοι· μητι αποκτενει εαυτον.
23 οτι λεγει· οπου εγω υπαγω υμεις ου δυνασθε ελθειν; και ελεγεν
αυτοις· υμεις εκ των κατω εστε, εγω εκ των ανω ειμι· υμεις εκ
24 τουτου του κοσμου εστε, εγω ουκ ειμι εκ του κοσμου τουτου. ειπον
ουν υμιν οτι αποθανεισθε εν ταις αμαρτιαις υμων· εαν γαρ μη
πιστευσητε οτι εγω ειμι, αποθανεισθε εν ταις αμαρτιαις υμων.
25 ελεγον ουν αυτω· συ τις ει; ειπεν αυτοις ο Ιησους· την αρχην ο τι
28 και λαλω υμιν; ειπεν ουν ο Ιησους· οταν υψωσητε τον υιον του
ανθρωπου, τοτε γνωσεσθε οτι εγω ειμι, και απ εμαυτου ποιω
29 ουδεν, αλλα καθως εδιδαξεν με ο πατηρ, ταυτα λαλω. και ο
πεμψας με μετ εμου εστιν· ουκ αφηκεν με μονον, οτι εγω τα αρεστα

12:

34 αυτω ποιω παντοτε. απεκριθη ουν αυτω ο οχλος· ημεις ηκουσαμεν
εκ του νομου οτι ο χριστος μενει εις τον αιωνα, και πως λεγεις συ
οτι δει υψωθηναι τον υιον του ανθρωπου; τις εστιν ουτος ο υιος
35 του ανθρωπου; ειπεν ουν αυτοις ο Ιησους· ετι μικρον χρονον το
φως εν υμιν εστιν. περιπατειτε ως το φως εχετε, ινα μη σκοτια
υμας καταλαβη· και ο περιπατων εν τη σκοτια ουκ οιδεν που
36 υπαγει. ως το φως εχετε, πιστευετε εις το φως, ινα υιοι φωτος

10:

19 γενησθε. Σχισμα παλιν εγενετο εν τοις Ιουδαιοις δια τους λογους
20 τουτους. ελεγον δε πολλοι εξ αυτων· δαιμονιον εχει και μαινεται·

266 ff.
(on 8:26 f.)

21 τι αυτου ακουετε; αλλοι ελεγον· ταυτα τα ρηματα ουκ εστιν
δαιμονιζομενου· μη δαιμονιον δυναται τυφλων οφθαλμους ανοιξαι;

22, 23   Εγενετο τοτε τα εγκαινια εν τοις Ιεροσολυμοις· χειμων ην· και   272–74
περιεπατει ο Ιησους εν τω ιερω εν τη στοα του Σολομωνος.

24 εκυκλωσαν ουν αυτον οι Ιουδαιοι και ελεγον αυτω· εως ποτε την
ψυχην ημων αιρεις; ει συ ει ο χριστος, ειπον ημιν παρρησια.

25 απεκριθη αυτοις ο Ιησους· ειπον υμιν, και ου πιστευετε· τα εργα
α εγω ποιω εν τω ονοματι του πατρος μου, ταυτα μαρτυρει περι

26 εμου· αλλα υμεις ου πιστευετε, οτι ουκ εστε εκ των προβατων

11 των εμων. Εγω ειμι ο ποιμην ο καλος. ο ποιμην ο καλος την

12 ψυχην αυτου τιθησιν υπερ των προβατων· ο μισθωτος και ουκ
ων ποιμην, ου ουκ εστιν τα προβατα ιδια, θεωρει τον λυκον
ερχομενον και αφιησιν τα προβατα και φευγει, — και ο λυκος

13 αρπαζει αυτα και σκορπιζει· — οτι μισθωτος εστιν και ου μελει

1 αυτω περι των προβατων. Αμην αμην λεγω υμιν, ο μη εισερχομενος δια της θυρας εις την αυλην των προβατων αλλα αναβαι-

2 νων αλλαχοθεν, εκεινος κλεπτης εστιν και ληστης· ο δε εισερχο-

3 μενος δια της θυρας ποιμην εστιν των προβατων. τουτω ο θυρωρος
ανοιγει, και τα προβατα της φωνης αυτου ακουει, και τα ιδια

4 προβατα φωνει κατ ονομα και εξαγει αυτα. οταν τα ιδια παντα
εκβαλη, εμπροσθεν αυτων πορευεται, και τα προβατα αυτω

5 ακολουθει, οτι οιδασιν την φωνην αυτου· αλλοτριω δε ου μη
ακολουθησουσιν, αλλα φευξονται απ αυτου, οτι ουκ οιδασιν των

6 αλλοτριων την φωνην. Ταυτην την παροιμιαν ειπεν αυτοις ο

7 Ιησους· εκεινοι δε ουκ εγνωσαν τινα ην α ελαλει αυτοις. Ειπεν ουν
παλιν ο Ιησους· αμην αμην λεγω υμιν οτι εγω ειμι η θυρα των

8 προβατων. παντες οσοι ηλθον προ εμου κλεπται εισιν και λησται·

9 αλλ ουκ ηκουσαν αυτων τα προβατα. εγω ειμι η θυρα· δι εμου
εαν τις εισελθη, σωθησεται, και εισελευσεται και εξελευσεται

10 και νομην ευρησει. ο κλεπτης ουκ ερχεται ει μη ινα κλεψη και
θυση και απολεση· εγω ηλθον ινα ζωην εχωσιν και περισσον

14 εχωσιν. εγω ειμι ο ποιμην ο καλος, και γινωσκω τα εμα και

15 γινωσκουσι με τα εμα, καθως γινωσκει με ο πατηρ καγω γινωσκω
τον πατερα, και την ψυχην μου τιθημι υπερ των προβατων.

17 δια τουτο με ο πατηρ αγαπα οτι εγω τιθημι την ψυχην μου,

18 ινα παλιν λαβω αυτην. ουδεις ηρεν αυτην απ εμου, αλλ εγω
τιθημι αυτην απ εμαυτου. εξουσιαν εχω θειναι αυτην, και
εξουσιαν εχω παλιν λαβειν αυτην· ταυτην την εντολην ελαβον

27 παρα του πατρος μου. τα προβατα τα εμα της φωνης μου

28 ακουουσιν, καγω γινωσκω αυτα, και ακολουθουσιν μοι, καγω
διδωμι αυτοις ζωην αιωνιον, και ου μη απολωνται εις τον αιωνα,

29 και ουχ αρπασει τις αυτα εκ της χειρος μου. ο πατηρ μου ο
δεδωκεν μοι παντων μειζον εστιν, και ουδεις δυναται αρπαζειν εκ

30, 31 της χειρος του πατρος. εγω και ο πατηρ εν εσμεν. Εβαστασαν
32 παλιν λιθους οι Ιουδαιοι ινα λιθασωσιν αυτον. απεκριθη αυτοις
     ο Ιησους· πολλα εργα εδειξα υμιν καλα εκ του πατρος· δια
33 ποιον αυτων εργον εμε λιθαζετε; απεκριθησαν αυτω οι Ιουδαιοι·
     περι καλου εργου ου λιθαζομεν σε αλλα περι βλασφημιας,
37 και οτι συ ανθρωπος ων ποιεις σεαυτον θεον.[1] ει ου ποιω τα
38 εργα του πατρος μου, μη πιστευετε μοι· ει δε ποιω, καν εμοι
     μη πιστευητε, τοις εργοις πιστευετε, ινα γνωτε και γινωσκητε
39 οτι εν εμοι ο πατηρ καγω εν τω πατρι. Εζητουν ουν αυτον παλιν
     πιασαι· και εξηλθεν εκ της χειρος αυτων.
40   Και απηλθεν παλιν περαν του Ιορδανου εις τον τοπον οπου
41 ην Ιωαννης το πρωτον βαπτιζων, και εμενεν εκει. και πολλοι
     ηλθον προς αυτον και ελεγον οτι Ιωαννης μεν σημειον εποιησεν
42 ουδεν, παντα δε οσα ειπεν Ιωαννης περι τουτου αληθη ην. και
     πολλοι επιστευσαν εις αυτον εκει.

11:

1   Ην δε τις ασθενων, Λαζαρος απο Βηθανιας, εκ της κωμης
3 Μαριας και Μαρθας της αδελφης αυτης. απεστειλαν ουν αι
4 αδελφαι προς αυτον λεγουσαι· κυριε, ιδε ον φιλεις ασθενει. ακου-
     σας δε ο Ιησους ειπεν· αυτη η ασθενεια ουκ εστιν προς θανατον
     αλλ υπερ της δοξης του θεου, ινα δοξασθη ο υιος του θεου δι αυτης.
5 ηγαπα δε ο Ιησους την Μαρθαν και την αδελφην αυτης και τον
6 Λαζαρον. ως ουν ηκουσεν οτι ασθενει, τοτε μεν εμεινεν εν ω ην
7 τοπω δυο ημερας· επειτα μετα τουτο λεγει τοις μαθηταις·
8 αγωμεν εις την Ιουδαιαν παλιν. λεγουσιν αυτω οι μαθηται·
     ρ α β β ι, νυν εζητουν σε λιθασαι οι Ιουδαιοι, και παλιν υπαγεις
9 εκει; απεκριθη Ιησους· ουχι δωδεκα ωραι εισιν της ημερας; εαν
     τις περιπατη εν τη ημερα, ου προσκοπτει, οτι το φως του κοσμου
10 τουτου βλεπει· εαν δε τις περιπατη εν τη νυκτι, προσκοπτει,
11 οτι το φως ουκ εστιν εν αυτω. ταυτα ειπεν, και μετα τουτο λεγει
     αυτοις· Λαζαρος ο φιλος ημων κεκοιμηται· αλλα πορευομαι ινα
12 εξυπνισω αυτον. ειπαν ουν οι μαθηται αυτω· κυριε, ει κεκοιμηται,
13 σωθησεται. ειρηκει δε ο Ιησους περι του θανατου αυτου· εκεινοι
14 δε εδοξαν οτι περι της κοιμησεως του υπνου λεγει. τοτε ουν
15 ειπεν αυτοις ο Ιησους παρρησια· Λαζαρος απεθανεν, καχαιρω ϑ[1].
     υμας, ινα πιστευσητε, οτι ουκ ημην εκει· αλλα αγωμεν προς αυτον.
16 ειπεν ουν Θωμας ο λεγομενος Διδυμος τοις συμμαθηταις· αγωμεν
17 και ημεις ινα αποθανωμεν μετ αυτου. Ελθων ουν ο Ιησους ευρεν
18 αυτον τεσσαρας ηδη ημερας εχοντα εν τω μνημειω. ην δε Βηθανια
19 εγγυς των Ιεροσολυμων ως απο σταδιων δεκαπεντε. πολλοι δε εκ
     των Ιουδαιων εληλυθεισαν προς την Μαρθαν και Μαριαμ, ινα

---

[1] Presumably the original gospel carried some such introductory clause
as "and Jesus said," if not v. 34a (απεκριθη αυτοις ο Ιησους).

20 παραμυθησωνται αυτας περι του αδελφου. η ουν Μαρθα ως
   ηκουσεν οτι Ιησους ερχεται. υπηντησεν αυτω· Μαριαμ δε εν τω
21 οικω εκαθεζετο. ειπεν ουν η Μαρθα προς Ιησουν· κυριε, ει ης ωδε,
22 ουκ αν απεθανεν ο αδελφος μου. και νυν οιδα οτι οσα αν αιτηση
23 τον θεον δωσει σοι ο θεος. λεγει αυτη ο Ιησους· αναστησεται ο
24 αδελφος σου. λεγει αυτω η Μαρθα· οιδα οτι αναστησεται εν τη
25 αναστασει εν τη εσχατη ημερα. ειπεν αυτη ο Ιησους· εγω ειμι
   η αναστασις και η ζωη· ο πιστευων εις εμε καν αποθανη ζησεται,
26 και πας ο ζων και πιστευων εις εμε ου μη αποθανη εις τον αιωνα·
27 πιστευεις τουτο; λεγει αυτω· ναι, κυριε· εγω πεπιστευκα οτι συ ει
28 ο χριστος ο υιος του θεου ο εις τον κοσμον ερχομενος. και τουτο
   ειπουσα απηλθεν και εφωνησεν Μαριαμ την αδελφην αυτης λαθρα
29 ειπουσα· ο διδασκαλος παρεστιν και φωνει σε. εκεινη δε ως
30 ηκουσεν, εγειρεται ταχυ και ηρχετο προς αυτον· ουπω δε εληλυθει
   ο Ιησους εις την κωμην, αλλ ην ετι εν τω τοπω οπου υπηντησεν
31 αυτω η Μαρθα. οι ουν Ιουδαιοι οι οντες μετ αυτης εν τη οικια και
   παραμυθουμενοι αυτην, ιδοντες την Μαριαμ οτι ταχεως ανεστη
   και εξηλθεν, ηκολουθησαν αυτη, δοξαντες οτι υπαγει εις το
32 μνημειον ινα κλαυση εκει. η ουν Μαριαμ ως ηλθεν οπου ην Ιησους,
   ιδουσα αυτον επεσεν αυτου προς τους ποδας, λεγουσα αυτω·
33 κυριε. ει ης ωδε, ουκ αν μου απεθανεν ο αδελφος. Ιησους ουν ως
   ειδεν αυτην κλαιουσαν και τους συνελθοντας αυτη Ιουδαιους
   κλαιοντας, ενεβριμησατο τω πνευματι και εταραξεν εαυτον, και
34 ειπεν· που τεθεικατε αυτον; λεγουσιν αυτω· κυριε, ερχου και ιδε.
35, 36 εδακρυσεν ο Ιησους. ελεγον ουν οι Ιουδαιοι· ιδε πως εφιλει αυτον.
37 τινες δε εξ αυτων ειπαν· ουκ εδυνατο ουτος ο ανοιξας τους οφθαλ-
38 μους του τυφλου ποιησαι ινα και ουτος μη αποθανη; Ιησους ουν
   παλιν εμβριμωμενος εν εαυτω ερχεται εις το μνημειον· ην δε
39 σπηλαιον, και λιθος επεκειτο επ αυτω. λεγει ο Ιησους· αρατε τον
   λιθον. λεγει αυτω η αδελφη του τετελευτηκοτος Μαρθα· κυριε,
40 ηδη οζει· τεταρταιος γαρ εστιν. λεγει αυτη ο Ιησους· ουκ ειπον
41 σοι οτι εαν πιστευσης οψη την δοξαν του θεου; ηραν ουν τον
   λιθον. ο δε Ιησους ηρεν τους οφθαλμους ανω και ειπεν· πατερ,
42 ευχαριστω σοι οτι ηκουσας μου. εγω δε ηδειν οτι παντοτε μου
   ακουεις· αλλα δια τον οχλον τον περιεστωτα ειπον, ινα πιστευ-
43 σωσιν οτι συ με απεστειλας. και ταυτα ειπων φωνη μεγαλη
44 εκραυγασεν· Λαζαρε, δευρο εξω. εξηλθεν ο τεθνηκως δεδεμενος
   τους ποδας και τας χειρας κειριαις, και η οψις αυτου σουδαριω
   περιεδεδετο. λεγει αυτοις ο Ιησους· λυσατε αυτον και αφετε
   αυτον υπαγειν.
45 Πολλοι ουν εκ των Ιουδαιων, οι ελθοντες προς την Μαριαμ και
46 θεασαμενοι ο εποιησεν, επιστευσαν εις αυτον· τινες δε εξ αυτων
   απηλθον προς τους Φαρισαιους και ειπαν αυτοις α εποιησεν

47 Ιησους. συνηγαγον ουν οι αρχιερεις και οι Φαρισαιοι συνεδριον,
48 και ελεγον· τι ποιουμεν, οτι ουτος ο ανθρωπος πολλα ποιει σημεια;
    εαν αφωμεν αυτον ουτως, παντες πιστευσουσιν εις αυτον, και
    ελευσονται οι Ρωμαιοι και αρουσιν ημων και τον τοπον και το
49 εθνος. εις δε τις εξ αυτων Καιαφας, αρχιερευς ων του ενιαυτου
50 εκεινου, ειπεν αυτοις· υμεις ουκ οιδατε ουδεν, ουδε λογιζεσθε οτι
    συμφερει υμιν ινα εις ανθρωπος αποθανη υπερ του λαου και μη
51 ολον το εθνος αποληται. τουτο δε αφ εαυτου ουκ ειπεν, αλλα
    αρχιερευς ων του ενιαυτου εκεινου επροφητευσεν οτι εμελλεν
52 Ιησους αποθνησκειν υπερ του εθνους, και ουχ υπερ του εθνους
    μονον, αλλ ινα και τα τεκνα του θεου τα διεσκορπισμενα συναγαγη
53 εις εν. απ εκεινης ουν της ημερας εβουλευσαντο ινα αποκτεινωσιν
54 αυτον. Ο ουν Ιησους ουκετι παρρησια περιεπατει εν τοις Ιουδαιοις,
    αλλα απηλθεν εκειθεν εις την χωραν εγγυς της ερημου, εις
    Εφραιμ λεγομενην πολιν, κακει εμεινεν μετα των μαθητων.
55   Ην δε εγγυς το πασχα των Ιουδαιων, και ανεβησαν πολλοι εις
    Ιεροσολυμα εκ της χωρας προ του πασχα, ινα αγνισωσιν
56 εαυτους. εζητουν ουν τον Ιησουν και ελεγον μετ αλληλων εν τω
    ιερω εστηκοτες· τι δοκει υμιν; οτι ου μη ελθη εις την εορτην;
57 δεδωκεισαν δε οι αρχιερεις και οι Φαρισαιοι εντολας ινα εαν τις γνω

12:

1 που εστιν μηνυση, οπως πιασωσιν αυτον. Ο ουν Ιησους προ εξ
    ημερων του πασχα ηλθεν εις Βηθανιαν, οπου ην Λαζαρος, ον
2 ηγειρεν εκ νεκρων Ιησους. εποιησαν ουν αυτω δειπνον εκει, και
    η Μαρθα διηκονει, ο δε Λαζαρος εις ην εκ των ανακειμενων συν
3 αυτω· η ουν Μαριαμ λαβουσα λιτραν μυρου ναρδου πιστικης
    πολυτιμου ηλειψεν τους ποδας του Ιησου και εξεμαξεν ταις θριξιν
    αυτης τους ποδας αυτου· η δε οικια επληρωθη εκ της οσμης του
4 μυρου. λεγει δε Ιουδας ο Ισκαριωτης εις των μαθητων αυτου,
5 ο μελλων αυτον παραδιδοναι· δια τι τουτο το μυρον ουκ επραθη
6 τριακοσιων δηναριων και εδοθη πτωχοις; ειπεν δε τουτο ουχ οτι
    περι των πτωχων εμελεν αυτω, αλλ οτι κλεπτης ην και το γλωσ-
7 σοκομον εχων τα βαλλομενα εβασταζεν. ειπεν ουν ο Ιησους·
    αφες αυτην, ινα εις την ημεραν του ενταφιασμου μου τηρηση
9 αυτο· Εγνω ουν ο οχλος πολυς εκ των Ιουδαιων οτι εκει εστιν,
    και ηλθον ου δια τον Ιησουν μονον, αλλ ινα και τον Λαζαρον
10 ιδωσιν ον ηγειρεν εκ νεκρων. εβουλευσαντο δε οι αρχιερεις ινα και
11 τον Λαζαρον αποκτεινωσιν, οτι πολλοι δι αυτον υπηγον των
    Ιουδαιων και επιστευον εις τον Ιησουν.
12   Τη επαυριον ο οχλος πολυς ο ελθων εις την εορτην, ακουσαντες
13 οτι ερχεται Ιησους εις Ιεροσολυμα, ελαβον τα βαια των φοινικων
    και εξηλθον εις υπαντησιν αυτω, και εκραυγαζον.
        ωσαννα,

ευλογημενος ο ερχομενος εν ονοματι κυριου,

    και ο βασιλευς του Ισραηλ.

14 [ευρων δε ο Ιησους οναριον εκαθισεν επ αυτο, καθως εστιν γεγραμμενον·

15   μη φοβου, θυγατηρ Σιων·

    ιδου ο βασιλευς σου ερχεται,

    καθημενος επι πωλον ονου.

16 ταυτα ουκ εγνωσαν αυτου οι μαθηται το πρωτον, αλλ οτε εδοξασθη Ιησους, τοτε εμνησθησαν οτι ταυτα ην επ αυτω γεγραμμενα

17 και ταυτα εποιησαν αυτω.]¹ εμαρτυρει ουν ο οχλος ο ων μετ αυτου οτε τον Λαζαρον εφωνησεν εκ του μνημειου και ηγειρεν

18 αυτον εκ νεκρων. δια τουτο και υπηντησεν αυτω ο οχλος, οτι

19 ηκουσαν τουτο αυτον πεποιηκεναι το σημειον. οι ουν Φαρισαιοι ειπαν προς εαυτους· θεωρειτε οτι ουκ ωφελειτε ουδεν· ιδε ο κοσμος οπισω αυτου απηλθεν.

20   Ησαν δε Ελληνες τινες εκ των αναβαινοντων ινα προσκυνησωσιν

21 εν τη εορτη· ουτοι ουν προσηλθον Φιλιππω τω απο Βηθσαιδα της Γαλιλαιας, και ηρωτων αυτον λεγοντες· κυριε, θελομεν τον

22 Ιησουν ιδειν. ερχεται ο Φιλιππος και λεγει τω Ανδρεα· ερχεται

23 Ανδρεας και Φιλιππος και λεγουσιν τω Ιησου. ο δε Ιησους αποκρινεται αυτοις λεγων· εληλυθεν η ωρα ινα δοξασθη ο υιος

24 του ανθρωπου. αμην αμην λεγω υμιν, εαν μη ο κοκκος του σιτου πεσων εις την γην αποθανη, αυτος μονος μενει· εαν δε αποθανη,

25 πολυν καρπον φερει. ο φιλων την ψυχην αυτου απολλυει αυτην, και ο μισων την ψυχην αυτου εν τω κοσμω τουτω εις ζωην αιωνιον

26 φυλαξει αυτην. εαν εμοι τις διακονη, εμοι ακολουθειτω, και οπου ειμι εγω, εκει και ο διακονος ο εμος εσται· εαν τις εμοι

27 διακονη, τιμησει αυτον ο πατηρ. νυν η ψυχη μου τεταρακται, και τι ειπω; πατερ, σωσον με εκ της ωρας ταυτης. αλλα δια

28 τουτο ηλθον εις την ωραν ταυτην. πατερ, δοξασον σου το ονομα. ηλθεν ουν φωνη εκ του ουρανου· και εδοξασα και παλιν δοξασω.

29 ο ουν οχλος ο εστως και ακουσας ελεγεν βροντην γεγονεναι·

30 αλλοι ελεγον· αγγελος αυτω λελαληκεν. απεκριθη Ιησους και

31 ειπεν· ου δι εμε η φωνη αυτη γεγονεν αλλα δι υμας. νυν κρισις εστιν του κοσμου τουτου· νυν ο αρχων του κοσμου τουτου εκβλη-

32 θησεται εξω· καγω εαν υψωθω εκ της γης, παντας ελκυσω προς

33 εμαυτον. [τουτο δε ελεγεν σημαινων ποιω θανατω ημελλεν αποθνησκειν.]²

---

¹ Possibly redactional (*Johannes*, p. 319) but Bultmann does not seem to embrace this possibility.

² Possible textual loss.

8: 30, 31   Ταυτα αυτου λαλουντος πολλοι επιστευσαν εις αυτον. ελεγεν   321–23
ουν ο Ιησους προς τους πεπιστευκοτας αυτω Ιουδαιους· εαν υμεις
32   μεινητε εν τω λογω τω εμω. αληθως μαθηται μου εστε, και
γνωσεσθετην αληθειαν, και η αληθεια ελευθερωσει υμας.
33   απεκριθησαν προς αυτον· σπερμα Αβρααμ εσμεν, και ουδενι
δεδουλευκαμεν πωποτε· πως συ λεγεις οτι ελευθεροι γενησεσθε,
34   απεκριθη αυτοις ο Ιησους· αμην αμην λεγω υμιν οτι πας ο ποιων
35   την αμαρτιαν δουλος εστιν. ο δε δουλος ου μενει εν τη οικια εις τον
36   αιωνα· ο υιος μενει εις τον αιωνα. εαν ουν ο υιος υμας ελευθερωση,
37   οντως ελευθεροι εσεσθε. Οιδα οτι σπερμα Αβρααμ εστε· αλλα
ζητειτε με αποκτειναι. οτι ο λογος ο εμος ου χωρει εν υμιν.
38   α εγω εωρακα παρα τω πατρι λαλω· και υμεις ουν α ηκουσατε
39   παρα του πατρος ποιειτε. απεκριθησαν και ειπαν αυτω· ο πατηρ
ημων Αβρααμ εστιν. λεγει αυτοις ο Ιησους· ει τεκνα του Αβρααμ
40   εστε, τα εργα του Αβρααμ ποιειτε· νυν δε ζητειτε με αποκτειναι,
ανθρωπον ος την αληθειαν υμιν λελαληκα, ην ηκουσα παρα του

6: 60   θεου· τουτο Αβρααμ ουκ εποιησεν. Πολλοι ουν ακουσαντες εκ των
μαθητων αυτου ειπαν· σκληρος εστιν ο λογος ουτος· τις δυναται
61   αυτου ακουειν: ειδως δε ο Ιησους εν εαυτω οτι γογγυζουσιν περι
τουτου οι μαθηται αυτου, ειπεν αυτοις· τουτο υμας σκανδαλιζει;
62   εαν ουν θεωρητε τον υιον του ανθρωπου αναβαινοντα οπου ην
63   το προτερον; το πνευμα εστιν το ζωοποιουν, η σαρξ ουκ ωφελει
ουδεν· τα ρηματα α εγω λελαληκα υμιν πνευμα εστιν και ζωη
64   εστιν. αλλ εισιν εξ υμων τινες οι ου πιστευουσιν. ηδει γαρ εξ
αρχης ο Ιησους τινες εισιν οι μη πιστευοντες και τις εστιν ο
65   παραδωσων αυτον. και ελεγεν· δια τουτο ειρηκα υμιν οτι ουδεις
δυναται ελθειν προς με εαν μη η δεδομενον αυτω εκ του πατρος.
66   Εκ τουτου πολλοι των μαθητων αυτου απηλθον εις τα οπισω
και ουκετι μετ αυτου περιεπατουν. ειπεν ουν ο Ιησους τοις δωδεκα·
67, 68   μη και υμεις θελετε υπαγειν; απεκριθη αυτω Σιμων Πετρος·
69   κυριε, προς τινα απελευσομεθα; ρηματα ζωης αιωνιου εχεις· και
ημεις πεπιστευκαμεν και εγνωκαμεν οτι συ ει ο αγιος του θεου.
70   απεκριθη αυτοις ο Ιησους· ουκ εγω υμας τους δωδεκα εξελεξαμην;
71   και εξ υμων εις διαβολος εστιν. ελεγεν δε τον Ιουδαν Σιμωνος
Ισκαριωτου· ουτος γαρ εμελλεν παραδιδοναι αυτον, εις εκ των
δωδεκα.

12: 37   Τοσαυτα δε αυτου σημεια πεποιηκοτος εμπροσθεν αυτων ουκ
38   επιστευον εις αυτον, ινα ο λογος Ησαιου του προφητου πληρωθη
ον ειπεν· κυριε, τις επιστευσεν τη ακοη ημων; και ο βραχιων
39   κυριου τινι απεκαλυφθη; δια τουτο ουκ ηδυναντο πιστευειν,
40   οτι παλιν ειπεν Ησαιας· τετυφλωκεν αυτων τους οφθαλμους και
επωρωσεν αυτων την καρδιαν, ινα μη ιδωσιν τοις οφθαλμοις και
41   νοησωσιν τη καρδια και στραφωσιν, και ιασομαι αυτους. ταυτα

ειπεν Ησαιας οτι ειδεν την δοξαν αυτου, και ελαλησεν περι αυτου.

42 ομως μεντοι και εκ των αρχοντων πολλοι επιστευσαν εις αυτον,
αλλα δια τους Φαρισαιους ουχ ωμολογουν, ινα μη αποσυναγωγοι

43 γενωνται· ηγαπησαν γαρ την δοξαν των ανθρωπων μαλλον ηπερ
την δοξαν του θεου.

13:

1–3 Προ δε της εορτης του πασχα και δειπνου γινομενου, ειδως   351 f.
ο Ιησους οτι παντα εδωκεν αυτω ο πατηρ εις τας χειρας, και   352 f.
(on 13:1–3)

4 οτι απο θεου εξηλθεν και προς τον θεον υπαγει, εγειρεται [εκ
του δειπνου] και τιθησιν τα ιματια, και λαβων λεντιον διεζωσεν

5 εαυτον· ειτα βαλλει υδωρ εις τον νιπτηρα, και ηρξατο νιπτειν
τους ποδας των μαθητων και εκμασσειν τω λεντιω ω ην διεζω-

6 σμενος. ερχεται ουν προς Σιμωνα Πετρον· λεγει αυτω· κυριε,

7 συ μου νιπτεις τους ποδας; απεκριθη Ιησους και ειπεν αυτω·

8 ο εγω ποιω συ ουκ οιδας αρτι, γνωση δε μετα ταυτα. λεγει αυτω
Πετρος· ου μη νιψης μου τους ποδας εις τον αιωνα. απεκριθη

9 Ιησους αυτω· εαν μη νιψω σε, ουκ εχεις μερος μετ εμου. λεγει αυτω
Σιμων Πετρος· κυριε, μη τους ποδας μου μονον αλλα και τας

10 χειρας και την κεφαλην. λεγει αυτω Ιησους· ο λελουμενος
ουκ εχει χρειαν νιψασθαι, αλλ εστιν καθαρος ολος· και υμεις

11 καθαροι εστε, αλλ ουχι παντες. ηδει γαρ τον παραδιδοντα

12 αυτον· δια τουτο ειπεν οτι ουχι παντες καθαροι εστε. Οτε ουν
ενιψεν τους ποδας αυτων και ελαβεν τα ιματια αυτου και ανεπεσεν,

13 ειπεν αυτοις· γινωσκετε τι πεποιηκα υμιν; υμεις φωνειτε με·

14 ο διδασκαλος και ο κυριος, και καλως λεγετε· ειμι γαρ. ει ουν
εγω ενιψα υμων τους ποδας ο κυριος και ο διδασκαλος, και υμεις

15 οφειλετε αλληλων νιπτειν τους ποδας· υποδειγμα γαρ εδωκα

16 υμιν ινα καθως εγω εποιησα υμιν και υμεις ποιητε. αμην αμην
λεγω υμιν, ουκ εστιν δουλος μειζων του κυριου αυτου, ουδε

17 αποστολος μειζων του πεμψαντος αυτον. ει ταυτα οιδατε,

18 μακαριοι εστε εαν ποιητε αυτα. Ου περι παντων υμων λεγω· εγω
οιδα τινας εξελεξαμην· αλλ ινα η γραφη πληρωθη· ο τρωγων

19 μου τον αρτον επηρεν επ εμε την πτερναν αυτου. απ αρτι λεγω
υμιν προ του γενεσθαι, ινα πιστευητε οταν γενηται οτι εγω

20 ειμι. αμην αμην λεγω υμιν, ο λαμβανων αν τινα πεμψω εμε

21 λαμβανει. ο δε εμε λαμβανων λαμβανει τον πεμψαντα με. ταυτα
ειπων Ιησους εταραχθη τω πνευματι και εμαρτυρησεν και ειπεν·

22 αμην αμην λεγω υμιν οτι εις εξ υμων παραδωσει με. εβλεπον εις

23 αλληλους οι μαθηται απορουμενοι περι τινος λεγει. ην ανακειμενος εις εκ των μαθητων αυτου εν τω κολπω του Ιησου, ον

24 ηγαπα ο Ιησους· νευει ουν τουτω Σιμων Πετρος και λεγει αυτω·

25 ειπε τις εστιν περι ου λεγει. αναπεσων εκεινος ουτως επι το

26 στηθος του Ιησου λεγει αυτω· κυριε, τις εστιν; αποκρινεται ουν ο

Ιησους· εκεινος εστιν ω εγω βαψω το ψωμιον και δωσω αυτω.
βαψας ουν [το] ψωμιον λαμβανει και διδωσιν Ιουδα Σιμωνος

27 Ισκαριωτον. και μετα το ψωμιον τοτε εισηλθεν εις εκεινον ο
σατανας. λεγει ουν αυτω Ιησους· ο ποιεις ποιησον ταχιον.

28 τουτο [δε] ουδεις εγνω των ανακειμενων προς τι ειπεν αυτω· τινες

29 γαρ εδοκουν, επει το γλωσσοκομον ειχεν Ιουδας, οτι λεγει αυτω
Ιησους· αγορασον ων χρειαν εχομεν εις την εορτην, η τοις πτωχοις

30 ινα τι δω. λαβων ουν το ψωμιον εκεινος εξηλθεν ευθυς· ην δε νυξ.

31, 1   Οτε ουν εξηλθεν, ειδως ο Ιησους οτι ηλθεν αυτου η ωρα ινα   351
μεταβη εκ του κοσμου τουτου προς τον πατερα, αγαπησας τους
ιδιους τους εν τω κοσμω εις τελος. <εγειρεται εκ του δειπνου>[1]

17:

1 και επαρας τους οφθαλμους αυτου εις τον ουρανον ειπεν· πατερ,
εληλυθεν η ωρα· δοξασον σου τον υιον, ινα ο υιος δοξαση σε,

2 καθως εδωκας αυτω εξουσιαν πασης σαρκος, ινα παν ο δεδωκας

3 αυτω δωση αυτοις ζωην αιωνιον. αυτη δε εστιν η αιωνιος ζωη, ινα
γινωσκωσιν σε τον μονον αληθινον θεον και ον απεστειλας

4 Ιησουν Χριστον. εγω σε εδοξασα επι της γης, το εργον τελειωσας

5 ο δεδωκας μοι ινα ποιησω· και νυν δοξασον με συ, πατερ, παρα
σεαυτω τη δοξη η ειχον προ του τον κοσμον ειναι παρα σοι.

6 Εφανερωσα σου το ονομα τοις ανθρωποις ους εδωκας μοι εκ του
κοσμου. σοι ησαν καμοι αυτους εδωκας, και τον λογον σου

7 τετηρηκαν. νυν εγνωκαν οτι παντα οσα δεδωκας μοι παρα σου

8 εισιν· οτι τα ρηματα α εδωκας μοι δεδωκα αυτοις, και αυτοι
ελαβον, και εγνωσαν αληθως οτι παρα σου εξηλθον, και επιστευ-

9 σαν οτι συ με απεστειλας. εγω περι αυτων ερωτω· ου περι του

10 κοσμου ερωτω, αλλα περι ων δεδωκας μοι, οτι σοι εισιν, και τα
εμα παντα σα εστιν και τα σα εμα, και δεδοξασμαι εν αυτοις.

11 και ουκετι ειμι εν τω κοσμω, και αυτοι εν τω κοσμω εισιν, καγω
προς σε ερχομαι. πατερ αγιε, τηρησον αυτους εν τω ονοματι σου

12 ω δεδωκας μοι, ινα ωσιν εν καθως ημεις. οτε ημην μετ αυτων,
εγω ετηρουν αυτους εν τω ονοματι σου, και εφυλαξα, και ουδεις
εξ αυτων απωλετο ει μη ο υιος της απωλειας, ινα η γραφη πλη-

13 ρωθη. νυν δε προς σε ερχομαι, και ταυτα λαλω εν τω κοσμω ινα

14 εχωσιν την χαραν την εμην πεπληρωμενην εν εαυτοις. εγω
δεδωκα αυτοις τον λογον σου, και ο κοσμος εμισησεν αυτους, οτι ουκ

15 εισιν εκ του κοσμου καθως εγω ουκ ειμι εκ του κοσμου. ουκ ερωτω
ινα αρης αυτους εκ του κοσμου, αλλ ινα τηρησης αυτους εκ του

16 πονηρου. εκ του κοσμου ουκ εισιν καθως εγω ουκ ειμι εκ του

17 κοσμου. αγιασον αυτους εν τη αληθεια· ο λογος ο σος αληθεια

18 εστιν. καθως εμε απεστειλας εις τον κοσμον, καγω απεστειλα

19 αυτους εις τον κοσμον· και υπερ αυτων [εγω] αγιαζω εμαυτον,

20 ινα ωσιν και αυτοι ηγιασμενοι εν αληθεια. Ου περι τουτων δε

[1] Some such phrase must have originally stood in the text (*Johannes*, p. 357).

ερωτω μονον, αλλα και περι των πιστευοντων δια του λογου αυτων

21 εις εμε, ινα παντες εν ωσιν, καθως συ, πατηρ, εν εμοι καγω εν σοι, ινα και αυτοι εν ημιν ωσιν, ινα ο κοσμος πιστευη οτι συ με

22 απεστειλας. καγω την δοξαν ην δεδωκας μοι δεδωκα αυτοις, ινα

23 ωσιν εν καθως ημεις εν· εγω εν αυτοις και συ εν εμοι, ινα ωσιν τετελειωμενοι εις εν, ινα γινωσκη ο κοσμος οτι συ με απεστειλας

24 και ηγαπησας αυτους καθως εμε ηγαπησας. Πατηρ, ο δεδωκας μοι, θελω ινα οπου ειμι εγω κακεινοι ωσιν μετ εμου, ινα θεωρωσιν την δοξαν την εμην, ην δεδωκας μοι οτι ηγαπησας με προ κατα-

25 βολης κοσμου. πατηρ δικαιε, και ο κοσμος σε ουκ εγνω, εγω δε σε

26 εγνων, και ουτοι εγνωσαν οτι συ με απεστειλας· και εγνωρισα αυτοις το ονομα σου και γνωρισω. ινα η αγαπη ην ηγαπησας με εν αυτοις η καγω εν αυτοις.

13: 31 [1]Νυν εδοξασθη ο υιος του ανθρωπου, και ο θεος εδοξασθη εν   349 ff.

32 αυτω· ει ο θεος εδοξασθη εν αυτω, και ο θεος δοξασει αυτον εν

33 αυτω, και ευθυς δοξασει αυτον. τεκνια, ετι μικρον μεθ υμων ειμι· ζητησετε με, και καθως ειπον τοις Ιουδαιοις οτι οπου εγω

34 υπαγω υμεις ου δυνασθε ελθειν, και υμιν λεγω αρτι. Εντολην καινην διδωμι υμιν, ινα αγαπατε αλληλους, καθως ηγαπησα

35 υμας ινα και υμεις αγαπατε αλληλους. εν τουτω γνωσονται παντες οτι εμοι μαθηται εστε, εαν αγαπην εχητε εν αλληλοις.

15: 1 Εγω ειμι η αμπελος η αληθινη, και ο πατηρ μου ο γεωργος

2 εστιν. παν κλημα εν εμοι μη φερον καρπον, αιρει αυτο, και παν το καρπον φερον, καθαιρει αυτο ινα καρπον πλειονα φερη.

3, 4 ηδη υμεις καθαροι εστε δια τον λογον ον λελαληκα υμιν· μεινατε εν εμοι, καγω εν υμιν. καθως το κλημα ου δυναται καρπον φερειν αφ εαυτου εαν μη μενη εν τη αμπελω, ουτως ουδε υμεις εαν μη

5 εν εμοι μενητε. εγω ειμι η αμπελος, υμεις τα κληματα. ο μενων εν εμοι καγω εν αυτω, ουτος φερει καρπον πολυν, οτι χωρις εμου

6 ου δυνασθε ποιειν ουδεν. εαν μη τις μενη εν εμοι, εβληθη εξω ως το κλημα και εξηρανθη, και συναγουσιν αυτα και εις το πυρ

7 βαλλουσιν, και καιεται. εαν μεινητε εν εμοι και τα ρηματα μου

8 εν υμιν μεινη, ο εαν θελητε αιτησασθε, και γενησεται υμιν. εν τουτω εδοξασθη ο πατηρ μου, ινα καρπον πολυν φερητε και

9 γενησεσθε εμοι μαθηται. καθως ηγαπησεν με ο πατηρ, καγω υμας

10 ηγαπησα· μεινατε εν τη αγαπη τη εμη. εαν τας εντολας μου τηρησητε, μενειτε εν τη αγαπη μου, καθως εγω του πατρος μου

11 τας εντολας τετηρηκα και μενω αυτου εν τη αγαπη. Ταυτα λελαληκα υμιν ινα η χαρα η εμη εν υμιν η και η χαρα υμων

12 πληρωθη. αυτη εστιν η εντολη η εμη, ινα αγαπατε αλληλους

---

[1] The λεγει Ιησους of the present text is naturally a redactional gloss, although I cannot find a specific indication of this.

13 καθως ηγαπησα υμας. μειζονα ταυτης αγαπην ουδεις εχει,
14 ινα τις την ψυχην αυτου θη υπερ των φιλων αυτου. υμεις φιλοι
15 μου εστε, εαν ποιητε ο εγω εντελλομαι υμιν. ουκετι λεγω υμας
δουλους, οτι ο δουλος ουκ οιδεν τι ποιει αυτου ο κυριος· υμας δε
ειρηκα φιλους, οτι παντα α ηκουσα παρα του πατρος μου εγνωρισα
16 υμιν. ουχ υμεις με εξελεξασθε, αλλ εγω εξελεξαμην υμας, και
εθηκα υμας ινα υμεις υπαγητε και καρπον φερητε και ο καρπος
υμων μενη, ινα ο τι αν αιτησητε τον πατερα εν τω ονοματι μου
17 δω υμιν. ταυτα εντελλομαι υμιν, ινα αγαπατε αλληλους.
18 Ει ο κοσμος υμας μισει, γινωσκετε οτι εμε πρωτον υμων μεμισηκεν.
19 ει εκ του κοσμου ητε, ο κοσμος αν το ιδιον εφιλει· οτι δε εκ του
κοσμου ουκ εστε, αλλ εγω εξελεξαμην υμας εκ του κοσμου, δια
20 τουτο μισει υμας ο κοσμος. μνημονευετε του λογου ου εγω ειπον
υμιν· ουκ εστιν δουλος μειζων του κυριου αυτου. ει εμε εδιωξαν,
και υμας διωξουσιν· ει τον λογον μου ετηρησαν, και τον υμετερον
21 τηρησουσιν. αλλα ταυτα παντα ποιησουσιν εις υμας δια το ονομα
22 μου, οτι ουκ οιδασιν τον πεμψαντα με. ει μη ηλθον και ελαλησα
αυτοις, αμαρτιαν ουκ ειχοσαν· νυν δε προφασιν ουκ εχουσιν περι
23 της αμαρτιας αυτων. ο εμε μισων και τον πατερα μου μισει.
24 ει τα εργα μη εποιησα εν αυτοις α ουδεις αλλος εποιησεν, αμαρτιαν
ουκ ειχοσαν· νυν δε και εωρακασιν και μεμισηκασιν και εμε και τον
25 πατερα μου. αλλ ινα πληρωθη ο λογος ο εν τω νομω αυτων
26 γεγραμμενος οτι εμισησαν με δωρεαν. Οταν ελθη ο παρακλητος
ον εγω πεμψω υμιν παρα του πατρος, το πνευμα της αληθειας
ο παρα του πατρος εκπορευεται, εκεινος μαρτυρησει περι εμου·

16: 27, 1 και υμεις δε μαρτυρειτε, οτι απ αρχης μετ εμου εστε. Ταυτα
2 λελαληκα υμιν ινα μη σκανδαλισθητε. αποσυναγωγους ποιησουσιν υμας· αλλ ερχεται ωρα ινα πας ο αποκτεινας υμας δοξη
3 λατρειαν προσφερειν τω θεω. και ταυτα ποιησουσιν οτι ουκ
4 εγνωσαν τον πατερα ουδε εμε. αλλα ταυτα λελαληκα υμιν
ινα οταν ελθη η ωρα αυτων μνημονευητε αυτων, οτι εγω ειπον
υμιν. Ταυτα δε υμιν εξ αρχης ουκ ειπον, οτι μεθ υμων ημην.
5 νυν δε υπαγω προς τον πεμψαντα με, και ουδεις εξ υμων ερωτα
6 με· που υπαγεις; αλλ οτι ταυτα λελαληκα υμιν, η λυπη πεπληρω-
7 κεν υμων την καρδιαν. αλλ εγω την αληθειαν λεγω υμιν, συμφερει υμιν ινα εγω απελθω. εαν γαρ μη απελθω, ο παρακλητος
ου μη ελθη προς υμας· εαν δε πορευθω, πεμψω αυτον προς υμας.
8 και ελθων εκεινος ελεγξει τον κοσμον περι αμαρτιας και περι
9 δικαιοσυνης και περι κρισεως· περι αμαρτιας μεν, οτι ου πιστευ-
10 ουσιν εις εμε· περι δικαιοσυνης δε, οτι προς τον πατερα υπαγω και
11 ουκετι θεωρειτε με· περι δε κρισεως, οτι ο αρχων του κοσμου
12 τουτου κεκριται. Ετι πολλα εχω υμιν λεγειν, αλλ ου δυνασθε
13 βασταζειν αρτι· οταν δε ελθη εκεινος, το πνευμα της αληθειας,
οδηγησει υμας εις την αληθειαν πασαν· ου γαρ λαλησει αφ

εαυτου, αλλ οσα ακουει λαλησει, και τα ερχομενα αναγγελει
14 υμιν. εκεινος εμε δοξασει, οτι εκ του εμου λημψεται και αναγγελει
15 υμιν. παντα οσα εχει ο πατηρ εμα εστιν· δια τουτο ειπον οτι εκ
16 του εμου λαμβανει και αναγγελει υμιν. Μικρον και ουκετι
17 θεωρειτε με, και παλιν μικρον και οψεσθε με. ειπαν ουν εκ των
μαθητων αυτου προς αλληλους· τι εστιν τουτο ο λεγει ημιν·
μικρον και ου θεωρειτε με, και παλιν μικρον και οψεσθε με;
18 [και· οτι υπαγω προς τον πατερα;] ελεγον ουν· τουτο τι εστιν
19 ο λεγει το μικρον; ουκ οιδαμεν τι λαλει. εγνω Ιησους οτι ηθελον
αυτον ερωταν, και ειπεν αυτοις· περι τουτου ζητειτε μετ αλληλων
οτι ειπον· μικρον και ου θεωρειτε με. και παλιν μικρον και
20 οψεσθε με; αμην αμην λεγω υμιν οτι κλαυσετε και θρηνησετε
υμεις, ο δε κοσμος χαρησεται· υμεις λυπηθησεσθε, αλλ η λυπη
21 υμων εις χαραν γενησεται. η γυνη οταν τικτη λυπην εχει, οτι
ηλθεν η ωρα αυτης· οταν δε γεννηση το παιδιον, ουκετι μνημονευει
της θλιψεως δια την χαραν οτι εγεννηθη ανθρωπος εις τον
22 κοσμον. και υμεις ουν νυν μεν λυπην εχετε· παλιν δε οψομαι
υμας, και χαρησεται υμων η καρδια, και την χαραν υμων ουδεις
23 αιρει αφ υμων. και εν εκεινη τη ημερα εμε ουκ ερωτησετε ουδεν.
αμην αμην λεγω υμιν, αν τι αιτησητε τον πατερα δωσει υμιν εν
24 τω ονοματι μου. εως αρτι ουκ ητησατε ουδεν εν τω ονοματι μου·
25 αιτειτε, και λημψεσθε, ινα η χαρα υμων η πεπληρωμενη. Ταυτα
εν παροιμιαις λελαληκα υμιν· ερχεται ωρα οτε ουκετι εν παροιμιαις
λαλησω υμιν, αλλα παρρησια περι του πατρος απαγγελω
26 υμιν. εν εκεινη τη ημερα εν τω ονοματι μου αιτησεσθε, και ου
27 λεγω υμιν οτι εγω ερωτησω τον πατερα περι υμων· αυτος γαρ
ο πατηρ φιλει υμας, οτι υμεις εμε πεφιληκατε και πεπιστευκατε
28 οτι εγω παρα του θεου εξηλθον. εξηλθον εκ του πατρος και
εληλυθα εις τον κοσμον· παλιν αφιημι τον κοσμον και πορευομαι
29 προς τον πατερα. Λεγουσιν οι μαθηται αυτου· ιδε νυν εν παρρησια
30 λαλεις, και παροιμιαν ουδεμιαν λεγεις. νυν οιδαμεν οτι οιδας
παντα και ου χρειαν εχεις ινα τις σε ερωτα· εν τουτω πιστευομεν
31 οτι απο θεου εξηλθες. απεκριθη αυτοις Ιησους· αρτι πιστευετε;
32 ιδου ερχεται ωρα και εληλυθεν [ινα σκορπισθητε εκαστος εις τα
ιδια καμε μονον αφητε·] και ουκ ειμι μονος, οτι ο πατηρ μετ
33 εμου εστιν. ταυτα λελαληκα υμιν ινα εν εμοι ειρηνην εχητε.
εν τω κοσμω θλιψιν εχετε· αλλα θαρσειτε, εγω νενικηκα τον
13: 36 κοσμον. Λεγει αυτω Σιμων Πετρος· κυριε, που υπαγεις; απεκριθη
Ιησους· οπου υπαγω ου δυνασαι μοι νυν ακολουθησαι, ακολου-
37 θησεις δε υστερον. λεγει αυτω [ο] Πετρος· κυριε, δια τι ου
δυναμαι σοι ακολουθησαι αρτι; την ψυχην μου υπερ σου θησω.
38 αποκρινεται Ιησους· την ψυχην σου υπερ εμου θησεις; αμην
αμην λεγω σοι, ου μη αλεκτωρ φωνηση εως ου αρνηση με τρις.
14: 1 Μη ταρασσεσθω υμων η καρδια· πιστευετε εις τον θεον, και εις

2 εμε πιστευετε. εν τη οικια του πατρος μου μοναι πολλαι εισιν·

3 ει δε μη, ειπον αν υμιν· οτι πορευομαι ετοιμασαι τοπον υμιν· και
εαν πορευθω και ετοιμασω τοπον υμιν, παλιν ερχομαι και
παραλημψομαι υμας προς εμαυτον, ινα οπου ειμι εγω και υμεις

4, 5 ητε. Και οπου εγω υπαγω οιδατε την οδον. λεγει αυτω Θωμας·

6 κυριε, ουκ οιδαμεν που υπαγεις· πως οιδαμεν την οδον; λεγει
αυτω Ιησους· εγω ειμι η οδος και η αληθεια και η ζωη· ουδεις

7 ερχεται προς τον πατερα ει μη δι εμου. ει εγνωκειτε με, και
τον πατερα μου αν ηδειτε. απ αρτι γινωσκετε αυτον και εωρακατε.

8 Λεγει αυτω Φιλιππος· κυριε, δειξον ημιν τον πατερα. και αρκει

9 ημιν. λεγει αυτω ο Ιησους· τοσουτον χρονον μεθ υμων ειμι και ουκ
εγνωκας με, Φιλιππε; ο εωρακως εμε εωρακεν τον πατερα· πως

10 συ λεγεις· δειξον ημιν τον πατερα; ου πιστευεις οτι εγω εν τω
πατρι και ο πατηρ εν εμοι εστιν; τα ρηματα α εγω λεγω υμιν
απ εμαυτου ου λαλω· ο δε πατηρ εν εμοι μενων ποιει τα εργα

11 αυτου. πιστευετε μοι οτι εγω εν τω πατρι και ο πατηρ εν εμοι·

12 ει δε μη, δια τα εργα αυτα πιστευετε. αμην αμην λεγω υμιν,
ο πιστευων εις εμε τα εργα α εγω ποιω κακεινος ποιησει, και
μειζονα τουτων ποιησει, οτι εγω προς τον πατερα πορευομαι·

13 και ο τι αν αιτησητε εν τω ονοματι μου, τουτο ποιησω, ινα

14 δοξασθη ο πατηρ εν τω υιω. εαν τι αιτησητε εν τω ονοματι μου,

15 εγω ποιησω. Εαν αγαπατε με, τας εντολας τας εμας τηρησετε.

16 καγω ερωτησω τον πατερα και αλλον παρακλητον δωσει υμιν, ινα

17 η μεθ υμων εις τον αιωνα, το πνευμα της αληθειας, ο ο κοσμος ου
δυναται λαβειν, οτι ου θεωρει αυτο ουδε γινωσκει· υμεις γινωσκετε

18 αυτο, οτι παρ υμιν μενει και εν υμιν εσται. Ουκ αφησω υμας

19 ορφανους, ερχομαι προς υμας. ετι μικρον και ο κοσμος με ουκετι
θεωρει, υμεις δε θεωρειτε με, οτι εγω ζω και υμεις ζησετε.

20 εν εκεινη τη ημερα γνωσεσθε υμεις οτι εγω εν τω πατρι μου και

21 υμεις εν εμοι καγω εν υμιν. Ο εχων τας εντολας μου και τηρων
αυτας, εκεινος εστιν ο αγαπων με· ο δε αγαπων με αγαπηθησεται
υπο του πατρος μου, καγω αγαπησω αυτον και εμφανισω αυτω

22 εμαυτον. λεγει αυτω Ιουδας, ουχ ο Ισκαριωτης· κυριε, και τι
γεγονεν οτι ημιν μελλεις εμφανιζειν σεαυτον και ουχι τω κοσμω;

23 απεκριθη Ιησους και ειπεν αυτω· εαν τις αγαπα με, τον λογον
μου τηρησει, και ο πατηρ μου αγαπησει αυτον, και προς αυτον

24 ελευσομεθα και μονην παρ αυτω ποιησομεθα. ο μη αγαπων
με τους λογους μου ου τηρει· και ο λογος ον ακουετε ουκ εστιν

25 εμος αλλα του πεμψαντος με πατρος. Ταυτα λελαληκα υμιν

26 παρ υμιν μενων· ο δε παρακλητος, το πνευμα το αγιον ο πεμψει
ο πατηρ εν τω ονοματι μου, εκεινος υμας διδαξει παντα και

27 υπομνησει υμας παντα α ειπον υμιν εγω. Ειρηνην αφιημι υμιν,
ειρηνην την εμην διδωμι υμιν· ου καθως ο κοσμος διδωσιν εγω διδωμι

28 υμιν. μη ταρασσεσθω υμων η καρδια μηδε δειλιατω. ηκουσατε
οτι εγω ειπον υμιν· υπαγω και ερχομαι προς υμας. ει ηγαπατε
με, εχαρητε αν οτι πορευομαι προς τον πατερα, οτι ο πατηρ
29 μειζων μου εστιν. και νυν ειρηκα υμιν πριν γενεσθαι, ινα οταν
30 γενηται πιστευσητε. ουκετι λαλησω μεθ υμων, ερχεται γαρ ο
31 του κοσμου αρχων· και εν εμοι ουκ εχει ουδεν, αλλ ινα γνω ο
κοσμος οτι αγαπω τον πατερα, και καθως ενετειλατο μοι ο πατηρ,
ουτως ποιω. Εγειρεσθε, αγωμεν εντευθεν.

18: 1   Ταυτα ειπων Ιησους εξηλθεν συν τοις μαθηταις αυτου περαν
του χειμαρρου του Κεδρων, οπου ην κηπος, εις ον εισηλθεν αυτος
2 και οι μαθηται αυτου. ηδει δε και Ιουδας ο παραδιδους αυτον τον
τοπον, οτι πολλακις συνηχθη Ιησους εκει μετα των μαθητων
3 αυτου. ο ουν Ιουδας λαβων την σπειραν και εκ των αρχιερεων
και [εκ] των Φαρισαιων υπηρετας ερχεται εκει μετα φανων και
4 λαμπαδων και οπλων. Ιησους ουν ειδως παντα τα ερχομενα επ
5 αυτον εξηλθεν και λεγει αυτοις· τινα ζητειτε; απεκριθησαν
αυτω· Ιησουν τον Ναζωραιον. λεγει αυτοις· εγω ειμι. ειστηκει
6 δε και Ιουδας ο παραδιδους αυτον μετ αυτων. ως ουν ειπεν αυτοις·
7 εγω ειμι. απηλθαν εις τα οπισω και επεσαν χαμαι. παλιν ουν
επηρωτησεν αυτους· τινα ζητειτε; οι δε ειπαν· Ιησουν τον Ναζω-
8 ραιον. απεκριθη Ιησους· ειπον υμιν οτι εγω ειμι· ει ουν εμε
10 ζητειτε, αφετε τουτους υπαγειν· Σιμων ουν Πετρος εχων μαχαιραν
ειλκυσεν αυτην και επαισεν τον του αρχιερεως δουλον και απεκοψεν
11 αυτου το ωταριον το δεξιον· ην δε ονομα τω δουλω Μαλχος. ειπεν
ουν ο Ιησους τω Πετρω· βαλε την μαχαιραν εις την θηκην· το
ποτηριον ο δεδωκεν μοι ο πατηρ, ου μη πιω αυτο;
12   Η ουν σπειρα και ο χιλιαρχος και οι υπηρεται των Ιουδαιων
13 συνελαβον τον Ιησουν και εδησαν αυτον, και ηγαγον προς Ανναν
πρωτον· ην γαρ πενθερος του Καιαφα, ος ην αρχιερευς του
14 ενιαυτου εκεινου· ην δε Καιαφας ο συμβουλευσας τοις Ιουδαιοις οτι
15 συμφερει ενα ανθρωπον αποθανειν υπερ του λαου. Ηκολουθει
δε τω Ιησου Σιμων Πετρος και αλλος μαθητης. ο δε μαθητης
εκεινος ην γνωστος τω αρχιερει, και συνεισηλθεν τω Ιησου εις την
16 αυλην του αρχιερεως, ο δε Πετρος ειστηκει προς τη θυρα εξω.
εξηλθεν ουν ο μαθητης ο αλλος ο γνωστος του αρχιερεως και
17 ειπεν τη θυρωρω, και εισηγαγεν τον Πετρον. λεγει ουν τω
Πετρω η παιδισκη η θυρωρος· μη και συ εκ των μαθητων ει του
18 ανθρωπου τουτου; λεγει εκεινος· ουκ ειμι. ειστηκεισαν δε οι
δουλοι και οι υπηρεται ανθρακιαν πεποιηκοτες, οτι ψυχος ην, και
εθερμαινοντο· ην δε και ο Πετρος μετ αυτων εστως και θερμαι-
19 νομενος. Ο ουν αρχιερευς ηρωτησεν τον Ιησουν περι των μαθητων
20 αυτου και περι της διδαχης αυτου. απεκριθη αυτω Ιησους· εγω

παρρησια λελαληκα τω κοσμω· εγω παντοτε εδιδαξα εν συναγωγη
και εν τω ιερω, οπου παντες οι Ιουδαιοι συνερχονται, και εν
21 κρυπτω ελαλησα ουδεν. τι με ερωτας; ερωτησον τους ακηκοοτας
22 τι ελαλησα αυτοις· ιδε ουτοι οιδασιν α ειπον εγω. ταυτα δε αυτου
ειποντος εις παρεστηκως των υπηρετων εδωκεν ραπισμα τω
23 Ιησου ειπων· ουτως αποκρινη τω αρχιερει; απεκριθη αυτω Ιησους·
ει κακως ελαλησα, μαρτυρησον περι του κακου· ει δε καλως, τι με
24 δερεις; απεστειλεν ουν αυτον ο Αννας δεδεμενον προς Καιαφαν
25 τον αρχιερεα. Ην δε Σιμων Πετρος εστως και θερμαινομενος.
ειπον ουν αυτω· μη και συ εκ των μαθητων αυτου ει; ηρνησατο
26 εκεινος και ειπεν· ουκ ειμι. λεγει εις εκ των δουλων του αρχιερεως,
συγγενης ων ου απεκοψεν Πετρος το ωτιον· ουκ εγω σε ειδον εν τω
27 κηπω μετ αυτου; παλιν ουν ηρνησατο Πετρος, και ευθεως.
αλεκτωρ εφωνησεν.

28   Αγουσιν ουν τον Ιησουν απο του Καιαφα εις το πραιτωριον·
ην δε πρωι· και αυτοι ουκ εισηλθον εις το πραιτωριον, ινα μη
29 μιανθωσιν αλλα φαγωσιν το πασχα. εξηλθεν ουν ο Πιλατος
εξω προς αυτους και φησιν· τινα κατηγοριαν φερετε του ανθρωπου
30 τουτου; απεκριθησαν και ειπαν αυτω· ει μη ην ουτος κακον ποιων,
31 ουκ αν σοι παρεδωκαμεν αυτον. ειπεν ουν αυτοις ο Πιλατος·
λαβετε αυτον υμεις, και κατα τον νομον υμων κρινατε αυτον.
ειπον αυτω οι Ιουδαιοι· ημιν ουκ εξεστιν αποκτειναι ουδενα·
33 Εισηλθεν ουν παλιν εις το πραιτωριον ο Πιλατος και εφωνησεν
τον Ιησουν και ειπεν αυτω· συ ει ο βασιλευς των Ιουδαιων;
34 απεκριθη Ιησους· αφ εαυτου συ τουτο λεγεις, η αλλοι ειπον σοι
35 περι εμου; απεκριθη ο Πιλατος· μητι εγω Ιουδαιος ειμι; το
εθνος το σον και οι αρχιερεις παρεδωκαν σε εμοι· τι εποιησας;
36 απεκριθη Ιησους· η βασιλεια η εμη ουκ εστιν εκ του κοσμου τουτου·
ει εκ του κοσμου τουτου ην η βασιλεια η εμη, οι υπηρεται αν οι
εμοι ηγωνιζοντο, ινα μη παραδοθω τοις Ιουδαιοις· νυν δε η
37 βασιλεια η εμη ουκ εστιν εντευθεν. ειπεν ουν αυτω ο Πιλατος·
ουκουν βασιλευς ει συ; απεκριθη [ο] Ιησους· συ λεγεις οτι βασιλευς
ειμι. εγω εις τουτο γεγεννημαι και εις τουτο εληλυθα εις τον
κοσμον, ινα μαρτυρησω τη αληθεια· πας ο ων εκ της αληθειας
38 ακουει μου της φωνης. λεγει αυτω ο Πιλατος· τι εστιν αληθεια;
Και τουτο ειπων παλιν εξηλθεν προς τους Ιουδαιους, και λεγει
39 αυτοις· εγω ουδεμιαν ευρισκω εν αυτω αιτιαν. εστιν δε συνηθεια
υμιν ινα ενα απολυσω υμιν εν τω πασχα· βουλεσθε ουν απολυσω
40 υμιν τον βασιλεα των Ιουδαιων; εκραυγασαν ουν παλιν λεγοντες·
19: 1 μη τουτον, αλλα τον Βαραββαν. ην δε ο Βαραββας ληστης. Τοτε
2 ουν ελαβεν ο Πιλατος τον Ιησουν και εμαστιγωσεν. και οι
στρατιωται πλεξαντες στεφανον εξ ακανθων επεθηκαν αυτου τη
3 κεφαλη, και ιματιον πορφυρουν περιεβαλον αυτον, και ηρχοντο
προς αυτον και ελεγον· χαιρε ο βασιλευς των Ιουδαιων· και

4 εδιδοσαν αυτω ραπισματα. Και εξηλθεν παλιν εξω ο Πιλατος
και λεγει αυτοις· ιδε αγω υμιν αυτον εξω. ινα γνωτε οτι ουδεμιαν
5 αιτιαν ευρισκω εν αυτω. εξηλθεν ουν ο Ιησους εξω, φορων τον
ακανθινον στεφανον και το πορφυρουν ιματιον. και λεγει αυτοις·
6 ιδου ο ανθρωπος. οτε ουν ειδον αυτον οι αρχιερεις και οι υπηρεται,
εκραυγασαν λεγοντες· σταυρωσον σταυρωσον. λεγει αυτοις ο
Πιλατος· λαβετε αυτον υμεις και σταυρωσατε· εγω γαρ ουχ
7 ευρισκω εν αυτω αιτιαν. απεκριθησαν αυτω οι Ιουδαιοι· ημεις
νομον εχομεν, και κατα τον νομον οφειλει αποθανειν, οτι υιον
8 θεου εαυτον εποιησεν. Οτε ουν ηκουσεν ο Πιλατος τουτον τον
9 λογον, μαλλον εφοβηθη, και εισηλθεν εις το πραιτωριον παλιν
και λεγει τω Ιησου· ποθεν ει συ; ο δε Ιησους αποκρισιν ουκ
10 εδωκεν αυτω. λεγει ουν αυτω ο Πιλατος· εμοι ου λαλεις; ουκ
οιδας οτι εξουσιαν εχω απολυσαι σε και εξουσιαν εχω σταυρωσαι
11 σε; απεκριθη Ιησους· ουκ ειχες εξουσιαν κατ εμου ουδεμιαν ει μη ην
δεδομενον σοι ανωθεν· δια τουτο ο παραδους με σοι μειζονα
12 αμαρτιαν εχει. εκ τουτου ο Πιλατος εζητει απολυσαι αυτον·
οι δε Ιουδαιοι εκραυγασαν λεγοντες· εαν τουτον απολυσης, ουκ ει
φιλος του Καισαρος· πας ο βασιλεα εαυτον ποιων αντιλεγει τω
13 Καισαρι. Ο ουν Πιλατος ακουσας των λογων τουτων ηγαγεν
εξω τον Ιησουν, και εκαθισεν επι βηματος εις τοπον λεγομενον
14 Λιθοστρωτον, Εβραιστι δε Γ α β β α θ α. ην δε παρασκευη
του πασχα, ωρα ην ως εκτη· και λεγει τοις Ιουδαιοις· ιδε ο βασιλευς
15 υμων. εκραυγασαν ουν εκεινοι· αρον αρον, σταυρωσον αυτον.
λεγει αυτοις ο Πιλατος· τον βασιλεα υμων σταυρωσω; απεκρι-
16 θησαν οι αρχιερεις· ουκ εχομεν βασιλεα ει μη Καισαρα. τοτε
ουν παρεδωκεν αυτον αυτοις ινα σταυρωθη.
17 Παρελαβον ουν τον Ιησουν· και βασταζων εαυτω τον σταυρον
εξηλθεν εις τον λεγομενον κρανιου τοπον, ο λεγεται Εβραιστι
18 Γ ο λ γ ο θ α, οπου αυτον εσταυρωσαν, και μετ αυτου αλλους
19 δυο εντευθεν και εντευθεν, μεσον δε τον Ιησουν. εγραψεν δε
και τιτλον ο Πιλατος και εθηκεν επι του σταυρου· ην δε γεγραμ-
μενον· ΙΗΣΟΥΣ Ο ΝΑΖΩΡΑΙΟΣ Ο ΒΑΣΙΛΕΥΣ ΤΩΝ ΙΟΥ-
20 ΔΑΙΩΝ. τουτον ουν τον τιτλον πολλοι ανεγνωσαν των Ιουδαιων,
οτι εγγυς ην ο τοπος της πολεως οπου εσταυρωθη ο Ιησους· και
21 ην γεγραμμενον Εβραιστι, Ρωμαιστι, Ελληνιστι. ελεγον ουν
τω Πιλατω οι αρχιερεις των Ιουδαιων· μη γραφε· ο βασιλευς των
Ιουδαιων, αλλ οτι εκεινος ειπεν· βασιλευς ειμι των Ιουδαιων.
22, 23 απεκριθη ο Πιλατος· ο γεγραφα, γεγραφα. Οι ουν στρατιωται,
οτε εσταυρωσαν τον Ιησουν, ελαβον τα ιματια αυτου και εποιησαν
τεσσερα μερη, εκαστω στρατιωτη μερος, και τον χιτωνα. ην
24 δε ο χιτων αρραφος, εκ των ανωθεν υφαντος δι ολου. ειπαν ουν
προς αλληλους· μη σχισωμεν αυτον, αλλα λαχωμεν περι αυτου
τινος εσται· ινα η γραφη πληρωθη. διεμερισαντο τα ιματια μου

εαυτοις και επι τον ιματισμον μου εβαλον κληρον. Οι μεν ουν
25 στρατιωται ταυτα εποιησαν. ειστηκεισαν δε παρα τω σταυρω
του Ιησου η μητηρ αυτου και η αδελφη της μητρος αυτου, Μαρια
26 η του Κλωπα και Μαρια η Μαγδαληνη. Ιησους ουν ιδων την
μητερα και τον μαθητην παρεστωτα ον ηγαπα, λεγει τη μητρι·
27 γυναι, ιδε ο υιος σου. ειτα λεγει τω μαθητη· ιδε η μητηρ σου.
και απ εκεινης της ωρας ελαβεν ο μαθητης αυτην εις τα ιδια.
28 Μετα τουτο ειδως ο Ιησους οτι ηδη παντα τετελεσται, ινα τελειωθη
29 η γραφη, λεγει· διψω. σκευος εκειτο οξους μεστον· σπογγον
ουν μεστον του οξους υσσωπω περιθεντες προσηνεγκαν αυτου
30 τω στοματι. οτε ουν ελαβεν το οξος [ο] Ιησους ειπεν· τετελεσται,
και κλινας την κεφαλην παρεδωκεν το πνευμα.

31   Οι ουν Ιουδαιοι, επει παρασκευη ην, ινα μη μεινη επι του
σταυρου τα σωματα εν τω σαββατω, ην γαρ μεγαλη η ημερα
εκεινου του σαββατου, ηρωτησαν τον Πιλατον ινα κατεαγωσιν
32 αυτων τα σκελη και αρθωσιν. ηλθον ουν οι στρατιωται, και του
μεν πρωτου κατεαξαν τα σκελη και του αλλου του συσταυρωθεντος
33 αυτω· επι δε τον Ιησουν ελθοντες, ως ειδον ηδη αυτον τεθνηκοτα,
34 ου κατεαξαν αυτου τα σκελη, αλλ εις των στρατιωτων λογχη
36 αυτου την πλευραν ενυξεν, εγενετο γαρ ταυτα ινα η γραφη
37 πληρωθη· οστουν ου συντριβησεται αυτου. και παλιν ετερα
38 γραφη λεγει· οψονται εις ον εξεκεντησαν. Μετα δε ταυτα
ηρωτησεν τον Πιλατον Ιωσηφ απο Αριμαθαιας, ων μαθητης
[του] Ιησου κεκρυμμενος δε δια τον φοβον των Ιουδαιων, ινα αρη
το σωμα του Ιησου· και επετρεψεν ο Πιλατος. ηλθεν ουν και
39 ηρεν το σωμα αυτου. ηλθεν δε και Νικοδημος, ο ελθων προς αυτον
νυκτος το πρωτον, φερων μιγμα σμυρνης και αλοης ως λιτρας
40 εκατον. ελαβον ουν το σωμα του Ιησου και εδησαν αυτο οθονιοις
μετα των αρωματων, καθως εθος εστιν τοις Ιουδαιοις ενταφιαζειν.
41 ην δε εν τω τοπω οπου εσταυρωθη κηπος, και εν τω κηπω μνη-
42 μειον καινον, εν ω ουδεπω ουδεις ην τεθειμενος· εκει ουν δια την
παρασκευην των Ιουδαιων, οτι εγγυς ην το μνημειον, εθηκαν
τον Ιησουν.

20: 1   Τη δε μια των σαββατων Μαρια η Μαγδαληνη ερχεται πρωι
σκοτιας ετι ουσης εις το μνημειον, και βλεπει τον λιθον ηρμενον
2 εκ του μνημειου. τρεχει ουν και ερχεται προς Σιμωνα Πετρον και
προς τον αλλον μαθητην ον εφιλει ο Ιησους, και λεγει αυτοις·
ηραν τον κυριον εκ του μνημειου, και ουκ οιδαμεν που εθηκαν αυτον.
3 Εξηλθεν ουν ο Πετρος και ο αλλος μαθητης, και ηρχοντο εις το
4 μνημειον. ετρεχον δε οι δυο ομου· και ο αλλος μαθητης προεδραμεν
5 ταχιον του Πετρου και ηλθεν πρωτος εις το μνημειον, και παρα-
6 κυψας βλεπει κειμενα τα οθονια, ου μεντοι εισηλθεν. ερχεται ουν
και Σιμων Πετρος ακολουθων αυτω, και εισηλθεν εις το μνημειον·

7   και θεωρει τα οθονια κειμενα, και το σουδαριον, ο ην επι της
    κεφαλης αυτου, ου μετα των οθονιων κειμενον αλλα χωρις εντετυ-
8   λιγμενον εις ενα τοπον. τοτε ουν εισηλθεν και ο αλλος μαθητης
    ο ελθων πρωτος εις το μνημειον, και ειδεν και επιστευσεν·
10, 11 απηλθον ουν παλιν προς αυτους οι μαθηται. Μαρια δε ειστηκει
    προς τω μνημειω εξω κλαιουσα. ως ουν εκλαιεν, παρεκυψεν εις
12 το μνημειον, και θεωρει δυο αγγελους εν λευκοις καθεζομενους,
    ενα προς τη κεφαλη και ενα προς τοις ποσιν, οπου εκειτο το
13 σωμα του Ιησου. και λεγουσιν αυτη εκεινοι· γυναι, τι κλαιεις;
    λεγει αυτοις οτι ηραν τον κυριον μου, και ουκ οιδα που εθηκαν
14 αυτον. ταυτα ειπουσα εστραφη εις τα οπισω, και θεωρει τον
15 Ιησουν εστωτα, και ουκ ηδει οτι Ιησους εστιν. λεγει αυτη Ιησους·
    γυναι, τι κλαιεις; τινα ζητεις; εκεινη δοκουσα οτι ο κηπουρος
    εστιν, λεγει αυτω· κυριε, ει συ εβαστασας αυτον, ειπε μοι που
16 εθηκας αυτον, καγω αυτον αρω. λεγει αυτη Ιησους· Μαριαμ.
    στραφεισα εκεινη λεγει αυτω Εβραιστι· ρ α β β ο υ ν ι (ο
17 λεγεται διδασκαλε). λεγει αυτη Ιησους· μη μου απτου, ουπω γαρ
    αναβεβηκα προς τον πατερα· πορευου δε προς τους αδελφους μου
    και ειπε αυτοις· αναβαινω προς τον πατερα μου και πατερα υμων
18 και θεον μου και θεον υμων. ερχεται Μαριαμ η Μαγδαληνη
    αγγελλουσα τοις μαθηταις οτι εωρακα τον κυριον, και ταυτα
    ειπεν αυτη.
19   Ουσης ουν οψιας τη ημερα εκεινη τη μια σαββατων, και των
    θυρων κεκλεισμενων οπου ησαν οι μαθηται δια τον φοβον των
    Ιουδαιων, ηλθεν ο Ιησους και εστη εις το μεσον, και λεγει αυτοις·
20 ειρηνη υμιν. και τουτο ειπων εδειξεν και τας χειρας και την
    πλευραν αυτοις. εχαρησαν ουν οι μαθηται ιδοντες τον κυριον.
21 ειπεν ουν αυτοις· [ο Ιησους] παλιν· ειρηνη υμιν· καθως απεσταλκεν
22 με ο πατηρ, καγω πεμπω υμας. και τουτο ειπων ενεφυσησεν και
23 λεγει αυτοις· λαβετε πνευμα αγιον. αν τινων αφητε τας αμαρτιας,
    αφεωνται αυτοις· αν τινων κρατητε, κεκρατηνται.
24   Θωμας δε εις εκ των δωδεκα, ο λεγομενος Διδυμος, ουκ ην μετ
25 αυτων οτε ηλθεν Ιησους. ελεγον ουν αυτω οι αλλοι μαθηται·
    εωρακαμεν τον κυριον. ο δε ειπεν αυτοις· εαν μη ιδω εν ταις
    χερσιν αυτου τον τυπον των ηλων και βαλω τον δακτυλον μου εις
    τον τοπον των ηλων και βαλω μου την χειρα εις την πλευραν
26 αυτου, ου μη πιστευσω. Και μεθ ημερας οκτω παλιν ησαν εσω
    οι μαθηται αυτου, και Θωμας μετ αυτων. ερχεται ο Ιησους των
    θυρων κεκλεισμενων, και εστη εις το μεσον και ειπεν· ειρηνη
27 υμιν. ειτα λεγει τω Θωμα· φερε τον δακτυλον σου ωδε και ιδε
    τας χειρας μου, και φερε την χειρα σου και βαλε εις την πλευραν
28 μου, και μη γινου απιστος αλλα πιστος. απεκριθη Θωμας και
29 ειπεν αυτω· ο κυριος μου και ο θεος μου. λεγει αυτω ο Ιησους· οτι
    εωρακας με, πεπιστευκας; μακαριοι οι μη ιδοντες και πιστευσαντες.

30   Πολλα μεν ουν και αλλα σημεια εποιησεν ο Ιησους ενωπιον των

31   μαθητων, α ουκ εστιν γεγραμμενα εν τω βιβλιω τουτω· ταυτα δε
      γεγραπται ινα πιστευητε οτι Ιησους εστιν ο χριστος ο υιος του
      θεου, και ινα πιστευοντες ζωην εχητε εν τω ονοματι αυτου.

[1]6:

28   τουτον γαρ ο πατηρ εσφραγισεν ο θεος. ειπον ουν προς αυτον·

29   τι ποιωμεν ινα εργαζωμεθα τα εργα του θεου; απεκριθη Ιησους
      και ειπεν αυτοις· τουτο εστιν το εργον του θεου, ινα πιστευητε
      εις ον απεστειλεν εκεινος.

[2]8:

26   πολλα εχω περι υμων λαλειν και κρινειν· αλλ ο πεμψας με αληθης
      εστιν, καγω α ηκουσα παρ αυτου, ταυτα λαλω εις τον κοσμον.

27   ουκ εγνωσαν οτι τον πατερα αυτοις ελεγεν.

[1] Bultmann speculates that this passage was originally a part of the now missing text which stood between 7:52 and 8:41 (*Johannes*, p. 164 n. 3, p. 238 n. 5).

[2] This passage is a misplaced fragment which perhaps had its original place in connection with 8:13–20 (*Johannes*, pp. 266 f.).

4

The Additions of the Ecclesiastical Redactor

Bultmann's proposal that the gospel has been subjected to redaction is not original,[1] nor does he claim it to be. The novelty of Bultmann's redactional theory consists in the way in which he relates it to the problem of the order of the gospel, maintaining that the same redactor(s) who found the gospel in fragments and assembled it in its present order also made certain additions that would make this original and dubiously orthodox document acceptable to the developing orthodoxy of the church of the early second century. Bultmann is careful not to go further than he believes his evidence allows in defining the exact nature of this redactional process. While it has become customary to refer to the "ecclesiastical redactor" in connection with Bultmann's theory, as often as not he himself speaks of a *Redaktion* (a redaction, editing, or process of editing) so as not to commit himself completely on the question of whether the editorial process was the work of one man or more than one.

Bultmann's criteria for identifying the work of the ecclesiastical redactor

1. Howard, *The Fourth Gospel*, pp. 3, 31 f., 38, 40, 63, 65, 67, 69, 75, 86, 98 f. 116 ff., 127, 299 f.; also above, p. 116 n. 1.

are mainly derived from context and content, not from style or vocabulary.[2] He does not regard this as a weakness of his redaction theory but believes that the criteria he adduces are quite objective and not at all subjective or arbitrary. The justification for the use of such criteria is two-sided. On the one hand, Bultmann is confident that he has comprehended the theological perspective of the evangelist and that this perspective is, on the whole, a consistent one. On the other, he assumes knowledge of certain tendencies toward an official ecclesiastical orthodoxy in the early church. Evidence for the latter is drawn from later writings of the New Testament and from the Apostolic Fathers and has been ably set forth and illuminated by modern scholarship.[3] Hence, the proposal that certain ideas expressed in parts of the Fourth Gospel are alien to the theological perspective and interests of the evangelist and are the work of a later churchly redactor is confirmed by the discovery that these very ideas are characteristic of an emerging early catholic orthodoxy. For example, a type of cosmic futuristic eschatology appears in Luke-Acts, the Pastorals, etc. and the idea of sacramental appropriation of the saving work of Christ, or the concept of φάρμακον ἀθανασίας, in Ignatius of Antioch.

By what route does Bultmann arrive at the conclusion that the Fourth Gospel has undergone redaction? As we have seen, there is first the internal evidence of the present order of the text, with the difficulties which it presents. Then, there are those sections which call attention to themselves because of their theological content. Finally, there is chapter 21. Because of its purpose and content (but not necessarily its style) and because the gospel already has its conclusion in 20:30 f., chapter 21 must be considered an appendix by a later hand. As such it affords clear evidence that the gospel was published by a redactor rather than by the evangelist. With chapter 21, 19:35 also comes under suspicion of being redactional along with all references to the disciple whom Jesus loved, although Bultmann does not, with Hirsch and others, ascribe every mention of this disciple to the redactor.[4]

The additions of the ecclesiastical redactor fall into five categories: (1) the sacramental, (2) the futuristic eschatological, (3) those which attempt at some point to harmonize the gospel with synoptic tradition, (4) those which lay claim to apostolic and eyewitness authority for the evangelist and therefore for his gospel, (5) and a miscellaneous group which are assigned to the

2. Cf. *Johannes*, p. 174 n. 8 and p. 175 n. 5 on 6:51b–58.

3. Note Bultmann's reference to W. Bauer, *Rechtgläubigkeit und Ketzerei im ältesten Christentum*, Beiträge zur historischen Theologie, 10 (Tübingen, J. C. B. Mohr, 1934) in his review of Dodd's book, *NTS, 1* (1954–55), 90.

4. *Johannes*, p. 4 n. 2, passim; *RGG, 3* (1959), 840–41; *ET, 4* (1937), 119 f.

redactor for a variety of textual and theological reasons. There are also a number of words and phrases which Bultmann excises as still later "tertiary" glosses. [5] Some of these lack the decisive support of the manuscript witnesses, hence judgments about them become matters of textual criticism.

SACRAMENTALISM

Before taking up Bultmann's assignment of sacramental passages to the redactor, I must note his understanding of the evangelist's position with respect to the sacraments.[6] Bultmann does not maintain that the evangelist simply opposes baptism and the Lord's Supper. The evangelist tolerates them. He reports that Jesus (like John) had baptized (3:22, 4:1) and indicates that entrance into the circle of Jesus' disciples was accompanied by baptism (4:1). But, assuming the excision of certain passages as redactional, he maintains a strange silence on the use of the sacraments in the church and does not report the institution of the Lord's Supper. John's misgivings about baptism and the Lord's Supper stem from the ecclesiastical misunderstanding and misuse of them as sacramental channels of grace. They are ultimately superfluous for him and have validity only insofar as the word is made present through them in a special way.[7] Hence, they can in no way be a substitute for faith and obedience.

5. The most important of these tertiary glosses is 2:15b, 16a, which is found in all manuscripts and which may stem from the ecclesiastical redactor (p. 86 n. 10); 4:2, also universally attested, is possibly from the redactor too (p. 122 n. 2). Other glosses identified by Bultmann include: the ἔγνω ὁ κύριος ὅτι of 4:1 (p. 128 n. 4); perhaps the parenthetical note at the end of 4:9: "For the Jews do not mix with the Samaritans" (p. 130 n. 5); possibly the statement "You have no bucket and the well is deep" in 4:11 (p. 132 n. 5); 6:18 (p. 159 n. 1); the participial phrase at the end of 6:23 (p. 160 n. 5); very significantly, the πολλά of 14:30, which leaves the way open for Jesus to say something further in chapters 15–17 (p. 349 n. 4, p. 487 n. 7); the phrase "except the feet" in 13:10 (p. 357 n. 5); πάλιν in 13:12 (p. 361 n. 7); possibly the phrase "because I go to the Father" in 16:17 (p. 444 n. 3); possibly the "more than these" of 21:15 (p. 551 n. 1); the characterization (chapter 21) of the Beloved Disciple as the one who rested upon Jesus' breast at dinner—beginning with the ἀκολουθοῦντα of 21:20 and continuing through the ὁ πέτρος of 21:21 (p. 553 n. 5). Also, "the spirit" in 3:34 (p. 119 n. 1) and "of sin" in 8:34 (p. 335 n. 7) are said to be tertiary glosses. References in parentheses are to Bultmann's commentary.

6. For Bultmann's general discussion of the sacraments in John, see *Johannes*, pp. 359 f., 370 f.

7. *Johannes*, p. 360: "Man kann sich also den Tatbestand [the evangelist's ambivalence toward the sacraments] wohl nur so erklären, dass sich der Evglist mit dem kirchlichen Brauch von Taufe und Herrenmahl zwar abfindet, dass dieser ihm aber infolge des Missbrauches verdächtig bleibt und dass er deshalb davon schweigt. In Wahrheit sind für ihn die Sakramente überflüssig . . . [The disciples are "pure" and "holy" through the word]. Hat sich der Evglist mit den Sakramenten abgefunden, so kann er sie nur so verstanden haben, dass in ihnen das Wort in einer besonderen Weise vergegenwärtigt wird."

There are several places in the gospel where Bultmann discerns a redactional reference or allusion to the Lord's Supper or baptism. (I have already discussed his assignment of 6:51c–58 to the ecclesiastical redactor because of the sacramental and eschatological concepts which it contains.[8]) The ὕδατος καί of 3:5 is assigned to the redactor,[9] who is said to have attempted to introduce into the discussion of rebirth and the spirit the traditional idea that rebirth occurs at baptism (Titus 3:5; Justin, *Apology* 50.66.1.). There is nothing about baptism elsewhere in this section, and the allusion to it here presents a problem both for the immediate context and for Bultmann's overall conception of the evangelist's theology. The ὕδατος καί of 3:8 (which Nestle puts in the apparatus as a *v. l.*) is poorly attested and is almost certainly to be regarded as an interpolation, presumably from a latter glossator rather than the ecclesiastical redactor. Unlike many scholars, Bultmann sees in 6:4 ("It was near the Passover, the feast of the Jews.") no attempt to relate the speech of Jesus in the latter part of the chapter to the Passover and thereby to its Christian counterpart, the Eucharist.[10] The assertion that the Passover feast of the Jews was near simply prepares the way for 5:1 ff. ("After these things there was a feast of the Jews . . .") and thus confirms the reversal of chapters 5 and 6. In any case the Eucharistic theme in the speech of Jesus (6:27 ff.) has been introduced redactionally (6:51c–58), and, if 6:4 were viewed as an attempt to connect the speech to the Eucharist, it too would have to be assigned to the redactor. But even if the evangelist were concerned with expounding the Eucharist he would not relate it to the Passover, since in the gospel the Eucharist is not related to Jesus' last meal, and that meal is not a Passover. Bultmann assigns 19:34b–35 to the ecclesiastical redactor, although different motifs appear in verse 34b and verse 35. He maintains that the issue of water and blood in verse 34b is reported as a miracle whose meaning "can hardly be other than that in the death of Jesus upon the cross the sacrament of baptism and the Lord's Supper have their origin." This is, of course, a common idea of early Christianity. Other interpretations of the meaning of this passage—e.g. that it is anti-Docetic—are regarded as untenable.[11] The washing of the feet in chapter 13 is often considered sacramental, but Bultmann has reservations about such an interpretation and does not assign it to the ecclesiastical redactor.[12]

8. Above, p. 141.

9. *Johannes*, p. 98 n. 2. Bultmann does not claim absolute certainty but maintains that the originality of ὕδατος καί is at least very doubtful.

10. Ibid., p. 156 n. 6.

11. Ibid., p. 525 n. 5. The reference to water and blood in I John 5:6, however, is said to be anti-Docetic rather than sacramental (ibid., p. 525 n. 6).

12. Ibid., p. 357 n. 5; pp. 359 f.

Although there is no mention during the Last Supper itself (chapter 13) of the institution of the Lord's Supper,[13] one cannot explain this curious omission by supposing that the evangelist assumed knowledge of the synoptic accounts and therefore did not feel called upon to report it. Why, then, did he report the prophecy of the betrayal or Peter's denial? The presentation of the last meal in John is complete, and at no point is there a place for the institution of the Eucharist, which, had it been included, would have been its high point. Why, then, does the evangelist omit the institution of the Lord's Supper? It cannot be maintained that the words of institution were suppressed because of their secret character;[14] neither does Bultmann wish to say that the institution of the Lord's Supper was ignored or that the evangelist was ignorant of it. Rather, he substitutes for it the prayer of Jesus in chapter 17. In doing so he places upon the lips of Jesus the principal theological motifs of the Lord's Supper: that the church is grounded in the sacrificial death of Jesus for his own, that it is the community of the New Covenant, and that it is bound to him in mysterious communion—albeit in a way somewhat different from that understood in the orthodox conception of the Eucharist. Bultmann deems it quite possible that the formulation of this prayer was influenced by the traditional form of the words of institution and perhaps, even, by the liturgical prayers which were used with it.[15]

APOCALYPTIC ESCHATOLOGY

Certain passages in the Fourth Gospel which reflect an apocalyptic eschatology are also assigned to the redactor. Bultmann does not, however, assign to the redactor all promises, to the believer, of a future existence after or beyond death, nor does he seek to interpret them in terms of an existentialism which limits eschatological existence to this life. The eschatological existence which the Jesus of the Fourth Gospel makes possible is a present reality, but not a present reality only. It is only the old apocalyptic worldview of Judaism which Bultmann believes is foreign to the Fourth Gospel and which he assigns to the redactor, not futurist eschatology per se. The future hope of the Fourth Gospel is said to be more closely akin to the Gnostic hope for an existence beyond death than to Jewish apocalypticism.[16] Nevertheless, in the farewell discourses, apocalyptic motifs are given a new interpretation under the control of the evangelist's distinct theological per-

13. For Bultmann's discussion of this problem see especially ibid., pp. 370 f.
14. Ibid., p. 360 n. 4.
15. Ibid., p. 371 n. 3.
16. Ibid., p. 465 n. 1.

spective, in which resurrection, parousia, and Pentecost are one.[17] The resurrection of Jesus, his coming again, and the coming of the Spirit are no longer
separate events along the time-line of salvation-history, but one and the same
event, made real for, and appropriated by, the congregation in the present.
The coming of Jesus to his own is the realization of eschatological existence
in the present life of the church. But in the disciples' following after Jesus,
the promise of a future existence with him beyond death is to be realized.
The traditional Jewish-Christian eschatological hopes are transmuted into the
present, and a new futurist eschatology is developed out of the Gnostic
Denkweise.[18]

Since I have already called attention to the long redactional section 6:51–
58, where, along with the sacramental interest, there appears an allegedly
non-Johannine futuristic eschatology ("and I will raise him up at the last
day": verse 54. Cf. also verses 39, 40, 44),[19] it will not be necessary to go
over this ground again. The single most important specimen of apocalyptic
eschatology is found in 5:28 f.:[20] "Do not marvel at this, for the hour is coming when all who are in the tomb shall hear his [the Son of Man's] voice,
and those who have done good shall come forth into the resurrection of life,
those who have done evil into the resurrection of judgment." The redactor
is said to have introduced these words so that the daring assertions of Jesus
in the preceding verses would not seem to stand in contradiction to traditional Jewish-Christian eschatology, which was becoming orthodox in the
early church. The redaction may very well begin in verse 27b ("and he has
given him authority to execute judgment, for he is the Son of Man"), which
does not really follow from what has immediately preceded but prepares
the way for verses 28 f. The Son of Man as apocalyptic judge is the necessary presupposition of verses 28 f., but such a concept is scarcely in accord
with the evangelist's understanding of the Son of Man as the revealer in his
earthly function. Bultmann notes that one would have expected only "Son"
in verse 27b, since in verses 21–26 only the Son is spoken of. It is just possible
that the ἀνθρώπου of verse 27 and no more is the redactor's gloss. Bultmann's
criteria for excising these verses as redactional are thus primarily theological.
Verses 28 f. are simply incompatible with the nonapocalyptic eschatology
of the evangelist, who, in verses 21 ff., speaks not of a future eschatological

17. Ibid., p. 451.
18. Ibid., pp. 447 f.; p. 451; p. 464, especially n. 1; p. 465 n. 1. Schulz, *Komposition und Herkunft*, attempts to show how the evangelist develops themes that are basically Jewish and apocalyptic through what is called Gnostic reinterpretation (above, pp. 93 f.). In effect his thesis is an extension of Bultmann's suggestion.
19. On the redactions of chapter 6, see Bultmann, *Johannes*, p. 162; above, p. 134.
20. For Bultmann's discussion of 5:28 f., *Johannes* pp. 195–97.

event but of an eschatological event already present in the work of Jesus. Furthermore, the teaching of a universal resurrection to life or judgment in verses 28 f. does not agree with verses 21 and 24 f., where it is said that only those whom the Father wills or only those who hear the Son are raised. The raising of the dead and the transformation from death to life spoken of in verses 21 ff. are present eschatological possibilities and not future eschatological events.[21] The spiritualizing of verses 28 f. in terms of verse 24 is said to be impossible in spite of the analogy of the Odes of Solomon (22:8 f.).[22] How the redactor reconciled his interpolation with the original text of the gospel, Bultmann can only guess. Perhaps he conceived of the κρίσις already present in the work of Jesus as the anticipation of the final judgment at the end of history, at which time the resurrection of all the dead would establish the truth of his word before all men. Bultmann notes that a precedent for this can be found in the Mandaean texts.[23] In conformity with his other excisions, Bultmann also removes the "in the last day" of 12:48 from the text of the original gospel and assigns it to the ecclesiastical redactor.[24]

CONFORMITY TO THE SYNOPTICS

The hand of the ecclesiastical redactor is also to be discerned in certain parallels to the synoptic gospels. Bultmann acknowledges that there are many passages similar to the synoptics which cannot be assigned to the redactor. Thus, similarity to the synoptics is not as sure an indication of redaction as sacramentalism or apocalyptic eschatology. Nevertheless, he believes that the redactor's orthodox tendency and interests can be seen in several attempts to conform the Fourth Gospel to the synoptics. The most important of these is the alleged redaction of the account of John the Baptist (chapter 1), which we have already discussed.[25] Also, the statement "For John had not yet been cast into prison" in 3:24 is said to be intended to harmonize the Johannine account, in which John and Jesus are portrayed as baptizing side by side, with the synoptic, in which Jesus does not begin his ministry until after the arrest of the Baptist. Bultmann assigns the passage to the redactor because in his view the evangelist is not interested in such harmonizations.[26] The pos-

---

21. Following Bultmann's interpretation, the τοῦτο of verse 28 refers not to the following ὅτι-clause but to what is said in verses 21 ff. about the raising of the dead. The ὅτι-clause is therefore causal (*begründend*) and not explicative.

22. *Johannes*, p. 196 n. 11.

23. Ibid., p. 197.

24. Ibid., p. 262 n. 7.

25. See above, pp. 121 ff.

26. Ibid., p. 124 n. 7.

sibility also arises that 12:14 f. is from the redactor,[27] since this report of
Jesus' riding into Jerusalem on an ass, a fulfillment of Old Testament
prophecy, can be construed as an attempt to bring the Johannine account
into line with the synoptics. Bultmann, however, rejects this possibility,
pointing out that the source could have been supplemented to bring it in
line with the synoptics before it came into the hand of the evangelist or that
the evangelist could have added verses 14 f. himself in preparation for what
is said in verse 16.[28] The verse 20:9 ("For they did not yet know the scripture, that it was necessary for him to rise from the dead.") is assigned to
the redactor. The δεῖ αὐτὸν ἐκ νεκρῶν ἀναστῆναι sounds un-Johannine and recalls
synoptic terminology or the language of the confessing church.[29] Finally, the
redactor's tendency to harmonize the Fourth Gospel with the synoptics appears in his appendix, chapter 21. For example, the report of the resurrection
appearance by the sea brings the Johannine account, which has heretofore
dealt only with resurrection appearances in Jerusalem, into line with the
Galilean tradition found in Matthew and Mark.[30]

THE BELOVED DISCIPLE AND THE ATTESTATION
OF THE GOSPEL

Bultmann does not think every reference to the Beloved Disciple must
be ascribed to the ecclesiastical redactor. Indeed, he believes that the figure
of the Beloved Disciple is an important creation of the evangelist. Only where

27. According to Bultmann (ibid., p. 319 n. 4) verse 16 must go with verses 14 f. If verse
16 must be assigned to the redactor, so must not only 12:14 f. but also 2:17, 22, and 7:39b,
for they contain the same motif of the disciples' initial lack of understanding and their
later recollection (2:17, 22), or the distinction between the period of Jesus' earthly ministry
and the time of his glorification in which the Spirit was given.
  When he wrote the part of the commentary which deals with the cleansing of the temple,
Bultmann thought that verses 17 and 22, which speak of the disciples' remembering a word
of scripture or a word of Jesus after the resurrection, were from the evangelist (p. 87 n. 3,
p. 89 n. 1). Apparently he later came to admit the possibility that these verses were from
the ecclesiastical redactor (Ergänzungsheft, pp. 86, 87, 89 n. 1, 90 n. 7). Cf. ibid., p. 229 n. 2
and 319 n. 4, where Bultmann deals with 7:39b and 12:14 ff. respectively; also pp. 530 f.
where he assigns 20:9 (which contains the motif of "not yet knowing the scriptures") to the
redactor.
28. In similar cases Bultmann decides that 12:25, 26, and 13:16, 20, traditional Herrenworte,
were not introduced by the ecclesiastical redactor from the synoptics but were either placed
here by the evangelist, who in turn drew them from some tradition, or were already in the
source which the evangelist was using: ibid., p. 325 n. 4; p. 352. (Each of these sayings occurs
in the context of a section which Bultmann believes is based on a separate traditional, probably written, source.)
29. Ibid., pp. 530 f.
30. Ibid., p. 543. Another apparent harmonization with the synoptics in 2:15 f. is assigned by
Bultmann to a tertiary glossator rather than to the redactor (p. 86 n. 10).

the Beloved Disciple is presented as a historical person, an eyewitness and
the author of the gospel, may one suspect that the hand of the redactor has
been at work. For, according to the redactor, the Beloved Disciple is both
an eyewitness and the author of the Fourth Gospel.[31] That this is actually
the case is, in Bultmann's judgment, impossible.[32] There is a sense in which
the evangelist does identify himself with the Beloved Disciple, but he thereby
makes no claim to having been an eyewitness and one of the circle of the
Twelve. The Beloved Disciple is in fact an ideal figure (*Idealgestalt*).[33] In
19:26, where Jesus leaves his mother in his care, the mother is Jewish Christianity, and the Beloved Disciple is the pagan Hellenistic church. In 13:21–30
and 20:2–10 the Beloved Disciple appears again as the symbol of the Hellenistic church over against Peter, who represents the Jewish church. Insofar
as the evangelist identifies himself with the pagan Hellenistic church, he
figuratively identifies himself with the Beloved Disciple.[34]

The redactor, like many readers after him, thus missed the point entirely
in attempting to make of the Beloved Disciple an eyewitness to Jesus and the
authoritative apostolic author of the gospel. To carry through the identification of this ideal figure with the evangelist, he added, in 19:35, an attestation
of the authenticity of the witness: "And he who has seen has borne witness, and his witness is true, and that one knows that he speaks truth, in
order that you also may believe." [35] The witness ("He who has seen," ὁ
ἑωρακώς) is the evangelist, to whom the redactor who writes this passage mis-
guidedly ascribes the role of eyewitness. That 19:35 is redactional is all the
more clear if one sees it in the light of 21:20 ff., especially 21:24. The Beloved Disciple, there identified with the eyewitness and author of the gospel,
is the same as the one who in 19:35 is said to have seen and borne witness.
That the evangelist merely desires to emphasize the reliability of his own witness in 19:35 is not possible since in that case one would have expected not
μεμαρτύρηκεν but μαρτυρεῖ. If 19:35 were ascribed to the evangelist, one would
have to suppose that he is here calling upon an eyewitness who delivered the
report to him.

31. Ibid., p. 369.
32. Ibid., p. 369 and n. 5. Bultmann does not go into the reasons why the evangelist could
not have been the Beloved Disciple and an eyewitness but refers to his own understanding
of the origin and interpretation of the gospel, which excludes this possibility.
33. Ibid., pp. 369 ff.
34. Ibid., p. 370.
35. The ἐκεῖνος cannot be the witness himself, but another who attests the truth of this
witness. Perhaps the text is corrupt at this point and should read "and we know that one"
rather than "and that one knows." Bultmann thinks that if the text is taken as it stands, the
ἐκεῖνος refers to Jesus himself. He rejects Goguel's suggestion that it refers to the publisher
of the gospel, who added verse 35 as well as chapter 21 (ibid., p. 526 and n. 4).

From 19:35 one moves naturally to chapter 21, which is crucial to an understanding of the process by which the gospel was published in its present form. Like many critics, Bultmann maintains that the evangelist closed the gospel with 20:30 f.[36] Chapter 21 is an addendum. The only question is whether it is the work of the evangelist himself or of a later redactor and publisher. Bultmann decides for the latter alternative. Not only is it extremely unlikely that an author would have added to his own work in this fashion, but the perspectives and interests reflected in this chapter are not those of the evangelist. One discovers here the same ecclesiastical interests and harmonizing tendencies which characterize the work of the redactor throughout the gospel. The apparent allegory of the net that does not tear despite the size of the catch of 153 fish (verse 11) symbolizes the indivisible unity of the church (cf. 10:16).[37] The sacramental interest of the redactor appears in the account of the resurrection appearance beside the sea (21:1–14), for the meal in which this scene culminates is no ordinary meal but, with its mysterious, cultic character, is a portrayal (*Abbild*) of the Lord's Supper.[38] The eschatology presupposed in verses 18 ff. is the primitive apocalypticism which the evangelist has sought to replace. Only in chapter 21, in agreement with the synoptics, do the disciples appear as fishermen. Also, only here are the sons of Zebedee mentioned. The appearance of the risen Jesus in Galilee, attested by Matthew and Mark, is mentioned only here in the Fourth Gospel, with no preceding report of the journey of the disciples to Galilee. Furthermore, 20:19–29 neither anticipates nor permits any further appearances of the risen Jesus. After the commissioning of the disciples (20:22 f.) it is scarcely understandable that they should go fishing in order to experience another appearance of the risen Lord. Jesus' word of 20:29 ("Blessed are those who have not seen and believe.") permits no more accounts of resurrection appearances.[39] Furthermore, 21:1–14 in its original form was an account of the

36. Ibid., pp. 542–47, for Bultmann's discussion of the problem of chapter 21. He admits that stylistic characteristics offer no proof of the secondary character of chapter 21 (p. 542), but nevertheless makes a thorough and careful analysis and presentation of the stylistic data of that chapter. While there are some distinct features of vocabulary, Bultmann does not claim that these are decisive for criticism, and admits that many only serve as an indication of the different content of chapter 21. He does, however, think some words and expressions are surprising in the light of the Johannine usage in chapters 1–20 (pp. 542–43, especially p. 542 n. 5). Ruckstuhl, *Einheit*, pp. 142–49, vigorously denies that the evidence of speech and style leads to any conclusion other than that the author of chapter 21 is also the author of the gospel.

37. Ibid., p. 549.

38. Ibid., pp. 549 f. According to Bultmann we find here the same sacramental interest of the redactor that is manifest in 6:51c–58.

39. *Johannes*, p. 543.

first appearance of Jesus, not the third, as the obviously redactional statement of verse 14 would have it.[40]

A new and altogether different interest also appears in chapter 21. No longer is the problem that of the existence of the disciples in the world, of revelation and faith, but of persons and their relationships in the church. The question of churchly rank and authority is introduced. Thus, in verses 20 ff. the Beloved Disciple, no longer an Idealgestalt, has become not only a historical person but also an authoritative, apostolic figure. In verse 24 this Beloved Disciple is designated as the author of the gospel. Verse 23 clearly implies that he is already dead and that the gospel with the postscript was published by another after his death. That the evangelist wanted to present himself as the Beloved Disciple in this sense and to prophesy his own death is, according to Bultmann, unbelievable.[41]

To the account of the resurrection the redactor joined two conversations of Jesus with Peter (verses 15–23) which to all appearances have little intrinsic relation to it. Except for the reappearance of the Beloved Disciple in verses 18–23, the other disciples are from this point on completely ignored. The theme of the first conversation (verses 15–17) is the commissioning of Peter as leader of the church and of the second (verses 18–22) Peter's relation to the Beloved Disciple. According to Bultmann these two sections are not integrally related but actually express different interests. The evangelist is really interested in the second conversation and by means of it makes the point that the Beloved Disciple is of equal rank with Peter, to whom the Lord has given the responsibility of church leadership. The redactor is not interested in Peter per se but only in carrying over his authority to the Beloved Disciple. "Thus vv. 15–17 are only a foil for vv. 18–23, where it is learned that after Peter had died as a martyr the Beloved Disciple stepped into his place as authoritative witness." Verses 15–17 were taken out of tradition—perhaps a written source—while verses 18–23 are the composition of the redactor.[42] The redactor brings in the Lord's own testimony to the apostolic authority of the evangelist and thereby attempts to give his gospel the highest possible authority in the church. The purpose of 21:15–23, and of the chapter as a whole, is to establish the ecclesiastical authority of the Beloved Disciple and his gospel.[43] It cannot be said that the redactor is concerned to portray the forgiveness and restoration of Peter, since his earlier denial is not mentioned.

40. Ibid., p. 546.
41. Ibid., p. 543.
42. Ibid., pp. 546 ff.
43. Ibid., pp. 547, 554 f.

Miscellaneous Redactions

At several points in John we find the suggestion that the disciples properly understand the Old Testament scriptures or a word or act of Jesus only after the resurrection (cf. 2:17, 22; 7:39; 12:14 ff.; 20:9).[44] In the latest revision of his commentary, Bultmann shows a tendency to assign such passages to the redactor, although in most cases he is hesitant about passing judgment. For example, he decides that 2:17, 22 could be assigned either to the redactor or to the evangelist. Then, after raising the possibility that 7:39b is from the redactor, he concludes that it is unnecessary to suppose this, since the relationship presupposed there between the Spirit and the glorified Christ is not foreign to the evangelist himself. The passage 12:14–16 is said to be probably original, but 20:9 is assigned to the redactor. Also, 12:33 ("Jesus said this, signifying by what way he should die.") is suspected of being from the redactor after having first been assigned to the evangelist.[45] Doubtless, Bultmann's suspicion stems from the observation that it is an editorial reflection upon a word of Jesus (12:32), relating it to his passion. In this respect it bears a certain similarity to the passages just cited. Verse 18:32 ("In order that the word of Jesus might be fulfilled, which he spoke signifying by what death he should die.") indicates the fulfillment of the word (and its interpretation) reported in 12:32. The statement of the Jews (18:31) that they are not allowed to put anyone to death is taken as confirmation of the death by crucifixion alluded to in 12:32 f. and as fulfillment of prophecy. Execution at the hands of the Romans would mean crucifixion. The redactional character of 18:32 is supported by its similarity to 21:19 ("This he said, signifying by what death he should glorify God."), which, as a part of chapter 21, must be from the redactor. If 18:32 is redactional, 12:33 cannot be original but must also be the work of the redactor.[46]

Because it asserts that "salvation is of the Jews,"[47] 4:22b, if not the entire verse, is assigned to the redactor. In view of 8:41 ff. and 1:11 (and in spite of 4:9) neither the evangelist nor the Johannine Christ could have said this. The Jesus of the Fourth Gospel, says Bultmann, is clearly set apart from the Jews.[48] Possibly 4:22a ("You worship what you do not know. We worship what we know.") is from the evangelist, but only if the "we" refers to the

44. Cf. above p. 220 n. 27 and the references to the commentary given there.
45. *Johannes*, p. 331 n. 4 (*Ergänzungsheft*, 1957); p. 495.
46. Ibid., pp. 495, 503, 505.
47. Ibid., p. 139 n. 6.
48. Ibid., p. 59, especially n. 2; cf. p. 34 n. 7.

followers of Jesus and the "you" to all others. If the "you" is taken to refer to the Samaritans and the "we" to the Jews, it must be excised as a gloss along with verse 22b. The ἀλλά of verse 23 scarcely makes for a suitable continuation if verse 22a is considered genuine, and this casts further doubt upon it.

As in chapter 21, ecclesiastical interest in the mission and unity of the church (10:16) is typical of the redactor.[49] Since the thought of 10:15—the relationship of the Father, the Good Shepherd, and the sheep—is continued only in verses 17 f., 10:16 is obviously an interruption and presumably an interpolation. The redactional character of verse 16 is confirmed by its allegorical application of the αὐλή of verse 1 to the Jewish people to make the point that not only among the Jews but in all the world the revealer finds his own. Since the idea of the unity of those who belong to Jesus is also contained in 11:52 and 17:20 (both of which are original with the evangelist), the redactor probably missed it in this context and thus added 10:16.

The awkward introduction of a proof text from the Old Testament may indicate the hand of the redactor, and Bultmann thinks that the scriptural argument or proof-text of 10:34–36 is probably to be assigned to the redactor. Such argument is elsewhere used by the evangelist (7:23, 8:17 ff.) but not in such a hard and fast way. In this instance the interpretation of the Old Testament passage is completely foreign to its original meaning. In addition, Jesus' self-citation in verse 36 ("I said, 'I am a son of God.'") corresponds neither to his statement in verse 30 ("I and the Father are one.") nor to the accusation of the Jews in verse 33 ("for you, being a man, make yourself God."). Bultmann thinks that 10:34–36 is a typical early Christian proof from scripture, and out of place in John. He suggests that the redactor got it from the apologetic tradition of early Christianity, which had to defend the divinity of Jesus against Jewish attack. If verses 34–36 were attributed to the evangelist, the passage, like 8:17 f., would have to be understood as a caricature of Jewish scriptural theology. With little hesitation Bultmann also assigns 7:38b ("As the scripture says, 'Out of his belly shall flow rivers of living water.'") to the redactor.[50] If this excision is made, 7:39 follows 7:37, 38a without interruption. Bultmann translates verses 37, 38a "If anyone thirsts let him come to me, and he who believes in me let him drink," the "he who believes in me" being read with the preceding clause rather than with the "as the scripture says . . ." The almost comical picture of the believer with rivers of living water flowing from his belly is eliminated, and the imagery is more intelligibly applied to Christ. The passage 7:38b is then understood as a redactional gloss prophesying the issue of water and

49. Ibid., p. 292.
50. Ibid., p. 228 n. 6, p. 229 n. 2.

blood from the side of Jesus in 19:34b, which is also assigned to the redactor.

We may simply mention several other words, phrases, and sentences which Bultmann assigns to the redactor: the superfluous ἐν τῷ πάσχα standing next to the ἐν τῇ ἑορτῇ in 2:32; τῆς Τιβεριάδος in 6:1; possibly the introductory clause of 8:12 ("Jesus then spoke to them, saying . . ."); the similar clause at the beginning of 12:44; possibly the translation in 9:7; 11:2, which betrays itself by the *kyrios* title and the attempt to identify Mary with the woman known from Mark 14:3–9 (Luke 7:37 ff.); possibly the ἐκ τοῦ δείπνου of 13:3. Finally, 18:9, which interprets the preceding statement of Jesus as the fulfillment of the word spoken in 6:39, is said to be a misinterpretation and is assigned to the redactor.[51]

We cannot conclude this survey of Bultmann's identification of redactional material in John without taking note of the way in which he says the redactor produced the appendix (chapter 21), namely, by weaving together traditional sources in much the same manner as the evangelist. Doubtless this source hypothesis helps explain why the main point of chapter 21, the attestation and authentication of the Fourth Gospel through the establishment of the author as an early eyewitness of equal authority with Peter, is not made more directly.[52] The original stories underlying the pericopes of verses 1–14 and 15–23 are said to stem from independent traditions. The resurrection account of verses 1–14 was originally a story of the first appearance rather than the third. Contextual analysis and other considerations show that verses 4b, 7, 8a, 9b, and 13 f. are glosses of the redactor, and verse 11a probably read ἀνέβησαν (οὖν) οἱ μαθηταὶ καὶ εἵλκυσαν κτλ originally. The redactor gives Peter and the Beloved Disciple a special prominence in verses 4b, 7, and 8a to prepare the way for verses 15–23, and in verses 9b and 13 his cultic sacramental interests emerge. The introduction of a Galilean resurrection appearance reflects the redactor's tendency to bring John into line with the synoptic tradition.[53] As I have noted, Bultmann's investigation shows that only verses 15–17 in the section 21:15–23 are traditional; verses 18–23 are the composition of the redactor. The traditional material, which relates the conversation between Jesus and Peter, merely serves as a foil to introduce the point about the Beloved Disciple, which is the evangelist's real interest.

51. Ibid., p. 91 n. 2 (*Ergänzungsheft*, 1957); p. 156 n. 2 (*Ergänzungsheft*, 1957), p. 253, p. 260 n. 2, p. 262 n. 2, p. 301 n. 4 and p. 302 n. 1, p. 355 n. 2, p. 495.

52. For the analysis of chapter 21, ibid., pp. 542 ff., especially 543–47.

53. Principally Matthew and Mark but also Luke 5:1–11, to which Bultmann believes John 21:1–14 is related.

The Validity and Significance of the Redaction Theory

The redactional material of the gospel is identified primarily by theological analysis, with contextual considerations playing a secondary role. Bultmann apparently assumes that a redactor would have imitated the style of the evangelist [54] and therefore makes little effort to show a stylistic difference between them. Even the contextual grounds for proposed redactions become fully apparent only when theological discrepancies have been pointed out.

I shall not attempt a thorough examination and evaluation of all of Bultmann's specific proposals. Ruckstuhl has contested every significant passage which Bultmann assigns to the redactor.[55] Unwilling to admit the possibility of more than a few minor secondary glosses in the present text of John, Ruckstuhl is therefore understandably opposed to the theory of ecclesiastical redaction as set forth by Bultmann. There is reason, however, for regarding Ruckstuhl's arguments against the redaction theory as less convincing than those which he advances against Bultmann's source theory. Bultmann claims fundamental stylistic support for the source theory (which Ruckstuhl is able to challenge) but does not attempt to adduce such support for the redactional additions. Such stylistic support as Ruckstuhl advances is of questionable value if one doubts that all redactions, especially relatively short ones, must show variations. In the case of most of Bultmann's redactions, the stylistic evidence seems to be ambiguous. Nevertheless, Ruckstuhl succeeds in raising significant objections to some of Bultmann's proposed redactions on other grounds.

It is very difficult, however, to believe that the case against any, or almost any, redactional material in the Fourth Gospel has been successfully made. Despite all representations to the contrary, chapter 21 seems to be a later addition to the gospel for which an editor is probably responsible.[56] Moreover, the possibility of redactional glosses at other points in the gospel cannot be easily dismissed (e.g., 3:24; 4:2, 44; 19:35). Our question is not, there-

54. Cf. Bornkamm, *ZNW*, 47 (1956), 163 f.
55. *Einheit*, pp. 134–79.
56. Here I agree with Bultmann against Ruckstuhl, pp. 134–49, and the skillful but to me unconvincing arguments of A. Kragerud, *Der Lieblingsjünger im Johannesevangelium, Ein exegetischer Versuch* (Oslo, Osloer Universitäts Verlag, 1959), pp. 13 ff. Chapter 21 cannot, however, be brushed aside as non-Johannine. It contains 30 Johannine characteristics of 13 different types (Ruckstuhl, p. 218). On the other hand, there are certain peculiarities of speech and style; cf. Kümmel, Feine-Behm, *Einleitung in das Neue Testament*, p. 142, and the literature cited there, especially Merlier, *Le quatrième Évangile*, pp. 149–74.

fore, whether the Fourth Gospel has been edited or contains any editorial material at all. Assuming that some editing is possible and even probable, we can only guess as to the felicity of Bultmann's characterization of it as "ecclesiastical redaction." In Bultmann's analysis the ecclesiastical redaction appears as a purposive attempt to bring the theologically acute and somewhat unconventional Gospel of John into closer conformity with the developing doctrine and practice of the early church or "early Catholicism," to use the term which now enjoys wide currency. In excising passages containing apocalyptic eschatology, sacramentalism, Old Testament testimony, or ecclesiastical problems and concerns, Bultmann removes an inappropriate veneer of later church theology from the original document. When taken in conjunction with his source and rearrangement proposals, which form the literary-critical groundwork of his understanding of the original Johannine theology, Bultmann's redaction theory seems quite plausible. I have already questioned the validity of the source and rearrangement proposals, and, to the degree that my criticisms have any validity, the redaction theory is also called into question. For if the evangelist did not work with sources in the clever and subtle way which the source theory proposes and the redactor did not substantially restructure the textual order, the case for the redactional additions becomes somewhat less persuasive. In fact, as I have noted, the rearrangement and redactional proposals in chapters 1 and 6 are closely interrelated.

It is, of course, not difficult to attack or reject Bultmann's redaction theory if one holds a different view of Johannine theology or a different view of the way in which theology developed in the early church.[57] Since in neither case is an alternative view clearly and positively established as preferable, and since I cannot possibly establish such alternative views here, it would be a question begging procedure to assume them in order to pronounce judgments upon the redactions. But it is not necessary to make any impeachable assumptions in order to pursue the inquiry I have already suggested, namely, into the intrinsic credibility of the redactional theory on the basis of the redactional material itself.

Of the sacramental passages assigned to the redactor the most important is

---

57. Bultmann believes that by the end of the first century there was already a trend toward an institutional understanding of gospel and church, i.e. "early Catholicism." The Fourth Evangelist stands entirely aloof from this trend as an independent theologian. Käsemann takes this position one step further with the proposal that the Johannine author is "Heretic and Witness" (*ZTK*, *48*, 1951, 292–311), a Christian thinker willing to use the weapons provided by Gnosticism in fighting the even more dangerous enemy of ecclesiastical institutionalism within the church. Käsemann has recently defended the propriety and usefulness of the term "Frühkatholizismus" in an article "Paulus und der Frühkatholizismus," *ZTK, 60* (1963), especially 75 n. 2.

6:51c–58, and I have already argued that this passage is not the work of the redactor. Of the redactor's attempts to conform the Fourth Gospel to the synoptics, the most extensive is to be found in 1:19–34, and again I have already argued that the synoptic element in this passage is not the work of a redactor. Although B. M. F. Van Iersel agrees with Bultmann that one must in this passage separate literary strata, he revises Bultmann's analysis and holds open the possibility that, as I have suggested, the distinction is not between evangelist and redactor, but between tradition and evangelist.[58] Of the redactional additions supposedly intended to introduce a more traditional eschatology, the most notable is 5:28 f. (with all or part of verse 27 being redactional also), which I must now consider further.

5:(27)28 f. occasions difficulty for Bultmann not because the Gospel of John presents no future eschatological hope (this is found in chapters 14–17) but because it sets forth an apocalyptic eschatology said to be explicitly denied in 11:23–26 ("I am the resurrection and the life") and generally contradictory to the view of the evangelist. Moreover, when the verses are removed, so are problems of interpretation. Until verse 27 only the Son is spoken of, but in verses 27–29 the Son of Man. While verses 28 f. speak of a general resurrection, the immediately preceding verses (24 f.) speak only of those who hear as receiving life.

Yet the excision of this passage as a later redaction also raises some questions.[59] Had a churchly editor been attempting to introduce here a more conventional eschatology, would he have written 5:(27)28 f.? What we find here is reminiscent of Daniel 12:2 or the doubtless Jewish apocalyptic of Matthew 25:31–46 and Revelation 20:11–15, although it lacks the detail of those passages. In the concept of a general resurrection, John 5:(27)28 f. agrees with these passages and with the view of II Baruch 50, 51. While Paul may assume a general resurrection and judgment (Romans 2:5 ff.; II Cor. 5:10), when he expounds the resurrection (I Cor. 15) he shows a tendency to identify it with the Christian eschatological salvation (cf. John 5:21, 25; 11:23 ff.), as do Ignatius (Smyrnaeans 7:1; Romans 2:2; 4:3) and the Didache (16:7), which explicitly denies the resurrection of all the dead and cites in support of this I Thessalonians 4:16. Further, there is nothing explicitly Christian in this Johannine passage, so that the possibility that it is a piece of traditional material appears strong.[60] Virtually no one denies that the evangelist drew upon tradition of one sort or another, and Bultmann

---

58. *NT, 5* (1962), 245–67.

59. Cf. Schweizer, *ET, 12* (1953), 354 f.

60. Schulz, *Untersuchungen*, pp. 135 ff. E. Schweizer, υἱὸς τοῦ θεοῦ, *TWNT* (seen in manuscript form) believes originally apocalyptic speech formulations lie behind 3:35 and 5:19–23.

has made his own views in this matter explicit enough. It is interesting that he sees in the farewell discourses the traditional themes of early Christian eschatology, which the evangelist has reinterpreted.[61] More than once the reader finds the coming again of Jesus mentioned (14:18–20, 21–24; 16:16–24). While Bultmann is, in my opinion, right in seeing here not the old parousia hope, but a reinterpretation, many readers of the gospel continue to see here the older eschatology in spite of the apparent correction of it in 14:22. The reason for this is the nature of the evangelist's speech itself, which is always more allusive than definitive, and this is nowhere more true than in relation to traditonal motifs. If the evangelist is working with tradition or traditional themes in chapter 5 also, it may be conceded that he does not assimilate the material as in the farewell discourses. This does not necessarily mean, however, that 5:(27)28 f. is impossible in the gospel or even in the context. In explaining how the redactor found it possible to reconcile his addition with what precedes, Bultmann says that he could have regarded the present judgment of the Son (5:24 f.) as the anticipation of the final judgment, and in support of this he cites passages from the Mandaean *Ginzā*.[62] There we also see a future judgment from which the elect are *exempt*, which

61. *Johannes*, pp. 447 f., 451, 477. Interestingly enough, in an earlier essay on "Die Eschatologie des Johannesevangeliums," Bultmann was less certain about the redactional origin of 5:28 f. (*Glauben und Verstehen, I*, 134–52; cf. p. 135 n. 1 and p. 144).

62. *Johannes*, p. 112 n. 1.
Ginzā, 323, 13 ff.:
> "Die wahrhaften und gläubigen **Nazoräer**
>   werden emporsteigen und die Lichtort schauen
> . . .
> Nicht werden sie zurückgehalten werden (in der Welt)
>   und im grossen Gerichte nicht zur Rechenschaft gezogen
>   werden.
> Über sie wird nicht das Urteil gesprochen werden,
>   das über alle Wesen gesprochen wird."

Ginzā, 512, 22 ff.:
> "Zum Gericht versammeln sich die Welten,
>   und ihnen wird Recht gesprochen.
> Recht wird ihnen gesprochen,
>   die nicht die Werke eines wahrhaften Mannes geübt haben.
> Du allein, Auserwählte, Reine
> . . .
> du wirst nicht zum Gerichtshofe gehen.
>   dir wird nicht Recht gesprochen werden,
> . . .
> da du die Werke eines wahrhaften Mannes geübt hast."

Citations refer to pages and lines in M. Lidzbarski, tr. and ed., *Ginzā, der Schatz oder das grosse Buch der Mandäer*, Quellen der Religionsgeschichte, 13, 4 (Göttingen, Vandenhoeck & Ruprecht, 1926).

is actually closer in this respect to what we find in John 5:28 f. than is the Jewish and primitive Christian idea of a general resurrection followed by a judgment for all. What is more, the Mandaean material, if it is relevant to the Fourth Gospel at all, is surely more clearly relevant to the evangelist than to an ecclesiastical redactor. That a piece of tradition should have Jewish apocalyptic and Mandaean affinities is by no means impossible if, as is now proposed, Mandaeism has its roots in sectarian Judaism contemporaneous with the origin of Christianity.[63] On the basis of Bultmann's own comprehension of the background and character of the gospel, 5:28 f. is entirely conceivable as traditional material which the evangelist did not find totally incompatible with his own viewpoint. Moreover, the passage may not really stand in tension with what precedes, but rather supplement it.

It is just possible that 5:28 f. refers to those who are really physically dead and simply says that they, too, will enter life or judgment—the characteristic Johannine alternatives—according to their deeds. That good or evil deeds correspond exactly to belief or unbelief is clear from John 3:18–21.[64] If this interpretation is correct, then 5:28 f. would answer the question about the destiny of those who died before the eschatological event took place (cf. I Peter 4:19 f.; Ephesians 4:8 f.).

The phrase "and I will raise him (it) up at the last day" in John 6:39, 40, 44, 54 also presents some perplexities when understood as ecclesiastical redaction. Unlike 5:28 f. this refrain seems to identify resurrection with the eschatological salvation. If this identification is a characteristic of distinctly Christian eschatology, this fact might favor redactional origin; but since it is also characteristic of the Gospel of John generally it says nothing decisive either way. That the redactional passages in chapters 5 and 6 understand resurrection differently does not, however, bespeak their common origin.

Also of interest is the phrase "in the last day" ($[\dot{\epsilon}\nu]$ $\tau\hat{\eta}$ $\dot{\epsilon}\sigma\chi\acute{\alpha}\tau\eta$ $\dot{\eta}\mu\acute{\epsilon}\rho\alpha$). Although it clearly refers to a future eschatological event, and thus seems to partake of the primitive Christian hope, in the New Testament it occurs in just this form only in the Gospel of John.[65] Whether the refrain is disruptive where it occurs in chapter 6 is difficult to say apart from a judgment about whether or not the evangelist could have written it at all. As Bultmann

63. Schulz, *Komposition und Herkunft*, 170–82; also *TR*, new ser. 26 (1960), especially 312–29 and the literature cited there by Schulz. For a rather Jewish presentation of resurrection and judgment, see *Ginzā*, 437, 22: "Dies ist die Skēnā, die für dich, Adam, und dein Weib Hawwā vor dem gewaltigen, ersten Leben gegründet ist, bis zum Tage dem Gerichtstage, bis zur Stunde, den Stunden der Erlösung, bis zum grossen Tage der Auferstehung."

64. Cf. Barrett, *St. John*, p. 219.

65. Close but not identical are Acts 2:17, II Tim. 3:1, Heb. 1:2, James 5:3, II Peter 3:3, I John 2:18.

himself indicates, it creates a greater problem in verse 44 than elsewhere. On the other hand, it is no more disruptive in verses 39 and 40 than in 54, already assigned to the redactor on other grounds. As for the phrase "in the last day" in 12:48, its presence improves the rhythm rather than destroys it.[66]

Instead of drawing any conclusions at this point, let us look now at the sacramental material assigned to the ecclesiastical redaction. The mention of "water" along with the Spirit in 3:5 is assigned to the redactor as a reference to baptism and an intrusion into this discussion of the activity of the Spirit. It is certainly true that water is simply mentioned and nothing is said about it. (The τοῦ ὕδατος καί of 3:8 is lacking in important manuscripts and is probably a gloss.) It is, nevertheless, questionable whether the water is an intentional allusion to baptism in view of the frequent occurrence of water as a soteriological symbol in the Fourth Gospel (4:14; 5:1–8; 7:37–39). The juxtaposition of water and Spirit in 7:37–39 is particularly interesting; it occurs even if 7:38 is assigned to the redactor. Whether or not 7:38 is retained as original, it is not immediately obvious that the water here alludes to baptism. Therefore it seems to me that the contextual argument for striking ὕδατος καί in 3:5 is stronger than the theological, even if one grants that Bultmann's view of the evangelist's attitude toward the sacraments is correct.[67]

More important than the redactional material in 3:5 is 19:34b–35.[68] Here we have two separate questions, the allusion to the sacraments said to be found in 34b and the attestation of the historical truth of the report in 35. They may be considered separately, although the occurrence of two redactional motifs side by side strengthens Bultmann's case. The assignment of verse 34b to the redactor rests upon the reference to the sacraments said to be found there and upon the fact that, while the appearance of the water and blood form the climax of the narrative, they are not specifically mentioned in the following Old Testament quotations. The latter reason can be appreciated by any interpreter, since it has nothing to do with an understanding of the sacramental views of the evangelist.

Since verse 35 is obviously a parenthetical note, both 19:34b and 35 are easily separable from the context. Bultmann's contention that they constitute a secondary addition is justified. That they are from an ecclesiastical redactor is somewhat less certain. According to Bultmann's own analysis, 19:34b, 35 has been inserted directly into the Passion source which the Fourth Evangelist

66. Bultmann displays the rhythm of 12:47 f., *Johannes*, p. 262; the assignment of the phrase "in the last day" to the redactor clearly cuts the last line short.

67. It is just possible that the ὕδατος καί is a scribal gloss in 3:5 as well as 3:8. In 3:5 it lacks the attestation of vg[harl 1023], Justin and Origen (partial).

68. On 19:34b–35 see especially Schweizer, *ET*, 12 (1953), 348–53.

used. There is therefore the possibility that the evangelist made the inter-polation himself,[69] and we must therefore ask whether 19:34b, 35 can be understood as his work. Putting aside the question of whether the evangelist could have alluded to the sacraments at this point, we may ask whether such an allusion is actually found in verse 34b. It is possible that the blood sig-nifies purification (I John 1:7, although Bultmann now ascribes this passage to the redactor), or at least the efficacy of the death of Jesus, while the water signifies the life-producing power of the Spirit (7:37–39). An anti-Docetic interpretation (I John 5:6) is excluded by Bultmann on the rather question-able grounds that here (in contrast to I John 5:6) not the blood but the water is the paradoxical element: "nicht nur Blut, sondern auch Wasser!"[70] I can-not, however, see any compelling reason to eliminate either of these inter-pretations, although neither of them self-evidently excludes a sacramental allusion. If an anti-Docetic emphasis and sacramental allusion is found here, this would bring the passage into line with our understanding of 6:51c–58.

As to 19:35, it is clear that we have here a secondary notation strikingly similar to 21:24, which Bultmann rightly ascribes to a redactor. Yet there are significant differences. In 19:35 the Beloved Disciple is not named and it is not really clear that he is meant, for the ὁ ἑωρακώς and the ἐκεῖνος are not further identified. It is not certain that they refer to the same person; although I can-not agree with Bultmann that this is impossible, since the ἐκεῖνος can be the same as the subject of λέγει with the meaning that the one who has seen is con-fident in the truth of his own testimony. If the evangelist is regarded as the author of 19:35, then the witness must be a figure standing behind the gospel rather than the evangelist himself, as Bultmann points out. If, however, the Johannine literature is the work of a school or circle of disciples,[71] we should not be surprised to find some indication of the real or alleged source of their distinctive witness. The obscurity of 19:35 tempts us to interpret it in the light of 21:24, but it is quite likely that 21:24 is in part a clarification of 19:35. Inasmuch as 19:35 does not identify the witness with the Beloved Disciple, it may be a misleading clarification.

Of the many remaining passages which Bultmann assigns to the ecclesias-tical redaction, perhaps two have received more attention than the rest, the statement of Jesus that salvation is of the Jews (4:22b, if not the whole verse) and the passage about the "other sheep" (10:16). Both of the pas-

---

69. Ibid., pp. 348 f.

70. *Johannes*, p. 525 n. 6.

71. So, recently, a number of scholars, Catholic as well as Protestant, including C. K. Barrett, A. Kragerud, F.-M. Braun, M.-É. Boismard, B. Noack, S. Schulz, and, in a sense, Bultmann also: *Johannes*, pp. 4, 76; earlier, *ZNW*, 24 (1925), 144 f.

sages are parentheses, and their excision improves the train of thought in both places. In 10:16 an idea which is not really foreign to the evangelist is introduced into Jesus' discussion of his role as the shepherd who lays down his life for his sheep. In 4:22, however, the idea that salvation is of the Jews is not only an intrusion into the context, but, according to Bultmann, an impossible theological idea for the evangelist. Bultmann is not the first to note the difficulty in reconciling it with the position generally taken toward the Jews. But 8:41 ff., which Bultmann cites as characteristic of John, does not mean that the Israelite nation as a whole has the devil as its father (verse 44); it need only apply to the present generation insofar as it rejects Jesus. Bultmann is probably right that the τὰ ἴδια of 1:11 does not refer to Israel, but this verse is from the prologue source. Therefore the fact that it does not use the *heilsgeschichtliche* terminology is not decisive in determining its meaning for the evangelist. On the other hand, 1:16, which is almost certainly from the evangelist, sets up a polarity between Moses and Jesus Christ. Although one can certainly not say that this implies that the one revelation emerges from the other, one must attach importance to the fact that the evangelist sees one over against the other, and not simply in a purely negative relation. This is clear also from the evangelist's presentation of Jesus as the King of Israel as well as his appropriation of Old Testament testimony.

The statement of 4:22 is not impossible for the evangelist if it only means that the Jews are the historic and geographic locus of the appearance of salvation. Nevertheless, one cannot be sure that the passage stems from the evangelist, especially in view of the contextual difficulties. On the other hand, an ecclesiastical redaction designed to prepare the gospel for acceptance in a developing orthodox (Hellenistic) church, where there was considerable controversy with the Jews, would have gained little by this statement. For example, in using the Old Testament, the second-century church tended to regard it as a Christian book rather than the revelation of salvation among the Jews. It is perhaps significant that chapter 4 contains some traces of the Samarian mission of the church (verses 35–38) whose exact meaning is not obvious. It may be that 4:22 is an aside which reflects the encounter of early Christianity with Samaritan and Jewish heterodoxy rather than a doctrinal codicil reflecting the Fourth Gospel's encounter with early Catholicism.

Instead of reviewing additional allegedly redactional passages, it will be more profitable to turn now to chapter 21, which is the key and cornerstone for any redactional theory. Two questions should be asked about chapter 21. First, to what extent does it actually embody the theological interests present in the redactional material within the gospel? Second, was the chapter composed and added in order to establish the authority of the Fourth Gospel in the church, as Bultmann believes?

In answer to the first question, while there are affinities between the views set forth in various passages assigned to the redactor and chapter 21, there are also some anomalies. There is doubtless an allusion to the Lord's Supper in 21:13, but it has little in common with the doctrine of 6:51c–58 if the sacrament is there presented as the medicine of immortality. The parousia expectation of 21:22 is introduced as a matter of course and somewhat incidentally, not as if the author were trying to emphasize a point. In 5:28 f.; 6:39, 40, 44, 54; and 12:48, resurrection or judgment are mentioned, but not the parousia of Jesus himself. The parousia is referred to in the Fourth Gospel, but in the original farewell discourses, where it is reinterpreted. I have already noted certain discrepancies in the eschatological redactional material within the gospel proper. While the resurrection appearance in Galilee brings John into conformity with Mark and Matthew as to geographical locus, this is scarcely done in a self-conscious way. (Of course, the Galilean resurrection appearance is in contradiction to Luke's gospel, in which so much is made of the Jerusalem resurrection appearances.) Neither the appearance in Galilee nor the presentation of the disciples as fishermen looks like a deliberate attempt to bring John in conformity to the synoptics. There is no conformity on the locus of the resurrection appearances within the synoptics, and the matter of the fishermen is relatively insignificant.

Bultmann's contention that the overall purpose of chapter 21 is to establish the authority of the gospel finds support in the text but is not unexceptionable. As we have seen, he believes that a redactor has used a traditional source or sources in verses 1–14 and again in 15–17, but that 18–23(25) is his own composition. The redactor has also made annotations in verses 1–14 which introduce the Beloved Disciple (verse 7, probably 4b), give a special role to Peter (verses 7, 8a), allude to church unity (verse 11) and to the Lord's Supper (verse 13), and round out the account, identifying it unmistakably as the third resurrection appearance (verse 14). Is it necessary to assign so much to the redactor? Admittedly there are minor obscurities, but is not this to be expected in a traditional story that has perhaps grown by accretion? The reference to the Beloved Disciple does not betray clearly redactional features, but recalls 20:1–10, where Peter and the other disciple also appear together. The 153 fish in the unbroken net may represent the unity of the church, but, Bultmann to the contrary notwithstanding, it is quite possible that such a bit of allegorization would have found its way into a traditional story.[72]

72. Note the many symbolic details in traditional narratives in the Fourth Gospel: the six water pots used for the purification rites of the Jews in 2:6 (semeia-source), the whip

I have already commented on the tenuous connection between verse 13 and the allegedly sacramental redactions in the main part of the gospel. It should be finally noted that Peter plays the leading role at the beginning of the story (21:2 f.) according to Bultmann's reconstruction of the source. Since, in this source, he so clearly dominates in the beginning, it is rather surprising that he should then disappear. Further, 21:15–17, which are regarded as traditional, follow quite well after 21:1–13. (Verse 14 is obviously a later addition, as Bultmann thinks.) This is particularly true if the later references to Peter are not excised as redactional. (I cannot see that the lack of any notice of Jesus having taken Peter aside effects any break in the account.) Verses 1–17 seem to me to form a continuous narrative interrupted only by verse 14. While verse 17 could be regarded as the end of the story and perhaps once was,[73] verses 18–22 form a fitting continuation and culmination when the phrase ἀκολουθοῦντα . . . ὁ Πέτρος is excised. Verses 23–25 may then be assigned to an editor, who presumably added chapter 21 and published the gospel. Perhaps the phrase in 21:20 f., which Bultmann ascribes to a tertiary glossator, ought also be assigned to the final editor, since it positively identifies and draws attention to the Beloved Disciple. As far as I can see only these verses fall readily out of the text and reveal the motivation which Bultmann ascribes to the entire chapter.[74] When they are removed, what we have is a resurrection narrative—indeed, a Johannine resurrection narrative—in which Peter's, or any disciple's, task becomes the dominant theme. At the end Peter's question about the fate of the Beloved Disciple evokes Jesus' word of verse 22: "If he remains until I come, what is that to you. *You* follow me." Certainly such a word of the Lord would have been relevant to a church in which the first generation was rapidly dying out and

---

of cords in 2:15 (special source), the 38 years of the invalid's sickness in 5:5 (semeia-source), the twelve baskets of leftover bread fragments in 6:13 (semeia-source). Cf. Bultmann, *Johannes*, p. 83 n. 5.

73. Peter, who appears as the leader of the disciples at the beginning of the story (21:3), would thus appear in the main role at the end. Verses 15–17, already identified by Bultmann as traditional are a good continuation of verses 1–13, but standing alone they are fragmentary and require an introduction. The recognition that verse 14 is redactional does not imply that the main narrative source that lay before the redactor ended after verse 13 (or 12). This is the only point at which he could have made the interpolation without its being an intolerable interruption.

74. There is also the possibility that 21:19a is from the redactor; it is just the kind of annotation that Bultmann ascribes to him in the gospel (cf. 12:33). If this sentence is a gloss of the editor who published the gospel, then the remaining material should be, as we have argued, traditional. At least it would be unnatural to regard it as the work of the redactor. Of course, 21:19 could be regarded as a tertiary gloss, but this would seem to be an unnecessary proliferation of hypothetical glossators.

people were concerned and distracted by the question of whether they would live until the parousia (I Thessalonians 4:13 f.). The disciple is not to be concerned that he may die, or even suffer martyrdom, while another lives until the parousia.[75] He has one calling, which may or may not end in martyrdom: "You follow me." That another disciple may have a different worldly destiny is irrelevant.

Thus a critical look at Bultmann's source and redaction theory casts doubt upon the view that chapter 21 was added to the gospel in order to establish the Beloved Disciple and his gospel as an ecclesiastical authority alongside Peter. It seems quite possible, even probable, that the question of the gospel's authority is only consciously injected in verses 23–25 and that the earlier rivalry of Peter and John, which has previous parallels in the gospel (e.g. 20:1–10), belongs to the Johannine or pre-Johannine tradition and does not reflect the particular ecclesiastical situation which produced Bultmann's redactor. Taken as a whole the chapter does not clearly manifest this redactor's theological interests nor the purpose which Bultmann attributes to it. It looks much more like a piece of Johannine tradition which was added, without ulterior motive, by whoever published the gospel.

It is difficult to make any assertions about either having established or disproved the theory of ecclesiastical redaction. Sweeping judgments would be inappropriate. There seems to be good reason to believe that the Fourth Gospel was published by a later editor who added chapter 21. There is, however, reason for doubting whether some of the material which Bultmann assigns to the redaction is secondary at all (1:22–24; 6:51c–58). In some cases the redactional material does not reflect a consistent outlook (5:28 f.; 6: 39, 40, 44, 54; 12:48; 21: 22; cf. also 6:51c–58 and 21:13). In other cases it is not easy to distinguish between a redactional annotation and one from the evangelist (19:34 f.; 11:2; 12:33; 18:9; 18:32), or to say whether an Old Testament quotation has been inserted by the original author or by a later hand (7:38b; 10:34–36). Moreover, an anomaly in the text often raises the question of tradition as well as redaction. Aside from the narrative tradition throughout the gospel and the apocalyptic tradition assimilated in the farewell discourses, Bultmann believes that the evangelist may have oriented chapter 17 (Jesus' departing prayer) around the traditional words of institution of the Lord's Supper, and perhaps around liturgical prayers associated with that occasion.[76] In Bultmann's view, a piece of tradition is sometimes the cause of a difficulty in the text (3:25),[77] and I have sug-

75. E. Schweizer, *Lordship and Discipleship*, Studies in Biblical Theology, 28 (London, SCM, 1960), 83.

76. *Johannes*, p. 371 n. 3.

77. Ibid., p. 122.

gested that 5:28 f. may be a relatively unassimilated traditional saying. Finally, it is to be observed that the material assigned to the ecclesiastical redaction shades imperceptibly into the tertiary glosses.[78] When taken as a whole the material assigned to the redaction does not present an entirely consistent picture, nor does it lend unqualified support to Bultmann's understanding of the motives and process involved in the editing and publication of the Gospel according to John.

CONCLUSION

At least three major questions are given sharp relief by Bultmann's solution of the literary problems of the Fourth Gospel. The first is naturally that of the composition and order of the gospel itself. How did it attain its present state? The second has to do with the implications of Bultmann's answer to this question for the understanding of the Fourth Gospel and its place in the development of early Christianity. The third concerns the significance, for Biblical exegesis as a theological discipline, of his elimination of the supposedly redactional element in the gospel. In this investigation, attention has been centered upon the first question, but it can scarcely be separated from the second. The third question takes us beyond the scope of this study, but I must attempt to say how it poses the question.

In raising questions about Bultmann's conception of how the gospel reached its present state, one inevitably raises a question for himself. If Bultmann's hypothesis is not entirely convincing, what is to be put in its place? We have already seen how alternative solutions of the problem of the composition of the Fourth Gospel are continually being advanced. Although one can perhaps speak of some general agreement about difficulties in the text, the author's use of some earlier tradition, and the need for rearrangement of the order of the text at a few points, even such agreement is by no means unanimous. The various proposals differ both in general conception and in detail. Although the existence of so many competing theories does not mean that no one is, or could be, correct, the situation is not very encouraging for the progress of research in this area. Of course, the idea that the gospel is a finished product and a literary unity still has its defenders. While the conclusions of this study may sometimes seem to point in that direction, it has not been possible to adhere consistently to this position. Not all the difficulties

78. Compare ἔγνω ὁ κύριος ὅτι (4:1), which Bultmann calls *eine schlechte Glosse* (ibid., p. 128 n. 4) with 11:2 (ibid., p. 302 n. 1), which he assigns to the ecclesiastical redactor. The term κύριος, said to be avoided by the evangelist until chapter 20, appears in both places. (It is a gloss also in 6:23.)

in the present text are explicable in terms of the intention of the evangelist.

We do not have another hypothesis about the composition of the Fourth Gospel to lay alongside of those already proposed. There is, however, one possibility that remains open. One hesitates to suggest it, for there is virtually no way in which it can be either demonstrated or excluded. Furthermore, it may appear to be an abandonment of the problem. Yet I think it quite possible, indeed probable, that the Fourth Gospel has been left to us in an unfinished state.[79] This suggestion is, however, not so far from Bultmann's own idea that the present text of the Gospel of John is the redactor's reconstruction of a document which he found in a fragmented or disordered state. We have already seen that the supposed disruption and restoration of the text is one of the least satisfactory aspects of Bultmann's literary theory. It is not a very convincing explanation of how an originally better text became the present poorer one. Very probably such an original text never existed, and thus such a reconstruction as Bultmann's is no reconstruction at all. Rather it brings to completion the task which the evangelist himself was never able to finish. Faure has pointed out that if the gospel is actually incomplete or unfinished, this accounts for both those qualities which have led some to call it a seamless robe and the perplexities and anomalies which have for so long plagued exegesis. It may provide the only satisfactory answer to such problems as the textual order of the farewell discourses, where chapter 14 and chapters 15 and 16 could each be taken as a separate discourse. Bultmann rightly rejects the suggestion that chapters 15 and 16 are a later addition by another author, but he is on much less firm ground when he brands as improbable the possibility that they are an alternative or supplementary edition by the same author which he never really incorporated into the text. As Bultmann himself has seen, the conception of a purposeful redactional reconstruction raises the difficult question of why the redactor should have put chapter 14 (with its conclusion in verses 25–31) at its present position.[80] The simple suggestion that for some reason the two sections were left side by side without being satisfactorily connected goes as far toward explaining their present position as any. Such a suggestion may also account for that other major anomaly of the gospel, the relative isolation of chapter 8 in its present position. It is true that this proposal leaves some questions unanswered, and that it is perhaps not so fruitful in facilitating the interpretation of the

79. This is, of course, not a novel suggestion. Cf., among others, A. Faure, *ZNW*, *21* (1922), 117; W. Grundmann, *Zeugnis und Gestalt*, pp. 6 f.; W. Wilkens, *Entstehungsgeschichte*, p. 172. W. F. Howard, *The Fourth Gospel*, p. 119; Kümmel, Feine-Behm, *Einleitung*, pp. 148 f. and the literature cited there.

80. *Johannes*, p. 349.

gospel. Nevertheless, it is a simple and credible historical hypothesis. Many books have been left incomplete.

The question of the theology of John in the development of early Christian thought is, in Bultmann's work, closely related to that of the composition of the gospel itself. For Bultmann regards the Fourth Evangelist as critical or skeptical toward some of the emerging beliefs, practices, and traditions of the early church. This critical posture is seen in his emphasis upon realized or present eschatology and his alleged rejection of primitive apocalyptic eschatology, his ambivalence toward the sacraments, his freedom from (or relative aloofness with respect to) the synoptics, his somewhat sparing use of the Old Testament,[81] his sense of distinct separateness from Judaism, and his refusal to find the locus of church authority in the Twelve or their successors. In many of these matters interpreters have long been perplexed or divided by a certain reticence, ambiguity, or contradiction in the Fourth Gospel, but Bultmann has now formulated a critical principle by which he eliminates certain passages which contribute to this situation and thus clarifies the evangelist's position. That is, he assigns to the redactor those passages which he deems irreconcilably contradictory to the central perspective of the evangelist. In excising passages embodying apocalyptic eschatology, sacramentalism, scriptural proof texts, or certain ecclesiastical concerns, Bultmann is not merely removing isolated and peripheral elements foreign to the evangelist's thought. They are all representative of that very significant developing strain of early Christianity which is now often referred to as "early Catholicism." Although we have seen that they themselves do not embody an entirely consistent point of view, we cannot deny that they often reflect the concerns of a broad spectrum of early Christianity as it is represented in the New Testament and other early Christian literature.

The idea that the Fourth Gospel stands opposed, or at least uncommitted, to this particular range of concerns gains support, as I have indicated, from the gospel as we have it. With the help of the redaction theory, the evangelist can be convincingly depicted as an independent and nonecclesiastical theologian who is skeptical of institutional traditions, beliefs, and practices, but whose work has been edited, ironically enough, in an attempt to bring it into line with the developing ecclesiastical orthodoxy. This attempt has failed insofar as it cannot conceal from the perceptive interpreter its artificial superimposition upon, and opposition to, the fundamental lines of Johannine thought.

81. According to Bultmann's source analysis, a number of the scattered Old Testament quotations in John fall in sections ascribed to sources or the redactor and thus do not reflect the deliberate choice of the evangelist.

In Bultmann's view, the evangelist has a uniform and coherent theological position, which is laid bare and expounded in the course of the commentary. But the fact that a consistent and unified theological exposition of a certain type can be derived from a reconstructed text of the Fourth Gospel does not eliminate the possibility of original incongruities or logical inconsistencies in the evangelist's thought. Bultmann's reconstruction of the gospel is only a hypothesis of literary, historical, and internal theological criticism grounded upon a distinctive grasp of the evangelist's theological perspective. The reconstruction presupposes and intends to demonstrate the truth of this preapprehension of the evangelist's theological position, but the very ingenuity and inner consistency of the whole scheme draw suspicion upon it. If Bultmann has accurately grasped the basic structure of Johannine thought, it is still questionable whether he thereby gains the right to effect serious alterations in the gospel in order to make it consistent with its own fundamental intention and, furthermore, to present the gospel thus purified as the original product of the evangelist. As an undertaking of historical and literary criticism such a program raises serious doubts, if my assessment of the redactions is in any measure correct.

Furthermore, the Johannine literature, while it clearly represents a particular religious and even theological milieu and perspective, does not contain unambiguous evidence that the author of the Fourth Gospel attained theological consistency. For example, the evangelist conceives of Jesus' death as exaltation or glorification. After the interpretation of his death in these terms, one is scarcely prepared for the resurrection stories which appear in chapter 20. Admittedly, their presence was demanded by the strength of the tradition in the church, but one may well ask whether they are consistent with the evangelist's understanding of the significance of the death itself. I do not think the evangelist would have seen any difficulty here, but the modern interpreter looking for theological consistency could reasonably raise such a question, for the hour toward which the gospel points is the hour of Jesus' death (2:4; 7:30; 8:20; 12:23,27; 13:1; 16:4; 17:1) and the fundamental purpose of the farewell discourses is the explanation of the meaning of this death. There is no more reason to expect the resurrection as a subsequent event than there is to expect the parousia if one agrees with Bultmann that in these discourses the traditional Christian eschatological categories and terms have been reinterpreted by the evangelist. Ancient religious literature, Christian as well as non-Christian, is not distinguished by systematic theological thinking, as Bultmann well knows. He himself has pointed out that Paul, whose epistles give more indication of a carefully defined perspective and a struggle for theological coherence than the Johannine writings, falls into self-contradiction. Commenting on Karl Barth's exegesis of I Corinthians 15:1–11, he says: "I can only understand the text as an attempt to make the resurrection of Christ believable as an objective historical fact. And I only see that Paul involves himself in self-contradiction through his apologetic, since what Paul says of the death and resurrection of Jesus in vv. 20–22 can certainly not be said of an objective historical fact." [82] If Paul can be said to have been capable of such inconsistency, so can John.

Bultmann's conception of the evangelist as theological thinker does not arise exclusively from his treatment of the problem of redaction, although it there comes into clearest focus. It is the fundamental axiom of his source theory and rearrangements, both of which demand this conception and, in the course of exegetical analysis, demonstrate it. So the literary problem of the Fourth Gospel cannot finally be separated from the question of the theological position and method of the evangelist himself. Perhaps this work will provide occasion and some stimulus for further consideration of certain problems of Johannine exegesis and theology such as eschatology,[83] sacraments,[84] the relation of John to the synoptics or the synoptic tradition,[85] the

82. "Karl Barth, 'Die Auferstehung der Toten,'" in *Glauben und Verstehen*, I, 54 f.

83. Cf. Meyer, "Eschatology." L. van Hartingsveld, *Die Eschatologie des Johannesevangeliums, eine Auseinandersetzung mit R. Bultmann* (Te Assen Bij, Van Gorcum, 1962) argues against Bultmann's interpretation of Johannine eschatology. He also summarizes Meyer's position and rejects his understanding of Johannine eschatology as reinterpretation. Cf. also D. E. Holwerda, *The Holy Spirit and Eschatology in the Gospel of John: A Critique of Rudolf Bultmann's Present Eschatology* (Kampen, J. H. Kok, 1959) and Bultmann's reply, "Zur Interpretation des Johannesevangeliums," *TL*, 87 (1962), 5–8. While the redaction theory may be exceptionable, Bultmann's judgment about the distinctive eschatological emphasis of the Fourth Gospel seems to me correct. Although the evangelist may not reject the primitive or traditional eschatology, his own interests lie in another direction, namely, to affirm the present eschatological reality (Dodd, *Interpretation*, pp. 148, 364–66; Hoskyns, *The Fourth Gospel*, pp. 270, 402; T. W. Manson, *On Paul and John, Some Selected Theological Themes*, Studies in Biblical Theology, 38 London, SCM, 1963, 114). C. K. Barrett, *St. John*, pp. 56–58, argues that the evangelist has not abandoned the traditional eschatology, but assumes there has been a significant shift in emphasis.

A novel proposal has been advanced by M.-É. Boismard, "L'Évolution du thème eschatologique dans les traditions johanniques," *RB*, 68 (1961), 507–24, who believes that the futuristic eschatology is to be found in an earlier literary layer of the gospel (e.g. in 12:46–50, 5:26–30, 14:1–3) while the present eschatology appears in later "relectures" of the earlier passages (3:16–19(21), 5:19–25, 14:15–23). In finding futuristic eschatology in the earlier literary stratum, Boismard agrees generally with Schulz (*Untersuchungen*). But while Schulz ascribes the earlier passages to tradition, Boismard thinks it quite possible that both earlier and later material stem from the same author.

84. Cf. Schweizer, *ET*, 12 (1952–53), 341–63; Wilkens, *ET*, 18 (1958), 354–70; and the other literature cited, p. 141 n. 75.

85. The discussion of the relation of John to the synoptics goes on with the trend toward denying John's dependence upon them, so that it is no longer possible to assume that John

relation to Judaism and the Old Testament,[86] the structure and order of the gospel,[87] the definition and relationship of tradition and interpretation,[88] and the question of redaction and secondary publication.[89] Only on the basis

---

knew them (D. M. Smith, "John 12:12 ff. and the Question of John's Use of the Synoptics," *JBL*, *82*, 1963, 58–64). J. A. Bailey, however, has attempted to demonstrate John's use of Luke as well as Mark in a recent monograph, *The Traditions Common to the Gospels of Luke and John*, supplements to *Novum Testamentum*, VII (Leiden, Brill, 1963). Certain special affinities between Luke and John cannot be denied, but I still prefer to attribute them to common tradition rather than literary dependence (with P. Parker, "Luke and the Fourth Evangelist," *NTS*, *9*, 1962–63, 317–36). Despite his theory of a direct literary relationship, Bailey must ascribe some of the similarities to common tradition. M.-É. Boismard, "Saint Luc et la redaction du quatrième évangile (Jn, IV, 46–54)," *RB*, *69* (1962), 185–211, thinks they are to be accounted for by Luke's editing of the Fourth Gospel! S. Mendner, "Zum Problem 'Johannes und die Synoptiker,'" *NTS*, *4* (1957–58), 282–307, analyzes John 6:1–30 and the synoptic parallels, concluding that John has been extensively edited to bring it into line with the other gospels *and* that Johannine material has been interpolated into the present redacted text of Mark! Mendner's ideas about the composition of the Fourth Gospel have been developed in a series of articles: "Johanneische Literarkritik," *TZ*, *8* (1952), 418–34; "Die Tempelreinigung," *ZNW*, *47* (1956), 93–113; "Nikodemus," *JBL*, *77* (1958), 293–323. He believes that the present text of the Fourth Gospel is the result of a very extensive redactional process.

Theologically more important than the question of John's knowledge or use of the synoptic gospels is the question of how he stands in relation to the synoptic tradition. To what extent does he know it or assume a knowledge of something like it? Hoskyns, pp. 58–75, has compiled a striking array of evidence to support his thesis that John assumed a widespread knowledge of something like the synoptic tradition about Jesus.

86. Cf. J. L. Martyn, "The Salvation-History Perspective in the Fourth Gospel" (unpublished Ph.D. dissertation, Department of Religion, Yale University, 1957). It is unfortunate that Martyn's contribution to the discussion of Johannine theology is not more widely available, since he deals with a question of fundamental importance. The two most recent studies of John's relationship to the Old Testament and Judaism do not investigate this problem: cf. Guilding, *Jewish Worship* and T. F. Glasson, *Moses in the Fourth Gospel*, Studies in Biblical Theology, 40 (London, SCM, 1963). Two briefer but nevertheless valuable investigations of the Old Testament in John are F. W. Young, "A Study of the Relation of Isaiah to the Fourth Gospel," *ZNW*, *44* (1955), 215–32, and N. A. Dahl, "The Johannine Church and History," *Current Issues in New Testament Interpretation, Essays in Honor of Otto A. Piper*, ed. W. Klassen and G. F. Snyder (New York, Harper, 1962), pp. 124–42.

87. Chapter 3 of this work represents a beginning in that direction. Cf. also Bussche, "La Structure de Jean I–XII"; and especially Grundmann, *Zeugnis und Gestalt*.

88. Regrettably, my book was already in press before the appearance of C. H. Dodd's *Historical Tradition in the Fourth Gospel*, announced for 1963 by Cambridge University Press.

89. The problem of redaction may be separated both from Bultmann's particular redactional theory and from the problem of rearrangement. The gospel could have undergone an editing which introduced numerous interpolations, including most of those proposed by Bultmann, without having been subjected to textual displacement and rearrangement. Needless to say, the gospel could also have been edited and published a generation or so after its composition, perhaps by a circle of the evangelist's disciples, with modest interpolations but without any attempt to revise the theological outlook of the gospel as a whole. Such

of a thorough reconsideration of such matters can a satisfactory revision of Bultmann's position or an advance beyond it be made. Some significant work in all of these areas has been done, but, in my opinion, a comparable comprehensive assessment of Johannine problems and interpretation of the gospel does not exist.

The third and final question raised by Bultmann's work concerns the role of higher criticism in biblical interpretation. *Das Evangelium des Johannes* is actually a commentary, not upon the canonical Gospel of John, but upon a hypothetical original document which Bultmann has constructed out of the materials provided by the traditional book. With its redactions and displacements, the present text is to some degree a corruption of pristine Johannine thought. Bultmann takes as the object of his exegesis only the gospel in its original form as he has restored it through the use of literary, historical, and theological criticism. The additions of the redactor and the traditional order, also his work, fall to one side and are not given consideration in the positive task of exegesis and interpretation.[90] It is this purified and reconstructed document which is the basis of everything that is said about the theology of John in Bultmann's magisterial *Theology of the New Testament*.[91] It is also this critically restored gospel which occupies a place of fundamental importance in Bultmann's total theological perspective,[92] so the question of the meaning and significance of the literary analysis for the inter-

---

more cautious redaction proposals have been made previously, e.g. Jeremias, *TB*, 20 (1941), 43–46.

I have been constrained, along with everyone who concedes the secondary character of chapter 21, to admit that the original author cannot be completely responsible for the present form of the gospel.

Those other than Bultmann who have recently espoused more or less extensive redaction theories include, as we have seen, S. Mendner and M.-É. Boismard (cf. also "Le Chapitre XXI de Saint Jean," *RB*, 54 (1947), 473–501), not to mention Hartke and Eckhardt; also F.-M. Braun (*Jean le Théologien*, pp. 24 f., 59) and J. N. Sanders ("St. John on Patmos," *NTS*, 9, 1962–63, 75–85). Merlier proposes to carry out an extensive separation of literary layers of the gospel based on an exhaustive analysis of the Johannine Greek. *Le quatrième Évangile*, however, presents only some observations based on literary-critical considerations (pp. 405–26).

90. Cf. *Johannes*, p. 4: "*Die Exegese hat selbstverständlich den vollständigen Text zu erklären*, und die kritische Analyse steht im Dienste dieser Erklärung. Anders liegt es nur da, wo sich Glossen einer sekundären Redaktion finden" (emphasis mine). In Bultmann's program, critical analysis serves the exposition of the complete text of the critically restored original gospel, whose content and order are themselves the product of critical analysis. Therefore the role of this analysis is much more determinative of the results of Bultmann's exegesis than he himself seems to allow.

91. Trans. K. Grobel, *II* (New York, Scribner's, 1955), 3.

92. See above, p. xv.

pretation of John could conceivably have rather far-reaching implications.

Insofar as Bultmann's criticism is only an attempt to recover the original form of an ancient document, it is a perfectly unexceptionable undertaking. The exposition of the theology of the original gospel forms a chapter in the history of early Christian thought, and only one question need be raised about it, namely, the question of its accuracy and the credibility of the literary-critical reconstruction upon which it is based. Yet the implications of Bultmann's work go beyond the bounds of literary criticism and historical interpretation. The way in which he appropriates his results in the exposition of the gospel's message and the incorporation of that message in his theology sets an impressive precedent for the use of modern critical analysis in the definition of the locus of the essential message of the biblical text. He has taken the gospel at what he discerns to be one particular stage of its literary development—namely, that between the weaving together of the sources and the final editing—as the authoritative document through which the revelatory word may be heard. One particular complex of literary strata, representing one stage in the gospel's development, is isolated by the methods of higher criticism, made the subject of interpretation, and held to be authoritative and, indeed, canonical.

What would be the possibilities inherent in this procedure if it were applied to other documents? Might it not justify turning to the synoptic gospels in order to seek out as authoritative that traditional stratum which gives, if not the life and teaching of the historical Jesus, at least his authentic kerygma? There is perhaps the possibility of distinguishing the latter by its literary or traditional form and theological content from the later accretions of the church which transmitted the tradition or the evangelists who composed the gospels? Might we not also feel justified in turning to the J document of the Pentateuch or to a reconstruction of the sayings of the original prophet Isaiah in order to seek out as authoritative those literary strata of the Bible which we can understand and appropriate on the basis of prior theological or hermeneutical principles and recover from the books in which they are now embedded with the tools of critical literary and historical reason?

Bultmann's procedure raises to a critical point the question of the role of higher criticism in making accessible the revelatory word assumed to be available in scripture. It is scarcely to be maintained that criticism should not play an important role in illuminating the message of the New Testament, but when this same criticism helps define the possibility of the speaking and hearing of the Word of God by putting aside certain sections of a New

Testament book as secondary corruptions of the document's original message, has it not overstepped its limits? My own reservations in this matter have been set forth by Bultmann himself.

> . . . the New Testament itself is revelation only insofar as it is kerygma or insofar as it "preaches Christ" (Luther); and this means that there is a criterion for determining the extent to which the New Testament statements speak as revelation. But this criterion can in no case be applied by a disinterested investigation in order to exclude this or that section of the New Testament as falling below the standard of genuine revelatory statements; for this criterion can always be effective only in faithfully hearing what the New Testament says. If one here and there fails to be addressed by the word of Christ, he of course does not have the right to say that it must be there or even to suppose that it could be. But he will ask himself whether his not hearing may not possibly have its basis in a not wanting to hear. If it cannot be denied in principle that there can be statements in the New Testament that are not revelatory, it nevertheless is not a meaningful task to name them.[93]

Lest there be any doubt about the applicability of Bultmann's statement, he continues by defining a situation exactly commensurate with the so-called redactional material in John:

> To be sure, certain New Testament statements can be named that speak of revelation in the form of a theological explication; and with respect to them the critical question to what extent the knowledge based in revelation is expressed in them in a conceptually adequate way is appropriate and necessary. However, the demand to say once for all and unambiguously what the word of God is must be rejected because it rests on the idea that it is possible to designate [as revelation] a complex of statements that can be found and understood with respect to their "content."

Bultmann wrote this in 1929. Has he since attempted to name the nonrevelatory passages in the Gospel of John and to eliminate them on the ground of their inadequate theological conceptuality? I do not think that this is his intention, but is it not the obvious implication of his Johannine criticism and interpretation? In actual practice, are not literary originality and theological adequacy made the criteria of revelatory possibility? In principle Bultmann would accept neither of these as adequate criteria. Yet for him the

---

93. "The Concept of Revelation in the New Testament," p. 90. *Cf. Glauben und Verstehen, III,* 34. I have slightly altered the translation.

authoritative character of the New Testament books really does inhere in their theological perspective and insight. Thus, while he refrains from making adequate theological formulation the criterion of revelation, he cannot understand as revelatory documents or, as in the Gospel of John, passages which contain inadequate or erroneous theological formulations.

Nevertheless, Bultmann himself is not willing to write off as much of the New Testament as he is unable to understand or appropriate. There is no real parallel with the Marcionite establishment of a canon in accord with a particular theological point of view. While Bultmann would not say that the traditional canon, in part a product of the early Catholicism which he does not espouse, guarantees the relevance and authority of any New Testament statement in any situation, he is not ready to abandon it. The right interpretation of the New Testament is, after all, his fundamental theological goal. He does not rest easy before portions of the Bible which he cannot appropriate as revelatory.

> Now it can and does happen that I encounter Biblical sayings which I cannot understand, and which resist or withstand—so to speak—my existentialist interpretation. Then I must be conscious that the method of existential interpretation is not a key which I can manipulate lightly, but that it is a method of asking, and perhaps in many cases I may be obliged to wait in patience. But all this does not refute the direction of my asking, for the asking has its origin in my existential aim and in the conviction that the Biblical word speaks to my existence.[94]

Bultmann's attribution of significance to the traditional canon is implicit in his intention to continue interrogating it and, if necessary, "to wait in patience." Yet this asking and this waiting take place within the context of a prior existentialist commitment, which guides his exegesis and theology. Bultmann gives no indication of a willingness to abandon this commitment.[95] He would still insist that it provides the proper prospective for understanding the New Testament's essential message.[96] Thus, there seems to be an un-

94. "A Chapter in the Problem of Demythologizing," p. 9. An indication of Bultmann's intention of interpreting the whole New Testament is found in his *Marburg Predigten* (Tübingen, J. C. B. Mohr, 1956). Only three of the sermons are on Johannine texts and three on Paul. Ten are on synoptic texts (all except one on sayings or parables of Jesus), with one each on Acts, Revelation, Genesis, and Lamentations.

95. This does not, however, mean that once an interpretation from this point of view is adopted it remains fixed and unalterable. Bultmann allows for a necessary openness to the future in biblical exegesis. Cf. "Is Exegesis without Presuppositions Possible?," especially pp. 295 f.; and *Glauben und Verstehen*, III, 142–50.

96. "The Problem of Hermeneutics," *Essays, Philosophical and Theological*, trans. James C. G. Grieg, The Library of Philosophy and Theology (New York, Macmillan, 1955), pp.

resolved tension in his position. If one is to enter into fruitful discussion with him, however, one cannot merely oppose him with some rigid doctrine of the canon, for that contains its own problems. He must rather raise the question of the appropriateness, adequacy, and application of the systematic and philosophical presuppositions which Bultmann has developed. At the same time he may be compelled to ask what justification still exists for attributing to the New Testament canon per se a unique significance in the life and teaching of the Christian church. Conversely, if the attribution of such significance or authority remains justifiable or even necessary, what is implied for the interpreter's responsibility to these documents? Does it come to an end when he discovers either later editorial insertions or theological assertions to which he must take exception? To give a negative answer does not solve the problem, but only defines the limits within which further discussion must take place.

My main purpose has been to set forth in detail that aspect of Bultmann's work which pertains to the composition and order of the Fourth Gospel [97] and to make some assessment of its validity by reviewing the scholarly discussion of it or subjecting it to direct critical examination. I have attempted to establish grounds and a position from which further and more definitive discussion and evaluation of Bultmann's work and the problems which it

---

234–61 (Cf. *Glauben und Verstehen, II*, 211–35, for the original German); *Jesus Christ and Mythology* (New York, Scribner's, 1958), pp. 45–59; also the important criticism of Bultmann's position in Schubert M. Ogden's *Christ without Myth: A Study Based on the Theology of Rudolf Bultmann* (New York, Harper, 1961). Ogden maintains that Bultmann's insistence upon the unique and indispensable nature of the Christ-occurrence stands in the way of the requisite complete demythologization and exhaustive existentialist interpretation.

97. There is some danger that in systematically setting forth Bultmann's literary analysis of the Fourth Gospel I have failed to do justice to the full range of probabilities which Bultmann ascribes to his various judgments. He shows different degrees of confidence or reservation in the assignment and rearrangement of material and often appears willing to let his judgments remain tentative. He occasionally changes his mind in the course of the commentary (cf. p. 215 and pp. 149 and 154 n. 8 on the position of 6:60–71) or revises a judgment in a later edition of it (on the status of 2:17, 22 cf. *Ergänzungsheft*, 1957, p. 86, p. 87, p. 89 n. 1, p. 90 n. 7; also see above p. 220 n. 27.

Nevertheless, the fact that Bultmann allows his entire exegesis and interpretation of John to rest upon his literary analysis is the strongest testimony to his commitment to it in substance, if perhaps not in every detail. In connection with a proposed rearrangement, Bultmann is not afraid to concede "Natürlich ist keine Sicherheit zu erreichen . . ." (*Johannes*, p. 216). When in doubt, however, he is often more certain of his own reconstruction than the present textual order. Typical of Bultmann's position is his statement on the rearrangement of chapter 6: "Kann die ursprüngliche Ordnung auch nicht mit Sicherheit wiederhergestellt werden, so muss doch der Versuch dazu gemacht werden" (*ibid.*, p. 163).

raises may advance. I do not at this point intend to raise further questions of criticism and interpretation or to chart the course of that advance.

While my reservations have been explicitly stated at the appropriate points, it may not be superfluous here to reiterate the very real and abiding value of Bultmann's critical proposals, a value which is by no means dependent upon their accuracy. Johannine interpretation has certainly been advanced by Bultmann's delineation of various literary strata in the gospel, by his identification of seemingly alien elements, and by those rearrangements which bring together the thematically related materials. Because of Bultmann's separation of the Offenbarungsreden, we are made keenly aware of the extent to which the Grund if not the Grundschrift of John is the revelatory self-disclosure of Jesus. Because of his identification of redactional elements, we can never lightly pass over the real theological tensions—if not contradictions—in Johannine thought. And if Bultmann assembles a discourse on light from passages gathered throughout the gospel, he makes us more than ever aware of the importance of this image in the evangelist's presentation of Jesus. It would not be difficult to give further evidences of his achievement.

No matter how negative the judgments against some aspects of Bultmann's work, Johannine criticism and interpretation have been immeasurably enriched by it. His work should call forth either our assent or an equally comprehensive and methodological exposition of the Fourth Gospel. Although it is not to be denied that interpretations of the gospel other than Bultmann's have been carried out in a competent, and to some extent convincing, manner, the whole task must be attempted again in the light of his work, which cannot be regarded as refuted until it has been superseded. Not until a comparably scientific exegesis of John appears can one rest easy with a substantially different interpretation of the theology of the Fourth Evangelist and his place in the development of Christian thought. A number of factors, such as the Qumran and Nag Hammadi discoveries, indicate that the time may soon be ripe for a fresh appraisal and interpretation of the Gospel of John. In the meantime, Bultmann's commentary remains a standard work, indispensable for an understanding of Johannine problems.

Bibliography

This bibliography contains only works which have been cited frequently or which have some direct bearing upon the problems dealt with in this book. All of Bultmann's more important books and articles pertaining to the Fourth Gospel have been included. The standard biblical texts, grammars, lexicons, and other reference works consulted in the preparation of this study are well-known and have been omitted in order to conserve space.

Although the original German has been consulted for every quotation and citation, I have referred to and quoted from the English translations of Bultmann's works where they are available.

Works by Bultmann

Bultmann, R., "Analyse des ersten Johannesbriefes," in *Festgabe für Adolf Jülicher zum 70. Geburtstag, 26, Januar 1927.* Tübingen, J. C. B. Mohr, 1927.

———, "Die Bedeutung der neuerschlossenen mandäischen und manichäischen Quellen für das Verständnis des Johannesevangeliums," *ZNW*, 24 (1925), 100–46.

———, "A Chapter in the Problem of Demythologizing," in *New Testament Sidelights, Essays in Honor of Alexander Converse Purdy*, ed. Harvey K. McArthur, Hartford, Hartford Seminary Foundation Press, 1960.

———, "The Concept of Revelation in the New Testament," in *Existence and Faith, Shorter Writings of Rudolf Bultmann*, trans. and ed. S. M. Ogden, New York, Meridian Books, 1960.

———, "Die Eschatologie des Johannesevangeliums," in *Glauben und Verstehen,*

Gesammelte Aufsätze von Rudolf Bultmann, Tübingen, J. C. B. Mohr, 1933–60, Vol. 1.

———, *Das Evangelium des Johannes, Kritisch-exegetischer Kommentar über das Neue Testament,* Abt. II, 15th ed. (with *Ergänzungsheft*), Göttingen, Vandenhoeck und Ruprecht, 1957.

———, *Glauben und Verstehen, Gesammelte Aufsätze von Rudolf Bultmann,* Tübingen, J. C. B. Mohr: Vol. 1, 1933; Vol. 2, 1952; Vol. 3, 1960.

———, *Gnosis, Bible Key Words from Gerhard Kittel's Theologisches Wörterbuch zum Neuen Testament,* trans. and ed. J. R. Coates, London, Adam and Charles Black, 1952.

———, "Hirsch's Auslegung des Johannes-Evangeliums," *ET, 4* (1937), 115–42.

———, "The Interpretation of the Fourth Gospel," *NTS, 1* (1954–55), 77–91.

———, "Is Exegesis without Presuppositions Possible?" in *Existence and Faith, Shorter Writings of Rudolf Bultmann,* trans. and ed. S. M. Ogden, New York, Meridian Books, 1960.

———, "Zur johanneischen Tradition," *TZ, 80* (1955), 521–26.

———, "Johannesevangelium," *RGG, 3* (1959), 840–50.

———, "Das Johannesevangelium in der neuesten Forschung, *CW, 41* (1927), 502–11.

———, "Johanneische Schriften und Gnosis," *OL, 43* (1940), 150–75.

———, "Die kirchliche Redaktion des ersten Johannesbriefes," in *In Memoriam Ernst Lohmeyer,* ed. W. Schmauch, Stuttgart, Evangelisches Verlagswerk, 1951.

———, *Primitive Christianity in Its Contemporary Setting,* trans. R. H. Fuller, New York, Meridian Books, 1956.

———, "The Problem of Hermeneutics," in *Essays, Philosophical and Theological,* trans. J. C. G. Grieg, The Library of Philosophy and Theology, New York, Macmillan, 1955.

———, "Der religionsgeschichtliche Hintergrund des Prologs zum Johannes-Evangelium," in *Eucharisterion, Studien zur Religion und Literatur des Alten und Neuen Testaments, Hermann Gunkel zum 60. Geburtstage,* ed. Hans Schmidt, Forschungen zur Religion und Literatur des Alten und Neuen Testaments, ed. R. Bultmann and H. Gunkel, new ser. 19, entire ser. 36, Göttingen, Vandenhoeck und Ruprecht, 1923, Vol. 2.

———, Review of *Ein Beitrag zur Mandäerfrage* by Hans Lietzmann, *TZ, 56* (1931), 577–80.

———, Review of *The Fourth Gospel in Recent Criticism and Interpretation* by W. F. Howard, *TZ, 59* (1934), 68 ff.

———, Review of *Johannes und die Synoptiker* by H. Windisch, *TZ, 52* (1927), 197–200.

———, Review of *Das Johannesevangelium,* 2d ed. by W. Bauer, *TZ, 51* (1926), 246.

———, *Theology of the New Testament,* trans. K. Grobel, 2 vols. New York,

Scribner's, 1951–55; 3d rev. German ed. *Theologie des Neuen Testaments,* Tübingen, J. C. B. Mohr, 1958.

———, "Untersuchungen zum Johannesevangelium," *ZNW,* 27 (1928), 113–63 and *29* (1930), 169–92.

OTHER IMPORTANT WORKS

Barrett, C. K., *The Gospel According to St. John: An Introduction with Commentary and Notes on the Greek Text,* London, S. P. C. K., 1955.

Becker, H. *Die Reden des Johannesevangeliums und der Stil der gnostischen Offenbarungsreden,* Forschungen zur Religion und Literatur des Alten und Neuen Testaments, ed. R. Bultmann, new ser. 50, entire ser. 68, Göttingen, Vandenhoeck und Ruprecht, 1956.

Bornkamm, G., "Die eucharistische Rede im Johannes-Evangelium," *ZNW,* 47 (1956), 161–69.

Braun, H., "Literar-Analyse und theologische Schichtung im ersten Johannesbrief," *ZTK, 48* (1951), 262–92.

Bussche, H. van den, "La Structure de Jean I–XII," in *L'Évangile de Jean, études et problèmes,* by M.-É. Boismard, F.-M. Braun, et al., Recherches Biblique, 3, Brouwer, Desclée, 1958.

Cullmann, O., *Les Sacrements dans L'Évangile Johannique, la vie de Jésus et le culte de l'église primitive,* Études d'histoire et de philosophie religieuses publiées par la faculté de théologie protestante de l'université de Strasbourg, 42, Paris, Presses Universitaires de France, 1951.

Dibelius, M., "Ein neuer Kommentar zum Johannes-Evangelium," *TL,* 67 (1942), 257–63.

Dodd, C. H., *The Interpretation of the Fourth Gospel,* Cambridge, Cambridge University Press, 1953.

Easton, B. S., "Bultmann's RQ Source," *JBL, 65* (1946), 143–56.

———, Review of *Das Evangelium des Johannes* by Rudolf Bultmann, *JBL, 65* (1946), 73–81.

Goodwin, Charles, "How Did John Treat His Sources?" *JBL,* 73 (1954), 61–75.

Grobel, K., Review of *Das Evangelium des Johannes* by Rudolf Bultmann, *JBL, 59* (1940), 434–36.

Grundmann, W., *Zeugnis und Gestalt des Johannes-Evangeliums, eine Studie zur denkerischen und gestalterischen Leistung des vierten Evangelisten,* Arbeiten zur Theologie, 7, Stuttgart, Calwer Verlag, 1961.

Guilding, A., *The Fourth Gospel and Jewish Worship: A Study of the Relation of St. John's Gospel to the Ancient Jewish Lectionary System,* Oxford, Clarendon Press, 1960.

Haenchen, E., "Johanneische Probleme," *ZTK, 56* (1959), 19–54.

———, "Aus der Literatur zum Johannesevangelium 1929–1956," *TR,* new ser. *23* (1955), 295–335.

———, "Neuere Literatur zu den Johannesbriefen," *TR,* 26 (1960), 1–43, 267–91.

Hirsch, E., "Stilkritik und Literaranalyse im vierten Evangelium," *ZNW*, *43* (1950–51), 128–43.

Howard, W. F., *The Fourth Gospel in Recent Criticism and Interpretation*, 4th ed. rev. by C. K. Barrett, London, Epworth Press, 1955.

Jeremias, J., "Johanneische Literarkritik," *TB*, 20 (1941), 33–46.

———, "Joh 6:51c–58—redaktionell?" *ZNW*, *44* (1952–53), 256–57.

Käsemann, E., "Aufbau und Anliegen des johanneischen Prologs," in *Libertas Christiana, Friedrich Delekat zum 65. Geburtstag*, ed. E. Wolf and W. Matthias, Beiträge zur evangelischen Theologie, Theologische Abhandlungen, ed. E. Wolf, München, Chr. Kaiser Verlag, 1957.

———, "Ketzer und Zeuge, zum johanneischen Verfasserproblem," *ZTK*, *48* (1951), 292–311.

———, "Rudolf Bultmann, Das Evangelium des Johannes," *VF*, *Theologischer Jahresbericht 1942–46* (published in 1947), pp. 182–201.

Köster, H., "Geschichte und Kultus im Johannesevangelium und bei Ignatius von Antiochien," *ZTK*, *54* (1957), 56–69.

Lohse, E., "Wort und Sakrament im Johannesevangelium," *NTS*, 7 (1960–61), 110–25.

Macgregor, G. H. C., and A. Q. Morton, *The Structure of the Fourth Gospel*, Edinburgh and London, Oliver and Boyd, 1961.

Menoud, Ph.-H., "Les Études johanniques de Bultmann à Barrett," in *L'Évangile de Jean, études et problèmes*, by M.-É. Boismard, F.-M. Braun, et al., Recherches Biblique, 3, Brouwer, Desclée, 1958.

———, *L'Évangile de Jean d'après les recherches récentes*, Cahiers théologiques de l'actualité protestante, 3, 2d ed. Neuchatel, Delachaux and Niestlé, 1947.

Michaelis, W., *Die Sakramente im Johannesevangelium*, Bern, BEG-Verlag, 1946.

Nauck, W., *Die Tradition und der Charakter des ersten Johannesbriefes, zugleich ein Beitrag zur Taufe im Urchristentum und in der alten Kirche*, Wissenschaftliche Untersuchungen zum Neuen Testament, ed. J. Jeremias and O. Michel, 3, Tübingen, J. C. B. Mohr, 1957.

Noack, B., *Zur johanneischen Tradition, Beiträge zur Kritik an der literarkritischen Analyse des vierten Evangeliums*, Publications de la Société des Sciences et des Lettres d'Aarhus, Série de Théologie, 3, København: Rosenkilde og Bagger, 1954.

Robinson, J. M., "Recent Research in the Fourth Gospel," *JBL*, 78 (1959), 242–52.

Ruckstuhl, E., *Die literarische Einheit des Johannesevangeliums, der gegenwärtige Stand der einschlägigen Erforschung*, Studia Friburgensia, new ser. 3, Freiburg in der Schweiz, Paulus-Verlag, 1951.

Schneider, J. "Die Abschiedsreden Jesu, ein Beitrag zur Frage der Komposition von Joh 13, 31–17, 26," *Gott und die Götter, Festgabe für Erich Fascher zum 60. Geburtstage*, Berlin, Evangelische Verlagsanstalt, 1958.

———, "Zur Frage der Komposition von Joh 6:27–58(59) (Die Himmelsbrotrede)," in *In Memoriam Ernst Lohmeyer*, ed. W. Schmauch, Stuttgart, Evangelisches Verlagswerk, 1951.

———, "Zur Komposition von Joh 7," *ZNW, 45* (1954), 108–19.

———, "Zur Komposition von Joh 10," in *Coniectanea Neotestamentica XI, in honorem Antonii Fridrichsen sexagenarii*, Edenda curavit Seminarium Neotestamenticum Upsaliense, Lund and Köpenhamn, Gleerup and Ejnar Munksgaard, 1947.

———, "Zur Komposition von Joh 18, 12–27, Kaiaphas und Hannas," *ZNW, 48* (1957), 111–19.

Schulz, S., *Komposition und Herkunft der Johanneischen Reden*, Beiträge zur Wissenschaft vom Alten und Neuen Testament, ed. K. H. Rengstorf and L. Rost, 5th ser. 1, entire ser. 81, Stuttgart, W. Kohlhammer, 1960.

———, *Untersuchungen zur Menschensohn-Christologie im Johannesevangelium, zugleich ein Beitrag zur Methodengeschichte der Auslegung des 4. Evangeliums, Göttingen*, Vandenhoeck und Ruprecht, 1957.

Schweizer, E., *Ego Eimi, die religionsgeschichtliche Herkunft und theologische Bedeutung der johanneischen Bildreden, zugleich ein Beitrag zur Quellenfrage des vierten Evangeliums*, Forschungen zur Religion und Literatur des Alten und Neuen Testaments, ed. R. Bultmann, new ser. 38, entire ser. 56, Göttingen, Vandenhoeck und Ruprecht, 1939.

———, "Das johanneischen Zeugnis vom Herrenmahl," *ET, 12* (1952–53), 341–63.

Wilkens, W., "Das Abendmahlszeugnis im vierten Evangelium," *ET, 18* (1958), 354–70.

———, *Die Entstehungsgeschichte des vierten Evangeliums*, Zollikon, Evangelischer Verlag, 1958.

———, "Evangelist und Tradition im Johannesevangelium," *TZ, 16* (1960), 81–90.

General Index

Abraham, 141, 157 f.; Jesus' sonship, 162

Acts, Book of, 100, 214, 247 n. *See also Index 2*

Aland, K., 88 n.

Albright, W. F., 110 n.

Ancient bookmaking, 100

Andrew, 161 n., 167

Annas, 175

Apocalypse (of John), 81, 86. *See also* Revelation, Book of

Apocrypha, 81

Apocryphal, writings: New Testament, 18, 178 n.; acts of the apostles, 80 n.

Apostolic Fathers, 214

Aramaic origin, 106; in *Offenbarungsreden*, 16; in prologue source, 61 f.

Arndt, W. F., xix

Authorship of Fourth Gospel, 2 f., 60; date of composition, 3; place, 3

Autographon of Fourth Gospel, 100 f., 176

Bailey, J. A., 234 n.

Baptism, 135, 216, 232; of Jesus, 52, 123 n., 124; in water and Holy Spirit, 120 f.; rebirth and Spirit, 216

Baptist: sect, 16, 38, 74, 87 n., 94, 96, 110 n., 127; tradition, 54. *See also* John the Baptist

Barrett, C. K., xv, 63 n., 79 n., 85 n., 86, 97, 111 n., 119, 126 n., 128 n., 134 n., 147 n., 149 n., 155 n., 172 n., 231 n., 233 n., 242 n., 253, 254

Barth, K., 242

Bauer, W., xvii, 252

Becker, H., 34 n., 79–83, 94, 132 n., 173 n., 161 f., 253

Beloved Disciple, 2 f., 118, 214, 220–23, 233, 235–37; as *Idealgestalt* or historical person, 221, 223; attempt to establish him as eyewitness and author of the gospel, 221, 223; death, 223

Ben Sirach, 103 n.

Bernard, J. H., 116 n., 126 n., 130 n., 172 n.

Bethany, 51

Black, M., 86 n.

Bodmer Papyrus *II (66) and XV (75)*, 159

Boismard, M.-É., 105 n., 124 n., 233 n., 242 n., 243 n., 244 n., 253, 254

Borgen, P., 113 n., 142 n., 143 n.

Bornkamm, G., xii, 60 n., 127 n., 142 n., 145, 146, 147 n., 150, 151 n., 253

Bousset, W., xii, 135 n.

Braun, F.-M., 85 n., 88, 108 n., 233 n., 244 n., 253, 254

Braun, H., 60 n., 253

Bread discourse. *See* Eucharist

Bread of God. *See* Ignatius

Brown, R. E., 142 n.

Büchler, A., 103 n.

Bultmann, R.: importance of literary theory, xi, 249; source theory, xiii f., 3–56, discussion and evaluation, 57–85, 107–115; displacement and rearrangement by redactor,

Bultmann, 72 f.; criticized by Bultmann, 77 f.
Noth, M., 89

Odeberg, H., 135 n.
Odes of Solomon, 17 f., 20, 80 n., 81 f., 145
Offenbarungsreden, xiii, 2, 6 f., 12 f., 15–34, 35, 57 ff., 63, 73, 76, 78 ff., 111, 113, 115, 134, 150 n., 164, 169, 249; rhythm, 5 f., 20, 22, 65; Aramaic origin, 16, 61 f.; Gnostic background, 16–19, 79 ff., 88, 109; and First Epistle, 17 n.; and Old Testament, 17, 18; theology, 18; mythological character, 18 f., 38, 63; revealer in, 19; formal and stylistic characteristics, 20 f., 79; evangelist's use, 21 f.; text reconstructed, 23–34; order, 73, 158; pattern in history of religions, 79–83. *See also* Evangelist; Prologue source
Ogden, S. M., 248 n., 251 f.
Old Testament: use and quotation, 12, 74, 76 ff., 83, 95, 103, 111 n., 144, 151 n., 220, 228, 232, 234, 237, 240, 243; quotation from memory, 76; testimonia source, 76, 123; text, 76; relation to source problem, 78; wisdom literature, 81; theophanies, 92; lectionary systems, 102 ff.; understood only after resurrection, 224; as indication of redaction, 225
Oral tradition, 51, 55, 72, 74 ff., 78, 86, 110 n., 112
Order of text. *See* Textual Order
Origen, 80 n., 232 n.
Orthodoxy and heresy in early church. *See* Early Catholicism
Ott, H., xvii n.

Papias, 106
Parable (*paroimia*). *See* Jesus
Paraclete, 90, 93, 98 n.; sayings, 169, 173
Parker, P., 88, 243 n.
Parousia, 90, 93, 218, 230, 235, 237, 241
Passion source, xiii, 13, 22, 44–51, 58 n., 86, 113, 120 n., 232 f.; relation to synoptics, 44 ff.; contextual evidence, 45 ff.; Semitizing Greek, 45; stylistic characteristics, 45, 47, 113; evangelist's use, 47; subsidiary criteria, 45; reconstruction, 48–51; narrative, 45 f., 74, 79, 97, 112 f., 114, 174
Passover, 97, 104, 128, 170 n., 171 n., 216; John as passover gospel, 97
Pastoral letters, 61 n., 214
Paul, xiv, 145, 228 n., 247 n.; as theologian, 241 f. *See also Index 2*
Pentateuch, 5, 14, 22, 89, 103, 245
Percy, E., 17 n.

Peter, 52, 106, 167, 169, 174, 221, 223, 226, 235 ff.; confession, 52; denial, 52, 169, 217; commissioning, 223; relation to Beloved Disciple, 223
Pharisees, 122, 133 f., 152, 154
Philip, 161 n., 167
Philo, 84 n., 95, 103 n., 104, 178
Pilate, 48
Poimandres, 80, 173 n.
Post-Bultmannian Era, 85–115
Prologue source, 2, 5–7, 16, 58, 61 f., 63 n., 64 n., 71, 79, 92, 234; versification and rhythm, 20 f., 61, 62; Aramaic origin, 61 f., Gnostic background, 61 f. *See also* Baptist; Gnosticism; John the Baptist; *Offenbarungsreden*
Pseudo-Clementines, 80 n.
Publication of Fourth Gospel, 117, 175–79, 237. *See also* Redaction

Qumran, 249; community, 94 ff.; scrolls, 110 n.; Manual of Discipline, 61 n.

Redaction (or redactor), 63 n., 64 n., 68, 76, 101 f., 106, 124 n., 243 n., 249; ecclesiastical (according to Bultmann), xii f., 2, 90, 111 n., 116–19, 119–79 *passim*, 213–38; purpose, 118, 213 f., 226, 235, 237; sacramental interest, 135 ff., 214, 215–17, 226; apocalyptic eschatology, 135 ff., 217–19; interest in church unity and other ecclesiastical matters, 164, 222, 225, 228, 235; criteria for identification, 213 f., 227; conformity to synoptics, 219–20; Beloved Disciple and the attestation of the gospel, 220–23; miscellaneous redactions, 224–26; use of sources, 226; validity and significance, 227–38; relation to source and rearrangement theories, 242. *See also* Sacraments; Eschatology; Synoptic gospels; Beloved Disciple
De regeneratione, 173 n.
Reitzenstein, R. xii, 84 n.
Rengstorf, K., 255
Resurrection, 129 f., 138 f., 150 n., 218 f., 229 ff.; of Jesus, 47, 52, 176, 220, 222 f., 224, 226, 235, 236, 242. *See* Eschatology
Revelation, 139 f.; as incarnation, 139; in cultus and history, 144 n.; in New Testament, 245–49
Revelation, Book of, 101 f., 106, 247 n. *See Index 2*
Revelation discourses. *See Offenbarungsreden*
Riesenfeld, H., 88 n.
Robinson, J. A. T., 88
Robinson, J. M., 95, 97, 254

Index 2: Scriptural References

DATE DUE

SEP 1 1994	
MAY 2 6 1995	
JUL 2 0 1995	
JAN 1 0 2001	
DEC 4 2000	